Shirley Smith: An Examined Life

Shirley Smith

An Examined Life

Sarah Gaitanos

Victoria University Press

For Stephanos, Thomas and Alexi

TE WHARE WĀNANGA O TE ŪPOKO O TE IKA A MĀUI
VICTORIA
UNIVERSITY OF WELLINGTON

Victoria University of Wellington
PO Box 600 Wellington
vup.victoria.ac.nz

First published 2019

A catalogue record is available from the
National Library of New Zealand

ISBN 9781776562176

The author gratefully acknowledges the assistance of

The Law Foundation
NEWZEALAND

Published with the assistance of

creative nz
ARTS COUNCIL OF NEW ZEALAND TOI AOTEAROA

Printed in China by 1010 Printing International

Contents

List of Illustrations

Sister Kathleen Cumming, New Zealand Army Nursing Service (NZANS), World War I

Shirley with David

Shirley's stepmother Margaret Elizabeth Smith, née Gibbs, called Meta

Mr Justice Smith

Shirley

Shirley with her brother Allan

David Smith, Richard Gibbs (Meta's father), Shirley and Allan at Taupō

Shirley's stepmother Meta at Taupō, about 1928

Shirley, Wellington, 1935, shortly before her departure for Oxford

Shirley, Wellington, 1935, in her debutante ballgown

Shirley, Oxford, about 1937

A postcard to Allan Smith from Munich, 1937

Wendelstein, Munich, on Shirley's European tour, summer 1937

Wendelstein, Munich, Shirley third from left, leaning against Martin Watkin

Hungarian State Wine Cellars, Budafok, Budapest; Shirley second from left

Hungarian State Wine Cellars, Budafok, Budapest; Shirley back row, centre

Vienna, with Roland Towers

Paris, with Martin Watkin

Wooden head of Shirley by sculptor Alec Miller, 1938

Shirley with her father, Geneva, 1938

David and Meta Smith, Grisons, Switzerland, 1938

Introduction

Shirley Smith was one of the most remarkable New Zealanders of the twentieth century, a woman whose lifelong commitment to social justice, legal reform, gender equality and community service left a profound legacy. This biography seeks to make her contributions known and acknowledged. Beyond that, it is the story of an extraordinary woman who appeals to the hearts and minds of those who knew and never knew her.

From the beginning, Shirley inspires sympathy as her formative years were clouded by loss. She was born in Wellington in October 1916. Three months later her mother died and her father, lawyer David Smith, joined the army and went to war, leaving the baby with her grieving maternal grandmother. That Shirley had no memory of her mother doesn't diminish the significance of the loss. In a sense she was always a motherless child.

Her 'darling daddy' came home safely. Shirley worshipped him. He remarried when she was seven and her brother Allan was born in 1924. Theirs was a privileged upbringing, especially after her father became a Supreme Court judge. But Shirley was a rebel. Her father often said she 'kicked against the pricks'.

The family moved to Auckland and Shirley was sent to boarding school in Marton. She was homesick and didn't fit in – even more so when she discovered communism – all described in detail in her letters home. But Nga Tawa gave her a purpose, to study classics at Oxford.

In 1935 she sailed for England and, on her nineteenth birthday, went to St Hugh's College, Oxford, to read Greats. Oxford, she said, was the most wonderful, transformative time of her life. She threw herself into its social, cultural and political activities, travelled in Europe, took lovers, joined the Communist Party and lived life at full tilt until she was stopped in her tracks by TB. She spent most of 1939 at Dr Rollier's clinic in Leysin in the Swiss Alps. Remarkably, despite her long absence, she graduated with a good Second.

Shirley was in Switzerland when war broke out. She managed to return to New Zealand at the end of 1939 and, after a difficult transition and further illness, was appointed lecturer in classics at Victoria and then Auckland University Colleges. In Auckland she was too liberal for many of her colleagues, and her loyalty to her professor irked those who opposed him in a department riven by factions. She survived her political battles and stayed on until she joined her husband in Wellington in August 1944.

She had married public economist Dr W. B. Sutch in June. Shirley retained her own name; she always called herself Shirley Smith and tried to get others to do likewise. In 1944 this wasn't understood by the world at large. She had strong feminist principles about being her own person and wished not to be defined in relation to the men in her life.

Shirley was very much her own person, but she was inevitably seen as the daughter of Sir David Smith and wife of Dr Sutch. Had her father and husband not been such forceful personalities with high public profiles, things would have been different.

Long before Shirley met Bill he had made his name as a brilliant public economist and a lightning rod for the Left. He was a radical thinker who fought for equality for women, but his idea of his own marriage was conventional. Shirley was disillusioned, as he may also have been, to find their expectations so wide apart. They were both strong, complex individuals and both exhibited paradoxical qualities. Through good and bad times, Shirley grew within the marriage.

Sutch's work for the United Nations Relief and Rehabilitation Administration (UNRRA) took them in 1945 to Sydney, where their daughter Helen was born, and in 1946 to London. In 1947 Sutch was appointed head of the New Zealand Mission to the United Nations. The family lived in New York for three years. It was the dawn of McCarthyism, an unnerving time for people of Shirley and Bill's leftish leanings. A record of a KGB file in the Mitrokhin Archive notes that in 1950, Soviet Intelligence recruited Sutch to what later became the KGB.

Back in Wellington in 1951, against a backdrop of local political upheaval, Shirley had a personal crisis. What was her purpose, beyond that of wife and mother? Her journal gives penetrating insight into her state of mind at this low point and shows how she worked herself out of it, addressing fundamental marital and feminist problems. She developed her ideas into radio talks and made her name as a public speaker on wider issues. She founded the Human Rights Organisation, co-founded the New Zealand Council for Civil Liberties, took on other campaigns, and started a law degree at Victoria University College.

In 1956 she reached a political turning point. This calls for both close scrutiny and a distant viewpoint. Historian Margaret MacMillan writes that humility is one of the most useful lessons the past can provide the present. She quotes British man of letters John Carey: 'One of history's most useful tasks is to bring home to us how keenly, honestly and painfully past generations pursued aims that now seem to us wrong or disgraceful.'[1] Shirley now realised she had been wrong in her political allegiance, albeit for sincere reasons.

She had been an active member of the Communist Party until she moved to Sydney in 1945. She never rejoined but remained in contact with Party leaders, and she defended Stalin publicly, despite private misgivings. Khrushchev's revelations about Stalin at the beginning of 1956 shocked her, but she hoped things could change. That hope shattered when the Soviet Union invaded Hungary. Correspondence with writer Elsie Locke, who left the Party at this time, shows the extent of her disillusionment. Of special interest is a letter Shirley wrote to Khrushchev that she called a 'Manifesto on Hungary'. New Zealand Security Intelligence Service (NZSIS) records are also of special interest, as Shirley took steps to clear the way for her husband's eventual promotion to Secretary of Industries and Commerce.

By then the family had moved to the house they built, designed by modernist architect Ernst Plischke, on Brooklyn hill. Shirley had graduated in Law (she was capped by her father Sir David Smith, retired

1 Margaret MacMillan, *The Uses and Abuses of History*, Profile Books, London, 2010, p.169.

from the Supreme Court and now Chancellor of the University of New Zealand). She worked in a law office and also returned to university as a lecturer, the first woman academic in New Zealand to join a law faculty. For a good part of 1958, prior to and just after Bill's appointment to head of Industries and Commerce, he was overseas for trade talks. His letters to Shirley during these months show their marriage in an intimate light.

At the age of forty-four, Shirley Smith set up her solo practice as a barrister and solicitor. Through the 1960s she was busy outside the home with her law work and campaigns. Helen was growing up and they were very close, too close, perhaps, for Helen's independent development. She went to Oxford, as her mother wished, and became more her own person. Helen's marriage to political scientist Keith Ovenden added another dimension to family dynamics. Helen and Keith's frank accounts portray a mother and mother-in-law with strengths and failings.

As a lawyer, Shirley Smith gave wise advice and people saw her as an icon. She ran a busy practice, employing two law clerks, three typists and other staff. She regularly appeared in the courts when it was still a male domain. Though she didn't wish to be seen either as a woman lawyer or a lawyer for women, she attracted clients because she was a woman and many of her clients were women. It was probably in family law that she made her biggest impact. She helped people in all sorts of ways that cannot be recorded or assessed.

Everything changed in September 1974 when, after a series of clandestine meetings with Russian spy Dimitri Razgovorov, Bill Sutch was arrested. He was tried for espionage and acquitted but unanswered questions and new revelations kept public interest alive. Apart from setting the scene, I recount the events from Shirley's point of view, or from a perspective that shows her involvement, perceptions and the psychological toll it had on her. How much did she know? I have gone as far as my sources allow me. There may well exist sources I haven't seen that go further, but those I have are revealing and in some respects troubling.

For all that, one can see the whole spy saga from the distance of the twenty-first century in a more understanding light. Shirley herself put it in perspective to her son-in-law Keith Ovenden following the publication of *Intersecting Lines: The Memoirs of Ian Milner*:[2]

Of course [Ian Milner] *belonged to the stratum, the generational level, of those who rebelled against received ideas of Britain as Home, Mother, the Empire on which the sun never set, and so on – also against capitalism which produced the Great Depression (is this one greater?), and saw the dawn of a new age, and peace and prosperity for all, in Socialism, leading to Communism, the expansion of the human spirit to realise its full potential . . .*

As you say, what [Vincent O'Sullivan] *says at the end about the motivation of those of us, for of course I was one of them, is good, by far the best part of the book. Whether Ian was in any way a minor Kim Philby or not, I have no idea. I would understand and not condemn him if he was. Thank God no one ever asked me to be a spy! I would probably have agreed.*[3]

Shirley continued to defend her husband's reputation after his death. Her commitment to Bill was 'a thing-in-itself', she said when he was alive, but she prided herself in dealing with truths and, as she articulated during the Hungarian crisis, perceptions of truth must change when the facts change. She posed the problem when she was asked to contribute to a history of the Classics Department at Auckland University College about the question of discretion. 'If my contribution to your history is to present an incomplete picture of how things were . . . should I contribute at all? The question is, is there an alternative between silence and telling the whole truth?'[4]

In the law, she said, truth was the most important thing. Was she gullible? On rare occasions when defending her Mongrel Mob clients she wondered what the truth really was, but she loved these young men. Though her own background was a world away from theirs, she had great rapport with them and understood why they rebelled against

2 *Intersecting Lines: The Memoirs of Ian Milner*, edited and introduced by Vincent O'Sullivan, VUP, Wellington, 1993.

3 SHSS to KWO, 10 February 1973, KWO papers.

4 SHSS to Peter Crawley, 11 July 1978, SHSS papers.

society. She constantly reminded the public that everyone was entitled to a fair trial. Her relationship with the Mob epitomised her role as a champion of the underdog.

While the vicissitudes of her later years included floods, muggings, burglaries and accidents, there are also happy family times with grandchildren, her pleasure in reading, poetry, art and theatre, and travel to many distant places, including back to her gods and heroes of Greece.

PEOPLE OFTEN ask me if I knew Shirley Smith. I did, briefly. When she was in her early eighties an old friend of hers and of my family, Helen Garrett, took me to her home in Brooklyn, known as the 'Sutch House'. I hoped Shirley would help me with the biography I was writing about theatre director Nola Millar and was surprised that she had little to say about Nola or Wellington's left-wing Unity Theatre. But Shirley herself was a character. She talked about the house and art collection, her friends in Greece and other interests.

I remember a moment between us, a pause in the talk when she looked me straight in the eye and I felt a connection. In my memory she had blue eyes, but one of her passports says they were grey and another, hazel. The problems of biography – but I do remember that look.

It wasn't until Shirley's daughter and son-in-law, Helen Sutch and Keith Ovenden, proposed the idea in February 2011, three years after Shirley's death, that I had any thought of writing her biography. Helen was just finishing reading *The Violinist*, my recent biography of Clare Galambos Winter, when she first phoned with the idea. She and Keith knew my other work and I had often discussed biography with Keith, who was also a biographer. I declined initially as I was working on another project, but when the situation changed I gave more thought to a biography of Shirley Smith.

Helen Sutch generously offered me first and sole access to Shirley Smith's papers, which are now housed in the Alexander Turnbull Library, but which I was privileged to begin reading at Helen and Keith's home in the Sutch–Smith house in Brooklyn, where Shirley had lived for almost 50 years, and where so much of her correspondence had its origins. While there, Helen and Keith also shared relevant letters from their own correspondence.

Apart from papers clearly identified as relating to Shirley Smith, I have not had access to the W. B. Sutch papers, which are also held in the Alexander Turnbull Library. Shirley had herself already promised Rosslyn Noonan, as Dr Sutch's biographer, first and sole access to them, a commitment also endorsed by Helen.

Helen and Keith didn't commission the biography but supported my applications for funding. I agreed to show them my manuscript and give them the opportunity to respond, but as an independent biographer, I was to write as I wished.

I read a selection of Shirley's writings. I was impressed. The project was interesting. Shirley Smith appealed to me.

The problem was, she appealed for many different reasons. Shirley's biography doesn't stand on a single attribute, achievement or purpose. She was her father's daughter, wife of her more famous husband, sister, mother, friend, advocate and always very much her own person. I came to see her life as a long, woven tapestry, rich and populated, its narrative driven by force of character. Motifs and textures stand out and recede, depending on the viewer and viewpoint. The subject invites one to pause at different stages, look close, step back and ultimately to stand far back to take in the whole picture.

The viewpoints within the narrative are also various. Shirley was a woman of her time, in some respects ahead of her time and, with age, more at home in her past. It is interesting to read her life story, written in later years, in the light of her earlier accounts and contemporary records. Through her diaries, oral interviews, public records and an extraordinary collection of letters, Shirley's voice reaches us across time.

The Greek hero Pericles famously said, 'What you leave behind is not what is engraved in stone monuments, but what is woven into the lives of others.' When you stand back and view the whole tapestry – that is the legacy of Shirley Smith.

Acknowledgements

THIS BIOGRAPHY has been a mighty collaborative effort. I have many people to thank, more than I mention below. To anyone I have overlooked, please forgive me.

In the first instance, I wish to thank Helen Sutch for the opportunity to write the biography of her mother. As explained in my introduction, Helen offered me first and sole access to Shirley Smith's papers, and I began reading these in their home, the Sutch–Smith house in Brooklyn, where Shirley had lived. Helen and her husband Keith Ovenden also made available relevant papers from their own collections, and welcomed me to their home for research purposes. Helen has generously permitted the use of photographs from her own and her parents' collections. I am deeply grateful to her.

Another family member who helped significantly at an early stage was Shirley's brother, the late Allan Smith. I spent many hours in his attic searching his father's extensive files, and many more discussing and recording Allan's family memories. Allan offered me what I wanted, including photographs, which I intend to deposit in the David Stanley Smith papers in the Alexander Turnbull Library.

My thanks also to Maureen Cassey who sourced and copied photographs from Shirley's maternal family.

A good friend on this project has been Vincent O'Sullivan. When I was deciding whether to do the biography he asked the key question, Are there letters? Letters are the bread and meat of biography, he said. And that clinched it. Vincent always brought focus to what mattered most and I am grateful for his generosity, knowledge and support.

An impediment for a biography of a barrister and solicitor might have been that I myself have no legal background. The first of many lawyers who came to my rescue was Barrister Phillip Green, who not only accessed and explained law reports but also offered me a room in his chambers in Sydney Street West, Thorndon, and was available to advise me when I needed it.

The material means for the work started with a seeding grant from the Lighthouse Cinema, thanks to the generosity of Dick Werry.

There followed a generous grant from Creative New Zealand that enabled me to work for six months on the project and to travel within New Zealand to carry out interviews and research archives.

I'm grateful to the Winston Churchill Memorial Trust for giving me a Winston Churchill Fellowship to undertake research overseas in Greece, Switzerland, England and the United States in 2012, and to the Stout Trust for its contribution to the trip. This was a vital opportunity to carry out in-the-field research to provide context and understanding related to relevant places, events and the character of my subject.

I was fortunate, too, in the people who provided hospitality, transport and local knowledge. These included Dimitrios, Stephanos and Natalie Gaitanos, who acted as interpreters in Greece and Switzerland, and, while in New York, Tony Garstang, who, in the teeth of approaching Hurricane Sandy, trudged with me in Shirley Smith's footsteps until the storm stopped us in our tracks.

The following year, 2013, I had the J. D. Stout Fellowship. I thank the Stout Trust and Victoria University of Wellington for this huge boost to the project. It provided financial security for a year and an office, and brought me back to the Stout Research Centre where I had worked on earlier books. My work has been infinitely richer for my association and friendship with colleagues there. Many are listed in my bibliography but others not mentioned were also important. I wish to thank particularly Lydia Wevers, director of the Stout Research Centre during my time there, for unfailing support and guidance; also Richard Hill, Anna Green and administrator Debbie Levy.

I continued to work at the Stout Research Centre as a resident scholar for the next two years. An example of a typical fruitful association that came from this extension was the opportunity to discuss my work with the 2015 Stout Fellow, social justice advocate Kim Workman. Among other things, Kim gave me the lead to a chain of contacts that became essential to my accounts of Shirley Smith's work with gang members.

Fortuitously that coincided with a grant in 2015 from the New Zealand Law Foundation towards research specifically related to Shirley Smith's work in the law, recording new interviews, transcribing previous interviews, archival research and writing. I am grateful to the

Law Foundation for this support and for their interest in my project. My thanks also to Tim Clarke for his much appreciated, personal donation.

I thank all the above organisations and individuals, and those who backed me with letters of support for funding and who promoted the project in other ways.

I wish to acknowledge everyone named in my bibliography, interviewees, correspondents, writing colleagues and people I consulted and others who shared their memories, knowledge and experience. I greatly appreciated the helpful staff at the Alexander Turnbull Library, and at other libraries, archives and other organisations that provided sources.

My thanks to the following copyright holders who allowed me to quote from unpublished material:
Mary Cassaidy and Tom Bayliss for Cecil Algie née Upton
David Garland for Peggy Garland
Jonathan Goldberg QC for himself
Margaret Hayward for herself
Robert Herrick for Margie Philips
Keith Locke for Elsie Locke
Piers Ovenden for Margaret Shirley Sutch
George Rosenberg for himself
Jane Shallcrass for Kate Shallcrass
Helen Sutch for herself, Shirley Smith, W. B. Sutch and David Smith
Alister Taylor for himself
Jonathan Temm for Paul Temm QC
Wellington Branch of the New Zealand Law Society for their oral history project, 'Hugo Manson with Shirley Smith', 1998

I apologise to any copyright holders I have failed despite my best efforts to identify or contact and would be pleased to hear from them.

I AM ESPECIALLY grateful to the people who read drafts and gave valuable expert advice, in particular Mary Brophy, Diedre Irons, Annabelle Woodhouse, Peter Woodhouse, Brian Easton, Rowena Cullen, Chris Maclean, John McGrath and Richard Hill. They not only made significant contributions to the book, but also by giving their time and attention so generously, they greatly supported me personally.

Victoria University Press publisher Fergus Barrowman encouraged and supported the project from the outset, challenging and guiding me through drafts and working collaboratively to the end. I'm grateful to my editor Madeleine Collinge for her sharp eye, judgment and efficiency, and for managing a smooth and satisfying editorial process, and to Tordis Flath for her excellent index. Finally, my thanks to the team at VUP, especially Jasmine Sargent, for their fine work.

I couldn't have written this book without my staunch friends and family, especially my husband Dimitrios (Taki), who lived with this book for eight years. I thank you all.

Notes on sources

BETWEEN 1992 AND 2002, Shirley Smith wrote her family history and the story of her life. Most of her reminiscences were written on her laptop in Warsaw in 1998 under subject headings, and these are dated. An earlier account, 33 typed pages starting with a 'Te Deum' is not dated (with the exception of the odd addition).

Sometimes Shirley had a specific reader in mind, as when she wrote about McCarthyism for her teenage grandson Piers, or her daughter Helen who suggested the topics. I felt also she was writing for unknown readers, which is not surprising – there had long been talk of her writing her biography. But for Shirley, the process of writing her memoirs as well as her journals and letters was rewarding in itself. She liked to write.

My references in the early part of the book to Sir David Smith's memoir refer to the manuscript I found in my search of his papers in Allan Smith's house. Sir David started writing his memoir in October 1966 and completed some 700 handwritten pages. This is now held by Helen Sutch and Keith Ovenden, who provided me with a typed transcript of the first 300 pages, the part most relevant to Shirley's life. An incomplete carbon copy of the original is in David Smith's papers in the Alexander Turnbull Library.

Shirley Smith's papers are also in the Turnbull collections and, where possible, I include reference numbers. It is an extensive collection and as I had done considerable work on them before they were deposited, I don't have reference numbers for them all. As far as I know, every source I identify as 'SHSS papers' is in the Alexander Turnbull Library.

Note on the text

I HAVE GENERALLY followed the convention of using names and spellings as they were used at the time, with the exception of Māori names. Outside quotations or official spellings, Māori names have macrons.

Abbreviations in the footnotes

AGS	Allan Gibson Smith
ATL	Alexander Turnbull Library
DSS	David Stanley Smith
KWO	Keith Ovenden
MES	Margaret (Meta) Elizabeth Smith
MHS	Margaret Helen Sutch
MSS	Margaret Shirley Sutch
PF	Personal File
SHSS	Shirley Hilda Stanley Smith
WBS	William Ball Sutch

1

Gathering threads

In the mid-1990s when Shirley Smith started her life story, she wrote with a sense of gratitude. Under the heading 'Te Deum' she acknowledged that she had been 'extraordinarily lucky'. She could have reviewed her life differently, starting as it did with tragedy, but she wanted to emphasise the positive.

I have been lucky in the sort of family I was born into: a family of intelligent, independent minded people, with high principles, a family who valued education, as much for girls as for boys, who never put girls down or told them there were things they couldn't do, because they were girls. A family who did not smack children (or hardly ever), who loved children, who cherished me because I had lost my mother. A family where men worked hard, honoured their wives and were faithful, and women who, in very different circumstances from one another, were faithful and fulfilled their responsibilities.[1]

Shirley valued these qualities above fame and fortune, though she knew that her family's prosperity was no small advantage. But had her mother not died, everything would have been different.

She wanted to give a true account of her life. Being truthful was a matter of principle and Shirley prided herself on her long-term memory. 'I am just letting my memory re-live the past, in a stream-of-consciousness way . . . regardless of any future use of this raw material.'[2] Fortunately her family also kept contemporary records.

1 SHSS memoir, 'Te Deum', undated (edited 1998), p.1, SHSS papers.
2 SHSS memoir, '23 Main Road, Wadestown' (follows 'Te Deum', edited 1998), p.24, SHSS papers.

SHIRLEY SAW herself as a Scot. Three of her grandparents were born and grew up in Scotland. The fourth, her maternal grandmother Emma White, was born in New Plymouth. Emma's parents Theophilus and Jane White were English. They arrived in New Zealand in 1853. While Shirley visited the ancestral homes of her Scottish forebears and wrote humorously that her father's Scottish ancestors were cattle rustlers – Border people rustling English cattle, so highly admirable and patriotic[3] – she wrote little of the Whites' origins. She didn't mention the secret she discovered in 1995: that Jane's father was William Shaw, the Yorkshire schoolmaster of Bowes Academy on whom Charles Dickens based his infamous schoolmaster in *Nicholas Nickleby*.[4]

Shirley's grandmother Emma told her about her young life in Taranaki, dancing, ice-skating (she called it 'rinking') and climbing Mount Egmont (now Taranaki), starting on horseback, camping at the base, then climbing to the top – wearing a long black dress.

The Whites attended St Mary's Anglican Church, where Emma married Duncan Cumming, father-of-four and six years a widower.

A Scottish Highlander from Inverness-shire, Duncan Cumming had started his working life as a teacher. Education for girls was highly valued in Scotland and Duncan always thought it important that women also should be able to work. His daughters were all qualified: Annie was a teacher, Kitty a nurse, and Eva, Shirley's mother, had an MA degree from Auckland University College.

3 SHSS, 'The Smith Family', undated (1992–98), SHSS papers. Shirley first learnt to use a computer in 1992 and wrote the Smith family history over the next years.

4 When Shirley wrote about the Whites in Warsaw on 17 June 1998 she didn't have with her the records her cousin Pam Pullar had gathered through her genealogical research, but she knew of the Dickens connection: SHSS to Elsie Locke, 23 May 1995, SHSS papers, ATL, MS-Papers-11369-039. The author found no other references to William Shaw in family papers but many elsewhere as another descendant, Ted Shaw, was active in his ancestor's defence. http://www.telegraph.co.uk/news/uknews/1316931/The-real-Squeers-was-no-Dickens-brute-claims-descendant.html (accessed 1 February 2018); 'Wearside Echoes: Dickens had twisted view of school head', Sunderland Echo, 15 June 2011, https://www.sunderlandecho.com/lifestyle/retro/wearside-echoes-dickens-had-twisted-view-of-school-head-1-347938 (accessed 29 May 2018). Jane White was described as 'a bright little lady, in no way like her portrait [Fanny Squeers in Nicholas Nickleby] drawn by the great novelist': 'Banking Reminiscences', *New Zealand Herald*, 30 March 1910, p.9, https://paperspast.natlib.govt.nz/newspapers /NZH19100330.2.97 (accessed 29 May 2018).

Duncan Cumming came to New Zealand in 1865, entered the Postal Service in New Zealand, and travelled around the country as Inspector of Post Offices until he became Chief Postmaster in Auckland and, finally, in 1907, Chief Postmaster and Controller General of the Post Office Savings Bank in Wellington.[5] On his retirement in 1908 he returned to Auckland, where he and his son William ran a successful land agency. Duncan died before Shirley was born, but he was a personal hero to her because he saved a widow and her children from destitution. On an inspection tour in the Far North, on finding a postmaster had died, Duncan assessed the widow's capability and appointed her postmistress. It was probably the first time a woman held such a position in New Zealand.

Emma brought up the four children of Duncan's first marriage as well as Eva, her only child. Shirley writes of her grandmother's excellent relationship with her stepchildren, who adored their younger half-sister.

Born in 1891, Eva Jane Cumming was, by Shirley's account, exceptional. She was Dux and winner of many prizes at Mt Eden Ladies' College, a private secondary school in Auckland. Among Shirley's relics of her mother were university tennis tournament medals, her Latin, French and English textbooks and photographs. And thick locks of her auburn hair.

Renowned Christian pacifist Ormond Burton told Shirley he remembered Eva well at Auckland University College. 'I gathered that he adored from a distance – he said she was lively and laughing, and always in a hurry, and he remembered her running to lectures with an inkbottle in her hand, leaving a trail of ink.'[6]

Shirley describes her mother as taller than her, 'slight but well formed, and with hazel eyes and a mass of curly auburn hair, a glorious colour. She was not strictly speaking beautiful, with typical White features – a strong nose – but she was so lively and laughing and high-spirited that everyone thought she was beautiful and her lovely personality shines

5 Obituary, Papers Past, Press, 7 February 1914, p.6, https://paperspast.natlib.govt.nz/newspapers/press/1914/2/7/6 (accessed 18 June 2018).

6 SHSS memoir, 'My Life – First Causes' (following 'Te Deum'), 16 June 1998, p.3, SHSS papers.

out of her photographs.' Of course, Shirley added, she was popular. Shirley's second name, Hilda, was after Eva's friend and tennis partner Hilda Bloomfield, who drowned with all her family on their way to Europe when their ship the *Empress of Ireland* collided with another in the St Lawrence River in Canada.[7]

THE SMITHS were high-principled, strong-willed, determined Presbyterians. Shirley said, in an interview with Neville Glasgow in 1989, 'Most of the members knew perfectly well what was right according to their lights, and they were going to stick with them, come hell or high water.'[8] Shirley believed she inherited these qualities and their principles. People said she was her father's daughter.

She had her father's smile, but not his gravitas. Photographs of the Hon. Sir David Stanley Smith, Judge of the Supreme Court of New Zealand, Chancellor of the University of New Zealand, Honorary D. Phil from Oxford University, show him according to the occasion in judicial wigs, gowns and ceremonial robes, every bit the distinguished man. As a young man too, Shirley recalled he cut a striking figure: 'He was not tall, but he was very good-looking, with the black hair, blue eyes and fair skin of his Celtic ancestry.'[9]

David's father, the Reverend John Gibson Smith, was one of the most beautiful men she ever saw, and his father, the elder David Earl Smith, was said to look like a patriarch from the Old Testament.[10] The last in a line of carpet weavers from Kilmarnoch in the Lowlands, he became a carpet designer, then manager of a woollen factory in Aberdeen, and able to provide his many children (fifteen, of whom thirteen survived to adulthood) with an academic education. John Gibson Smith went to King's College of the University of Aberdeen. He failed Mathematics (which was then compulsory for a Bachelor of Arts) and therefore his

7 *Poverty Bay Herald*, 1 June 1914, p.4.
8 SHSS to Neville Glasgow, interview, broadcast on Radio NZ, 18 January 1989, published in *Directions: New Zealanders Explore the Meaning of Life*, Shoal Bay Press, Christchurch, 1995, pp.186–201.
9 Complexion medium. Hair med brown. Height 5'6½", eyes blue . . . Certificate of Discharge from NZEF, 18 October 1919.
10 Middle name Earl (spelt Curle in 'notes on the ancestry of Marjorie Milne on her Smith side' by DSS).

degree. Shirley adopted his belief that 'the Smiths can't do maths'. John then switched to Theology at the United Presbyterian Theological Hall in Edinburgh and entered the ministry.

He married Ann Gibb, a primary-school teacher of Highland ancestry. Shirley saw herself in the mould of her Gran'ma Smith – short and stubby. There was a double Smith–Gibb connection, as John's sister, Jean Smith, married Ann's brother, James Gibb, who was also a Presbyterian minister. The Gibbs had emphatic views on everything. Shirley wondered how they came to be so sure of themselves and their views on life, and she wondered about this quality in herself. She thought of her grandmother as 'the Generalissima'.

Both couples emigrated to New Zealand, where James Gibb was Minister at the First Church in Dunedin and John was Minister of the North Dunedin Presbyterian Church. Shirley's father, David Stanley Smith, was born in the manse on 11 February 1888. His middle name 'Stanley' was after the explorer who found Dr Livingstone in the African jungle. When he married Eva, they called themselves the Stanley Smiths and Stanley became Shirley's third name.

David's brothers James (Jim) and George, and his sister Annie Ethelwyn (Wynnie) were also born in Dunedin. When David was six, his father was called to Invercargill, where two more children, Lorna (called Tom) and Fiona (called Woey), were born. The youngest, Alison, was born much later. She was just seven years older than Shirley.

A minister's salary was moderate and David recalled they heard often the admonitions 'Waste not, want not' and 'A fool and his money are soon parted'. But they had a happy family life with wonderful summer holidays on Stewart Island, fishing and cooking on an open fire.

In 1902 David started his secondary education at Southland Boys' High School, then one of the country's top schools. The following year the family moved to Wellington when John was called to St Andrew's (now St Andrew's on The Terrace). At the same time, James Gibb was called to St John's in Willis Street. Many years later Shirley was shown a parish paper from the church archives that announced that 'the giants from the South have arrived'.[11]

11 SHSS, 'The Smiths', undated (1992–98), p.7, SHSS papers.

Home was now the manse at 84 Hill Street. David attended Wellington College, where he did well and set his heart on becoming a doctor, but there was no money to put him through medicine in Dunedin. His mother decided he should become a lawyer: he could live at home while he studied at Victoria, and after two years he could combine study with office experience and so earn money to help the family before he qualified.

His mother managed the family finances and all worldly matters, leaving her husband to contemplate the world of God and get on with his writing, including a book, *The Christ of the Cross*, which caused a furore. Shirley explained that he was a freethinker who questioned the doctrine of redemption: that by his death on the cross, Christ had saved all mankind. These ideas from a minister were scandalous in 1908. John Smith's livelihood and position at St Andrew's were threatened when his fellow ministers in the Presbyterian Church charged him with heresy. He put his case before the Presbyterian General Assembly, a compromise was reached and, according to David, he remained minister at St Andrew's.

Shirley heard a lot about this furore when she was young. A cartoon showing a traitor (Carpus, his anonymous accuser) stabbing her grandfather in the back stuck in her memory, but she never understood what it was about. She never read his book. What impressed her was that he stood up for what he believed and was true to his convictions.

David entered university life to the full and made a name for himself in debating, student politics and sport. He also developed what he described as 'a sense of the need to give voluntary service and of the need to pull together in giving it, not with any idea of personal gain but because it was in accord with the basic values of the good life.'[12] He and a friend set up and ran classes for boys who had had to leave school at primary age. He prepared them for their Proficiency Certificate to enable them to get promotion in the Public Service. Shirley thought this was 'marvellous'.[13]

12 DSS, memoir, p.67, DSS papers.

13 This is from the oral history of Shirley Smith with Hugo Manson on 4 November 1988 commissioned by the New Zealand Law Society, Wellington Branch, side 1, ATL,

At one stage David was interested in the Labour movement. In January 1913, after the collapse of the Waihi Strike, he attended, as an observer, a 'Red Feds' conference, set up by that militant side of the movement to see if unity within the Labour ranks could be achieved. He wrote that he didn't feel at home with the brusque types of men who were there and he found himself in opposition to their purposes:

Notwithstanding the Christian atmosphere in which I was then enveloped, I had ambitions to succeed in a worldly way, encouraged in them, too, by the attitude of my mother who greatly wanted, in good Scottish fashion, that her eldest son should succeed in the world. I wanted to succeed in my profession, perhaps also in politics, to have an appropriate house and to be able to travel. No matter how much I wished to give voluntary service to help other people, and I did, I saw that my ambitions required money and that to make the amount I wanted, I should need to be able to control my own activities, to work as long and as hard as I wanted to work and to keep, subject to taxation, the rewards of my own efforts. So, deep down, I knew that my basic attitude was unsympathetic to the economic objectives and methods of Labour. After that Conference, I never sought further acquaintance with Labour men for any political or economic purpose.[14]

Soon after this David was again an observer, this time as a keen amateur photographer, and the outcome was very different. The occasion was the New Zealand University Easter tennis tournament.

The leading lady tennis player was Eva Cumming from Auckland. As I watched her play, I was attracted, and my camera came into play. But when I met her, with the light shining on her auburn hair, with 'eyes of gold and bramble dew' and her merry and spontaneous laugh, I was enchanted. So when she had returned to Auckland, with the Women's Singles and the Combined Doubles to her credit, I started a correspondence, sending her photographs of the tennis tournament.[15]

OHInt-0082-02.
14 DSS memoir, pp.62–63, DSS papers.
15 Ibid, p.26.

He visited her in Auckland, met her family, and found that he and Eva shared interests in the arts, in prose and poetry, and in social and moral questions. 'She filled my heart and mind and I fell in love with her.' Eva charmed his family and to everyone's delight, in October 1913, they became engaged.

But the outbreak of war created problems. Should they marry? Should he enlist? 'I cannot say that I wanted to enlist in the N.Z.E.F. My whole life had been directed towards peaceful work in a peaceful society. Though at College I had helped to organise a Social Service League, I had not joined the Officers Training Corps.' Then there were family needs. His father was a diabetic and in August 1914 the family doctor thought he might not live more than six months, and that it was David's duty to look after the family. Another factor was his work. In 1915 David became a partner at Charles Bruce Morison. C. B. Morison's two sons, both clerks in the office, had enlisted and Morison himself was ill. David was needed in the office. 'In all the circumstances, Eva and I decided to marry.'[16]

David's father married them at Knox Church in Parnell, Auckland, on 23 November 1915. After a honeymoon in the Bay of Islands the couple set up home in the house David had already built at 100 Upland Road, Kelburn. They were happy, but the shadow of the war was always in the background. Over the next year, David and some friends formed a New Zealand Returned Soldiers' Association to coordinate the activities of the local associations that were springing up around the country. David drafted its Constitution.[17]

SHIRLEY WAS BORN at 100 Upland Road on 10 October 1916. It was, Shirley says, a difficult birth. Two months later, in December, with Eva's agreement, David enlisted in the NZEF with instructions to report for the 30th Reinforcements the following March.[18]

Why he decided to enlist now when he had new family responsibilities, he didn't explain in his memoir. There was no conscription and married

16 Ibid, p.27.

17 Ibid, p.78. He writes that the only alteration it had ever required was the change of the word 'Soldiers' in the name to 'Services' in order, more naturally, to include women.

18 Ibid, p.38.

men were not expected to enlist. The lists of casualties included his great friend Allan MacDougall, who went to Oxford as a Rhodes Scholar, joined the army early in the war and was killed in August 1916. David thought Allan a man of the highest moral judgment and later named his son after him. One can understand David's moral predicament when people like Allan MacDougall gave their lives in what was now portrayed as a fight for good over evil.

Shirley never asked her father why he went to war. Most of her life she thought it was because Eva died and only learnt otherwise when she found a letter, dated December 1916, from Eva to her half-sister Annie. (It was a great thrill to Shirley to find a letter handwritten by her mother, the nearest thing to her mother's voice, expressing her love and fears. The pages have been opened, read and folded away again many times.) From her sickbed, Eva wrote that she had been diagnosed with appendicitis and there was talk of an operation. Her mother Emma was staying with them and David was home on holiday, helping with the baby.

The thought of David at the war is something I can't quite face up to at present but it's something we've got to live out. I shall always be very very truly glad we were married: this year has been worth anything even tho' it will hurt more now when he goes. And we have Shirley.

. . .

Colonel McDonald seems to think he should go in as an N.C.O. and if he gets his commission he will be about 10 months in camp – which prospect does not delight him. He wanted to know from the Defence yesterday what were his chances of getting away as a private with the Artillery. But those ranks are absolutely full of trained men. . . . these are David's last holidays before he goes into camp. . . .

We have advertised for a furnished room with use of kitchen at Trentham, so that I can be near David: then later I do want to go to Featherston too. . . .[19]

Eva's mother stayed on, and Willie Cumming, Eva's half-brother, was also there on Sunday 14 January when early in the morning

19 Eva Smith to Annie Mayer, December 1916, SHSS papers.

Eva's pain became acute. The family doctor was away and David had difficulty getting another doctor, who finally arrived about 9 am. He decided to do an appendectomy later that morning in the Thorndon Private Hospital. Shirley wrote, 'What happened was that when Dr Patterson saw her appendix, he realised that it was perfectly healthy: he then proceeded to make the long incision necessary to remove her gall bladder, which he rightly now saw as the problem. She died while he operated. The death certificate says that she died of shock.'[20] Eva was twenty-five.

20 SHSS memoir, 'My Life – First Causes' (following 'Te Deum'), 16 June 1998, p.3, SHSS papers.

2

Loss

A PRIVATE interment for Eva was held in the Karori Cemetery. David recalled in his memoir how he and 'Mithermie' (Eva's name for her mother that David also adopted) were both shattered. 'Even some weeks later when I thought I had regained my composure, I would find myself suddenly, almost hysterical.'[1]

Friends offered Emma their beach house at Plimmerton as a place to take Shirley. She later told Shirley that without her to look after, she would have gone mad.[2] On hearing the news, Emma's step-daughter Kathleen (Kitty) Cumming, who had rejoined the New Zealand Army Nursing Service in England (having earlier served on the hospital ship *Maheno* at Gallipoli), immediately sailed home.[3] With 'Nannie' and Auntie Kitty, Shirley was in good hands, but, as is now known, infants are sensitive to their emotional environment and also suffer from separation from their mothers in ways that have far-reaching psychological effects.[4] Shirley's need for love and intimacy through her life was perhaps deepened by this early loss.

David auctioned everything he and Eva had bought for their new home: furniture, carpets, piano, gramophone and records, ornaments, glassware, cutlery and crockery, bedding, kitchenware, cookbooks, pot plants, camera – 'the WHOLE of the SUPERIOR and NEW FURNITURE, contents of 7 rooms, all purchased from the leading

1 DSS memoir, p.80, DSS papers.

2 SHSS memoir, 'My Life – First Causes', undated (1990s), SHSS papers. The friends were Herbert Evans, known as Bertie, and his wife. Evans was later Solicitor General. Photos show David and Bertie with their babies Shirley and Harold in prams. Shirley and Harold remained lifelong friends.

3 Auckland Museum, http://www.aucklandmuseum.com (accessed 18 June 2018). Kitty had been on home leave, having earlier served as a nursing sister in the Mediterranean on both hospital ships *Maheno* and *Marama*, for which she received the Royal Red Cross.

4 Work on attachment by Winnicott, Bowlby and Balint, 'Dunedin Longitudinal Study'.

warehouses, in the city. . . . This is a beautifully furnished home, and everything is the best.'[5] In March, two months after Eva's death, David went into camp in Trentham. His parents moved from the manse into his Upland Road house and he arranged for his mother-in-law and the baby to live at Kenilworth, a boarding house in Hill Street. David saw as much of Shirley as possible. He visited Emma and Shirley on leave and Emma took Shirley to see him in Trentham.[6] He was due to go overseas in July 1917, but he was kept back to train a later reinforcement. His departure was further delayed because he left camp to run the firm when his partner C. B. Morison became ill. When he returned to camp, now at Tauherenīkau, he arranged for Emma and Shirley to live in the Salvation Army Hostel in Featherston, and again, spent as much time as possible with Shirley.

Finally, on 10 July 1918, with the rank of Company Sergeant Major to the 40th Reinforcements, David farewelled his parents from the troopship *Tahiti*: 'Now cheerio to everybody. I'm hopeful of a very good trip and a speedy return, but of course it's a bit hard leaving you all. I commend Shirley to you all. *Goodbye* from your loving son, David.'

THE VOYAGE went well until the ship joined a large convoy at Sierra Leone, where all the troopships came down with influenza. The *Tahiti* was the worst afflicted. Writing from No. 3 New Zealand General Hospital in Codford, Wiltshire, soon after arriving in England, David described how he succumbed on the second day and for several days had a temperature of between 104 and 105 degrees.

The natural strength of my heart pulled me through this but I was just on the verge of going right out, when Col. Allen saw me lying on the deck one morning . . . and I was taken that day to his cabin. I was also put into a hospital for dangerous cases organised that day. By dint of spongings and stiff whiskeys for three days, they got my temp down . . . But I was left so weak – far weaker than the proverbial kitten . . .

Very few people even thought I'd pull through. There was one time when

5 *Evening Post*, 28 February 1917, p.12, http://paperspast.natlib.govt.nz (accessed 26 September 2018).

6 DSS to parents and sisters, 8 March 1917, DSS papers.

I felt like hanging on for little Shirley's sake only. We had really to fight hard for our chances.[7]

Over 70 died on the *Tahiti*. David suffered from deafness, lapses of memory and a 'lack of grip', which lasted months. Though he found writing difficult he wrote a twelve-page account detailing the troopship's disorganisation and inadequate medical supplies and provisions. Men who pulled through the fever then died on the decks for lack of nutrition. (He sent his account to George Dixon, to be shown also to his friend Bertie Evans, and to the Government Statistician Malcolm Fraser, a Cumming relative.) When a Court of Inquiry was held and he wasn't called as a witness, David assumed that the whole thing had been whitewashed.

He also wrote to the relatives of the men in his Company who died. 'I think they will like to know the last about those dear to them and to feel that they were not passed by unnoticed. Our O.C. is not literary at all . . . other officers died. So I expect there's just about me left.'[8]

He had the highest praise for the nurses. He had met some of them in New Zealand through Kitty Cumming, including Matron McNie, who was in charge of the whole hospital, and Sister Grigor in charge of the isolation wards. Some of the nurses had even met Shirley. 'It's quite charming to find that my little girl predisposes people to be kind to her Daddy.'[9]

On 28 September he wrote that isolation had been lifted that day but 10,000 Americans who had just arrived had gone down with it.[10]

By the time his family received these letters, the epidemic had become a pandemic. It reached New Zealand in October. In Shirley's memoir

7 DSS to parents, 15 September 1918, as recounted in his memoir, pp.85–86, DSS papers.

8 DSS to parents, 21 September 1918, DSS papers.

9 Ibid.

10 DSS to parents, 28 September 1918, DSS papers. David added, 'Sister Grigor . . . says that all the bacteriologists of allied countries will be chasing this new germ, which our Rgt. introduced, with all the might of their bug-chasing brains in the endeavour to discover some serum or anti-toxin for it.' The influenza pandemic was first observed in Kansas in January 1918. In August a more virulent form appeared in Britanny, Sierra Leone and Boston. It didn't receive wide press attention until it moved to Spain, which was not involved in the war and had no wartime censorship, hence it became known as the 'Spanish Flu'.

she wrote, 'While the 'flu was raging in New Zealand, Nannie and Auntie Kitty were doing their best to prevent the baby catching it. They took me up to Rotorua, on the theory that the thermal fumes would ward off infection: they also burnt a substance giving off protective fumes (it was believed), in my room at night. (Creosote, I think.)'[11] In fact Shirley and Nannie moved to Rotorua to join Kitty, who was nursing in the new hospital for returned servicemen whose numbers included influenza patients.[12]

Ironically, the influenza that nearly killed David kept him from active service and assured his survival. When he was well enough he took sick leave, which he spent with his relatives in Scotland and Cambridge. Most significant, as far as Shirley's future was concerned, was his father's much younger sister, Sarah Milne, in Cambridge. One of few women doctors of her time, Sally, as she was called, had been a medical missionary in India, where she met her husband, Charles Milne, also a doctor. She then ran a civilian practice while he was in charge of a military medical unit in Egypt.

While staying with the Milnes, David sent Shirley a postcard of Girton College, Cambridge: 'This is the kind of college you might like to go to when you are big. Love from Daddy "Davit".'[13] This card to his two-year-old little girl in New Zealand stands out among others that were usually amusing pictures with messages in her own language. (David had a much younger sister, just seven years older than Shirley, and his family letters show how well he related to children.) He also sent photos of himself – 'Baby will have a copy of each' – and proudly showed off photos he received of Shirley in return.

Three days after the Armistice, David was in Sling Camp, New Zealand's main training camp in England, on the Salisbury Plains. The war was over, but training remained in full swing. 'We are all to be fully trained evidently,' he wrote to his family on 19 November.[14] As

11 SHSS memoir, 'My Life – First Causes', revised 1998, p.8, SHSS papers.

12 Kitty was in Rotorua 17 September 1917–28 February, 1919. NZ Defence Force Personnel Records, Kathleen Susan Cumming, Archives NZ, AABK 18805 W5537 0030841.

13 DSS to SHSS, 13 October 1918, SHSS papers.

14 DSS to family, 19 November 1918, DSS papers. David wrote in his memoir that he was

the 40th Reinforcements was one of the last to arrive, they were the last to be demobilised.

Before Christmas, an outbreak of measles put him back in quarantine, at Larkhill Military Hospital Isolation Ward. He had much time to ponder his and Shirley's future. On 16 April 1919 he wrote to his mother that he had written to Mrs Cumming:

I have said that two facts seem to stand out.

1 That I want to see Shirley.

2 That she (Mrs C) is apparently both for her own sake and Shirley's the person to continue looking after the little girl.

I have said also that these facts seem to suggest some kind of establishment run by her and me, seeing that Boarding houses are bad.

I have said also that I am merely making a suggestion and I have asked her frankly for her views.[15]

Eventually, on 27 July 1919, David embarked for New Zealand on the *Hororata*. Shirley recalls his arrival in Wellington about two months later:

I was dressed up in my best white frock, given a little Union Jack, and taken down to the wharf to meet the ship. I have a clear memory of the huge side of the ship, and the rows and rows of uniforms, topped with smiling faces, and Nannie and Kitty calling excitedly, 'There's Daddy, wave your flag for him!' And I remember what no-one could ever have told me, my dismay and confusion, because which of those smiling faces was Daddy? How could I tell?[16]

Shirley thought this was her first authentic memory, but then remembered an earlier one, of a stay in New Plymouth with Nannie's

at Codford Military Hospital 11 September–14 November 1918; Sling Military Camp 14 November–11 December 1918; Larkhill Military Hospital Isolation Camp 11 December 1918–20 May 1919 (because of an outbreak of measles); and again at Sling 20 May–27 July 1919 when he embarked on the *Hororata* for New Zealand.

15 DSS to Ann Smith, 16 April 1919, DSS papers.

16 SHSS memoir, 'My Life – First Causes', revised 1998, p.9, SHSS papers.

friend Mary Newton King at Broadlands. Shirley recalled waking in the night, calling for Nannie and finding her gone. 'A kind woman came and tried to soothe me, told me that Nannie had gone to see some friends and would be back before long . . . Nothing registered with me but that Nannie, my sole anchor, wasn't there, and I screamed for her and wouldn't stop. They had to send for her. I have the vividest memory of this.'[17]

Now she had her father. Initially David lived with her and Nannie at Kenilworth in Hill Street. Shirley recalled meeting him as he came home for lunch: 'He used to pretend to be blind, and would hold out his stick . . . and I would take the end and lead him home.'[18]

The three of them moved to a rented house in Kelburn, then to another in the Glen. Shirley had no memories of living together with both her father and Nannie, but she remembered a holiday together at Paihia, where David and Eva had spent their honeymoon. Her father drew in the sand a huge figure of a man with his feet towards the water, and they watched him being slowly washed away by the incoming tide. 'This was a regular beach entertainment put on by Daddy. But what happened only at Paihia, while we were on the beach, was that a small float plane, like a beautiful white bird, came in and landed on the sea near us. My first aeroplane.'[19]

David lived with Emma and Shirley for just over a year. He explained years later why the arrangement ended: after his partner died, David had to work day and night to restore the fortunes of the firm. Nannie wanted to talk. Shirley understood that he found this intolerable because Nannie's talk 'flowed like a river . . .'[20]

17 SHSS memoir, 'With Nannie' (following 'Te Deum'), revised 1998, p.9. SHSS papers. Broadlands is now a public park.

18 Ibid. It was the fashion for men to walk with elegant sticks. Electoral Roll 1919 lists Emma Cumming and David Stanley Smith both at 28 Hill St, confirming Shirley's memory.

19 Ibid.

20 SHSS memoir, 'My Life – First Causes', revised 1998, p.9, SHSS papers. David Smith was also Chairman of the Executive of the RSA for four years, and a member of the New Zealand Alliance 1921–22: *Auckland Star*, 4 April 1928, p.10. He was also vice-president of the NZRSA between 1920 and 1924, during the busiest period of the association's affairs: *Evening Post*, 4 April 1928, p.12, Papers Past. C. B. Morison died in January 1920:

David bought a section at what would become 23 Wadestown Road in Wellington's newly subdivided hillside suburb of Wadestown. He built a house made up of two flats, with the intention of Shirley and Nannie living in one and he in the other. Meanwhile, he shared a room with a friend in a boarding house in Hobson Street. Shirley and Nannie moved to a flat with Kitty Cumming in Rawhiti Terrace, Kelburn.

Auntie Kitty was Shirley's first heroine. Though as a child Shirley couldn't have understood the significance of her war medals – the 1914 Star (Mons Star), British War Medal and the Royal Red Cross – she remembered Kitty in her nursing sister's uniform as 'a noble and magnificent figure. I could not imagine anything better than to follow in her footsteps. She never married: she was reported to have said . . . that she had never wanted a husband, but she would have liked a little daughter: well, she got me, for a time.'[21]

Naturally Shirley's hero was her father. She eagerly anticipated Sunday outings with him, wearing the Saxe blue outfit – frock, coat and cap – that Nannie had made her for such occasions. 'I remember the delight with which I hailed the appearance of my father, young as he was then and handsome, with his black hair and blue eyes. I thought he was wonderful, and loved him dearly.'

He drove her in his new Tin Lizzie (Model T Ford) around the Wellington coast, with a stop for afternoon tea on the way. Sometimes they visited his mentor, Sir Frederick Chapman. 'I used to be sat in a small room, probably a study, where a fire burned in the grate, and I was provided with milk and biscuits, and two books – always the same, as I recall: Struwwelpeter and Baron Munchausen.'[22] The horror stories didn't bother her. She thought that her father was courting one of Sir Frederick's three daughters and never quite believed that he wasn't.

The close connection between the families continued down the generations. One of the daughters, Vera, married David's great friend Siegfried Eichelbaum – their daughter Ann married Wolfgang

Obituary. *Free Lance*, 13 January 1920, p.10.

21 SHSS memoir, 'My Life – First Causes', revised 1998, pp.8–9, SHSS papers. Kitty Cumming died of heart failure on 29 October 1931: Auckland War Memorial Cenotaph.

22 SHSS memoir, 'With Daddy – The Chapmans' (following 'Te Deum'), p.19, SHSS papers.

Rosenberg, their son George Rosenberg worked for Shirley in the 1970s, and their friendship lasted until her death.

After her husband's death, Emma Cumming had sold her Auckland house to make herself available to her large family, and this she continued to do. Shirley first sensed the romance of travel in Auckland when she stayed with Emma's sister, Ellen, and saw white steam and whistles rising from the Newmarket junction to Ely Avenue.

She felt at home on the Main Trunk between Auckland and Wellington. The Ladies' Carriage had a nurse in attendance who helped with babies and small children: 'She was always dressed in spotless white: did it stay spotless? Trains were stoked with coal, and the smoke was filthy and pervasive. It was always a problem, when there was a tunnel; there was a frantic rush to put the windows down.'

Nannie had a routine for travelling:

She paid for the use of two pillows, in clean white covers, from the kiosk on the platform and carried them, with her rugstrap, into the carriage . . . she aimed to get to the carriage early and secure the end seats. I do not recall her ever failing. She then turned the second-to-end one to face the end, and filled up the space between with our suitcases. When it was time to sleep, the rugs and pillows were placed so that we could have our heads on one seat and stretch out towards the other . . . I do not recall anyone ever objecting to this somewhat excessive claim on the seats, for the payment of one and a half tickets.

The journey itself was wondrous:

Fire-blackened stumps of trees on the blasted land below the central mountains, in the moonlight, looking like a landscape on the moon; the old Maori women, with their shawls over their heads, and moko on their chins, sitting on the platform at Te Awamutu, watching the train go through, at night; being taken to watch the engine's water tank being filled from the 'elephant's trunk' on the platform – I used to wonder, where was the rest of the elephant? – seeing One Tree Hill take shape in the distance, or the marvellous sight of Wellington harbour bursting into view as the train raced out of the tunnel through the hill below Wadestown.[23]

When they stayed with Auntie Annie and Uncle Don Mayer, they travelled by train to Mercer, then took a launch on the Waikato River to Orton and the Mayers' dairy farm. Once the launch hit a sandbank and their suitcase, piled on top of the others, was pitched into the water. This, and its rescue by the boatman, added to the drama of the river, all of which made a deep impression on young Shirley.

On the farm were calves and piglets. And Shirley had children to play with, her cousins Duncan and Barbara. When the Mayers moved to the farm next to Uncle Willie Cumming at Ardmore near Frankton Junction, there were more cousins, Isobel and Marjorie. They all referred to Shirley as 'Granny's girl'. She felt loved and secure.

From my mother's family I got a lot of love. I don't mean I didn't get a lot of love from my father's family, but my mother's family were my close family during the first six years of my life when I was living with my grandmother. I spent most of my time with her family. . . . four step-children. We never regarded the 'step' as significant in any way at all, or the fact that I was only half a cousin, not a real cousin. Those cousins were really my brothers and sisters.[24]

Back in Wellington, at their flat in Rawhiti Terrace, Shirley's relationships with other children weren't so happy. The landlady's daughters who lived upstairs taunted and rejected her. Shirley's memories of Queen Margaret Kindergarten were also unhappy, except for her teacher, Miss Grace, whom she would later envisage as Katherine Mansfield's Māori princess friend, Maata.

At Kelburn Normal School, Shirley took a stand against sexual discrimination. 'I had long admired the shiny leather schoolbags that the boys carried, cater-cornered across their backs. Knowing that I was

23 SHSS memoir, 'With Nannie', pp.10–11, SHSS papers.

24 SHSS to Neville Glasgow, interview for National Radio, broadcast January 1989, published in *Directions: New Zealanders Explore the Meaning of Life*, Shoal Bay Press, Christchurch, 1995, pp.186–201.

soon going to school, I asked, when do we get my schoolbag? Oh, I was told, those are for boys, girls carry attaché cases. I desperately desired a bag and saw no reason for the discrimination: I got my bag.'[25]

But at school, too, she was unhappy, 'at least in the playground, where bullying and terrorising of the small fry was a normal part of this Normal school.' In the classroom she had no difficulty, but one incident filled her with horror. To punish a small boy, the teacher made him stand on a table, with the children all watching, took what seemed to be an endless bandage and bandaged him from the feet up, turning him into a cocoon. Seeing his face disappear, Shirley wanted to call out, but didn't dare.

She took to skipping school. She recalls 'lying out in the sun on the long grass on top of some bank in Kelburn, and watching white clouds blown across the blue sky, and persuading myself that I could hear the earth turning.' Her Primer II report for the term ending 18 August 1922 noted that she had been absent 23 days. Her absences prompted a visit to her father from a truant officer. She nevertheless made good progress. Her report described her as a 'bright little pupil but inclined to be over-anxious.'

Some of her absences were attributed to dancing classes, others to tonsillitis. Her tonsils were removed on the kitchen table without adequate anaesthetic and when she came to, blood was streaming from her mouth. 'I screamed and screamed, as much from the fright of the bleeding as the pain.' Years later it was found that they had not been removed from the roots and had re-grown, become infected and had to be removed again.

25 SHSS memoir, 'Kelburn' (following 'Te Deum'), undated, p.16, SHSS papers.

3

Little Red Fed

In January 1922 David announced his engagement to Margaret Elizabeth Gibbs. Shirley was 'disappointed'. She added that she was lucky to have 'an extremely intelligent and very kind stepmother', but it took years to see her in that good light.

Meta, as she was called, was the eldest of three daughters of Richard Wain Gibbs, Government Auditor of the Bank of New Zealand. She and David had known each other since university when they worked together on the Students' Association executive and the Christian Union. Meta graduated with an MA Honours in Mental Science, then took up teaching. Her last position was headmistress of Archerfield, a girls' private boarding school in Dunedin. Back in Wellington, she did voluntary work for the Federation of University Women and the YWCA. Besides her intellectual qualities, David found her sympathetic and fun.

Shirley had little opportunity to get to know her future stepmother. Following their engagement, Meta spent most of the year on a trip to Europe with her parents – her second world trip.

The wedding took place in January 1923. Shirley was hurt when she learnt that Meta's niece Betty Batham was to be the flower girl and, worse, that she herself wasn't even to attend. Soon after the wedding, when she was in Auckland with Nannie and Auntie Kitty, David telephoned to say he was coming up by train to collect her and would Nannie please have her ready. Though she knew it was coming, Nannie was heartbroken. She told Shirley, '– and he did not call me "Mitheree"', which Shirley thought the unkindest cut.[1]

1 SHSS, 'Re-marriage, the Gibbs Family' (following 'Te Deum'), pp.20–22, SHSS papers. (David spelt it 'Mitherie'.) From then on David called Emma Cumming 'Nannie'.

But she wasn't sad at leaving. She supposed it was because she was going to live with her adored father.

He told her a few years later that he had felt it was time she was removed from Nannie and Auntie Kitty because they spoilt her. Possibly on the same occasion, he raised the subject of his remarriage. 'What came through clearly to the child was that he felt he had to justify himself to Eva's daughter for taking unto himself another wife, after losing his one true love.' She said she understood it would be unreasonable to expect a man, however devoted he was to his first wife, to remain without one from the age of twenty-eight until death. At six she may have thought differently, but she later wrote, 'I never doubted their love; it was the food of my childhood.'[2]

The adults would tell Shirley about her wonderful mother and she grew up cherishing this knowledge, visualising her, idealising her. Every night before she lay down to sleep she kissed the photograph of her mother that hung above her bed.

Also in her bedroom was a metal trunk with her mother's clothes. Nannie and Kitty had kept them for Shirley and sent the trunk with her when she left them, and it sat there in her room. No one ever mentioned it, but later, after her half-brother Allan was born and Shirley was 'banished' to a downstairs bedroom, she would secretly open the trunk. When her parents were out at night, she would try on some of the garments.

There were big roomy bloomers, white cotton, which did up at the waist with a button . . . camisoles, a number of very pretty white cotton tops, with lace and ribbons . . . There were beautiful evening dresses: these I did not try on. There was a tennis skirt, long and heavy. . . . I would keep my ears cocked for the sound of the car, as it came up the hill, and turned into the garage. Back went everything into the trunk, out went the light. I was never caught.[3]

2 Ibid.

3 SHSS memoir, 'Wadestown – Twenties', 24 June 1998, p.8, SHSS papers. At the end of World War II, when clothes rationing was still in force, Shirley took the evening dresses with her when she joined her husband, Bill Sutch, in London. She had them altered and wore them in Paris.

Like the picture above her bed, the trunk of clothes in her room was not something forbidden, yet she behaved and thought as though it was. In her father's household there was little talk about her 'wonderful' mother. When Shirley suggested to her father that they tend her mother's grave as she used to do with Nannie, he was horrified. Shirley never went again.

But the ghost of Eva was present, even if no one spoke of her.

FOR SOME TIME after leaving Nannie, Shirley was afraid at bedtime. Her father always came to kiss her goodnight, but as soon as he returned to the drawing room she would call for him again, and he would come. 'He came again and again, how often I can't say, but I marvel to remember how return he did, with never a word of reproach, to comfort and reassure me. He must have been very conscious that a six-year-old had been taken away from the only mother she had ever known; but how many men would have been so patient?'[4]

In the morning she would go into her parents' bedroom when the maid brought their morning cups of tea, hop into bed with her father who sang to her and told stories. Then she had to take a cold bath. This was a shock. She found a way around it then, but years later she willingly adopted the routine. Most of her life she started the day with a cold plunge.

Shirley didn't go to school for the first year of the new marriage. The idea was to help her settle into her new home and get to know her new 'Mummy', and to give her a break after her unhappy time at Kelburn School before starting a new school. Meta, being a teacher, kept her up with her lessons. Shirley didn't remember these, only that when they ended, Meta would take her to sit in the sunny little front hall and read to her. 'She also produced a small china box, very pretty . . . and allowed me to take one butter ball, a kind of boiled sweet I thought delicious. One chapter and one butterball.'[5]

Early in the year, Meta had a visit from a woman who had known Eva

4 SHSS memoir, 'Life in Wadestown' (following 'Te Deum'), undated, pp.25–26, SHSS papers.
5 SHSS memoir, 'Re-marriage – the Gibbs Family' (following 'Te Deum'), undated, p.22, SHSS papers.

and wanted to check on Shirley. She wrote to reassure Mrs Cumming: 'She is still the same bright happy quaint little lassie, and Mrs David is very sweet with her, in such a really nice way. Certainly I think that Shirley's individuality will not be repressed . . . I do hope she grows up like her mother . . .'[6]

But Shirley was difficult. Her father affectionately called her his 'little Red Fed'. He said that she was the most stubborn child he had ever met and that 'Shirley always kicks against the pricks.'[7] 'I didn't set out to be difficult,' she told an interviewer in 1984, '– my father regarded me as difficult, but I think I must have a bit of him in me. He always did exactly as he wanted.'[8]

As far as Shirley was concerned, Meta was the problem. She thought of herself as a poor little girl with a horrid stepmother. 'I had a lot of girls' books of my mother's that had been saved for me: one was called *Bad Little Hannah*, and it appeared, by the end, that she had only been "bad" because she was so unhappy with her stepmother. I identified with bad little Hannah, although I don't remember being very bad, only unhappy.'[9]

Yet she was sympathetic towards her stepmother in some respects. After living with Nannie and Auntie Kitty, some of her father's patriarchal rulings seemed unfair and she spoke up for Meta in these instances. 'It was not that she sought my sympathy, it was natural for me to feel it.' To her father's credit, he allowed her to speak freely when she saw an injustice. 'He never punished me and never put me down.'[10]

6 Winnie V. Thompson to Emma Cumming, 8 April 1923, SHSS papers.

7 There are many references to this, including 'Wadestown – Twenties', 24 June 1998, p.3, SHSS papers. 'It is hard for you to kick against the pricks' was a Greek proverb used in the Bible in Acts 9:5 or 26:14 (but not in the original Greek manuscript). It refers to an oxen's resistance to the correcting prick or goad as it tilled the soil. When the ox kicked against the pricks, the pricks bit deeper. The animal thereby inflicted further pain upon itself.

8 SHSS, interview with Victoria Main, 'The Crusades of Shirley Smith', W5, pp.12–13, 23 March–5 April 1984.

9 SHSS memoir, 'Life in Wadestown' (following 'Te Deum'), undated, p.27, SHSS papers. In this book by L. T. Meade, eight-year-old Hannah struggles with the question of whether to be good or bad.

10 SHSS memoir, 'Wadestown – Twenties', 24 June 1998, p.3, SHSS papers.

Meta had sacrificed much to be a housewife and mother. She had been a professional woman, she was older than David, more widely travelled, more modern in her thinking – and she didn't like housework and cooking. They had a live-in maid but, except when they brought in a cook for dinner parties, Meta cooked the meals. She had no experience of cooking before she married and never enjoyed it. Shirley recalled a painful Sunday dinner:

. . . and for Dad there was only one Sunday dinner, roast beef and Yorkshire pudding, with roast vegetables, followed by apple pie and cream. The beef was always a deboned sirloin, and it was always tough. On this occasion, after sharpening the carving knife, Dad attacked the beef, threw down the carvers, and said, 'tough again!' Mum dropt her head, and wept. I was dreadfully embarrassed, slipped down from my chair, went up to Dad and whispered in his ear 'Go and kiss her and say you're sorry', and left the room.[11]

Early in the marriage, Meta was asked to go back on the staff at Wellington Girls' College. 'Mum would have loved to do this. She referred the request to Dad, who said, No, it was not proper for a professional man's wife to take a job, even if it would be a return to her own profession. So Mum stayed at home.' Fortunately – as David controlled the household finances – she had some independent income. Shirley would remember Meta telling her, 'Remember, it is essential for a married woman to have some money of her own.'[12]

On 13 October 1924, three days after Shirley's eighth birthday, her half-brother Allan was born. Though Shirley felt banished when she was moved to a downstairs bedroom, her baby brother captured her affection and pity. As he grew, he was found to have bow legs and wore bands to pull them into shape; this in turn made him knock-kneed, so he was put into irons to straighten them in the opposite direction. When he learnt to walk, it was with the aid of two sticks and he couldn't

11 SHSS memoir, 'Life in Wadestown' (following 'Te Deum'), undated, p.26, SHSS papers.
12 SHSS memoir, 'Wadestown – Twenties', 24 June 1998, p.18, SHSS papers.

climb stairs. By then Meta was pregnant again. 'I have this clear and awful memory of pregnant Mum carrying him, irons, sticks and all, up and down stairs.'[13]

The new baby was stillborn. This sadness was borne quietly. Only after the birth of his own son, Hugh, did Allan learn from his father of this other baby whose name coincidentally was to have been Hugh.

Shirley remembered Allan fondly: 'and Dad thought of a pet name for him – Homiti, which being translated, meant "little Smith man": Hom, from homo, Latin for man, miti, the Maori for Smith, and iti, the Maori for little.'[14]

Shirley's sympathy for Allan grew. He suffered from incontinence for years, not helped by medical advice that it could be psychologically controlled. Meta had a child-friendly approach, at odds with David's. 'He had to be brave, not cry, not show fear, be a man. . . . I had no such problems; I was a girl.'[15]

And as Allan once said, 'Shirley is the child of the most loved wife.'[16]

Shirley's extended family now included Meta's, and she saw a good deal of them. Alternating with visits to David's parents, the Smiths visited Meta's widowed father every second Sunday for high tea. Shirley thought Grandpa Gibbs a crusty old man. She hated him because he teased her. Exchange visits with Meta's sisters and their families, the Bathams and Skinners, who lived in Dunedin, included a trip to Dunedin for the Great Exhibition in 1925 and a summer holiday in Nelson with other Gibbs relatives.

David was always attentive to his own large family and on that holiday in Nelson they took with them his sister-in-law, Nellie Smith, to give her a much-needed holiday from Eltham where her husband Jim was a minister. She brought her four-year-old son, Neil. Shirley thought him a peevish child, but as adults they grew close, brought together by their socialist politics.

She loved her visits to Gran'ma and Gran'pa Smith. 'I would run

13 Ibid, p.5.
14 SHSS memoir, 'Life in Wadestown' (following 'Te Deum'), undated, p.29, SHSS papers.
15 SHSS memoir, 'Wadestown – Twenties', 24 June 1998, p.6, SHSS papers.
16 Ibid.

down the path and the steps ahead of the others, and at my knock, the door would fly open, and there would be Gran'ma, beaming, with her arms wide open for the hug I always got.' Gran'pa Smith wrote poetry and gardened. He created a water folly Shirley loved. On their Sunday drives, he always led the singing. She thought him 'a lovely, generous man'. She always remembered what he said to her on one occasion when she was being emotional: 'Remember, Shirley, a dry light burns brightest.'[17]

David's sisters, Fiona and Wynnie, figured largely in Shirley's upbringing. Lorna did not, but she would haunt Shirley. The story Shirley tells is that when Eva and David were engaged, Lorna went to stay with the Cummings in Auckland.

After a lovely time, the return to Kelburn was too much. To start with, she dressed in the frock she had worn in the mornings. 'What are you thinking of?' asks Gran'ma. 'Go and take that off and get into your working dress. Get a bucket and clean the bathroom.' Lorna did as asked, so far as filling a bucket of water was required, and from the top of the stairs poured the contents of the bucket on Gran'ma, who was standing below, no doubt still issuing orders. And that was that. Lorna spent the rest of her life in Porirua.[18]

If this says more about Shirley than what actually happened, it explains her view of 'Generalissima' Gran'ma Smith. (Shirley naturally identified with Lorna – was the story told to her as a warning?) But in fact, it wasn't until 1919, when David was in England, that Lorna's state of mind became serious. He wrote to his mother:

I feel awfully sorry for her and for the rest of us too. It is hard. I do hope she will get completely over her lapses. It's a mystery to me to understand what has brought her to this stage. Have you any idea? And what has the doctor said?

17 SHSS, 'The Smith Family', undated (1992–98), p.12, SHSS papers. Shirley gave this example of John Smith being a rationalist, not an enthusiast.

18 SHSS memoir, 'Wellington to end 1928', 27 July 1998, SHSS papers.

I suppose it's not necessary to ask you to buck up and face these inevitable things quietly.[19]

His fear of word getting out was a normal concern at a time when mental illness carried such stigma and Porirua (synonymous for the mental hospital there) was a place of dread, but David took Shirley as a small child to see Lorna. Shirley remembered the first time, waiting in a wooden reception hall with chairs around the walls. 'We had to wait quite a long time, but eventually there appeared, in the doorway at the far end of the room from the entrance, a vision. A tall elegant woman in a long white dress, her long dark hair wound around her head like a crown. This was Auntie Lorna . . . I thought she was beautiful.'[20]

Later, before Allan was born, David, Meta and Shirley drove to Porirua, picked Lorna up and took her to 100 Upland Road for afternoon tea with her mother. Tea was served on the front lawn and everything went well until it was time to go. 'Auntie Lorna did not want to go. She was persuaded into the car by false pretences. . . . as soon as she realised that we were on the road to Porirua, she became extremely agitated, and when Dad would not turn back, she hammered on the back seats and cried, "Take me back to 100 Upland Road!"' For Shirley, in the front with her parents, it was dreadful, with Lorna repeating her cry all the way.

Shirley couldn't recall anyone mentioning Lorna ever again. She didn't know if anyone ever visited her; she knew only that her aunt died at a comparatively young age of pneumonia. (She died in 1927, aged 31 or 32.) She never asked her father about her but she did ask her Aunt Fiona, who just looked strained and said, 'She *was* odd.'[21]

Her memory of Lorna was one of the reasons Shirley later took special interest in mental health issues in her work as a lawyer.

19 DSS to family, 16 April 1919, DSS papers, replying to letters posted two months earlier from his mother and Wynnie.
20 SHSS memoir, 'Wellington to end 1928', 27 July 1998, SHSS papers.
21 Ibid.

DAVID SMITH, by this time no longer a Christian believer, had left the Presbyterian Church, but kept some of their customs. Though theirs wasn't a Calvinist household, Sundays were for rest and recreation – family visits and Sunday drives. When he bought a Willys-Knight with a detachable canvas hood, their Sunday drives took them further afield, around the Wellington coast, up the Hutt Valley and over the hills to the Kāpiti Coast. These were jolly expeditions – there was always a picnic and usually a swim in the river or sea, and singing all the way home – but on one occasion, driving from Trentham 'over the Moonshine', Shirley saw in the valley below an encampment where a few bedraggled men were milling about miserably in the rain. Her father explained that it was a relief work camp for the unemployed. (This was towards the end of the 1920s, an early sign of the Depression.) Shirley was appalled that they lived there away from their families in such pitiable conditions. She was shocked on another drive, over the flats of Rongotai and Strathmore, to be told that the concrete boxes she saw were houses, recently built for the poor.

Shirley learnt about 'the poor' at Sunday School, Bible Class and at church: 'For ye have the poor with you always, and whensoever ye will ye may do them good' (Mark 14:7). Along with teachings about truth, righteousness and compassion, and the good shepherd who defended the weak, she learnt that Jesus was a bold rebel. That appealed – in the 1960s she gave a radio talk about this. Though Shirley later rejected the Church, she consciously based her moral code on the Christian teachings she learnt as a child.

Ironically it was Meta, an Anglican, who guided Shirley's religious upbringing. Meta had moved to the Presbyterian Church when she married, and she took Shirley to the little Presbyterian church in Wadestown. Shirley took her Presbyterianism very seriously: it was her tribe. Granddaughter of a Presbyterian minister, she was also the great-niece of the Very Rev. Dr James Gibb DD, the best known and most controversial Presbyterian leader of his time.[22] Seeing Shirley as a good

22 James Gibb had brought about the union of the independent Northern and Southern Churches in 1901 and was elected as the first Moderator of the United Presbyterian Church of New Zealand. The University of Aberdeen conferred on him the honorary degree, Doctor of Divinity. He had been militant during the war, encouraging clergy to

Presbyterian in the making, he exhorted her to always remember that she was a 'strong little Scotch woman Presbyterian'.

James Gibb had co-founded Wellington's Queen Margaret College in Thorndon in the spirit of Scottish Presbyterian schools for girls. Naturally it was to be Shirley's new school. In 1924 a close friend of her parents, Irene Wilson, became headmistress. '. . . life within the school was full and happy in 1924 and there was a coherence about it . . . To the girls Miss Wilson was attractive in every way – young, modern . . . frank, energetic and in command of every situation. . . . Girls had for her a deep and healthy respect.'[23] Shirley recalled, 'She was a wonderful teacher and a wonderful headmistress and she really created that school, made it . . . into something significant.'[24]

Shirley's end-of-year school report in 1924 showed she was generally doing very well.

In 1925 schools were closed until April by an outbreak of infantile paralysis. Shirley stayed with Nannie and the Mayers at the farm they had moved to at Ardmore, near Papakura, next to Uncle Willie Cumming's farm. Auntie Annie, an ex-schoolteacher, supervised the work schools sent them to do from home. These were happy times, roaming on the farm barefoot until they were called in for meals.

And she was happy at school, too, when it reopened:

23 Wadestown Road
'Cliffton'
16th April 1925

Dear darling Dad,

How are you getting on with your work. It is splendid at school, Joan Goodwin is a new girl, and she is a darling, and is my best friend. She is in form III and I am in form II. There are two new girls I have to look

serve, but after the war he became an outspoken pacifist. He founded the New Zealand Branch of the League of Nations Union.

23 Mollie D. Gambrill, *A History of Queen Margaret College*, Board of Governors, Queen Margaret College, Wellington, New Zealand, 1969, p.73.

24 This is from the oral history of Shirley Smith with Hugo Manson on 4 November 1988 commissioned by the New Zealand Law Society, Wellington Branch, side 2, ATL, OHInt-0082-02.

after, Elna and Betha Wright; and they follow me round like dogs, and on the first day I could not play – just for them. They come from Johnsonville.
With love from your darling Shirley Whirley-bolby-bus.[25]

She was back at Ardmore in September with Nannie, Auntie Kitty, the Mayers and Cummings, including her uncle Duncan Cumming and his family who lived in South Africa. (She would get to know her South African cousins later at Oxford.) After writing home, mostly about calves, dogs, cats and kittens, she added, 'To Daddy. I am not getting all nervy and excited, don't you worry about that!'[26] Her father apparently did worry about that.

She now wore spectacles, which did nothing for her self-esteem. But having 'best' friends at Queen Margaret's helped her settle at home. Her new best friend, Marjorie Shoosmith, was quite different from anyone she had met before. Marjorie's whole family seemed exotic. Her parents came from English and Scottish merchant families, but were both born and married in Russia, and Marjorie had been born there. They fled the Revolution in 1917. Shirley was entranced by Marjorie's stories of her parents smuggling her out at night, wrapped in blankets, leaving behind their possessions and escaping to England where Mr Shoosmith then worked for British Intelligence. The girls swore eternal friendship. Their lives would take them on different paths, but they always kept in touch.

School reports show Shirley was bright and doing well academically. Her Term II report in 1926 typically shows she was top of the class in English, reading and history, and in most subjects she was near the top, always with the exception of arithmetic. Principal Irene Wilson makes the following additional remarks:

Conduct *Good, but a little too assertive.*
Diligence *Keenly interested; lacks steadiness.*
Progress *Very good; but Shirley needs to learn patience and humility.*[27]

In 1927 she passed her Certificate of Proficiency, the award school

25 SHSS to DSS, 16 April 1925, SHSS papers, ATL, MS-Papers-11404-01.
26 SHSS, 21 September 1925.
27 Queen Margaret Term II report, 1926, SHSS papers, ATL, MS-Papers-11404-01.

inspectors gave to children who passed Standard VI (Year 8).

IN THE NEW YEAR, 1928, while staying with Nannie and the Mayers on their farm at Ardmore, Shirley was admitted to the isolation ward in Hamilton's public hospital with scarlet fever. The disease was then, in the days before antibiotics, serious and often fatal. She was discharged six weeks later. 'Oh, you don't know how spiffing it is to be out of that hospital!' she wrote to her family in Wellington. She then had a fortnight's seaside holiday with Nannie at Narrow Neck on Auckland's North Shore, which her father agreed was necessary to complete her recuperation.

Shirley didn't mention this illness in her recollections, nor that she was taken out of school for most of that year on account of her deteriorating eyesight. Her eye specialist, Dr L. D. Cohen, thought the problem would be solved by her avoiding close-up work. (Allan Smith, who had the same condition and treatment, could never understand how their father was taken in by this idea.) She was back with the Mayers in June, then sent to a farm on the Ōtaki River, owned by an acquaintance of her father. Shirley stayed with the manager's family. A new bike gave her some independence, but she was much happier when she was back at the Mayers in September.

When Shirley was home, she went for solitary early morning runs to Wilton's Bush and up Tinakori Hill. 'There were beautiful open grassy hillsides, down which you could roll quite a distance, great fun, and wonderful views.' The trig was then overgrown with mānuka, all flattened by the wind. 'A child could lie on the top, as on a bed, and bounce . . . And when the wind became a gale, you could lean back into it, trust yourself to it, and it would hold you up. . . . I also climbed every bank that seemed possible: I adored climbing, banks or trees . . .'[28] Later she wondered if wandering alone in the hills in the wild northerlies helped stiffen her back. 'How difficult to work out what made one the person one now is.'[29]

THE PATTERN of life at home included her father's periodic absences.

28 SHSS memoir, 'Wadestown – Twenties', 24 June 1998, p.19.
29 SHSS to MSS, 29 December 1974, MSS papers, ATL, MS-Papers 9268-015.

He had become an expert on Māori land law, and he dealt with most of his firm's work that came before parliamentary committees. The work often concerned petitions by Māori regarding their grievances over land confiscations following the wars of the 1860s. When Prime Minister Gordon Coates set up a commission, presided over by Justice William Sim, to enquire into their grievances, David Smith was offered the brief to represent the Taranaki, Waikato and Bay of Plenty iwi.

Shirley had almost no contact with Māori in her daily life, but her father talked to her about his clients and sometimes took her to meetings with them.

When he did, it remained with me as an important memory. It was clearly brought home to me at this stage the importance of the Maoris as the first inhabitants of New Zealand and of the importance of their claims.

He told me how Sir Maui [Pōmare] *had been his mentor in the Taranaki land claims in the late 1920s, and had translated for him at a great gathering of the country people at the Urenui marae; how he had been humbled by the consciousness that all these people depended on him and him alone. He was proud of finding a way around the restrictive terms of reference so that he could bring in individual claims.*[30]

David told her a lot about that. She understood that his part in the Commission's finding that the wars in Taranaki and the Waikato were unjustified was the beginning of justice for Māori. In recognition of this, his clients presented him with some splendid feather cloaks and other taonga, which they had at home for a time, until protocol demanded they be returned.[31] Later, when Sir Māui was ill with tuberculosis, David took Shirley to see him at his home in Belmont, Lower Hutt. Later still, Lady Pōmare visited the Smiths to present her tall teenage grandson, also called Māui. These people made a deep impression on Shirley.

Following the Sim Commission, David was appointed to the

30 SHSS to Louise Pōmare, 8 April 1995, Cecilia Johnson papers.

31 Sir David wrote in his memoir: 'It is true to say, I think, that this Native Affairs Commission of 1926–1927 is regarded by both Maori and Pakeha alike as one of the most important in Maori affairs and as one which made a substantial contribution to the improvement of racial relationships in New Zealand.'

Supreme Court Bench. When he took this up on 26 April 1928 he was, at the age of 40, the second youngest judge to be appointed in New Zealand (the youngest since colonial times). He was often away on circuit. Shirley wrote to him, usually addressing him 'Dearest old Judgey Dad', and in one, adding a PS: 'Don't send too many people to gaol!'[32]

David now had the annual six-week judicial holiday in December and January when the courts closed. At the end of 1928 the Smiths camped at Taupō on the land David's partner Gordon Morison had inherited from his father, on the riverside opposite the wharf. There was a fishing shack with one bedroom, which no one had used in years. The family loved the place and, when the estate was subdivided, David Smith bought the site, one acre of the fifteen.

Despite missing so much schooling in 1928, in 1929 Shirley topped her class in most subjects. As Puck in the school's production of *A Midsummer Night's Dream*, she fell in love with Shakespeare. She was also entralled by poetry (Palgrave's *Golden Treasury*) and English language and grammar (according to J. C. Nesfield). She had friends. She was happy.

AT THE END of 1929, after her father became a resident judge in Auckland, the family moved to Auckland. Shirley was devastated at having to leave the life she now enjoyed.

About this time she started to build a better relationship with her stepmother. 'I suddenly had a flash of insight and enlightenment and decided she was an extremely nice woman and she and I were going to be friends. It worked out extremely well after that. She talked to me as a person, not as a child.'[33] But she now clashed with her father. He thought some of her behaviour – chatting away to a male hotel servant, not wearing gloves and stockings – reflected badly on him. He told her later that he was amazed at her independence. 'He couldn't understand how I could do and say what I thought was right and didn't care what

32 SHSS to DSS, 15 October 1928, SHSS papers, ATL, MS-Papers-11404-01.

33 SHSS to Neville Glasgow, interview, broadcast on National Radio on 18 January 1989, published in *Directions: New Zealanders Explore the Meaning of Life*, Shoal Bay Press, Christchurch, 1995, p.191.

people thought.'[34]

With the move to Auckland, the social distinctions that came with her father's position were more apparent than in Wellington. They lived first in a hotel, then at Bishop's Court in Parnell for a year, and finally bought a huge property in Victoria Avenue in Remuera. They had staff: a gardener, a mechanic for the cars, a live-in maid and a cook for occasions when they entertained. Shirley's parents established themselves in the upper echelons of Auckland society.

By contrast, her farming relatives had little to show for their hard work as the Depression kicked in. One of the children's jobs was making toilet paper: cutting newspaper into squares, which they then threaded together and hung on a nail in the outhouse lavatory. Even there, Shirley picked up a sense of class distinction. There were subtle hints that that the neighbours were not quite 'our' kind of people. But she also knew that dairy farmers did not move in the circle of Supreme Court judges. The accent Shirley acquired in the Waikato was noticed and banned when she came home.

Shirley always kept in touch with her farming relatives, but summer holidays were now spent at Taupō. Nannie joined them there once, but the visit wasn't a success. Meta's family often stayed, including Shirley's step-cousin Betty Batham, and Shirley brought friends but not her Mayer and Cumming cousins. Shirley's brother Allan said he never met them.

They saw a good deal of Nannie though. She had settled in Auckland and was one of the reasons David moved there. Living close to Nannie was expected to be some compensation for Shirley. Their house in Victoria Avenue was near Nannie's in Remuera Road. The whole family used to visit her for Sunday afternoon tea.[35]

But nothing made up for leaving her friends. Shirley would be grateful for her one year at St Cuthbert's College, but at the vulnerable age of thirteen she felt once again an outsider.

She took out her misery on the family, and in later life was always

34 This is from the oral history of Shirley Smith with Hugo Manson on 4 November 1988 commissioned by the New Zealand Law Society, Wellington Branch, side 2, ATL, OHInt-0082-02.

35 AGS to author, interview, 28 February 2011, track 2.

perceptive about disruptive children whose behaviour reflected feelings of alienation. Writing in 1995 to a friend about a difficult son, she explains, 'The trouble is, the more the one who is odd man out gets the blame, maybe quite justifiably, for what he does or how he behaves, the worse he is likely to get, because what he is reacting against is feeling he is out of favour. What he needs is reassurance that he is a member of the family.'[36]

In Shirley's case, however, it was decided that boarding school was the answer.

36 SHSS to Jenny Sivitos, 6 February 1995, SHSS papers.

4

Nga Tawa

THE CHOICE of Nga Tawa for Shirley is surprising. The small Church of England school in the Rangitīkei town of Marton largely attracted farmers' daughters who had little interest in education. And yet the school prospectus stated that they prepared girls for the entrance examinations to Oxford and Cambridge. This was based on only one girl having gone from Nga Tawa to Oxford, but for Shirley's parents the possibility may have been significant.

Shirley thought they chose Nga Tawa for its playing fields. 'They thought that what little Shirley needed was to get out in the open air and run about.'[1] Many girls had their own ponies at school and Shirley had horse-riding lessons at one stage. She took up lacrosse, an English game she had not played at her Presbyterian schools.

Nga Tawa was as English as her previous schools had been Scottish. Most of the teachers were recruited from England and were neither successful academics nor great teachers. The headmistress, Miss Frances Helen McCall, wanted to turn out young ladies, but her English recruits who thought this would be an easy task found the 'wild colonial girls' too hard to handle and left when they finished their three-year contracts. Comparing Nga Tawa with St Cuthbert's, Shirley found the discipline was as lax as the academic standards.

Shirley's parents would have liked the idea of her being transformed into a 'lady' and Miss McCall's aspiration to send girls forth into the world 'equipped, not only with a sound education . . . but with a desire to serve others, and to use their knowledge for the benefit of their Country and of the Empire'.[2]

1 SHSS to Neville Glasgow, first broadcast on National Radio, 18 January 1989, published in *Directions: New Zealanders Explore the Meaning of Life*, Shoal Bay Press, Christchurch, 1995, pp.186–201.

2 Miss F. H. McCall's report in *The Diocesan Chronicle*, February 1931.

For Shirley, Nga Tawa was like a prison sentence. She never fitted in. Part of her Presbyterian ethic was to do well academically. She had a natural love of learning and her studies proved a refuge from loneliness, but it wasn't done to work hard at Nga Tawa.

Aged fourteen and, at under five feet, one of the smallest in the school, she went into Middle V, a class where she was a year younger than the average age and two classes ahead of most of the new girls. The girls in Studholme, her boarding house, didn't invite her to join their groups of friendships – 'crews'. If you weren't in a crew you were non-existent, but nobody wanted her and she was too proud to join the 'crewless'.

Her letters home ached with misery:

22 February 1931
My Darlingest dear Daddy,

Thank you ever so much for your letter. I loved getting it 'cos I'm so homesick. This place is alright but it's nothing like home. Oh Daddy I do want you.

. . . Today after dinner the new girls had to go over to Miss McCall's cottage; we went in separately and she asked me how I was getting on and was so jolly nice that I couldn't help crying. I know it was silly but she was so nice and sort of reminded me of home.

I'll do my best, Daddy, trust me. I'm going to work like a Trojan, but I'll be very careful of my eyes, and play lots of games too.

. . .

We have just had fire drill. We have it every day and it is becoming rather a nuisance, specially at night when bed is so warm. Bed is the place I like best here. You remember I used to hate going to bed? I look forward to it now.

. . . Please give lots and lots of love to Mummy and Allan and Daddy, I can't say what I feel, except that I'm always your own lovingest Shirley-wirley.[3]

3 SHSS to DSS, 22 February 1931, SHSS papers, ATL, MS-Papers-11404-01.

21 June 1931

Daddy, I've discovered what I don't like about this school . . . It's not the school or the mistresses, or the lax state of work, but the girls. They can make you feel absolutely awful – as if you were the stupidest, silliest, most unworthy person there ever was. I daresay it's mostly my imagination, but it is awful sometimes. I only mention this because I wanted to tell you the reasons. I'm not whining . . .[4]

Her father's quick reply prompted an outpouring:

27 June 1931

My darlingest Daddy,

Thank you ever and ever so much for your letter. Oh Dads I feel such a rotter; you see you're absolutely right, and I'm so utterly wrong. I am just what you have said. I do like shining over everyone, and I do like being admired, and I'm most awfully critical of other people, and I don't suppose that I've ever really thought that other people's ideas are really justifiable as I think my own are. And, Daddy, I am so stupidly self-conscious – everything I do or say, I sort of see it written in a book, just as if I was some silly book character. Do you understand that, Daddy? 'cos it's so hard to explain. And I always wonder what other people are saying about me.

I have thought a lot about myself, I'm afraid, to try and find out what I'm really like – to sort of know myself, and it makes me feel very conscious of what I'm saying and doing all the time; I seem to be analysing my thoughts and actions all the time. And I have half realised what I have been doing all along, but it hasn't made me any humbler; I want to stop and I can't. I go and analyse the very action of stopping.

I have tried to make me an ideal – it was from religion, but I go and do something unworthy every minute of the day. Do you know, I'm even wondering what you'll think of this letter, and even of my inserting this very question? But I'm telling you everything truly and sincerely to the very best of my ability, and that doesn't affect the spirit of this whole confession. Oh dear, that's a silly thing to put. Never mind, you know what I mean.

I have tried to be friendly with people I don't like and very patient with

4 SHSS to DSS, 21 June 1931, SHSS papers, ATL, MS-Papers-11404-01.

everybody – and the next minute I go and snap someone's head off. You see Daddy dearest, as you said, I am difficult, and very very difficult I'm afraid.

About the critical spirit, I was reading the Bible last night 'cos I thought that might help, and I found something . . . just by chance . . . about don't judge your neighbour and think you are justified in doing so because probably you are just as bad yourself. . . like don't try to take the mote from your neighbour's eye while you've still got a beam in your own . . .

Well, darling Daddy, that's all I know about myself I think, and now I'll tell you about the things we've been doing which might interest you.[5]

In a post-script, she mentioned that the school was to hold a mock election and she was to be the candidate for Communism. 'So now I've got to get up on a soapbox and make speeches . . . if you can spare the time could you please tell me about Communism and how you go about speaking in public? Very *Urgent*!'[6]

THE MOCK ELECTION was an annual event, but it was the first time there was to be a Communist candidate. Recalling how she became 'hooked on Marxism', she told Hugo Manson how Miss McCall threw this bombshell at the meeting of the political studies group. It was hard enough finding anyone prepared to stand for Labour. When no one proposed a Communist candidate, Miss McCall said that she would choose one.

I was cowering down sitting on the floor in her study. She stood at her favourite place by the fireplace where she could get a few inches more height, standing on the hearth. She deliberately looked in the opposite direction from me to start with and sort of looked all round the room and then she swung her arm and pointed in my direction and said, 'We shall have Shirley Smith as the Communist candidate.' People were amazed, I was new, I was insignificant . . .[7]

5 SHSS to DSS, 27 June 1931, SHSS papers, ATL, MS-Papers-11404-01.
6 Ibid.
7 This is from the oral history of Shirley Smith with Hugo Manson on 4 November 1988 commissioned by the New Zealand Law Society, Wellington Branch, side 3, ATL,

The other candidates were all sixth-formers. (In later years Shirley thought this must have occurred in her last year.) Whether or not Miss McCall planned it with Shirley in mind, it gave her a chance to shine. Her history teacher, Rita Mary Johnson, discreetly showed her pamphlets about Stalin's first Five-Year Plan in the Soviet Union. Shirley was sold, especially on the idea of collective farming. Thinking of her relatives in Waikato who got together with their neighbours at haymaking time to build one another's haystacks together, she thought it was the answer. 'It's what I'd been waiting to hear all my life,' she told Hugo Manson.[8]

She put up notices announcing when she would address the school, and where – on stage in the hall or outside where she could stand on a balcony above her listeners. It was fun.[9] The election itself was thrilling – Shirley wrote eight pages describing it to her parents. After polling, there were more speeches that were judged by the local Rangitīkei MP, Mr Eliott, a Conservative. In her letter home Shirley wrote of her performance:

They said I tossed back my head then, and later on when I got a tough question, but I didn't know I did. It was awful at first – everything silent and my voice booming forth . . . Then I forgot all that I was going to say, and plunged into Russia, correcting and contradicting all the things about it that the others had said, then compared it with the Br. Empire and said something about the Principals of C and the rotten state of social order today, etc. and was just going to sit down when the first question came, and then I had a regular torrent. . . . Mr Eliott summed up. I'm going to tell you what he said, I simply must, but I don't want you to think I'm 'skiting'. He said, 'By far the ablest and best exposition of her party's platform was given by the Communistic candidate.' Then he pulled us all to pieces in the order in which he considered we had come in speechifying. . . . the order of the poll reversed.[10]

OHInt-0082-02.

8 Ibid.

9 Ibid; SHSS to family, 19 July 1931, SHSS papers, ATL, MS-Papers-11404-01.

10 SHSS to family, 8 August 1931, SHSS papers, ATL, MS-Papers-11404-03.

She made her mark all right, and she convinced herself. But as she now saw herself as a communist she was even further beyond the pale as far as the girls at Nga Tawa were concerned. She desperately wanted to belong.

In the third term she was so unhappy that Meta wrote to Miss McCall to say she and Shirley's father were 'thoroughly distressed and disturbed on her account'. Shirley was now entirely alone.

She does not say very much about it, but I quote this from her last letter: 'Sundays here are horrible: it's much worse now we are having such fine weekends, because everyone is scattered in crews all over the grounds, and there is nowhere that you can go without finding a crew there as well. So I am writing in one of Studholme's windows with the sun full on my back. It is very warm and fairly comfortable and quite the best I can do. There isn't anyone else in Studholme.'

You will agree that such isolation must destroy a child's confidence and happiness and hinder new development. Do you think matters will be any better next year? We will be most grateful if before half term you will give us your candid opinion about the child. We know her faults . . . but such treatment cannot go on for too long and we are feeling disturbed and responsible.[11]

Miss McCall tactfully took things in hand. Shirley wrote home that the girls in her dorm made much of her birthday. 'And do you know what? You'd never guess though. Cecily Bell sent for me, and [I] went in fear and trembling, and what she did was to wish me many happy returns, and present me with a wee parcel! . . . Oh! I was *thrilled*! I still am. Wasn't it simply marvellous of her?'[12]

Shirley had a crush on Cecily Bell, which Meta sensibly put in a positive light when she forwarded Shirley's letter to David: 'I feel perfectly delighted that she has had such a jolly birthday – also that she is lavishing her affection on Cecily. Things aren't so bad when she has

11 Draft MES sent DSS of her letter to Miss McCall, October 1931, SHSS papers, ATL, MS-Papers-11404-03.

12 SHSS to DSS, 11 October 1931, SHSS papers, ATL, MS-Papers-11404-03.

someone to love!'[13]

This last comment was spot on. Shirley soon transferred her affection to an athletic boy at Wanganui Collegiate, expressing her feelings into what she called 'Attempts at Poetry Inspired by Michael' in her Journal marked '1932–34, Strictly Private'.

Miss McCall arranged for Shirley to be taken into a crew, but Shirley's memory of Nga Tawa was that she was always an outsider. She took a defiant attitude and all her life she presented a self-image of one who didn't care what people thought of her:

I found I could be self-sufficient. I found I could walk into a room full of people where nobody was going to be friendly to me and not care. Maybe I cared, but I didn't show it. And I survived, and I didn't lose my self-respect. I don't know why. Perhaps it was part of this being a little Red Fed that came out. I've always been, my father would have said, headstrong, obstinate, opinionated, determined to stick to what I believed was right. This was jolly good training in sticking up for oneself and sticking to one's guns in the teeth of what was really a pretty unpleasant and unhappy environment.[14]

But Shirley did want to be liked, admired and accepted, and it mattered not only that she was right, but that she was seen to be right.

Shirley had little understanding of economic hardship, though the Depression saw Nga Tawa's school roll plummet. As judges' salaries were fixed and prices fell, David Smith's real income rose during those years. He increased his personal contributions to philanthropic organisations and both he and Meta did voluntary social work, but Shirley knew little of that at the time. Her experience of poverty came in glimpses – the labour camp for the unemployed, housing for workers, country children walking to school barefoot. In the summer of 1931–32, one of her farming uncles warned, 'Next winter we shall hit rock bottom – then there will really be trouble.' Shirley wondered what he meant. She was

13 MES to DSS, 16 October 1931, SHSS papers, ATL, MS-Papers-11404-03.

14 SHSS to Neville Glasgow, interview, broadcast on National Radio, 18 January 1989, published in *Directions: New Zealanders Explore the Meaning of Life*, Shoal Bay Press, Christchurch, 1995, pp.186–201.

at school at the time of the Queen Street riots of 14 April. She recalled reading about it with 'a shiver of excitement, almost pleasurable'.[15]

In her submission to the Royal Commission on Social Security in 1970, Shirley reflected on the influences that shaped her views of what she later saw as New Zealand's two races, the rich and the poor:

My family was not only comparatively well-off, it was Presbyterian, imbued with the Calvinist notion that material success was a sign of Divine Grace – 'Success' was the outward visible sign of virtue: the other side of the coin was that if you were poor, you were undeserving. It was also taken for granted that everyone had free will to choose and was responsible for his choice. You could choose to be thrifty, hard-working, ambitious, and thus succeed; or you could choose to be improvident, lazy, aimless, and thus fail.[16]

As a teenager she probably questioned such thinking, however. In Auckland she went to church every Sunday with Meta, either to Knox Church in Parnell or to St Andrew's at the top of Constitutional Hill. 'I used to judge a sermon on its intellectual content and my stepmother and I used to discuss it learnedly as we came home for our Sunday dinner.'[17] She would write to her freethinking grandfather about questions of interpretations, while her great-uncle James Gibb kept her steamed up about the importance of being a Presbyterian and not belonging to 'any of those other sects'.[18] She became very partisan at school, fighting for her 'sect'.

Whatever questions she had then or later about her religion, the work ethic was ingrained. Her terms of success would change, but her identity was deeply rooted in Presbyterianism. 'I love the Presbyterian Church, I feel that they are my tribe . . . it's got nothing to do with

15 SHSS, Submission to the Royal Commission to Enquire into Social Security, 1970, Submission no. 107, Archives NZ, Ref. No. COM7 7.

16 Ibid.

17 SHSS to Neville Glasgow, interview, broadcast on National Radio, 18 January 1989, published in *Directions: New Zealanders Explore the Meaning of Life*, Shoal Bay Press, Christchurch, 1995, pp.186–201.

18 James Gibb to SHSS, 7 March 1934, SHSS papers. John Gibson Smith died 23 April 1933, days after he last wrote to Shirley on 11 April, sending a photo of himself and a Westcott & Hort Greek Testament.

religion,' she told Hugo Manson in 1988.[19]

None of this sat well with the Anglican girls at Nga Tawa.

At the end of her second year at Nga Tawa, Shirley passed matric with good marks. Meta conveyed her hope that she would be someone in her own right.[20] Her father's aspirations for his daughter weren't limited by her being a girl – except when it came to the law.

In school holidays, when her father came home for lunch, he went over what had happened in court in the morning and asked the family for their views. 'If it was a traffic accident he would use the cutlery on the table to set up the intersection, with napkin rings for the cars. I thought it was fascinating and I said, "Dad, I would like to be a lawyer." He was really quite shocked. He said, "Oh no, it's no career for a lady. It is much too sordid".'[21] When she recalled this many years later, she was amazed that, for once, she didn't challenge him.

Oxford was another matter. The oldest university in the English-speaking world, an international forum for learning, intellectual and moral debate, Oxford was proudly elitist, admitting only top scholars, the best minds, the crème de la crème and, until relatively recently in its history, only men. But David Smith saw Shirley's future at Oxford.

Shirley would later say that the initiative came from her headmistress at Easter 1933 when she invited her parents to her cottage and proposed that Shirley should be prepared for the Oxford entrance examination with a view to going directly to Oxford from school. She should study classics. Shirley's father and Miss McCall agreed classics was by far the best education for life. Shirley was called for and told what was decided.[22]

19 This is from the oral history of Shirley Smith with Hugo Manson on 4 November 1988 commissioned by the New Zealand Law Society, Wellington Branch, side 2, ATL, OHInt-0082-02.

20 SHSS to MHS, 1968: 'I suppose I've conveyed to you my urgent hope, that you would do something and be something as yourself and in your own right . . . Gran'ma conveyed to me her similar feeling, combined with her total aversion to housework!'

21 SHSS to Neville Glasgow, interview, broadcast on National Radio, 18 January 1989, published in *Directions: New Zealanders Explore the Meaning of Life*, Shoal Bay Press, Christchurch, 1995, p.197.

22 SHSS to Peter Crawley, in her memoir, 'Classics Department, AUC 1942 – 2nd term 1944', 1979, SHSS papers, ATL, MS-Papers-11404-70.

Shirley thought the decision was made for her then, but though at this stage her conception of Oxford was scarcely more than a dream, that dream had been nurtured for some time. It's clear from her letters that there had been discussions since she finished matric. The goal was assumed; the question was how it could be achieved. Shirley wrote to her parents on 19 February 1933 – weeks before Easter – that Miss McCall had made her give up history so that she could focus on classics in preparation for the Oxford entrance exam in March 1935. But if her parents couldn't afford the full cost of Oxford she was to sit Junior Scholarship in 1934, in which case she had to continue taking a wider range of subjects.[23] That was soon settled. What made it all possible was the arrival of a brilliant new classics teacher, Miss Ann Young, who had taken the Classical Tripos, the equivalent at Cambridge of Oxford's Literae Humaniores, also known as Greats.

Shirley saw what Miss Young had to offer and she was hungry to learn. When the class played up, as they did for new teachers from England, Shirley took a stand and made it clear she wanted to learn. She complained to her parents:

. . . the rest of the form object to my trying to absorb knowledge; their idea is that we are here for knowledge to be pushed into us while we resist as hard as we can. . . . they said that if I tried to be intelligent, it showed them up as duds. . . . It's rather hard to work in the sort of atmosphere they have here. I'll do my best, Dads and Mum![24]

At one point her classmates attacked her physically, throwing dictionaries at her. For the rest of the year Shirley worked in this atmosphere, but she had a goal. She was dazzled by the prospect of Oxford.

In her last year, except for divinity and English, Shirley worked solely with Miss Young. The painful memories stayed with her, but she said that Nga Tawa was like the curate's egg: in parts it was pretty good. She enjoyed lacrosse, cricket and gym. As a prefect and head of Studholme House, she made friends with the other prefects, most importantly with

23 SHSS to family, 19 February 1933, SHSS papers.
24 Ibid.

the head prefect Cecil Upton, from Auckland.

The year ended with Shirley's father giving the prize-giving speech. Asked for her advice tips, she replied succinctly:

Do not speak at length.

Let me examine your speech before you give it.

But remember, the school will forgive any sort of speech as long as it's short.[25]

THAT YEAR, 1934, David Smith chaired the Commission that investigated Maori Land Farming Schemes operated by the Maori Land Boards, the Native Trustee and the State.[26] During that time the Smiths moved back to Wellington.

In Taupō they had extended the bach, adding a living room, bedrooms and a bigger veranda. Shirley and Allan always slept in tents – that was part of the Taupō experience. So was the early morning swim. They sailed a heavy clinker 16-footer and David put in a tennis court. Allan's memory of Shirley at Taupō was that she liked to get away on her own to sunbathe, read and swim, and sometimes she had friends to stay. One was Helen Coates from Auckland, who was also a close friend of Cecil Upton. The Uptons had their own place at Taupō and they all got together.

Helen and Cecil enrolled at Auckland University College in 1935, intending to join Shirley at Oxford after they graduated.

To everyone's delight Shirley had passed her Oxford entrance exam and been accepted for St Hugh's College. Founded in 1886, St Hugh's had a radical tradition that surely appealed to Shirley. It was probably impressed on her that St Hugh's had a reputation for turning out trailblazers, women who made their mark in the world, often on behalf of women. One can imagine she saw herself in this light when

25 SHSS to DSS, 18 November 1934, SHSS papers.

26 The Inquiry, which met between April and October 1934, investigated the schemes that Sir Āpirana Ngata, Minister for Native Affairs (later Maori Affairs), had set up and administered, which had been subject to many complaints from the Auditor General. By Sir David's account, the Inquiry was 'strenuous, demanding and charged with political dynamite', and it led to the resignation of Sir Āpirana Ngata.

she considered her future, but she had much to do in the short term.

Shirley was due to leave for England in August. Meanwhile she had two terms at Victoria University College under Professor John Rankine Brown, who had taught her father classics, and who would later take her on to his staff when she returned from Oxford. She thought him 'a dear old thing, a very good scholar . . . who actually calls me "Shirley" when he forgets. I don't mind – I loathe being called Miss Smith.'[27]

Less complimentary about her fellow male students, she wrote to Cecil about the Freshers' welcome:

I thoroughly enjoyed myself at first and wasn't critical of my partners as I was only too thankful to have any, but later I did long for the sight of a good-looking, or even passable looking boy. . . . I was glad I went, because it gave me a bit of self-confidence I badly needed, especially after a party I'd been to the night before when I'd been exceptionally dumb even for me, and felt completely hopeless and helpless. But Oh Cecil! What boys! It was nothing to be pleased with really.[28]

In preparation for adult life Gran'ma Smith gave Shirley two lessons:

One day, she showed me all the shining wood in the dining room, chairs, table, mantelpiece and so on, and instructed me in how to polish furniture, which must be done regularly once a week. . . .

The last thing I remember her doing is instructing me in the keeping of accounts. She took me into the bedroom she shared with Gran'pa, and told me to look at the shelves above the head of the great big bed . . . There were rows of little black-covered account books. She took one down, and showed me the items entered, most orderly, each with its cost beside it: 'There, Shirley, in those books there is entered every ha'penny I have spent since the day I was married,' she said proudly. . . . She intended, no doubt, to encourage me in thrifty ways and careful use of money; but alas, the effect it had on me was to induce only horror . . . I was so horrified that I have never kept a household account in my life.[29]

27 SHSS to Cecil Upton, 16 March 1935, SHSS papers.
28 Ibid.
29 SHSS, 'The Smith Family', undated (1990s), p.15, SHSS papers.

Nor did she ever polish furniture.

THE OLDER GENERATION was dying out. Gran'pa Smith had died in 1933. Shirley would not see Gran'ma Smith again, nor Great-uncle James Gibb, whose parting words were, 'Shurrley, niver give a thing to they Anglican!'[30] Auntie Kitty had died of heart failure in 1931, in her early fifties, leaving Shirley a small inheritance. Since Kitty's death, Nannie had taken Uncle Willie's children into her home, as their mother had died. They recall Shirley was still 'Nannie's girl'. Everything she did was the best.

30 James Gibb to SHSS, 7 March 1934; SHSS, 'The Smith Family' p.11, SHSS papers. The last time Shirley saw James Gibb was before she went to England. He died on 24 October 1935.

5

To Oxford

BEFORE SHIRLEY left for Oxford, her father had a serious talk to her about looking after herself and conducting herself appropriately, in the first instance on the ship. Her constant reassurances to him about her health show she understood his anxiety, but he was also concerned that she would lose her head in matters of the heart. Shirley promised not to commit herself to anyone until she had completed her degree.

As the *Ruahine* left Auckland on 17 August 1935, Shirley watched from the deck until the last sight of land disappeared. The cabin she shared with a school friend, Deirdre Williams, was full of cards and telegrams, gifts of confectionery and so many flowers that it was like a florist's shop.

'Here on the ship time is meaningless,' she wrote to her family a week later. 'There's just morning, noon and night and we feel cut off from both the past and the future. And the present consists of a day at a time. It seems nothing is real but the ship.'[1] She quickly formed a group that included Deirdre's friends Godfrey and Mick Hall from a sheep station in South Canterbury. Mick was going up to Cambridge, Godfrey to the Royal College of Agriculture at Cirencester for a year. Shirley liked them, especially Godfrey, who was keen on her but had a fiancée back home. At twenty-four, he impressed Shirley as 'a MAN'. When she broke her spectacles, she experienced her non-spectacled state as a transformation, as she saw herself in the admiring eyes of the opposite sex, then found herself in the arms of Fourth Officer Mark Young. 'The Fourth is the best officer so far,' she wrote to her parents.

Before landing at Panama she wrote home that a typical day started with the Fourth's wake-up call through her porthole to join him for a swim, and ended with dancing or a party, with all the fun and activities

1 SHSS to family, 25 August 1935, SHSS papers.

in between. 'It's dashed good. All the lads are nice, and there are hardly any girls except us.' And in the margin, a scribbled afterthought: 'Deirdre and I are going ashore with the Fourth and Second!'[2]

On the night of 25 September they reached Southend. They saw nothing but lights in the fog as they came up the Thames and docked at the Royal Albert Docks at 1.30 am. They all felt 'frightfully blue' because the voyage was over. Leaning over the rail, Shirley thought that whatever happened in her future, these six weeks had made her life worth living. When she said goodbye to Mark, assuming her shipboard romance was over, he persuaded her that it wasn't and, believing him to be 'honest through-and-through', she agreed to meet again.

SHIRLEY'S GREAT-AUNT and great-uncle, Sally and Charlie Milne, met Shirley when she disembarked next morning. Aunt Sally, Gran'pa Smith's youngest sister whom David had befriended during the war, became Shirley's *in loco parentis* until she turned twenty-one.

Sally and Charlie Milne were deeply religious and their four daughters were also dedicated to a Christian path. Ruth, a qualified doctor, was serving as a medical missionary at Swatow, on the south coast of China; Carrie was a medical student in London; Marjorie had been an Anglican nun in India and was back in England, recovering from an illness; and Betty, the youngest, kept house for her parents at Greystones in the village of Witham, Essex. She and Marjorie were there to welcome Shirley and help her adjust to English life. They took her to Chelmsford and Colchester, and introduced her to London.

As well as the thrill of seeing London's famous sites, Shirley discovered New Zealand House, which became another home from home. It was then simply an office on The Strand, where visitors picked up their mail and usually bumped into someone they knew.

Shirley was there chatting away on 10 October, her nineteenth birthday, the day she was to go up to Oxford, and so missed both her meeting at Paddington Station with the escort arranged for her and the train they were to have caught. She arrived on the next train, alone, unknown and late for dinner.

2 SHSS to family, 6 September 1935, SHSS papers.

So began what became the 'the most wonderful transforming experience' of her life.[3] She recalled she was 'happy and at home at St Hugh's from the beginning.'[4] She was undaunted, even when a woman at dinner in Hall the first night answered Shirley's question, 'What subject are you studying?' with 'Do you mean what School am I reading for?'

She learnt that at Oxford undergraduates were never 'students' and females were 'women', never 'girls' – except in relation to the other women's colleges in which case 'Lady Margaret Hall are ladies, Somerville are women, St Hugh's are girls, St Hilda's are hussies!!'[5]

And she learnt that proctors were 'progs' and principals 'prinks'. The principal of St Hugh's was Miss Barbara Elizabeth Gwyer, sister of the Chief Justice of India. Shirley explained to her father that Miss Gwyer was 'something of a personage in Oxford – a great woman. We have every reason, and certainly are, proud of our Prink'. Shirley met her after dinner that first night.[6]

Shirley was then taken to the Lawn, an elegant Georgian stone house across the garden from the main college building. She met the other freshers, about eleven of them, and their house don, Miss Dorothea Gray. She was both Shirley's classics tutor and her 'moral tutor' (a new term in the 1930s), responsible for her moral and intellectual development.

'The Gray', as they called her, was in her second year as tutor and in charge of the Lawn. She inspired respect and was an inspiration to Shirley. Lame from polio, she was said to have climbed Mt Snowden and dug at archaeological sites, and she was a powerful canoeist. 'Whatever she did, she did as if it were completely natural, with no hint of physical limitations overcome: this gave her courage quite another dimension: there was no self-regard in it. Her thrust was upon the world outside, with no backward look at where she'd started from.'[7]

3 SHSS to Dr Kenyon, Principal, St Hugh's College, 26 February 1967, St Hugh's Archive.
4 SHSS to Dr L. F. E. Edwards, St Hugh's College, 9 March 1993, SHSS papers.
5 SHSS to Helen Coates and Cecil Upton, 15 April 1936, SHSS papers.
6 SHSS to family, 21 February 1936, SHSS papers; SHSS journal, 1935, p.26, SHSS papers.
7 SHSS, obituary for Dorothea Helen Forbes Gray, *St Hugh's College Chronicle*, 1985, pp.48–49, St Hugh's Archive; copy of unedited obituary, 30 January 1985.

Miss Gray didn't allow her disability to define her. Furthermore – and equally impressive in Shirley's eyes – she admitted no limited idea of womanhood. She impressed on Shirley the idea that whether one was a man or a woman was not important, 'the important thing was to be a person'. A woman was a sovereign person in her own right, not subject to men who had rights over them. (Victorian women had been defined in law as 'not persons'.) Shirley resolved to establish her identity as a person in her own right, not as the daughter, wife or sister of her male relatives. The sense of personhood as impressed on Shirley by Miss Gray would be a guiding light for life.[8]

Dorothea Gray had the greatest influence on Shirley and her good opinion mattered most. She was clear, direct and incisive, 'she pounced, but she had the gift of pointing out the error equally of one's ways and one's proses with such patent objectivity that one accepted her corrections without the least doubt of her goodwill.'[9]

While Dorothea Gray guided Shirley's moral and intellectual development, her course itself was the key. Greats – *Literae Humaniores*, literally the more humane literature – was a medieval discipline, a synthesis of reason and virtue based on the idea that a classical education was essential for a proper understanding of the values and virtues of Western civilisation. The course was an Honours degree with two sets of 'public examinations' (set by the university rather than individual colleges). The first, Honour Moderations (Mods), at that time the only Oxford degree in Latin and Greek languages, came at the end of the first five terms and covered Life, Language and Literature of Greece and Rome. The second part of the course was philosophy and ancient history.[10]

8 Ibid; Professor Ngaire Naffine, Shirley Smith Address 23 November 2016, 'Manliness, Male Right and the Criminal Law: the uses of Criminal Law in the formation of the character of the male legal person'. As Professor Naffine explained, Victorian women were defined in law as 'not persons'. They had no legal existence. The law brutalised men by enshrining the sense that they could rightfully assert their will over women. Dorothea Gray's view that Shirley adopted can be understood in this light.

9 SHSS, obituary for Dorothea Helen Forbes Gray, *St Hugh's College Chronicle*, 1985, pp.48–49, St Hugh's Archive.

10 This is from the oral history of Shirley Smith with Hugo Manson on 4 November 1988 commissioned by the New Zealand Law Society, Wellington Branch, side 3, ATL, OHInt-0082-02.

Greats was the most difficult course at Oxford.

Shirley started with a huge disadvantage. Decades later, Miss Gray recalled that she had accepted Shirley 'on a hunch' and found she knew 'practically nothing' when she admitted her to Greats.[11] Undergraduates were expected to arrive with enough knowledge of Latin and Greek to tackle the extensive reading lists. Miss Gray thought Shirley would never catch up with her Greek reading.

That seems not to have worried Shirley. She wrote exuberantly to her parents at the end of the first week:

Oxford is marvellous, and it's thrilling having lectures in great oak-panelled dining-halls or lecture-rooms with portraits hanging all round. We go to various different colleges for lectures – we classics people have none at St Hugh's. . . . it seems to me that I'm hardly behind at all with the proses and unseens, though I certainly haven't done as much reading as most of them . . .[12]

The first week she made friends at the Lawn over cocoa elevenses, teas and suppers. The girls Shirley mentioned in her first letters became long-term friends. They included the College beauty Sheila Wilson; Megan Edwards, very 'county'; Edna Edmunds, a grammar-school girl from Gloucestershire who later married Denis Healey (a politician who would hold high office in the British Labour Party, including Deputy Leadership) and became a best-selling author; Marcia Gillett, whose friendship with Shirley grew later in life; and, most significantly, Phoebe Llewellyn Smith. The youngest of a brilliant family, Phoebe was multi-talented. She opened doors for Shirley, especially in art. Phoebe and Shirley were among only four freshers from St Hugh's who read classics.

Having bought her cap and gown, furnishings for her room and a second-hand bicycle, Shirley was set to discover Oxford.

11 Dorothea Gray to Theodora Cooper, 1967, regarding Helen Sutch's application to St Hugh's, St Hugh's Archive. 'I think this is good blood and promising.'

12 SHSS to family, 17 October 1935, SHSS papers.

I stood at Carfax and looked down the High, beautiful in the pale sunlight of autumn, and could hardly believe it – here I was, in Oxford. It was real, it was true . . . I had done it! I could do anything! . . . from the moment I arrived in Oxford, I was gloriously happy, I enjoyed everything. I did not miss New Zealand, my family or friends. I rejoiced in having got away.[13]

On the first Sunday in term she was invited to a large Victorian League tea and dinner at Cherwell, the home of physiologist John Scott Haldane and his wife, the first of many visits. Shirley later got to know their daughter, writer Naomi Mitchison, and their famous son, scientist J. B. S. Haldane (Jack). Shirley felt honoured by the attention she received, especially from Mrs Haldane, who regularly asked Shirley to accompany her to plays. Shirley thought Mrs Haldane 'one of the kindest and most charming old ladies' she'd ever met.[14]

On that first Victorian League gathering, Shirley met several Rhodes Scholars, including New Zealanders Ian Milner, Lester Moller and Norman Davis.[15] Norman and Lester both invited her to tea at their rooms at Merton. Also in her first week she met New Zealander John Mulgan, who had recently started work for the Clarendon Press (the Oxford arm of Oxford University Press, which also had a London office). John's mother, a friend of Annie and Kitty Cumming, had written to him of Shirley's arrival. He dutifully invited Shirley to lunch, then reported home that he wondered at her temerity, not only in going from Nga Tawa to Oxford but to do classics. Did she know what she was taking on?[16]

John Mulgan had recently graduated with a First from Merton. He introduced Shirley to one of his younger Merton friends from Yorkshire, Frank Harley, who was reading Greats. Their mutual love for classics

13 SHSS memoir, 'Oxford', 2 October 1998, SHSS papers.

14 SHSS, Journal, 1935, p.35, SHSS papers. The introduction to the Haldanes came initially through David and Meta's friend Dr Grace de Courcy (the author's great-great-aunt). When Shirley met the Haldanes they had staying with them another New Zealand friend of her parents, Dr Ada Paterson. She and Grace de Courcy both knew Shirley's background.

15 SHSS to family, 17 October 1935, SHSS papers.

16 Vincent O'Sullivan, *Long Journey to the Border, A Life of John Mulgan*, Penguin Books (NZ) Ltd, 2003, p.178; further discussions with Vincent O'Sullivan.

was a strong bond between Shirley and Frank, but in the short term Shirley was more interested in the social life she found with Frank and his friends. Like him, they came from Leeds Grammar School, all at Merton on county scholarships. Shirley joined their otherwise all-male pub-crawling jaunts on the outskirts and surrounding countryside of Oxford. Part of the thrill was the risk of discovery – they were not permitted to drink out of cCollege. She found Oxford full of contradictions regarding alcohol and sex. Women were forbidden to drink in their own college and not allowed to invite men who were not fathers or brothers to their rooms, but they were allowed to visit men in their rooms.

Other bids for her attention came from Oxford's many clubs and societies. Shirley joined the Lacrosse Club and the British University League of Nations Union. She teased her parents about the October Club – 'definitely Communist – I think I'll join'. All Oxford was discussing the Italo–Abyssinian question but it seemed to her academic and unreal.

She continued to attract the attentions of the New Zealand Rhodes Scholars. Norman Davis often took her to the cinema and theatre, and to tea at Merton where he took her worldly education in hand. The first lesson was to recognise a good sherry. 'He had a row of sherry bottles with the labels covered, he'd pour a little of each into glasses. . . . He did the same with cigarettes. I had to be able to recognise a good tobacco – essential.' The third discipline was an outdoor one and of great value: he took her on the Cherwell and taught her to punt.[17]

And Norman took her walking in Wytham Woods and lectured her on the meaning and origin of words and how languages evolved. Shirley was fascinated. On one of their walks he said, 'I think I'm falling in love with you.' A little later he asked her to marry him – but she had to understand, he said, there would be no children. He couldn't put a woman through that agony. She told him she was sorry but she couldn't possibly face marriage without children. Norman said he understood. Shirley was relieved.[18]

17 SHSS to James McNeish, interview, 4 May 1998, James McNeish papers.
18 Ibid.

She kept in touch with her friends from the *Ruahine*. Godfrey Hall drove over to Oxford from his college at Cirencester to take her for Sunday drives into the green rolling countryside of Oxfordshire and Gloucester and the ancient villages of the Cotswolds, which she loved. They planned to take a car trip in Devon with his brother Mick and Deirdre Williams at the Easter vacation in 1936. In the event, Deirdre pulled out, but Shirley still went. The trip was a great success. She recorded it in detail in a journal, copies of which her father circulated around friends and relations, including Helen and Cecil, who thought her letters to them much more interesting.

She wrote to them about Mark Young, off again across the ocean. In just her third week at Oxford, Shirley's bubble of euphoria had burst. She confided in Cecil that her feelings for Mark overshadowed all else:

It is damn hard for us to know how much to believe of what men say, as you said. . . . It may be my imagination but from his last letter before he sailed, I've got an idea his ardour is abating. It's only from reading between the lines and there may be nothing in it, but I'm quite prepared and won't be in the least surprised if it is so. Meanwhile of course, and it is his fault, I've become so keen on him that I can't work and feel restless and miserable and unsatisfied all the time. . . . I'm not a bit interested in the work, I've no ambitions, except that I don't want to make a fool of myself by getting ploughed, and I think of – and want – Mark desperately the whole time.[19]

She had thoughts of a rose-coloured cottage somewhere in England, with Mark and a few children. She thought the shame of failing ('getting ploughed') was all that weighed against that dream, but it was enough – she didn't seriously think of giving up Oxford for Mark. But neither did she give up Mark for Oxford.

Helen Coates wrote that she had never been so keen on anybody that she had felt that void Shirley described in Mark's absence. 'You really sound a CHANGED WOMAN. By the way, what are your

19 SHSS to Cecil Upton, 28 October 1935, SHSS papers.

serious opinions of this parking racket?'[20] Helen was curious about sexual practices at Oxford.

Replying to Shirley's later account of the very good time she was now having, Cecil wrote:

I was so thrilled to see that your conquests are continuing on land. To what do you attribute your success . . . Have you changed an awful lot? Sometimes I feel you are quite different, and I don't know you at all. . . . As you can probably tell, I am in the fit of depression which usually follows your letters, which however I look forward to more than anything else. How I'd love to be with you.[21]

Shirley attributed most of her success with men to breaking her spectacles on the *Ruahine*, but thought 'colonial freshness' helped. She pined to have a 'real yarn' with Cecil. She was friendly enough with girls in the Lawn and the classics freshers, but not intimate. 'They're all really awfully decent, but I can't imagine myself unburdening my heart to any of them – nor wanting to. I feel rather like the cat that walked by herself.'[22]

In the new year she wrote that she didn't know what she thought about Mark any more. He just didn't seem real. 'Sometimes I still get all het up about him, but I don't know whether it's really him or a myth of my own making. I do know I haven't fallen for anyone else. Then of course I don't know what he's thinking. His ship only reached NZ on December 29th, so I can't possibly hear from him until the beginning of February.'[23]

She considered the possibility that he had a girl in every port; on the other hand, he had 'a transparent sort of honesty'. But had it been just a phase? She was leaving the problem until he came back. Meanwhile there were more immediate questions at Oxford: how far should a girl go?

20 Helen Coates to SHSS, 2 December 1935, SHSS papers.
21 Cecil Upton, 7 January 1936, SHSS papers.
22 SHSS to Cecil Upton, 18 January 1936, SHSS papers.
23 Ibid.

I'm afraid my feelings have rather skewed around from what I have said before, but we're always learning! . . . All the same I quite agree that when the passionate part of your nature has *been stirred up, it's most awfully disturbing. That's why I couldn't work last term. I'm hoping to do a bit more concentration this term on the world of books instead of that of men, but I still get the longing now and again for a good park – the most awful frustrated feeling as you say, which can't be healthy – and then of course a good old park only makes you feel worse. But do you think that to stop the business at a friendly kiss would solve the problem? I find I get the 'frustrated passion' feeling without even so much as a kiss to rouse it. I used to be tormented by it before I even left N.Z. – and you know the stage my experience was at then! That was partly what made me think I was passionate by nature, but now I know that I feel completely cold and unmoved unless I'm really keen on the man – and I rather think that Mark is still the only man with whom I feel really moved, and who gives me a real pleasure in it. So I wonder if I am truly in love with him? But if one doesn't* know, *I suppose it means one isn't. What a muddle! . . . I shall probably go mad from repressions and inhibitions if I'm not physically satisfied – and sometimes I feel I can't do without it much longer.*[24]

She continued in her next letter to Cecil and Helen:

Life's rather difficult these days. One day I feel I want to be a chaste Dickensian heroine (Agnes or Rose in Oliver Twist) and the next I go all Nell Gwynnish – or worse! . . .

– I hope to Heaven you burn these letters – I should hate anyone else to read them, even in a hundred years' time. . . . But my considered opinion (I think, though I may change my mind tomorrow) is that petting and parking generally is a bad thing. It's only, as you said, Cecil, working up to one end and object which is not likely (for us, at least, I hope) to be accomplished, and only makes you feel more of a frustrated woman than ever. I would appreciate a nice innocently natural state of society, where you all fulfilled your natural impulses as you breathed and ate, and there were no conventions or artificial restrictions – I don't say no morals, because

24 Ibid.

you'd probably have them, but a different set, with different applications. No sophistication – especially no sophisticated nastiness – but all as innocent and healthily lustful as animals.[25]

She wrote home the same day:

By the way, don't be running away with the idea that I'm keen on Norman, or any of these lads. I'm just getting a little of the fun and attention I never had before, and it's very pleasant to the neglected little Cinderella I felt I was in New Zealand! The lad I like best is Mark, who sails the ocean blue, and I like him a lot, but it's nothing to worry about. Trust me, Daddy darling, I have *got my head screwed on the right way. I have been complimented on the air of calm confidence and competence I show in managing my life – which you of course will think is hooey . . . as it seems to me, but at least I don't seem to be giving the opposite impression.*[26]

On 10 March Shirley received a sharp rebuke from her father, unusually by airmail, to which she replied:

Please, Daddy, don't believe that I just went head over heels for the first person who cared at all about me. Unfortunately I've never gone head over heels at all – wish I could. I didn't on the ship, but when I'd left it, for several weeks . . . I thought I had, chiefly because I wanted to. You're quite right of course not to take it seriously. But I am still pretty sure that the exception to the rule does apply to Mark; though it would be much easier if it didn't. Anyway I shall know soon. I'm going up to London at the beginning of this vac to meet him and after that I may be able to tell you more certainly how things are.[27]

She wrote next from Aunt Sally's during the Easter vacation, that she had 'tootled off down to the docks. It was quite an adventure but everything was all right.'[28] Meta asked whether going down to the

25 SHSS to Helen Coates and Cecil Upton, 2 February 1936, SHSS papers.
26 SHSS to family, 2 February 1936, SHSS papers.
27 SHSS to DSS, 10 March 1936, SHSS papers.
28 SHSS to family, 31 March 1936, SHSS papers.

docks was quite wise, to which Shirley replied, 'Anything reasonable is "done" in London . . . and certainly no "danger" in talking to Mark in his cabin. Rest assured . . . I always *think* before I do things, and I really don't think you need worry very much about me.'[29]

She then received her father's reply to her letter of 10 March:

We are not taking your preoccupation with the Fourth too seriously. Looked at from the outside, the thing is too queer for words. We all make tacit assumptions but your tacit assumption that you are cool-headed and hearted ought to be re-examined . . . you really must examine this cock-suredness of yours about yourself. It certainly gives me pause and makes me anxious. People of depth are less sure of themselves, I think – at least their method of expression is not that of the dogmatic affirmative about their own abilities and powers. . . .

The very least you can do, if you have regard to those who have sent you abroad, is to do nothing and bind yourself not at all until your university days are over. God knows I hope you will be happily married some day, but for Heaven's sake, make sure that you and your mate have common interests, ideals, outlook and educational background and that the depth and intensity of each of these is about the same. And you ought to think more than twice if the mate with such common interests is wandering the earth so that you can't share them with him most of the time.[30]

Shirley replied on 11 May:

My preoccupation with the Fourth isn't 'queer', I think, Dads. Maybe silly, and all that, but quite ordinary. I certainly have no intention of binding myself in any way before I go down from Oxford – that has always been taken for granted. And really you needn't worry about the Fourth (actually the Third now), Dads, though he is a darling.

I have taken to heart and quite agree with all your requirements for a mate, but you do seem to have left out love. (Or am I being romantic and sentimental?) Am I to understand that if two people fall in love with each

29 SHSS to parents, 14 April 1936, SHSS papers.
30 DSS to SHSS, 23 April 1936, SHSS papers.

other whose interests etc. are not as much the same as they ought to be, they ought not to marry, and that conversely, that it is all right to get married if the common interests etc. are satisfactory, but there isn't the real thrill of love? I'm not trying to pick holes or be impertinent but I really would like to know what you think about it.[31]

Two months later she wrote to the family:

. . . I'd like to tell you that my Romance of the Sea is, and has been for a wee while, a void and a nullity. If you don't mind, I won't pour out details; but I have written Finis. . . . I don't regret that affair in the least, and I've learnt a lot – chiefly not to take myself seriously even when I feel serious. (darlings, it was my first little flutter – you can understand I went a bit off the deep end, thinking, as I did, that no one would ever look at me twice. Please forgive me for the anxiety I caused you, and look at it, as I'm sure you won't find difficult, as more humorous than anything else.) There is no Other Man, you may be relieved to hear! . . . When I say Norman, Godfrey, Mick, Monty (Harvie), Donald, Frank, John (Reeves) or any other name except Lester, I mean a good old platonic relationship, though, I'm afraid, sometimes one-sided – poor old Norman hasn't quite recovered, but he really is a brick. Lester signifies something not quite so platonic, but never serious. He is a great relief and a jolly good sort. We get on very well, but we'd never break our hearts over each other. . . . And a little bit of demonstration of affection (sounds awful but words are difficult here – I think it's the demonstrativeness rather than the affection) is a great help and cheer along. You know you miss awfully the people to whom you can show affection, and who show it to you – I do anyway. So Lester rather takes the place of Family, dearest Daddy and Mums, strange though it may sound! Just an outlet.[32]

To Cecil and Helen she wrote that she had again seen Mark and it was all off. 'I honestly am delighted that it's all over – it was quite impossible. He attracted me physically, but his mind didn't help. Now

31 SHSS to DSS, 19 June 1936, SHSS papers.
32 SHSS to family, 11 August 1936 (from St Leonards-on-Sea), SHSS papers.

I begin to understand – you see he's Public School and County, would probably have been Army if he'd had any money, and that's the sort of mind they've all got, made up for them before they're born.'[33]

But days later she was all stirred up again when a letter arrived from Cecil, written in July, with news that she and Helen had met Mark in Auckland and really liked him, and that she and Helen were both coming to Oxford in 1937. Shirley immediately replied that she was thrilled about them coming to Oxford. About Mark she wrote, 'It's sickening how you can put a man out of your life one day and he walks back in the next! I'm all upheaved again, blast it.'[34]

Then Shirley learnt that Mark was to marry an English girl he'd been engaged to all along. In December she wrote to Cecil that it really was over. 'One misses an object of affection (within reach!) more than anything else. I think that having people who are fond of you when you can't feel any warmth of emotion only makes you more alone than ever.'[35] It was her second Christmas in England and she was homesick.

33 SHSS to Cecil Upton and Helen Coates, 14 August 1936 (from St Leonards-on-Sea), SHSS papers.
34 SHSS to Cecil Upton and Helen Coates, 20 August 1936, SHSS papers.
35 SHSS to Cecil Upton, 19 December 1936, SHSS papers.

6

Turning 'Pink'

SHIRLEY LATER joked that she spent her first two years at Oxford pub-crawling and attending sherry parties and her last two devoted to politics. In fact, most of her time was spent studying. And she was always interested in politics and always enjoyed a party.

During her first winter when she and her friends in the Lawn gathered in the evenings around one another's fires, drinking cocoa and roasting chestnuts, they were more interested in poetry than politics. 'We read T. S. Eliot, who was new, and Dylan Thomas, who was newer; but we all agreed they faded out under Shakespeare's sun.'[1] She was nevertheless forming and changing her political opinions and redefining where she stood on the political spectrum.

To start with, she was a pacifist. After joining the British University League of Nations in her first week, when everyone was talking about Mussolini's invasion of Abyssinia, she attended the League's study groups. At their Armistice Day peace meeting she sold literature on their hot issues, 'Does Capitalism Cause War?' and 'Organising Peace'.

The desire for peace unified people of all classes at Oxford and throughout Britain, from the monarch downwards. King George V told his former Prime Minister David Lloyd George that he would 'go to Trafalgar Square and wave a Red Flag' himself in protest if there were any question of war over Abyssinia.

On Christmas Day 1935, at Aunt Sally's, Shirley listened to the Empire broadcast and the King's last speech, knowing her family at home would also be listening. 'I felt almost like weeping in parts, from pure sentimentality!' she wrote to her father. 'See how imperialistic I am becoming . . . But the atmosphere affects my heart rather than my

1 SHSS, 'Reminiscences for St Hugh's Centenary Book', 1986, SHSS papers, ATL, MS-Papers-11404-35.

brain; though I have definitely dropped Communism . . . Politically, I'm nothing at the moment.' The Labour Party's victory in New Zealand shocked and alarmed her – 'and this from an ex-communist!'[2]

Reporting in January 1936 on a study group she attended at Wadham College (which included almost every political club in Oxford), she found the Labour speakers intense and the Liberals flippant. 'I find my sympathies with the Liberals these days . . . I don't like intensity unleavened by any sense of humour.' The meeting's sympathies were also with the Liberal speaker:

When, for instance, after the theme had been declared open for discussion, one painfully serious comrade said 'the capitalists must be crushed and oppressed' there was a general murmur of laughter. When a North countryman with a gorgeous accent asked 'And how will ye croosh and oppress us?' there was more mirth; but when the comrade said 'by taking away your right of voting and – and – (with a rush) by putting you in concentration camps' there was a general roar. I felt sorry for the comrade, as a matter of fact – he didn't laugh. It's frightening to think you can find fanatics like that (and there are lots like him) even in Oxford. The discussion was quite good, the communists as usual talking in vague generalities – 'the vast masses of the people' and tags like 'the dictatorship of the Proletariat' and the more liberal minded laughing at them and occasionally saying something sound.[3]

She had earlier dismissed a Russian film as propaganda: 'The idea was to show how happy the people are under the Soviet – and the result was almost an American slapstick comedy.'[4] A debate at the Union on the motion 'That this House dislikes Soviet Russia and all it stands for' left Shirley 'unconvinced either way'.[5]

At the end of 1935 when the Seventh Congress of the Communist International called for a popular united front against fascism, Oxford's communist October Club disbanded and its members joined the Oxford

2 SHSS to MES, 1 December 1935, SHSS papers.
3 SHSS to family, 26 January 1936, SHSS papers.
4 SHSS to family, 21 November 1935, SHSS papers.
5 SHSS to family, 21 February 1936, SHSS papers.

University Labour Club and changed their image. Denis Healey noted, 'From that moment communists started shaving, tried to avoid being drunk in public, worked for first class degrees, and played down their Marxism-Leninism. As a result, membership of the Communist Party increased rapidly on both sides of the Atlantic.'[6] At the same time the merger of the communists with the Oxford University Labour Club moved the Labour Club further left.

The threat of war grew nearer on 7 March 1936 when Hitler, having defied the Treaty of Versailles and rearmed Germany unopposed, marched into the Rhineland. At this point the Conservative British Government announced plans to build up its defence forces in readiness for war. Shirley wrote:

It was nasty to see 'Germany invades Rhineland' on the hoardings . . . but what really makes me despair is the White Paper on re-armament. I feel . . . that there was some hope for peace while Britain kept sane, but now that Britain has caught the madness of others and has joined in a race for which it is difficult to see more than one end, I can't help feeling that the bottom has dropped out of things. . . . If we are not going to fight, why arm? . . .

St Hugh's has sent a letter of protest . . . to Mr Baldwin, which I signed with great emphasis. The Principal's signature also lent weight. I had dinner on High the other night and the Prink graciously discussed international affairs with me. She is an ardent pacifist . . .

Wherever one goes people are discussing 'what they're going to do in the war' quite seriously. May I be a V.A.D. [Voluntary Aid Detachment] *or some such thing?*[7]

In her view, nothing was worth fighting for, although she saw a place for an international army under the League of Nations.

She was hesitant to show her politically conservative family, who had apparently found her previous interest in communism a bit much,

6 Denis Healey, *The Time of My Life*, Penguin Books, England, 1990, p.35. Healey continued, 'It was from the earlier generation, particularly at Cambridge, that the Soviet Union recruited its spies.'

7 SHSS to family, 8 March 1936, SHSS papers.

how attractive she found the radical left. When she joined the Labour Club early in 1936 she justified it to her parents, saying that they had such good speakers, like the secretary of the Young Communist League – 'But don't worry, he didn't bring in Communism at all.' She heard political leaders of all parties address Oxford clubs, including Labour Party leader Clement Attlee – 'clever but unsound'.[8] Later in the year she hung on the fire escape outside the Union to hear Winston Churchill talk 'tommyrot' to a full house.

She regretted that she couldn't afford to join a three-week student tour for the Moscow Theatre Festival in the summer vacation of 1936. She knew many, including Norman Davis, who had been on these popular student tours of Russia.[9] Instead, she visited Scotland and Wales, staying with Smith relatives near Aberdeen and a well-to-do family in Abergavenny. Both experiences made her more conscious of the English class system. Travelling second class on a steamship to Aberdeen (the cheapest way), she got into discussion with a fellow passenger and was surprised to find he could reason as well as any Oxford man. In England she had learnt that country people and 'the lower orders' were a people apart. 'Steady solid folk, perhaps, the backbone of old England, and all that, but essentially not thinking creatures. But in Scotland it's quite different.'[10] She remarked later that she got on better with Scottish fishermen than with county people in Wales.

The following incident highlights her disenchantment with the landed gentry. On a drive to Tintern Abbey and down the Wye Valley, passing through desolate mining villages, she asked her driver what she thought of the miners' strikes and was told smartly, it was their own fault. Shirley was indignant: 'Doesn't it seem reasonable that these people should strike for better wages . . . and not see their children

8 SHSS to parents, 14 June 1936, SHSS papers. 'There's still that inconsistency between his demand for collective security and disarmament. It's what we would like, but they're practically mutually exclusive.'

9 New Zealanders James Bertram, Charles Brash and Ian Milner went together before the Stalinist trials and purges. James Bertram was a member of the Society for Cultural Relations with the Soviet Union and he initiated the Oxford branch of the Independent Labour Party. Milner became a committed Marxist; Bertram was a Presbyterian turned socialist. Shirley knew them both.

10 SHSS, journal, 16 July 1936, p.13, SHSS papers.

deformed by malnutrition?'[11]

Back at Oxford, the Junior Common Room at St Hugh's welcomed the hunger marchers walking to London from the north to draw attention to their poverty. When they passed through Oxford, Shirley turned out with hundreds of others to butter bread and make tea for their evening meal. The face-to-face contact with skilled workers, unemployed since Britain's wool and cotton industries were 'ruined by the failure of capitalism', made a deep impression on Shirley and her companions.[12] The marchers' suffering drove home the reality of Britain's unequal society and was visible evidence that the government's economic policies had failed.

In 1970, in her submission to the Royal Commission on Social Security, Shirley wrote about a later revelation, in the autumn of 1938, that showed her what sort of people 'workers' were, and how they lived:

In election canvassing, I knocked on the doors of damp cottages down by the gasworks in Oxford, only a stone's throw from Pembroke College; I saw people who had never had a chance of health or education or of finding out what they were capable of. What had been hidden to me at home was revealed to me in England; that 'workers' were people; but I saw how crippled they were by being treated as less equal than others.[13]

But she really didn't know them as people. As John Mulgan observed, communism at Oxford was a parlour game. Even Party members didn't rub shoulders with working-class people, since the university branch was separate from the town branch. They knew there were millions of victims of capitalism, but only understood that as an abstraction.

With the exception of college servants, the closest to working-class people Shirley knew at Oxford were her Yorkshire friends and they were from lower middle-class backgrounds. She thought that

11 SHSS, journal, 28 August 1936, p.90, SHSS papers.

12 Ian Milner noted that in the mid-1930s nearly one third of the people of Great Britain were forced to live on a diet below the bare minimum set by the British Medical Association as necessary for normal subsistence. (Shirley referred to the marchers passing through Oxford, in which case they were not the Jarrow marchers.)

13 SHSS, Submission to the Royal Commission to Enquire into Social Security, 1970, Submission no. 107, 1970, p.5, Archives NZ, Ref. No. COM7 7.

despite being Oxford men, they remained victims of the English class system, 'psychologically crippled by their inferiority complexes'. One, an excellent mathematician, used to infuriate her by saying, 'Fancy me going out with the daughter of a judge!'[14]

In her journals, letters and memoirs, Shirley gave no inkling of how she related to her domestic servants at college. 'Scouts' were an important part of life at Oxford. Her scout would have delivered a bucket of coal to her room every day, kept her fire going, dusted and swept her room, washed up tea cups, probably made her bed, perhaps even provided emotional comfort. One can imagine Shirley chatting familiarly to her scouts, but did she take an interest in them as people? In all that she wrote about Oxford in journals and letters to friends and family at the time and reminiscences in later years, she never mentions them.

WHILE SHIRLEY became more conscious of Britain's unequal society, that wasn't the deciding factor in her joining the Communist Party in 1937. In September 1936 she wrote to Meta, 'I am now quite certain I'm no Communist, chiefly because I'm determined on Evolution as opposed to Revolution; and I'm equally certain I'm no Fascist . . . and I'm really not terribly attached to the competitive capitalist system, so I suppose I'm orthodox Labour.'[15]

The civil war in Spain was the hot issue. Influenced by *New Statesman and Nation* editor Kingsley Martin, who had been anti-war but now took a strong line against fascism, she dropped pacifism and supported the Government Popular Front.

England and France's non-intervention treaty showed that they feared the 'Moscow peril' more than fascism. The League of Nations was now seen to be ineffective. John Mulgan, having spent the summer of 1936 as an observer at the League in Geneva, described it as 'paralytic' as a moral force for collective security. New Zealanders held their head up when the leader of the New Zealand delegation in Geneva, High Commissioner William (Bill) Jordan, took an independent stand and

14 Ibid.
15 SHSS to MES, 15 September 1936, SHSS papers.

voted to censure Italy for its scorched-earth policy in Abyssinia. It was the first time New Zealand had opposed the 'mother' country.

Shirley never felt that she had to go to Spain, but she desperately wanted to do something. At St Hugh's, where evening discussions were now political, the Junior Common Room instituted four bread-and-cheese lunches a term, sending the money they saved to Republican Spain.

Encouraged by her family's compliments about her writing, she wrote home:

I feel most strongly that the only way to bring any permanent concord into this unholy mess of a world is by education, in the best and the widest sense, and that the ability to write is still a valuable weapon for the task. (Please Daddy, is it still just a dream of youth to want to improve the world? At least it's not Communism now!)[16]

In the new year, which she spent studying at Witham, Shirley confronted a deeper crisis as she questioned her fundamental beliefs. Her subject was 'On the Nature of Things', the epic poem by Latin poet and philosopher Lucretius. She wrote to her father of her thinking as she grappled with its ideas:

Now I understand what Lucretius felt when he gloried in the freedom of the Epicurean philosophy, and in the loss of fear rising from his conviction that man was wholly mortal. But I felt that I must make the very most of every moment of life, waste nothing, be prodigal of giving and eager to accept all things. And I felt very much weighed down by my twenty already passed years! And as never before, I realised how much I had unconsciously depended on the reality of God and Immortality and the absolutes of truth, goodness and beauty. . . .

But now I know what it would be like to be a materialist. It's very exhilarating and certainly tempting, but I know I could never accept it . . . It's very hard to reconcile a personal God with any Reason, and yet it appears a personal God is essential to Christianity. Personal survival after

16 SHSS to family, 5 October 1936 (from 'Pound Cottage', Meg Oswald's home), SHSS papers.

death seems also eminently unreasonable – though it's a belief I've always clung to blindly because I so hate it not to be true.

. . . I've reached no conclusion. I only wish I could be utterly convinced of something, fairly soon, too.[17]

Shirley always defined herself by her convictions. She needed certainty in a belief system. If her religion didn't stack up, she had to find something else that did. Could it be a political belief? Oxford was teaching her to think, she loved the world of ideas (she was fortunate to have Cyril Bailey at Balliol College as her lecturer on Lucretius), but questions and doubts were also unsettling. She was impatient to find answers.

In Shirley's first year, her moral tutor Miss Gray had noted her 'over-rapid and facile thinking', adding 'but there is power in it'.[18] After Mods (the exams at the end of the first part of her course) in 1937, Miss Gray reported that Shirley had worked with untiring zeal and had been rewarded by increasing proficiency. 'She is not a scholar, and her judgment is at times over-hasty and unsound; but she is prepared to use it with independence and defend it with spirit.'[19]

Despite thinking her not a scholar and her judgment unsound, Miss Gray wrote personally to Shirley that her Mods results were very satisfactory. She had obtained a good Second with first-class marks on some papers, including her Special Subject, Greek Sculpture.

On 3 April 1937, with Mods behind her, Shirley and about 200 others packed into boat-train carriages labelled 'Anglo-Hellenic tours', destined for Marseille. There they boarded a 'rusty tub of a boat' and set sail for Athens. So began her lifelong love affair with Greece.

Shirley's party included Phoebe Llewellyn Smith and other friends from St Hugh's. Their study tour leader was Shirley's tutor in Greek Sculpture, Stanley Casson. Don of New College and reader in Classical Archaeology, Casson had published books on both classical and modern sculpture. He opened Shirley's eyes to Greek sculpture and she was

17 SHSS to DSS, 9 January 1937, SHSS papers.
18 Dorothea Gray, in Shirley's first year reports, St Hugh's archive, Oxford.
19 Dorothea Gray, Hilary term, St Hugh's archive, Oxford.

thrilled to be introduced to Greece by someone of his knowledge and experience.[20]

Shirley always remembered passing through the Corinth Canal at sunrise, seeing Athens from the sea and the port of Pireaus with its ships of all sizes and nationalities. Then came the thrill of the Acropolis and having Casson as a guide in the Acropolis museum, where she came face to face with statues familiar to her from her studies. 'It was most exciting – even casts give nothing of the real essence of an original.'[21]

Of Crete's Knossos, the ancient Minoan palace restored by Arthur Evans, she wrote, 'Some archaeologists don't like it but it is well done. . . . It is the most thrilling place.'[22] She would return to Knossos on many trips to Crete in later years.

In Cyprus they visited the museum in Nicosia where she was absorbed by the Cypriot pottery with its Greek, Egyptian and Assyrian, Byzantine and Persian influences. In Rhodes, they found themselves in the Middle Ages with the Knights of the Crusades. She loved the early Rhodian pottery – magenta on cream – and the poppies that grew around the encircling castle walls – and much more. 'Rhodes was really magnificent.'[23]

Kos was the only dull day, but she thought the mules splendid beasts. Samos was beautiful – fertile, covered with vines, olives, corn and almond trees ('*amigdala*, a green fruit with a soft juicy kernel which you eat – rather good') and she found the sea – its deep translucent Mediterranean blue – was better there than anywhere. At the end of the day the Pythagorean Society treated their party to a magnificent reception in the Town Hall. 'They regarded Britain as the Great Big Brother, Champion of Liberty and us as honoured ambassadors. Makes

20 Other experts she mentioned in her travel journal included an older Wykeham professor in ancient history, John (later Sir John) Myres; Professor Fleure, from Manchester University, an eminent archaeologist who had worked with Sir Arthur Evans; also two writers and former suffragists, H. W. Nevinson (a prominent supporter of the Republicans in Spain) and his wife Evelyn Sharp. Another writer and a committed socialist was Naomi Mitchison, daughter of Mrs Haldane, who had been so kind to Shirley at Oxford; and a Marxist from Bristol University.

21 SHSS, journal, April 1937, SHSS papers.

22 Ibid.

23 Ibid.

you realize that it is rather a responsibility to be British, and makes you feel worse than ever about Abyssinia.'[24]

Summing up Greece, she wrote to her family, 'the places were magnificent and always far exceeded expectations. . . . I'm just aching to go back . . . And it really is most exciting coming back and hearing places you've seen mentioned in lectures.'[25]

INSPIRED BY what she had seen and learnt in Greece, Shirley looked forward eagerly to her first lectures for Greats (the second part of her course after Mods). 'One begins to get a glimpse of the freedom that comes from knowledge and understanding and some notion of the value of a trained mind, and therefore to want to achieve it . . .' She expected to get on 'without outside urging and be my own pin-prick . . .'[26]

The course was divided between philosophy and ancient history. Ancient history was treated as an introduction to research, using first sources, ancient Greek and Roman authors, Herodotus, Thucydides, Tacitus, Cicero and so on. The emphasis was on methodology: how one evaluated the materials and reached conclusions was more important than a correct answer. Shirley chose for her specific periods the fifty years of Athens's glory and the early Roman Empire.[27]

Herodotus especially is fascinating as a writer . . . I have one Wade Gery of Wadham for my history tutor. . . . He's an iconoclast and heretic as far as Ancient History is concerned . . . but that's a characteristic of Oxford. . . . one's always awake with such as Wade Gery – we learnt with Casson how essential it was to be on the lookout for plausible fallacies . . . Our philosophy man, [J. L.] *Austin, is rather the same sort.*[28]

24 Ibid.
25 SHSS to family, 7 May 1937, SHSS papers.
26 Ibid.
27 This is from the oral history of Shirley Smith with Hugo Manson on 4 November 1988 commissioned by the New Zealand Law Society, Wellington Branch, side 3, ATL, OHInt-0082-02; SHSS to Andreas Sivitos, 23 November 2000.
28 SHSS to family, 7 May 1937, SHSS papers.

Her philosophy course, Logic and Moral Philosophy, posed big questions: What is truth? What is the relationship between appearance and reality? In what sense can different minds be said to share a common experience? Should punishment be designed to fit the crime or the criminal?

Unlike Ancient History, the course covered an enormous range, starting with Plato and Aristotle; then they skipped to Descartes and covered the development of philosophy to the present day. They could bring the theories of Marx and Engels into essays. What wasn't done was simply to reproduce what philosophers had said. Answers had to be based on knowledge, but what mattered most was how one used the knowledge.[29]

She would always agree with her father that philosophy was the best kind of university education anybody could have. Later, looking back on her work in the law, she saw the value of having developed habits of thinking, the importance of logic and attention to evidence in reaching a final position, but added that it was valuable for anything in life.[30]

The discipline was especially valuable for someone of Shirley's temperament. While she was learning that an enquiring mind and thinking things out for herself were what mattered, her natural impetuosity sometimes inclined her to jump quickly to conclusions. 'She much prefers judging to thinking,' philosophy tutor John Austin (who would go on to become a celebrated British philosopher) noted at the end of the Trinity term in 1937. And he thought her too ready to repeat things she didn't understand.

By then she had joined the Communist Party and was undergoing the next stage of her conversion. As a condition of entry, she had to undergo serious political re-education that prescribed what to think and how to behave. She would have to learn to follow the Party line as dictated by Moscow, whatever it was. The cause was greater than the individual – unless that individual was the Party Leader. The thinking was, 'Joe was

29 This is from the oral history of Shirley Smith with Hugo Manson on 4 November 1988 commissioned by the New Zealand Law Society, Wellington Branch, side 3, ATL, OHInt-0082-02; SHSS to Andreas Sivitos, 23 November 2000, SHSS papers.

30 Ibid.

right, because he was Joe.' This ideology obviously conflicted with the discipline she was studying, but these were confusing times.

On 12 May 1937 Shirley attended the coronation of George VI. She travelled down to London the day before, rose early to take the seat she had booked in Pall Mall and, stocked up with sandwiches, apples, chocolate and cigarettes, began the long wait for the procession. She looked hopefully around at the other New Zealanders in her stand but didn't know anyone.

When at last the procession started, she was disappointed. 'I wanted to be swept off my feet and really enjoy it, but it never came to that, not in the Mall anyway.' She herself led the cheering for the New Zealanders when the Escorts of Offices from the Colonial and Dominion contingents passed by. 'Luckily the rest took it up, but I was sick of the lethargy. I mean, if one's going to a Coronation, one ought to do it properly. They hadn't even the excuse of being Socialists like me, most of them, I'll bet.' The state coach she thought pretty awful, 'just one mass of gilt and tritons and horns'. The King, upright and glum, looked straight ahead in his Cap of Maintenance, which didn't suit him – 'perhaps he looked better in a Crown'. At the end of the procession everyone waited around to hear the service from the Abbey, broadcast over a loud speaker. She heard it quite well except when the bands of the infantry detachments marched along the Mall to the Abbey. When the New Zealanders came along, she yelled out 'Hurrah!' and again the others took it up 'and the noise was so great that they turned the Abbey service off!'

It was an odd day, she concluded. 'I'm glad to have seen the Pomp and Pageantry of the British Empire – but once is enough.'[31]

Inside the Abbey with the New Zealand delegation to the eighth Imperial Conference was Shirley's future husband, economist Dr William Ball Sutch, private secretary and economic advisor to New Zealand's Minister of Finance Walter Nash.

31 SHSS to family, 14 May 1937, SHSS papers.

At Oxford in the spring and summer of 1937, Shirley threw herself into activities with the Labour Club, where meeting after meeting was devoted to the civil war in Spain. The issues seemed clear: Nazi Germany and Fascist Italy supported General Franco's military coup; Britain and France's Non-Intervention Pact helped the aggressors. Only the communists took a clear and unequivocal stand against fascism. As she explained in her memoir for St Hugh's centenary book, this was why she joined the Communist Party: '. . . it was the duty of each and every one of us to do his or her bit to repel Fascism and by presenting a united front against the Nazis now, prevent the world war which would otherwise inevitably break out . . . many of my friends and I joined the Communist Party.'[32]

Spain wasn't clear and simple – some who went there to fight for the Republicans returned bitterly disillusioned – but Shirley felt part of the greater sense of riding the wave of history:

We also believed that fascism and nazism were the last despairing convulsions of the capitalist system, and that when this final crisis was resolved, the great day of socialism would dawn, bringing, in Lenin's words 'bread and roses' to all mankind. We joined the Left Book Club, regarded John Strachey's 'Why You Should be a Socialist' as unanswerable and lapped up the Red Dean's [Dean of Canterbury, Hewlett Johnson] *reports on his visits to the USSR. We began to read the classics of Marxism, starting with the* Communist Manifesto *. . . I found Marx's exposition of the dialectic brilliant and convincing . . . I still think it is.*[33]

32 SHSS, St Hugh's: One Hundred Years of Women's Education in Oxford, ed. Penny Griffin, Macmillan Press, 1986, pp.123–24. To Shirley's chagrin, her entry was attributed to Shirley Sutch.

33 Ibid. SHSS continued, 'Lenin's "Materialism and Impirico-Criticism" was, however, a great disappointment. I approached it with excitement, thinking I would find all the answers to the philosophical questions which enthralled: alas, the book begged them.' Shirley recalled that she read *The Communist Manifesto* at the same time as J. B. S. Haldane. This may refer to conversations she had at Cherwell, but also points out that great thinkers such as J. B. S. Haldane were persuaded. He became a Marxist and supported the Communist Party, but did not join the Party until 1942.

One of the problems philosophy posed was '"I could have chosen otherwise." Is this ever true?'[34] Many socialists chose not to join the Communist Party, but in Shirley's case it seems to have been inevitable that she would. The political environment at Oxford swirled with conspiracy theories, lies and propaganda on all sides, and many were taken in by 'plausible fallacies' and the hope they offered. While Shirley later admitted that they had been naïve and blinded to the realities of the USSR, she asserted that Oxford communists had nothing to apologise for and she was proud of what they tried to do.[35]

WHEN SHE first told her parents that she had joined the Party, she made light of it:

Did I tell you that I'd gone definitely Pink this term? Conservatives continually give me a pain in the neck, and Labour people only now and then. Fascism is anathema to me, and as the Oxford Communists are affiliated with the Labour Club anyway, I didn't have to choose between them. At present I'm only a Socialist on vague general grounds but I simply must read up the theory of Socialism with all speed. On very general grounds I do like the Socialist attitude to colour and sex – I mean everyone is taken on their own merits . . .[36]

She was conscious of a colour bar in England, but not among her socialist and communist friends. Her new best friend was an Indian called Ravi Batha, who was 'very intelligent and charming'.

And yet she was going to the College dance with Norman, who was not a communist. They planned to find digs together in Munich or Vienna later in the summer vacation, after her grand tour of cultural capitals of Europe. She convinced her father that she could use money her mother left her to travel and joined a National Union of Students

34 A question in Moral and Political Philosophy, Second Public Examination, Trinity term 1936, SHSS papers.

35 SHSS to James McNeish, 7 February 1999, James McNeish papers.

36 SHSS to family, 28 May 1937, SHSS papers. In her memoir for St Hugh's Centenary Book (1986) Shirley wrote that by joining the Communist Party, she and many of her friends automatically became part of the Labour Club, but her correspondence at the time shows that she first joined the Labour Club.

(NUS) tour that included Munich, Vienna, Budapest, Venice, Geneva and Paris.

SHIRLEY'S LETTERS and postcards from Europe in the summer of 1937 convey the Nazi menace. The tour's visit to Munich coincided with Hitler's. On 18 July 1937, the day Hitler opened the 'Great German Art Exhibition' that showcased 'Aryan' art, Shirley sent her brother Allan a postcard especially issued for the occasion. The next day the exhibition of 'Degenerate Art' opened. One can imagine how she must have felt at this use of art for the purpose of Nazi propaganda. But Shirley was blissfully happy in Munich. 'Having a grand time,' she wrote to Allan. 'There are some jolly good sorts on this trip . . . Munich is a very pleasant town and has the best beer I've ever drunk.'[37]

The tour ended in Paris where, at the World Exposition, she saw the monumental pavilions of Germany and Russia confront each other as two great rivals. And she saw Picasso's great mural, *Guernica*, Spain's sole exhibit, depicting the destruction of the Basque town by aerial bombing in April that year. She never forgot this horrific portrayal of war. At the same time she described her life as 'very rich and wonderful'. She was meeting interesting and charming people and making new friends, chief among whom was her tour leader, Martin Watkin.

Two years down from Oxford, now teaching in a private school in Surrey, Martin Watkin was the main reason for her present happiness. 'This is a very different thing from anything I've known before,' she explained to her father. She and Martin discussed and defined 'primary rules of life', and they were helping each other to live up to their ideals. 'And now he loves me, and you can see that with the basis this love has, it's very different from anything that's been offered me before.

'But I can't truly say I love him.'[38]

The trouble for Shirley was, when she returned to Switzerland to study at Hergiswil on the shores of Lake Lausanne after her tour, she met a law student called Hans Reichenbach. She described Hans more

37 SHSS to AGS, postmarked Munich 18 & 26 July 1937, SHSS papers, ATL MS-Papers-11404-04. The author hasn't found the journal Shirley kept on this trip,

38 SHSS to family, 3 September 1937, from Alpenhof Grafanasat, Post-Schwaz, Tyrol, Austria, SHSS papers.

specifically, his 'honesty, sincerity, love of sound thinking and hatred of superficiality . . . I quite forgot to tell you how beautiful Hans is . . . like a Greek Apollo'.[39] She had stayed with him in Zurich – not in his bed, she added.

Her plan to return to Munich or Vienna and find digs with Norman fell apart when he was suddenly offered a professorship in English at the University of Kuma in Lithuania. Instead, she stayed in a student hostel in the Austrian Alps, overlooking the Inn Valley. There she read Plato and Herodotus by day and in the evening she practised speaking German with the innkeeper and his family and other guests, and she wrote letters. She continued her serious heart-to-heart with her father:

. . . what matters, as you say, are the principles by which one guides one's behaviour in every sphere, which keep you on the right path while you're evolving your philosophy, and here, Daddy darling, I am in complete agreement with you and shall always be, for I do believe 'that the cardinal principles of the best life do not change', and I do believe in the supremacy of character; and most ardently, that to keep a fine standard is the most important thing in life; . . . and it had seemed to me too that honesty and unselfishness are the essence of character. I had added courage; but I see that that is really implied in honesty; for sometimes one needs supreme courage to be honest. . . .

I live this creed. I am always trying to live it better. I've only been growing to this knowledge gradually, and learning it through my own experience . . . I'm sure I've been helped immensely by the family I'm lucky enough to have; sub-consciously, at any rate, even when I've seemed an ungrateful little rebel. . . . Of course in lots of ways I'm still very unsure of what I think, and I'm even less sure now than I was a month ago.[40]

Her father replied:

Well you are a very precious daughter and I do so appreciate your love and candour. I feel you have been growing up this last year and I feel, too,

39 Ibid.
40 Ibid.

after reading this letter that you have, and deserve our complete trust and confidence. Of course, things are not so simple always as they seem, and I don't think it expedient to make all your doings known. I suppose if you were a married woman and had plighted your troth, you wouldn't think it expedient to spend a night in another man's hut, alone with him, though all was most virginal. There would be something wrong somewhere if you thought you ought to do that.

Well I can't say much about Martin or Hans but I am so glad you are finding life deep and rich and wonderful. They seem to have touched life for you with finer issues and to have extended sympathy on a deeper basis and you seem to have responded in that way in their eyes in a manner different from that which you have previously experienced. I feel you are getting down to root principles and I am glad. Yet I am glad, too, that you are holding back. You will need another two years . . . You need not be in a hurry. Emotions are not constant, either for men [or] *women. If they were, you would not have moments of ecstasy . . . man is more liable to change than woman. Wait for some testing times and see how you both feel. And this is possible, that though emotion wavers, falls as well as rises, you may recognise with your mind that you and another are fit mates, on the deepest basis of common ideals, mutual and also diverse interests and mutual attraction, and you may take the plunge with an assured faith that all will be well.*

I would prefer that you did not pass on any of this letter as coming from me.[41]

When Martin met Shirley on her return to England, things became more serious. Strapped for cash, they wandered in the streets and parks, getting to know each other. 'We're very much living in the present because the future is so horribly insecure.'[42]

'Life is so good and I'm so happy I'm afraid it can't last,' she wrote days later to her father. 'I feel like the Greeks who became scared of the wrath of the gods if their good fortune grew very great.'

At the same time, the European situation, and now war in the Far East, looked worse than ever. 'I can't see much future for my generation,

41 DSS to SHSS, 21 October 1937, SHSS papers.
42 SHSS to MES, 20 September 1937 (from Witham), SHSS papers.

can you? . . . but as I said, in my private life I am selfishly and gloriously happy.'[43]

When Helen Coates and Cecil Upton arrived soon after, Shirley met them off the ship and they all took a flat together in Earl's Court for ten days. Martin joined them for a weekend and stayed a night there with Shirley.[44]

TURNING TWENTY-ONE at the beginning of her third year at Oxford, Shirley's immediate financial situation improved as she came into her inheritance from Auntie Kitty and received gifts of money from her family. She bought books of verse, a Gauguin print, a new bicycle, new shoes and a posh coat. And she threw a sherry party, hiring a dancing teacher's floor on condition that numbers didn't exceed sixty. They did, when a group of Tom Harrisson's Mass Observers gatecrashed, claiming to be social anthropologists carrying out scientific research. She tried to rally her guests to observe the observers, but they were more interested in partying.[45] The Mass Observers gave her party notoriety, with both student publications, *Isis* and *Cherwell*, reporting it, but if anything came of their research she never heard of it.

For the rest of the term she was torn between academic work and politics, on one hand grappling with philosophical abstractions in her studies, on the other rushing round being practical in the Labour Club, and she had recently been roped into taking a part in a play for the Experimental Theatre Club – 'ridiculous incomprehensible surrealist . . . great fun.'[46]

'Your last letters gave us an idea of a breathless and hurried existence,' her father wrote. 'Having often let myself feel like that I ought to have nothing to say – and I'm not going to say anything. You can think it out for yourself.'[47]

43 SHSS to DSS, 24 September 1937 (from Witham), SHSS papers.

44 Cecil referred to this in a letter to Shirley nine months later.

45 SHSS, 'Reminiscences for St Hugh's Centenary Book', 1986, SHSS papers, ATL, MS-Papers-11404-35. Shirley couldn't recall whether the observers were absorbed into the party and never saw or heard of any monograph on the manners and customs of an expatriate's 21st birthday party at Oxford in 1937.

46 SHSS to MES, 23 November 1937, SHSS papers.

47 DSS to SHSS, 6 January 1938, SHSS papers.

Shirley had by now studied Marxist texts and applied them in her political tasks, but her political education was ongoing. Each college had its small cells. In many ways being a comrade was like belonging to a religious sect. Betty Brodie, also at St Hugh's, would have had Shirley in mind, among others, when she recalled 'very red' members of the Labour Club who 'saw the world in Manichean terms and cherished an ill-formed and idealized form of Russian communism'.[48]

48 Betty Brodie, *St Hugh's: One Hundred Years of Women's Education in Oxford*, ed. Penny Griffin, Macmillan Press, 1986, p.123.

7
TB

With Cecil Upton and Helen Coates both at St Hugh's, life at Oxford was better than ever for Shirley. They met her larger circle of friends. Helen's love affairs were always a talking point – Shirley and Cecil were almost prudishly critical. Reflecting in December 1937 on her first term at St Hugh's, Cecil wrote to Shirley, 'What has made it all complete and bound together the component parts has been my friendship with you. I can't tell you how much it means to me – and I have a feeling that we have found something that neither of us will ever lose. I hope that you feel the same.'[1]

When Cecil and Helen's friend Rona Lewis arrived from Auckland, her flat in London became a base for them all. Shirley had heard a lot about Rona. Of the three friends, Shirley ultimately remained closest to Rona in her political thinking, but at the time they were all ardent socialists.

Shirley's bubble burst soon after the arrival of her parents on 7 May 1938. David Smith's sabbatical gave him and Meta the chance to travel for a year and Shirley had longed for their visit. She planned to accompany them through Europe in the summer.

They spent their first evening together at her parents' hotel in Oxford. As well as catching up with each other, they looked forward to what they would do together. Russia was a possibility, but Meta wasn't keen.[2]

One can imagine their mixed emotions on being reunited after nearly three years. The girl David had farewelled was now the same age as Eva had been when he first met her. But Shirley was alarmingly thin

1 Cecil Upton to SHSS, undated (December 1937), SHSS papers.

2 Shirley and her parents no doubt discussed this and questions of freedom that recur in Shirley's correspondence with Meta. (After David spoke to Sir Bernard Pares of the Institute of Slavonic Studies at London University about conditions in Russia, they

and she had a persistent throat infection and a swelling under her jaw that she had noticed some weeks earlier. That she made light of all this added to his concern.

The next day Shirley walked them to St Hugh's and took them punting on the Cherwell. In the afternoon they all took a bus to Chipping Campden in the Cotswolds to see David's cousin Alec Miller, a well-known sculptor who agreed to carve a wooden head of Shirley. David and Meta left for London the day after and Shirley was to join them, but she was too ill. They returned to Oxford where David took things in hand, meeting doctors and specialists. It was decided that her tonsils, which had been partially removed in childhood, should be removed again once the glandular problem was diagnosed. Dr Crook, the college doctor, suspected a tuberculous process was going on and referred Shirley to Dr William Stobie, a gland specialist who happened to be in Oxford.

After further consultations, Shirley entered the Acland Nursing Home, a private hospital in Oxford. Her neck was put in a plaster splint and her tonsils were to be removed in a week, but two weeks later she had still not had her tonsillectomy and treatment of her gland remained undecided. Her father saw another expert in London and urged further delays. Shirley vented her frustration to friends far and wide. 'To get the doctors finally under your thumb – or at least fairly tractable, and then to find a father standing firmly in your way must be galling to say the least of it,' replied Helen Coates.[3]

As her Oxford friends headed off for the summer vacation, Shirley felt the fates had conspired against her. She resented what she saw as her

dropped the idea. The secret trials and executions of military and party leaders, and the administrative purges had created conditions that he thought would greatly restrict their liberty and actions (DSS memoir, p.250). Stalin's liquidation of the Kulaks by famine was known, although it had been denied; the trials in 1936 of Old Bolsheviks, and the purges and exile of dissenters to gulags where millions perished were also reported. Shirley believed that the Soviet Union was making a peaceful transition to a new order.

3 Helen Coates to SHSS, 28 June 1938 (from St Hugh's), SHSS papers. A general surgeon in Oxford added his agreement that they should get on and remove her tonsils, and this was put to David, adding that the patient was 'getting restive'. The shadow of Eva hung over her. Shirley said her father was always pessimistic about health, and it seems he feared her going into an operation when she was run down, and while a diagnosis of her glandular problem remained uncertain.

unnecessary captivity, hated her confinement in bed and the cast on her neck. Her father blamed her for allowing her health to run down. Her relationship with Martin Watkin was unsettled, but as far as her father was concerned, her love life was part of the problem.

She left hospital with her tonsils still intact, and was sent to stay with the Millers at Chipping Campden. Her parents were thrilled with Alec's head of Shirley and she found the Millers congenial, especially her cousin Alistair, who was then publishing his first novel. Helen Coates's reply to Shirley's letter from Chipping Campden shows that Shirley was happier, except for her enforced celibacy:

Glad relations with Ma and Pa are now on a more satisfactory plane. They are definitely right about our taking ourselves too seriously. . . .

Who *is Alastair*[sic] *Miller, the Ideal Man?? . . .*

H. L. Mencken says that all women fall short of their ideal man, and usually their final 'choice' is making the best of a bad bargain. . . .

However, H. L. Mencken apart, quit saying you're 'too dull and ordinary' for anyone. Ridiculous standpoint. We all have our own particular method and attraction, which given the right circumstances, we can exploit on almost any man. An unscrupulous statement, but still . . .

About you and Somerset Maugham saying that love is sex . . . well of course a hell of a lot of it is, and it's a pretty marvellous part. But without other things, it soon becomes sordid and disgusting. . . . You can only achieve perfect union, if you have a similar outlook, more or less similar ideas and ideals, and similar instincts. But it's no good having that without the sex part . . .

I think there always has to be something missing.

The big trouble – or one of them – is that a woman always wants to spiritualise a love-affair more than a man. That is what you do, I think, isn't it.[4]

Shirley's tonsils were finally removed on 7 July. She returned to the Millers to recover before further surgery to remove the gland in her neck on 26 July.

4 Helen Coates to SHSS, 1938, SHSS papers.

Her father wrote to his friend and colleague, Arthur Fair, that Shirley had 'overworked and overplayed, over-lived herself in the atmosphere of this ancient but very free University. Result bad tonsils and glands.'[5] (Fifty years later he put it more kindly: 'Being young and eager to put the world to rights in double-quick time, she had over-taxed her strength in extra-curricular left-wing activities, mostly political . . .')[6]

His blame upset her more than learning that her gland was TB infected. This was confirmed on 4 August, the day after she came out of hospital. Her father received the pathology report, then went to see her in college:

I was in bed and he sat on the end of my bed and lectured me for half an hour, non-stop, on the life style I must have been living to have got so run down. The College doctor, a nice woman, said that either I had drunk some TB infected milk, or I had run myself down. Naturally I preferred the milk theory, but to be honest, I have to admit that if the 'burning the candle at both ends' was not the whole cause, it probably was at least the partial cause.

There was no arguing with Dad, and I didn't try: I just sat there against my pillows and took it, with tears running down my face. My distress did not affect Dad in the least. He went on and on.[7]

Shirley agreed not to mention her tuberculosis to Nannie. The shock would be too great.

It was decided that her parents would take Shirley to Switzerland, where she was to recuperate and study in the mountains while they continued their travels. They all left London on 10 August, Shirley feeling wretched as her father continued to lecture her.

I had the sensation that I was sinking deeper and deeper into a clear greeny-blue sea, and I said to myself, If I don't do something, I'll drown. So I called

5 DSS to Arthur Fair, 26 July 1938, DSS papers.
6 DSS memoir, p.243, DSS papers.
7 SHSS memoir, 'Leysin', 26 August 1998, SHSS papers. Bovine TB (scrofula), 'the king's evil' was popularly thought to be cured by the touch of royalty.

up all my courage and answered Dad back. And at once I had the sensation of rising swiftly from the deeps into the air . . . There was no comeback from Dad, and he gave up lecturing me.[8]

From Geneva (where Shirley met up with Hans) they took the train east to Disentis, a town near the headwaters of the Rhine in the Canton of Grisons. They stayed several days, relaxing and exploring the mountain countryside. Shirley was to stay at Curaglia, the tiny village above the Lukmanier Pass that drops to Ticino en route to Italy. After seeing her parents off, Shirley moved into Hotel Kurhaus Lukmanier.

She wrote cheerfully to her parents to say that she was 'feeling twice the woman she was' and that the air was really wonderful. She had met all the guests and had provided much merriment with her attempts to converse in German, not surprisingly since the Swiss-German dialect in this remote area was quite different from anything she had ever studied. In the village she picked up a little Romansch. No one spoke more than a few words of English.

Hitler's manoeuvres on the Czech border had Europe on high alert. Amid rumours of war, Shirley's father wrote from Berlin telling her to return to England without delay. A day or two later he felt that the line taken by the British Cabinet with the Runciman investigation would postpone war.[9] He phoned her and put her mind at rest about staying. She had cash in hand if she needed to leave at short notice and had worked out the timetables for the quickest routes back to England.

I don't think I can do any more now but wait and see. It's all very nasty, and if I'm not bombed here, in France or the Channel, I expect I'll be bombed in England. What a life! Do you wonder we take politics seriously? If there is some kind of war, and I get back to England, I'll do some kind of war work. There'll be conscription of women anyway, in all probability.[10]

8 SHSS memoir, 'Leysin', 26 August 1998, SHSS papers.

9 DSS memoir, quoting his letter to his mother, 31 August 1938, DSS papers. Shirley did postpone her departure, reaching England only two days before Chamberlain made his 'peace in our time' arrangement with Hitler at Munich on September 29.

10 SHSS to DSS, 4 September 1938, SHSS papers, ATL, MS-Papers-11404-05.

A week later Shirley was worried that things seemed to be working up again. 'I listen to the BBC news every night, and as well get rather more leftish news from Martin, and the Daily Worker, which arrives at irregular intervals from Oxford. . . . I should be very sorry to leave here early, but I think I may come back [to England] soon unless the tension is relaxed.'[11]

The next day, 12 September, she heard Hitler's speech at Nuremberg. Shirley wrote to Cecil on 14 September that she was coming back: 'The tension is ghastly and Papa even phoned from London to say come back today – but I must see Hans and Norman first . . . Am going to Zurich on Friday, then to Geneva where I'll meet Norman (on his way to Bulgaria) on Sunday.'[12]

On 18 September she wrote to her father from Zurich:

It's all right when one forgets the fuss, as I managed to do most of the time yesterday with Hans. I'm going to Geneva this morning to meet Norman who is departing for Sofia. I must see him again if we're all going to be wiped out. Then I shall come back to London, probably arriving on Thursday unless something happens suddenly, in which case I'll come earlier. I'm very fit and brown.[13]

Norman Davis wrote to Shirley from Sofia, where he was Professor of English:

After I left you on Wednesday morning I naturally had no time to sleep . . . As I had feared, after so pleasant a stay in Geneva in your company I was somewhat oppressed by loneliness for a bit;

. . .

I hope last Tuesday night had no ill effects on your delicate constitution – you had perhaps a little more alcohol than you had intended (I don't mean to suggest that it was noticeable – it wasn't . . .) I hope also that your various acquaintances have been entertaining you properly. I envy them their good fortune: but you already know how I feel about you, so there is

11 SHSS to DSS, 11 September 1938, SHSS papers, ATL, MS-Papers-11404-05.
12 SHSS to Cecil Upton, 14 September 1938, SHSS papers.
13 SHSS to DSS, 18 September 1938, SHSS papers, ATL, MS-Papers-11404-05.

no point in rubbing it in. Anyhow, by this time the old 'serenity' has set in again – you gave it its worst shake-up for years.[14]

One of the 'acquaintances' Norman referred to was Martyn Finlay, an observer at the United Nations. Helen Coates had earlier written to Shirley about him, having met him in London with a bunch of socialists from the London School of Economics who all idolised Harold Laski. 'Mart was corker – typical NZ, but not typical in socialism and keenness for music.'[15]

Remembering their first meeting, Shirley wrote to Martyn Finlay in 1994, '. . . it amazes me sometimes how happy we could be in the thirties, under the shadow of war, which we all knew was coming, unless a miracle occurred. I have the clearest memories of Geneva, and Dick Campbell, and Jean McKenzie, and Robert Dell and the journalists' pub, and you. . . . Well, it was the end of the world, wasn't it?'[16]

ON THE NIGHT of 26 September, Shirley and Martyn Finlay left Geneva together and travelled back to London by train. It occurred to both of them separately that they got on exceptionally well, but their thoughts were not of the future. After Shirley introduced him to her father on arrival in London, Martyn went his own way.

That evening Martin Watkin dined with Shirley and her parents. While Shirley's relationship with Martin worried her father, all their futures hung in the balance as they heard Chamberlain's speech.

Gran'ma Smith wrote urging David and Meta to return immediately and bring Shirley with them. If war broke out, she imagined Shirley being one of the first to volunteer for War Service, especially if they weren't there to restrain her. That was exactly what Shirley had in mind, but it was her not her father but Ruth Keay, her communist friend and mentor at St Hugh's, who dissuaded her. 'Whatever happens, I don't think there is any need to rush you to the Women's Territorials!' Ruth wrote on 29 September.

14 Norman Davis to SHSS, 24 September 1938, SHSS papers.
15 Helen Coates to SHSS, 28 June 1938, from St Hugh's, SHSS papers.
16 SHSS to Martyn Finlay, 23 October 1994, Martyn Finlay papers.

. . . the best thing for you to do is to read the Daily Worker and [illegible] *and believe nothing unless it comes from Party sources. I know when one's isolated one often gets taken in by the other people's propaganda. . . . The war scare in Britain is definitely worked up to make people believe that Collective Security means war.* We *know it doesn't. If we can beat Chamberlain and guarantee Czechoslovakia, there won't be war. That is our line. But if Chamberlain gets away with his Four Power Pact (we oughtn't to be discussing the possibility of defeat but this is just to help you with your private affairs), there will be war of course, but not for Britain immediately . . . So don't be carried away, and don't let your parents take you home to NZ or anything silly like that. There is of course a slight possibility of war now, and it is up to us to prevent it. . . .*

Get in touch with the Party if you can. Go and demonstrate and then you won't get defeatist . . .[17]

On 'Black Wednesday', London prepared for the worst. David Smith wrote a month later of the strangeness of going about a city whose citizens were convinced it would be largely in ruins in four days.

I thought it. Everyone I met thought it. The people were going about their business with set faces. Very little was said in the streets or buses or tubes. There were no smiles. . . . I walked down Kingsway. Two Jewish girls were distributing pamphlets purporting to show how necessary it was for Britain to fight Germany. I got one. . . . I went to Her Majesty's Stationery Office, also in Kingsway. It was besieged with people buying air-raid precaution pamphlets. I bought one. In Piccadilly, Burlington House had been made a sandbag distribution centre. . . . People were queued up at various places waiting for their gas masks. In the parks, trenches were being frantically dug. I got the impression of a most desperate last minute attempt to protect the civilian population.[18]

17 Ruth Keay to SHSS, 29 September 1938, SHSS papers. Shirley's father in fact advised her to stay in England and do what she could to help the country, after first finishing her degree if possible. DSS to SHSS, 24 September 1938 (from Glasgow), SHSS papers.

18 DSS memoir, p.263–65, quoting his letter to Arthur Fair, 28 October 1938 (from the Duchess of Richmond en route to Quebec), DSS papers.

In the late afternoon, before they knew Chamberlain was returning to Munich, Shirley and her parents joined the exodus of cars leaving London and drove to Oxford. Meta recorded in her diary that the next evening they sat with Shirley by the fire in Helen and Cecil's study, then, in warden Miss Salt's study, heard the wireless news of the reception of the 'great four' – England, France, Germany and Italy – at Munich. They learnt the result next day: No War.

The Sudetenland was relegated to Germany between 1 and 10 October 1938. Meta, in her diary entry for 1 October, notes 'Arguments and discussions all day about rights of Chamberlain's deeds'. Shirley recalled in 1990 how she and her friends were sure that the forced surrender of the Sudetenland would lead to war:

How well I remember the appalling performance of the Runciman Commission, and my horrified shock when mentor (until then) Kingsley Martin wrote that in order to preserve peace, the Sudetenland must be given up: how ashamed we were by the treaty-breaking betrayal by Britain and France, and how we wished that Benes would accept the Soviet Union's help and stand firm.[19]

David and Meta, having brought forward their return home, now postponed it and travelled around Britain, returning to Oxford on 13 October. They took Shirley, Helen and Cecil out for a farewell dinner and then to the Oxford Union Debate. The motion was 'That this House deplores the policy of His Majesty's Government in pursuing peace without honour'. Sir David later wrote in his memoir:

It was a sparkling and vivid yet very earnest debate. Of the student speakers, my wife, my daughter Shirley and her left wing friends thought that Christopher Mayhew, for the motion, (and subsequently Minister of Defence in Mr Attlee's first Cabinet) was the best – while I thought that Edward Heath, also for the motion, (and now Prime Minister of Britain) had a special force and appeal and was clearly the best.[20]

19 SHSS to Fred Turnovsky, 1 August 1990, referring to his chapters on the betrayal of Czechoslovakia in his recently published memoir, SHSS papers, ATL, MS-Papers-10540.
20 DSS memoir, p.263, DSS papers. The motion was carried by 340 votes to 256.

Next morning Shirley saw her parents off on their train for London. They did not hear from her until they arrived in New Zealand on 23 December.

THE CLIMAX of the Labour Club's political activities at Oxford was the campaign against the Munich Agreement and this was the main issue in the Oxford by-election in autumn 1938. Shirley canvassed for Popular Front candidate Sandie Lindsay against Conservative candidate Quintin Hogg. Lindsay lost, but greatly reduced the Conservative majority.

Shirley sent off a spirited account of the campaign to Norman Davis. In his sardonic way, he took her to task. After referring to more volatile goings-on in Sofia – rumours of a pogrom and student protests against the continuance of the conditions of the Treaty of Neuilly – he continued:

. . . this however is all very local, and of no interest to one so much concerned with the major issues as you are. (I should be interested to hear the Communist apologia for the recent speech of General Belyayeff about the army, and the Changufeng business in general.) About your remarks about Munich, I share, of course, with all decent men your detestation of the bargain. On the other hand, stories of hoaxes, frame-ups, put-up jobs, and what you will bring home to one the essential gullibility of the Communist enthusiast, who is apparently every bit as vulnerable to propaganda on his own side as is the Great Chief Blimp. However this will fill you with either righteous anger or pitying disgust; as a palliative, may I ask you to supply me with as much left 'literature', or anyhow propaganda, as you can find time to send. I should be especially glad to see an occasional copy of the Daily Worker, *whenever it contains anything of special interest. I do not propose to become a convert, but I should like to see what your comrades are thinking (or at any rate saying); I get the N.S.&N.* [New Statesman and Nation] *every week but you will agree that it would be refreshing to see something somewhat 'lefter'. One special request, however: please wrap anything of that sort very carefully so as to conceal the name. This country has the jitters about Communism, ever since your pals blew up a cathedral*

in 1925 and killed 150 people (they were unlucky enough to miss the King after all). This of course was just an instance of the peaceful gradualist policy which you expounded to me, and it is very wrong-headed of the Bulgarians to object to a hundred or two murders; but they do, and if there were any sort of suggestion that I had any connection with red flags and what not I should have to leave at once. If things are wrapped, however, or better still, enclosed as cuttings in letters, they will be quite safe, as letters are not opened.[21]

He wrote that he probably wouldn't have a chance to get back to England for a long time. Shirley had no idea Norman was involved in British intelligence work.

About this time, her affair with Martin Watkin finally ended. She wrote to her parents, 'You can rest calmly in the knowledge that all is over now. I'm learning how difficult it is to break off something which had seemed permanent. Makes you feel as if your eiderdown has been pulled off on a cold night. However it's quite all right. I rejoice in my peace.'[22]

That week, she discovered another tubercular gland in her neck.

THIS TIME things moved fast. She saw Dr Chandler, a London TB specialist who happened to be in Oxford, who said that the gland must come out immediately. The main question was about convalescence. Dr Chandler advised a long convalescence at a sanatorium in the best possible climate. He recommended Montana or Leysin in Switzerland. Shirley chose Leysin, where Dr Auguste Rollier ran his famous sun clinics. This, of course, was subject to her father's agreement. He had told her that if she had any further TB trouble, she should return to New Zealand, but he was still at sea. He didn't get the news until the end of December.

Shirley assured her parents that she had been careful, 'going to bed early, drinking Horlicks, eating oranges, not overworking, going for a walk every day, and so on. I honestly have a clear conscience.

21 Norman Davis to SHSS, 26 November 1938, SHSS papers.
22 SHSS to parents, 1 December 1938. SHSS papers, ATL, MS-Papers-11404-04.

. . . I was feeling very fit last term, and actually put on weight.'[23] Her doctors, tutors and the principal all wrote to persuade him not to have her sent home. Aunt Sally Milne wrote that she thought a Swiss clinic was extravagant, but advised against a long sea voyage without medical supervision. She reported that Shirley wanted to use her own money from her trust and had written to her solicitor about it. 'Shirley has quite definite views of what she wants, and is "of age"!'[24]

Dr Crook decided to speed things up. She contacted Dr Rollier, who agreed to take Shirley at any time. 'I told him that she was inclined to take her health too lightly and asked him to be on his guard about it,' Dr Crook assured Shirley's father.[25]

Dr Chandler thought she could continue her studies from the clinic and expected that in six months' time she would be strong enough to come back to Oxford and take her exams. The St Hugh's warden, Miss Salt, reinforced this idea when she in turn wrote to Shirley's father:

[Dr Chandler] *was very emphatic that she should be happy and not have to worry about not taking her exam. She would be very disappointed if this could not be, and I am writing to you just on her behalf. She could return home after her exam – and I think she should be able to manage this. I would see that she is specially looked after.*

I must say in Shirley's favour, she has been wonderfully good this term. So the gland is not her foolishness at all. I have just seen her in the Acland where she is wonderfully bright having had yesterday her operation. It is most wretched for her, but she is so good and plucky. She will remain in the Acland for about 10 days. I hope you will forgive this letter but I am anxious for Shirley.[26]

The emphasis on her happiness struck Shirley as funny under the circumstances, but it helped that people were kind and concerned and showed they really cared. Her tutor, Miss Glover, hoped her father

23 SHSS to parents, 9 December 1938 (from Oxford), SHSS papers, ATL, MS-Papers-11404-04.
24 Sally Milne to DSS, 8 December 1938, SHSS papers, ATL, MS-Papers-11404-04.
25 Dr Crook to DSS, 5 January 1939, SHSS papers, ATL MS-Papers-11404-04.
26 Miss S. F. Salt to DSS, 9 December 1938, SHSS papers, ATL, MS-Papers-11404-04.

would let her continue her studies and return to Oxford to sit Greats.

I think it would be a great advantage to Shirley to have taken this exam. . . . She has a quick critical mind, and is very good at fighting her way through a difficult discussion, writing a clear sensible essay at the end. She could be trusted to learn a lot by working at her books by herself and I would of course coach her by correspondence. I should expect her not to fall below a third, and I think she might get a second even yet.

If at any point her doctor thought that her work was exhausting her, she should have to stop at once; and if they felt that a longer period of convalescence would be good, she would have to give up the idea of taking Greats this year. . . .

I am very sorry she has to be away from College next year. We all like her so much.[27]

As soon as he received these letters, her father sent off a sympathetic cable to Shirley and a second to Dr Crook requesting 'sanatorium convalescence permanent cure Switzerland if desirable', and he wrote to all concerned, agreeing to the course they recommended. To Dr Crook he commented that Shirley needed 'the regular hours and the proper treatment of an institution and needs it in an atmosphere which tends to induce willing submission.' He agreed that if she were permitted to study, it would give her an interest in life but that study and examinations should be ruled out if they interfered with her cure. 'The argument against Switzerland is purely financial and that must be faced.'[28]

Her father left it for her to choose where she went. Dr Crook recommended as much comfort as Shirley could afford, and insisted on a separate room and the best of cooking. Dr Rollier ran 36 clinics in Leysin. Shirley chose Clinique Miremont, the second most expensive. With meals and medical attention, it came to 17 francs a day (£6 a week).[29]

27 Mary Glover to DSS, 13 December 1938, SHSS papers, ATL, MS-Papers-11404-04.
28 DSS to Dr Crook, 2 January 1939, SHSS papers, ATL, MS-Papers-11404-04.
29 DVD: 70 clinics and sanatoriums, at its height in the 1930s close to 6,000 residents, of which 3,000 were TB patients attended by 300 nurses and 50 doctors.

She was relieved that her father told Nannie. She had felt uncomfortable about the deception, though she knew her grandmother would take it hard. When she recovered from the shock, she offered her savings towards Shirley's expenses. 'I think Shirley must have the very best we can do for her, don't you?' she wrote to David.[30] (He persuaded her to keep her savings for Shirley's use on her return to New Zealand.)

On leaving Acland Nursing Home, Shirley stayed with the Millers over Christmas, then went to the Milnes at Witham. As an atheist as well as a communist, she found the Milnes 'so evangelical . . . a sick sinner is especially tempting.'[31]

Shirley was now as zealous about communism as they were about Christianity. After her visit, Charles Milne replied to a letter from David that they were very sorry about his sad and disappointed tone about Shirley:

Like you we had been puzzled and perplexed at what we thought were her perverse ideas about politics and some other things. I tried many times to have a reasoned argument with her about these things. I have read a very great deal about Russia, Communism and Socialism and although I have my ideas more or less clear to myself, I was never able to cope with her. She simply flatly contradicted all my arguments and as she had many readymade shibboleths derived from her intercourse with people who were accustomed to discussing these matters I was simply left high and dry without anything to say. . . .

What she needs is deep, patient and impartial thinking, not the casting away of unpalatable facts, but studying them and letting them penetrate into her mind and soul. At present she has a self-protective system that brushes aside all objectives to her sentiments – I will not call them convictions. I'm sure if she would stop for a year reading any of Gollancz's red books and read History as a philosophical study and not for propaganda, she would have a different point of view.[32]

30 Emma Cumming to DSS, 23 January 1939, SHSS papers, ATL, MS-Papers-11404-04.
31 SHSS to DSS, 20 January 1939, from Leysin, SHSS papers, ATL, MS-Papers-11404-04.
32 Dr Charles Milne to DSS, 1 February 1939, SHSS papers, ATL, MS-Papers-11404-04.

Aunt Sally plied her with books on Faith and True Inwardness. Forgetting that David too was an unbeliever, she wrote to him:

[Shirley] *will just need to work through it all, but whatever she may think, the heavenly Father will keep an eye on her, as in Francis Thompson's 'Hound of Heaven', unceasing, unresting, footsteps ever nearer, and finally the joy of yielding to the Divine Love.*

She is so very intense about everything – nothing of the Laodicean about her! When she does yield her will eventually, she will do something fine – à la St Paul (on a lesser scale).[33]

33 Dr Sally Milne to DSS, 26 January 1939, SHSS papers, ATL, MS-Papers-11404-04.

8

Leysin

AT DR CROOK's insistence Shirley travelled to Leysin first class with a companion, Cecil Upton's sister Peggy. They stayed in Paris and Geneva, then took the train east along the lake shore to Lausanne, Montreux and Simplon, changing at Station Aigle to an electric alpine railway that took them above the blanket of low cloud to Leysin. The new four-storey Clinique Miremont stood out in the centre of numerous clinics scattered around the sprawling village, all distinguished by their sunny south-facing balconies.

Shirley soon appreciated her good fortune in coming to Leysin. Its inhabitants had for centuries been known for their longevity. The combination of altitude, cool dry mountain air and exceptional hours of sunshine provided what Dr Rollier considered the 'best sun radiation imaginable', ideal for his 'Sun Cure' for tuberculosis. He had arrived in 1903 and built a world-renowned medical centre with specialist clinics for lung patients and others, such as Clinique Miremont, for bone, gland and skin tuberculosis.[1]

Besides sun therapy and fresh air, Dr Rollier's cure centred on rest, good nutrition and occupation. This last was novel in medical terms. Rollier's holistic approach put great store on morale. Every patient had to work at something. Some learnt a language, others an instrument, while others plied their trades. He equipped clinics with light machinery so they could be productive, and this in turn helped them pay for their treatment. It was not only practical; it also helped them remain positive and confident. Shirley was deeply impressed by the creative ways he accommodated everyone's needs. She had her academic work.

1 *Leysin, 100 Years of History 1860–1960* – DVD produced by Véronique Bernard and Pierre-Alain Frey; brochures, *Clinique Miremont, and The Sun Cure* from SHSS papers. Leysin's microclimate comes from its southerly aspect and shelter from cold wet winds by high mountains to the north, east and west, plus the proximity of Lake Geneva below.

She wrote cheerfully to her father:

Rollier himself had a look over me when I arrived, and patted me on the shoulder and said 'c'est favourable'. I am allowed to read as much as I like . . . As for me personally, everything is fine. I feel, of course, extremely well! . . . You will be pleased to hear that Rollier disapproves of alcoholic liquor. On the other hand, smoking is permitted. Poor Daddy! However it costs too much, so I won't.[2]

Dr Rollier explained that it was useless to treat the disease without overcoming the cause, and he agreed with her father that the cause of her infection was that her resistance had been lowered because her general health was run down. His remedy was to build it up. The first part of the cure was total bed rest and he insisted that to get better she had to eat everything.

The cuisine was excellent: simple breakfast and two dinners that included a starter, often soup, a main meal of meat and vegetables, then salad, dessert and fruit. 'I have to lie back and do nothing afterwards for some time to recover. However they all say the more I eat the quicker I'll get better, so I do my best.'[3] The midday dinner was served in bed in her room. In the evening, patients were wheeled in their beds via a huge lift to the dining room and lined up on each side of a long table (although their food was on bed tables).

Dining together was considered good for morale, but, on her first night, seeing her fellow patients who had come to dinner in their beds and realising she was one of them reduced Shirley to tears. That they were all laughing and talking made it worse: '. . . how pathetic they were, pretending that all was normal and well. My neighbour eventually noticed my tears and asked what was the matter. Nothing, I said, the tears still running down. . . . I behaved more sensibly after that, but it was a relief when I was allowed to come down to dinner under my own steam and sit sensibly at a table.'[4]

When she got to know people, she learnt something important.

2 SHSS to DSS, 20 January 1939, SHSS papers.
3 SHSS to family, undated (about 8 February 1939), SHSS papers.
4 SHSS memoir, 'Leysin', 26 August 1998, SHSS papers.

To me at first the illness seemed the reality, what I saw was an illness with a human face, so to speak. What I learnt was that the humanity was the essential part, the illness just an adjunct. They were first and foremost people. This may seem too obvious for it to be a revelation, but that is what it was for me. While my two terms at Leysin affected my Oxford degree, they gave me a good deal else.[5]

Her attitude towards her own illness was courageous. Nowhere in any of her letters home did she show signs of self-pity and Dr Rollier's reports always noted her excellent spirits, even in the face of setbacks. Writing to her brother, she referred to her first setback simply as still having 'local trouble' in her neck but continued light-heartedly:

That same aged and broken down sister is burgeoning forth into new youth and health in this heavenly spot. . . . The sun is simply glorious and the snowy mountains all round are magnificent. Far down below I can see the Rhône Valley, and across it is the group of peaks called Les Dents du Midi. Directly opposite . . . is a rather less aetherial and more solid looking range, Le Chamossaire. . . . We are quite closed in by mountains, so there is practically no wind, and the sun feels hotter than you'd think possible in the middle of winter. There is snow two or three feet deep in the village and all round; and just opposite my verandah there are gentle slopes where people ski all day . . .[6]

When she had adjusted to the altitude and cold air, Shirley was introduced to the sun therapy. The early morning air was considered best for sun exposure. She was wheeled in her bed out to her private veranda, screened from the view of her neighbours. Wearing only a loincloth – a three-inch-wide strip of white fabric held in place by white tapes around the waist – and covered head to toe by a sheet, she was slowly and methodically exposed to the sun. The first week, only her feet were exposed, five minutes in, five minutes out, repeating the routine

5 Ibid.
6 SHSS to AGS, 29 January 1939, SHSS papers.

three times. The second week it was ten minutes in, five minutes out for the feet, and five in and five out from the ankles to the knees; the third, fifteen minutes in, five out for the feet, ten in and five out for the lower legs, and the five minute regime for the upper legs, all repeated three times. This progressed to thirty minutes in, five out for the whole body except the head. Each session ended with the nurse rubbing her down vigorously using a rough glove and bottle of mentholated spirits. Shirley found it felt wonderful.

The sun, bracing air and exhilarating view produced, as the brochure promised, the mental tonic considered important in the cure. Such value was put on happiness that when Shirley awoke to see the snow below her veranda marked by delicate footprints of small animals, she wondered if they were created for the patients' pleasure.

Part of the treatment was the 'Silence'. The entire village observed it – holy calm fell over Leysin from two to four o'clock. Cars were stopped outside the village and even the horses wore special slippers. Shirley usually slept.

After a week or so she was allowed up for an hour after the Silence to go for a walk, either to the village on her level or up the railway line to Leysin-en-haut to visit Gwenllian Moss, formerly of St Hugh's, in one of the cheaper clinics. Gwenllian had had a kidney removed in England and now her other kidney was infected. It gave Shirley a sense of perspective when, soon after she arrived, it was found that another gland had swollen up – the 'local trouble' she mentioned to her brother Allan. She assured her family that it wasn't serious; neck glands were considered minor in Leysin where there were people with legs, spines, tummy glands and kidneys out of action. The doctors told her she had *la plus petit maladie.*

Though a surgeon himself, Rollier was totally opposed to surgery in most cases of TB. Shirley had complete trust in him. Her father sent her names of surgeons, but she replied that surgery had done little except cost money.

I've been having compresses of various kinds since the first week, and last week without any pain or trouble at all the old scar opened – just a tiny opening – by itself and a lot of pus came away. . . . Now I am having more compresses to bring out the rest . . . They will make sure it is completely cleaned out, and of course I will stay a bit longer, till they are satisfied that I'm quite OK, and then they will let me go with instructions about looking after myself, and the expectation of being healthier than ever before in a month or two. This is not a pretty picture seen through my incorrigibly rosy spectacles (as I fear you may think) but cold sober fact – or if at least not fact accomplished yet, at any rate the well considered opinion of experienced doctors. So be of good cheer. You have had such a worrying and trouble-full time since you returned that I can't bear to think of you being caused worry and trouble by me too.[7]

What worried Shirley was that she had missed so much work since first becoming ill the previous year. She had permission to sit Schools (final exams) by special decree, exempting her from residence, the idea being that she would return early enough for preliminary coaching with her tutors, but the latest gland trouble meant that returning early was unlikely. Furthermore, her regimen left little time to study. Mornings were best, but the sunbath routine meant she couldn't get into anything, at least not in the early weeks. She wasn't supposed to read during the Silence, then came her afternoon walk, and then people came to see her . . .

She had attracted a following that included a German film producer, two Irish girls, an arty young person interested in socialism, an English padre, a Portuguese fascist lawyer and an English public-school boy. Most spoke some English but she wanted to improve her French (which she spoke with her nurses) and German. They would be useful if, as she feared, she got a bad degree.

She wished she had someone with whom she could discuss philosophical problems, questions like, 'Has anyone the right to be rendered happy?' 'Can there be a criterion of truth?' and 'Is political liberty an end or only a means?' After launching into a little lecture to Meta on the meaning of 'freedom', she laughed at herself: 'Oh dear, I feel I am quite insufferable. At best I suppose I merely amuse you. But

7 SHSS to family, 21 February 1939, SHSS papers.

. . . apart from any interest I take in practical politics and in immediate issues, I have these questions forced upon me by my reading in Moral and Political Philosophy and even Metaphysics. The beauty of academic work for Greats is that it can never be purely academic.'[8]

Miss Glover would have set her written work and given feedback, but Shirley thought that would be counter-productive under the circumstances. She nevertheless managed to keep up her extensive correspondence. To Allan, who had been sent to Wanganui Collegiate School despite protests from Shirley about how unhappy he would be at boarding school, she sent cheerful messages:

Yes, I am tucked away in Switzerland, and also in bed. It is very comfortable and I am very happy; except when I think of all the work I ought to be doing. It is quite heavenly to do nothing all day. It's just one glorious round of meals, sleep, and a little reading and writing letters. . . . I have been told to take a lesson from the cow, and learn to be placid and just chew the cud all day.[9]

But chewing the cud just wasn't in her nature. 'Even here, I wish the day was twice as long. I think I was just born to be in a rush. If I "haven't enough time" here, I never shall have,' she wrote to Meta.[10]

She confided in the same letter that she had received a marriage proposal, by post, from Martyn Finlay, the 'brilliant' law student from Dunedin she had met in Geneva the previous year, who had worked under Laski and got his PhD and was now in America on a Harvard Fellowship. 'I shall certainly think pretty hard about this one . . . If Daddy sees this he will probably throw a fit – "didn't I tell that girl not to get involved in anything like this until she's finished at Oxford?" But please, say I, How could I help getting a letter? And having got it, how could I not think about it? I'm not the sort of girl who can send letters back without a reply.' She added that Martyn shared her outlook on life, 'a fundamental condition for Husbandhood for Shirley. . . . He's no Apollo, but I like him.' They both planned to return to New

8 SHSS to family, 26 March 1939, SHSS papers.
9 SHSS to AGS, 5 March 1939, SHSS papers.
10 SHSS to MES, 13 March 1939, SHSS papers.

Zealand at the end of the year, war and disease permitting. But she still found herself 'hankering for Martin (with an 'i') so you never know what might happen.'[11]

Hans Reichenbach, to Shirley's amazement, had given up law and gone off to Peru to start 'publishing or something'. 'The sound sober sensible Hans! But I was always conscious of hidden depths, unplumbed at any rate by me.'[12]

At Easter, Cecil Upton arrived. Shirley was allowed to take a sleigh to the station to collect her. 'It was simply heavenly to see her – now I feel I can't bear to let her out of my sight.'[13] Cecil stayed at a *pension* close to Clinique Miremont, so she could easily visit Shirley. (Only pulmonary consumptives were not admitted to the clinic.) There was much to talk about, not least politics.

Two weeks earlier, Hitler had taken Czechoslovakia. Shirley assured her parents that being close to the French border, Leysin was the last part of the country that Hitler would get to, and anyway, he wouldn't turn his attention to Switzerland until he'd finished with eastern Europe, 'so I'm all right for the moment . . . but it's much more risky now than in September, naturally.'[14]

Cecil was with her when they heard on 1 April that the Spanish Republic had surrendered. This, in Shirley's memory almost half a century later, was devastating: 'None of us who were emotionally involved will ever feel anguish of quite that kind again. The loss of a great hope was an essential part of it, and we could never hope so greatly again.'[15]

When she next wrote home, Cecil had been and gone.

11 Ibid.

12 SHSS to family, February 1939, SHSS papers; Hans Reichenbach to SHSS, 24 July 1938, SHSS papers.

13 SHSS to family, 26 March 1939, SHSS papers.

14 Ibid. Shirley had just read *Fallen Bastions: The Central European Tragedy* by G. E. R. Gedye, which convinced her that Britain wouldn't go to war while Chamberlain remained in power.

15 SHSS, 'Reminiscences for St Hugh's Centenary Book, 1986', SHSS papers, ATL, MS-Papers-11404-35. While Shirley conflates two events, the International Brigades' withdrawal at the end of 1938 and the Republic's surrender, her devastation on both occasions was no doubt as described.

As for me, I progress with unexciting regularity – the doctor's even given up looking at my chart, it bores him so. Every Saturday Rollier says, 'bonjour mademoiselle, mais oui, ça va très bien – ça diminue beaucoup – alors, au revoir, mademoiselle', and every Wednesday Wasserfallen says much the same thing. . . . As for general health, I'm the Pride of the Clinic – not to mention for good behaviour.[16]

She had a respectable tan. 'The trouble is, I stop at my ribs, so that above I am as pale as the lily and below I'm as brown as the berry! What will I look like in a bathing suit?'[17]

She was losing interest in Greek and Roman history, but said philosophy still had a grip.

I suppose it would be a pity to plough, but I'm afraid I'm going to. I don't even seem to care. Can this be me? I want to go to the London School of Economics, I want to learn shorthand and typing, I want to learn lots of languages, including Maori. But what of Pisistratus and Nero? Their names touch no answering chord.

However I am still me . . . Politics is still life itself to me. And heavens, how it is for everyone, so horribly literally. Life I mean, or Death.[18]

After expounding her views on what would happen in Europe, she returned to her present tranquil life:

The snow went in a twinkling, about a week ago, and now the grass is brilliant emerald, and patterned with white and purple crocuses, yellow primulas, tiny pale violets, and pink-tipped daisies. I wandered over the Corbelets, the common ground in front of the clinics . . . trying not to tread on the flowers, looking at the surrounding mountains still all snowcapped, while the sun and a light breeze kept me both warm and cool . . . Briefly, it was heavenly. Then I came back and joined a crowd on Carl's balcony where Bernard, our Portuguese count, was making everyone roar with laughter . . . Carl, Norwegian sailor boy whose father owns a beer factory –

16 SHSS to MES, 15 April 1939, SHSS papers.
17 Ibid.
18 Ibid.

he's a pet but a noisy one. So you see, as long as life is undisturbed by wars and rumours of wars, it is very pleasant.[19]

She now looked forward to returning to New Zealand, to renewing her acquaintance with young Allan. 'Then there's the distinctly attractive prospect of getting to know Mart Finlay better. If only there isn't war. That'll break everything, of course.'[20]

To her stepmother's enquiry about whether Leysin had changed her fundamental world view, she replied that even a year of chewing the cud wouldn't make any difference. 'But though I couldn't profess any religion without being dishonest, I do believe in many, though not all, of the Christian ideals. It's because I believe, as Plato did too, that everyone has a spark of the divine (in a slightly different sense) in them, that I think as I do; not in spite of it.'[21]

THOUGH SHIRLEY reported that her gland was almost better, it actually took a long time to return to normal. Any thought of her returning to Oxford in time to study and have coaching with her tutors before Schools was now out of the question. While she feared she wasn't doing enough work, Dr Rollier told her she was the only patient he had ever had who was overworking. He regarded her time away at Oxford as more or less lost, but thought it in her best interests to go anyway, providing she returned to the clinic after Schools. Shirley's father agreed to this.

By 30 May she was in Oxford, having flown from Lausanne to Basel ('thrilling, flying very low under the clouds, bumping about'), then to London, the whole journey from Leysin taking just seven hours. Schools began on 1 June. 'Honestly I don't know anything and only hope I get a Fourth. College says they'll be quite satisfied if I do . . .'[22]

After exams she was confident that she hadn't failed, but still feared disappointing her father with anything less than a Second.

19 Ibid.
20 SHSS to MES, 30 April 1939, SHSS papers.
21 Ibid.
22 SHSS to parents, 30 May 1939, SHSS papers.

With several weeks before her oral exam, *viva voce*, she was finding it 'very pleasant to lie around in the garden, and be punted on the river by a stalwart young man, and be entertained almost as an equal by the dons! – makes me realise that (with luck) one is now a graduate.'[23] Helen Coates had finished her English Language and Literature exams. Together they wrote letters and 'yapped and yarned like old times'; and Shirley caught up with other friends, some of whom, she reminded her father, were not leftists. But her best friends were communists, and they happened to be Party members: 'I won't get going on Communism and -ists now – but just you wait!'[24] The political climate at Oxford was feverish.

Many men had already started military training, including her friend Frank Harley, who had corresponded with Shirley throughout her illness. Another admirer invited her to Commem Ball . . . Dr Rollier said, No. She was disappointed but Rollier's word was law.

She met up with Martin Watkin and his friends again. More importantly, her relationship developed with Kenneth Wright, one of the 'red rabbler' Yorkshire men she had met when she first arrived in Oxford.

Her oral exam was brought forward to 13 July so that she could return sooner to Switzerland (normally the women did theirs after the men). 'I've got to go and stand before a lot of hoary old gentlemen and answer all and any questions they see fit to put to me,' she explained to Allan, '– and if I can't answer, so much the worse for me!'[25]

Back in Leysin, she got her results: BA Oxon Class II Honours. It was a good Second. A Second in Oxford's most demanding course in the Humanities was considered a fine achievement in any circumstances, but considering her inadequate preparation when she started and her long illness, it was thought remarkable. Miss Glover thought it 'a most excellent performance. I think you are equal to anything you put your mind to . . .'[26]

Of only five graduates in Greats from St Hugh's in 1939, two got

23 SHSS to MES, 10 June 1939, SHSS papers.
24 SHSS to DSS, 15 June 1939, SHSS papers.
25 SHSS to AGS, 27 June 1939, SHSS papers.
26 Miss Glover to SHSS, 30 July 1939, SHSS papers.

Thirds, two Seconds and Phoebe Llewellyn Smith got a First, the third First from St Hugh's in the whole decade.[27]

SWITZERLAND was now on a war footing. Rumour had it Hitler's next coup would be on 15 August. All the Germans had left Clinique Miremont. Carl Christiansen, the Norwegian 'sailor boy', was one of the few remaining patients she knew.

She was given leave for a week when Kenneth Wright visited. They stayed in the little town of Thonon on the French shore of Lake Geneva. Back in Geneva, they met up with Helen Coates and her fiancé, Canadian Rhodes Scholar John Garrett. Helen and John then stayed with Shirley for a couple of days in Leysin. They were there with her on 22 August when Stalin signed his non-aggression pact with Hitler.

Shirley was initially shocked by the pact, but justified it to her father a week later, declaring it was a measure of self-defence forced on Russia by the imperial powers.

. . . because of course Chamberlain and Co. had obviously not given up their ultimate idea of turning Hitler on to the USSR. It was a glorious slap in the eye for them to have their intended tool and their intended victim sign a non-aggression pact. But any suggestion that it means that Russia and Germany are getting together is ridiculous . . . It is a superb piece of work. Meanwhile Chamberlain and Co. are clearly preparing to give in again to 'Save Peace'.[28]

Two days later, on 1 September, Germany invaded Poland. Britain sent Hitler an ultimatum, then declared war on Germany on 3 September.

Shirley later described hearing the Town Crier's call-up for Swiss forces just after Britain's declaration.

27 St Hugh's Register of Students, 1936–H.T. 1941; St Hugh's Archive; St Hugh's College Chronicle, 1939–40, p.15. The three other graduates in Greats from St Hugh's were Joan Pye (a Second), Ruth Keay and R. D. Wise (both Thirds). Helen Coates got a Second in English Language and Literature.

28 SHSS to DSS, 30 August 1939, SHSS papers.

All the nurses disappeared, but . . . most of them soon returned. More serious was the announcement that a 20-mile cordon had been imposed around France. . . . I had a flight already booked, but this meant I could not return by air, or, for that matter, by any other means. I was not unduly worried: I thought of staying in Switzerland throughout the war and 'helping the Swiss' . . . until an Englishman, also in the clinic, told me that he had heard on his wireless that the British Embassy had arranged for a train to take British subjects . . . back to Britain, to be paid for later. [29]

Doctors Wasserfallen and Rollier declared her cured and agreed to her leaving. When she told the manager of the clinic that she would be leaving on this train from Geneva, then going from Dieppe to Calais by ferry, he was horrified. '"Mais vous ne pouvez pas passer la Manche!" he exclaimed. I smiled and said, "Il faut passer aussi L'Atlantique et La Pacifique."'[30]

She left Leysin on 12 September. From Geneva she sent a postcard to Carl. He replied:

I am missing you Shirley girl it was so nice to have you here to get a good 'chat' with you whenever I liked. . . . thank you very much for the two months you were here and especially for the last three weeks in 23. You were terribly nice to me Shirley. But I think it was just as well you went now. I could easily have fallen in love with you and as you don't like 'capitalists' it would probably have been a great misfortune to me. . . . I was very fond of you little girl, and you know under these circumstances it is a bit hard when a good friend is leaving. . . . You must marry Kenneth one day and come to Norway when the war is over. . . . I did not ask you for a kiss until the last evening but . . . all the time I was just on the point to ask.[31]

29 SHSS, 'Beginning of War and Return to NZ', 24 August 1998, SHSS papers.

30 Ibid.

31 Carl Christiansen to SHSS, 13 September 1939 (from Leysin), SHSS papers. Carl wrote to Shirley in 1945 that he was discharged from Dr Rollier's clinic, then joined an underground movement in Norway, was arrested by the Gestapo and spent years in German concentration camps, the last ten months in Dachau near Munich. He was starved but survived.

Eventually, after standing in a queue at the British Consulate that went around the block, Shirley obtained her special visa for the train through France. She was told to take enough food and drink for two days. She bought a paperback, rye bread and cheese and a thermos, which she filled with milk, and went several hours early to the station to secure a window seat in a birdcage compartment. All the seats were already taken, and the corridors were packed.

The trip took longer than expected, with delays and hold-ups. No one was allowed out at stations, although they could buy food and drink through the windows. Passengers without seats slept on the floor in the corridor. This made it difficult for anyone moving through the train to use the lavatory, but that problem was eliminated early on when the water supply ran out. When they eventually reached Dieppe and transferred to the ferry, Shirley took one look inside and opted for the cold but fresh open deck where she slept in a nest of lifebelts. At least she wouldn't be trapped if they were torpedoed.

When she arrived in London she went straight to Aunt Sally's and slept for 24 hours.

SHIRLEY MADE a provisional booking with the New Zealand Shipping Company to travel home via Panama, but cancelled this when her father cabled her to 'travel neutral' via the United States. She booked a passage with the Holland Amerika line across the Atlantic, but was told at the Matson line office that all berths across the Pacific were booked. There was apparently no other way to go, but she heard she'd have no trouble booking from the States and decided to take her chances.

'England is all blackout, gas masks, gloom and puzzlement, otherwise you wouldn't know a war was on – except for rising prices, profits, cost of living, terrific wage and employment cuts,' Shirley wrote to her parents.[32] She went up to Oxford for graduation on 19 October. Most of the men graduating with her were in uniform. St Hugh's was to be turned into a hospital.

She collected references from her college principal, Miss Gwyer, and

32 SHSS to parents, 6 October 1939 (from Witham), SHSS papers.

her house don, Dorothea Gray. The principal referred to her 'sturdy independence of character, self-reliance and excellent capacity for work', and also her good sense and cheerfulness. Dorothea Gray had 'nothing but admiration' for her 'concentration and cheerful courage . . . sound judgment, good sense and infectious enthusiasm'. (In 1967 Dorothea Gray would recall Shirley as one of her 'most satisfactory undergraduates'.)[33]

From her tutor Mary Glover, Shirley later received a more specific reference that acknowledged how much work she had done on her own, with very little help from tutors, and how much she had matured during that time, adding, 'She is always liked; she has courage and steadiness and a sense of humour, and strong common sense also.' Miss Glover anticipated a distinguished career for Shirley.[34]

It was a time of partings and breakups. Shirley later argued that Stalin was forced to sign a pact with Hitler for self-protection, but many others left the Communist Party Great Britain (CPGB) because of the pact. She doesn't mention her response to the Soviet invasion of Poland on 17 September 1939, or the progressive annexations that followed. All in all, they must have provoked deep soul-searching. Even top Communist Party leaders in Britain were divided. When the Comintern ordered the CPGB to campaign for peace and not support what it described as an imperialist war, Harry Pollitt, General Secretary of the CPGB, and J. R. Campbell, editor of the *Daily Worker*, both opposed this change and were forced to resign in October. The CPGB then supported strikes and denounced the government for its pursuit of war.

Shirley was called to the Party's headquarters in London and given a message to deliver to New Zealand headquarters in Auckland, to the effect that the present war was an imperialist war, not to be supported. She learnt it by heart and, after flushing it down the lavatory, said it over every night, like prayers.

She spent her last nights in London with her Yorkshire Oxford friend

33 B. E. Gwyer, Principal, 17 October 1939; D. H. Gray, 21 October 1939, SHSS papers; D. H. Gray to Theodora Cooper, Tutor in Economics), 1967 (about accepting Shirley's daughter Helen Sutch), St Hugh's College Archive.

34 Mary Glover, 27 November 1939, SHSS papers, ATL, MS-Papers-11404-31.

Kenneth Wright. Kenneth wanted to marry her. Shirley didn't accept, but neither did she reject his proposal.

Shirley embarked on the *Statendam* at Southampton on 23 October and arrived safely in New York. Her relief must have been all the greater on learning that, despite its neutrality, the Holland Amerika ship that departed after hers was sunk. She had no one to meet her, knew not a soul in New York, had no US dollars, and she had to get herself and her luggage – crates of books and four years' impedimenta – across the States to San Francisco to catch the *Monterrey*, the ship on the Matson line, on which she had no booking. A longshoreman gave up his lunch hour to help her and she managed to book berths on both the *Monterrey* and the trans-continental train.[35]

On arriving in San Francisco, she was told the longshoremen were on strike and there was no telling when her ship would sail. The other problem was that her heavy luggage, which she expected to find on the docks having come on ahead of her by train, wasn't there. She searched in vain until she learnt it had been sent by sea, via the Panama Canal, direct to New Zealand. With only the clothes she had with her, she eventually set sail, travelling economy class.

On 25 November, after a mercifully uneventful voyage, her ship came to dock in Auckland. She was shocked to see it was just like any other little Pacific Island port. All her family were there to meet her.[36]

35 SHSS to Miss Helene Hanff, 9 April 1978 (a fan letter), SHSS papers.

36 SHSS memoir, 'Beginning of the War and Return to NZ', 24 August 1998, SHSS papers; SHSS passports.

9

Bill

Practically the first thing that happened on Shirley's arrival in Auckland in November 1939 was that a waterside worker very nicely asked her for a date 'and I saw the changes that had already been brought about, how the world of "The Doll's House" and "The Garden Party" was vanishing.'[1] But as soon as she was reunited with her family, including Allan, who had been taken out of school to meet her, she was in trouble with her father. He was exasperated that she hadn't reformed her political views and critical of what he saw as her irresponsible behaviour, all of which made her homecoming miserable. She wrote to Kenneth Wright:

My darling Kenneth,

This is my fourth evening in this country and my God am I homesick for England – and you. The place isn't as bad as might be, and I met some political pals this morning who seem to be pretty fine, but I'm dead beat and there have been family upsets ever since I arrived. First, an attaché case went missing through the fault of an agent of my uncle's who was supposed to be seeing my things through the Customs, and though it turned up this morning (Monday), Dad had seized on the defection as another proof of my irresponsibility. Then today he grasped the fact that I actually am a stubborn radical (which I told him last year) and will continue to operate as such in New Zealand and I have practically been told that as such I am no longer any daughter of his. Actually, practically speaking, it's an advantage, but it doesn't make a very pleasant homecoming. He also seems to regard my returning as an act of cowardice – thinks I should be V.A.D.-ing it in France; health (which fussed him so before) now apparently being of no importance. Of course I must be an awful disappointment to

1 SHSS, Submission to the Royal Commission to Enquire into Social Security, 1970, Submission no. 107, p.6, Archives NZ, Ref. No. COM7 7.

him as a daughter. He likes to be proud of anything that's 'his' and I only let him down all the time. . . .

Still my two main reasons for coming back still hold. My grandmother Nannie is really glad to see me (I'm staying with her) on account of the fact that I'm my mother's daughter, of course, but as long as she's happy the reason doesn't matter. And then I am going to need a good bit of a holiday before I begin to feel really healthy again. I'm just a wreck at the moment. . . . I just had to get in touch with you a wee bit . . . because I felt so wretched and wanted to be with you so much. Even scrawling this has helped a lot. Goodnight, darling Kenneth – my love, Shirley.[2]

As a record of her homecoming, it causes pause for thought, especially about her comment that Nannie was glad to see her – 'on account of the fact that I'm my mother's daughter, of course'. And it did matter. Shirley always wanted to be loved and valued for herself.

Apart from revealing family tensions, the letter is a record of her delivering her message to the Communist Party head office. The 'political pals' she met were the Party's national secretary Gordon Watson, 'a very able young man', and unionist Stan Roscoe, whom she also liked and admired. Recalling their meeting years later, Shirley said she and Gordon Watson were both worried about the Pact and the direction not to support the war, but decided they had to follow the Party line.

This all took much longer than she expected and she was late for her next engagement, which involved Allan. She explained frankly where she had been. Allan recalled her defiant attitude, practically spitting in his face that she was a courier for the communists. 'I thought that a pretty despicable thing. . . . She thought it was time I grew up and joined her progressive views.'[3] As for her father, '. . . oh dear . . . Dad thought I'd left all that behind.'[4]

Nothing and no one could shake her convictions. 'I remember how

2 SHSS to Kenneth Wright, undated, SHSS papers, ATL, MS-Papers-11369-217.
3 AGS to author, interview, 25 February 2011, track 4.
4 This is from the oral history of Shirley Smith with Hugo Manson on 4 November 1988 commissioned by the New Zealand Law Society, Wellington Branch, side 3, ATL, OHInt-0082-02.

impervious I was when I was a true believer,' she reflected in 1993.[5]

Shirley then got into trouble with Nannie. Martyn Finlay was in Auckland and he invited Shirley to meet him at his hotel.

I arrived back in Remuera later than Nannie expected, and naturally I explained where I'd been and with whom . . . Oh dear! I'd been to see a man *in a* hotel, *how awful, what would people think? Did I talk to him in the lounge? I lied without hesitation. What would she have thought if she'd known I'd talked to him in his* room? *I received a lecture on proper behaviour for young ladies. This was a foretaste of what life back in the bosom of the family was going to be like.*[6]

Shirley and Martyn went out together when she was back in Wellington and there was more talk of marriage. Having completed his fellowship studies at Harvard, Martyn had returned to New Zealand with Ian Milner, with whom he now shared a flat on The Terrace. Martyn joined a prototype law reform committee in the office of Attorney-General Rex Mason. His friends included Jack Lewin of the Public Service Association and economist Bill Sutch, who was a private secretary to the Minister of Finance, Walter Nash.[7]

Shirley joined the family at Taupō for Christmas and, as she recalled to Hugo Manson in 1988, that's where things really went wrong. The Bathams – Meta's sister's family from Dunedin – were there, and Allan and a school friend. The boys teased Shirley pitilessly. She described a characteristic incident: she was given some bacon to cook on a trench fire outside, but, having never cooked anything, she didn't know what

5 SHSS to Amanda Rosenberg, 19 November 1993, SHSS papers. This was in reference to Shirley's friend Cath Kelly, George Rosenberg's aunt. Shirley had just read Rory Maclean's book *Stalin's Nose: Across the Face of Europe*, an exposé of the crimes of the Stalinist regimes in Eastern Europe, ending in Moscow: 'Some of the horrors I had no doubt about, even before they were confessed . . . But there was so much more I didn't know. . . . I suppose it would be useless to give it to Cath. I remember how impervious I was when I was a true believer.'

6 SHSS memoir, 'Beginning of War and Return to NZ', 24 August 1998, p.8, SHSS papers.

7 http://www.michaelbassett.co.nz/article_finlay.htm

to do. She used lots of fat. When it caught fire the family rushed out, saw the flames and howled with laughter.[8]

She developed an itchy heat rash all over her body. The doctor diagnosed it as a nervous disorder and ordered her to bed.

Back in Wellington, Shirley started to make a new life for herself. Her parents had sold the house in Wadestown Road and she lived with them in the top flat they rented at 29 Rawhiti Terrace, Kelburn, just along the road from where she had lived with Nannie and Kitty, close to the city and university.[9]

Seeking relief from disapproval at home, Shirley found new friends whose political opinions she shared. Lois Suckling, who founded the Sex Hygiene and Birth Regulation Society (now the New Zealand Family Planning Association), brought young left-wingers together over tea in glass teacups in her open parlour. It was there Shirley first met Wolfgang Rosenberg, a Jewish Berliner who had escaped Hitler's Germany.[10] At the Wellington Central circle of the Left Book Club she met leading public servants and academics.[11] Some of the same people belonged to the Peace and Anti-Conscription Council, which organised stop-the-war meetings in January 1940. Shirley probably met pacifist Reverend Ormond Burton about this time.

At Communist Party meetings Shirley got to know Elsie Freeman (later Locke), who was Wellington provincial secretary of the National Committee of the Communist Party of New Zealand (CPNZ), the only woman on the committee. So began one of Shirley's most significant friendships, important to both her and Elsie on many levels.[12]

8 This is from the oral history of Shirley Smith with Hugo Manson on 4 November 1988 commissioned by the New Zealand Law Society, Wellington Branch, side 4, ATL, OHInt-0082-02.

9 The flat belonged to Malcolm Fraser, 'Uncle Malcolm', a Cummings relative who administered Shirley's mother's estate. He was Government Statistician 1911–32.

10 SHSS to Elsie Locke, 9 July 1990, SHSS papers, ATL, MS-Papers-11369-039.

11 A. R. Perry, Labour MP Martyn Finlay, Bill Sutch, F. L. W. Wood, businessman Fred Turnovsky, Ian Milner, among others. (Professional rather than working-class people.)

12 Some months later, Elsie developed a lump in her neck that was diagnosed as bovine tuberculosis. She was admitted to Wellington Hospital, where the lump was lanced and she was discharged, believing herself cured. Elsie's marriage to Fred Freeman ended, she moved to Christchurch and married Jack Locke on 7 November, the anniversary of the Russian Revolution.

But the most important person to enter Shirley's life at this time was economist Bill Sutch.

In December 1939, unionist Stan Roscoe (whom she had met at the Communist Party office in Auckland) took Shirley to Parliament to introduce her to Bill Sutch. But on this first meeting Shirley wasn't particularly drawn to Bill.[13]

She met Bill for the second time early in 1940 when her father took her to a lecture at the Institute of International Affairs in the Dominion Farmers' Building. Her father had told her that the Institute was being harassed by new members with unorthodox ideas and she now realised that one of them was Bill Sutch. Afterwards, when everyone gathered downstairs in the foyer to chat, Bill approached her. As she was talking to him, the certainty came over her that 'this was the man for me'.[14]

He was very vital, full of nervous energy, had most of his hair at that stage. He was good looking I thought, not tall but very well built. I just got mown down. He wasn't setting out to attract me in any way but some sort of chemistry worked at that point. I always remember how my heart felt when he looked up at the staircase . . . and there was a woman hanging over the bannister and he said, I want you to meet my wife.[15]

Allan remembered Shirley telling him that she had met the most marvellous man, but it was too late – he was married.[16]

Bill and his wife Morva invited Shirley to their home in Easdale Street, Kelburn. Since refurbishing the house in the modernist style Bill admired they held 'open house' afternoons, and Shirley became a regular visitor. With the Sutches she found further relief from the atmosphere at home. It seemed to her that she and Bill felt and thought

13 This is from the oral history of Shirley Smith with Hugo Manson on 4 November 1988 commissioned by the New Zealand Law Society, Wellington Branch, side 4, ATL, OHInt-0082-02.

14 SHSS 24 August 1998, 'WBS meets SHSS', SHSS papers.

15 This is from the oral history of Shirley Smith with Hugo Manson on 4 November 1988 commissioned by the New Zealand Law Society, Wellington Branch, side 4, ATL, OHInt-0082-02.

16 AGS to author, interview, 28 February 2011, track 5.

alike on almost everything.[17] And Bill spoke with authority on many subjects of interest to Shirley. He talked about economics in human terms – he always said that economics was about people. His father, a builder and joiner, was a strong unionist and, though Bill had come far from his working-class origins, he remained their strong advocate.

Bill Sutch had been close to policy-makers since 1933 when he joined the Ministry of Finance under Gordon Coates in the 'Coalition' government. As an economic advisor and secretary to Finance Minister Walter Nash, Sutch had been associated with the Labour Government's economic nationalism and monetary policy reform and the Social Act (1938), which sought to ensure that every New Zealander enjoyed a minimum standard of living. Based on the idea of the nation as a family, the legislation was the most comprehensive system of public health, pensions and superannuation in the world and the first of its kind. In 1970 Shirley described the Act as she saw it in her submission to the Royal Commission on Social Security: '. . . all would be assured that they would be supported in the vicissitudes of life by the family, and on the basis of equality.'[17]

Sutch was a charismatic public speaker and Shirley, like many others, found him inspirational. He was a leading member of the Left Book Club, the Progressive Publishing Society and the Wellington Co-operative Book Society (Modern Books). She joined all these groups.

MEANWHILE David Smith decided Shirley needed a job. When lobbying his friends proved fruitless, he decided she should do a course in shorthand and typing at Banks Commercial College. Shirley had no interest in being a secretary, but she wanted to learn to type. She bought a second-hand portable typewriter and had started the course when another gland swelled with infection under her jaw.

Her father allowed her to apply Dr Rollier's treatment of rest, open air, occupation for the mind and good food, all of which she had at home in Rawhiti Terrace. Her bed was moved out to the sunny veranda overlooking the harbour. She slept there until it got too cold. Meals

17 SHSS to Rosemary Vincent, 'Mongrels lawyer takes it quietly', News Feature, *New Zealand Times*, 27 November 1983, p.9.

were brought to her. With her typewriter and Pitman's manual she got on with the cure.

The gland subsided, but Shirley felt lethargic and depressed. She attributed all her woes to coming home and living in what she called 'an atmosphere of restriction and criticism' after four years of freedom. When the family moved into their new house at 10 Sefton Street in Wadestown, Shirley was in a state of inertia. She lay around the house all day, went to bed early, wrote long letters to her Oxford friends, now scattered. The men were now soldiers. She must have spent what little money she had on sending them food parcels, books and other things. 'I thought you told me you couldn't knit,' wrote Frank Harley on receiving a balaclava. Two weeks later he added, 'You talk of living for the European mails, but you have probably no idea of the intense delight I feel when I get a letter from you.'[18]

It was during this time that she decided Kenneth Wright, who had proposed marriage before she left England, was 'the one'. She wrote to him that she would marry him.[19] But mail in wartime took months to cross the oceans, and by the time her letter arrived Kenneth had written her off. He replied that he was about to marry a girl from Bristol. Fortunately, when Shirley eventually received this news, things were looking up for her.

At the end of 1940, she got a job. It came about when Professor Rankine Brown invited Shirley and her parents to lunch.

Over lunch, the Professor said to Dad, without preamble, 'What would you say to Shirley coming to be an assistant to me?' What would Dad say? What would he say to someone who was offering his daughter a job? What but Yes, Yes, Yes. . . . Neither of them even looked at me. . . . But this is not to say that I would have said anything but Yes, too.

So this was the end of the Return. I was now starting out on a life of my own.[20]

18 Frank Harley to SHSS, 18 March and 1 April 1940, SHSS papers.

19 Phyl Vincent to SHSS, 10 October 1940, SHSS papers. Phyl, a friend of SHSS in Remuera, was replying to SHSS telling her that Kenneth Wright was 'the one'.

20 SHSS memoir, 'Beginning of War and Return to NZ', 24 August 1998, SHSS papers.

She taught Greek and Latin at Stage I level, and Greek Art (as part of Greek History, Art and Literature), which especially pleased her, as she had taken her special paper in Greek Art at Oxford. But her salary of £200 per annum was not enough to live on. Helen Garrett (née Coates, now married to John Garrett) wrote from Edmonton, Canada, where she was finding life slow and marriage not easy:

The Rankine Brown offer is good, though miserly in salary, I should think. What a cheek to act on the assumption that you wish to live on your family! . . . I do sympathise with your wanting to get out of the house atmosphere for at least half *the day. . . . And keep the Beatrice Webb line about marriage in mind – it can wait, and don't you worry.*[21]

Responding to Shirley's comments on the state of the world, Helen wrote:

I don't know whether I'm prepared to follow you in always supporting the Relatively Better, except in smaller and more immediate actions and reactions. For larger issues, I prefer to try to examine – with plenty of healthy doubt and skepticism – What It May Lead To.

. . .

I hope I don't annoy you saying this, but from the reading I have been doing lately, especially of Eastman, I think that the distinction between Socialism and Stalinism must be made. The awful problem is whether any *attempt to establish Socialism will lead in the end to Stalinism. If a peaceful attempt is made right after this war, as you and I both hope it will, nicht? then I hope and think that this will not be the end result.*[22]

Cecil Upton wrote from London that she was still with the Marxists but no longer had blind faith in Stalin. Whatever Shirley thought, she was relieved when Hitler's attack on the Soviet Union in June 1941 brought the Russians into the war. Now she could openly support 'our

21 Helen Garrett to SHSS, 12 December 1940, SHSS papers.

22 Helen Garrett to SHSS, 18 September 1941 (from St Andrew's College, Aurora, Ontario), SHSS papers. The book Helen referred to by Max Eastman was *Stalin's Russia and the Crisis of Socialism*.

boys' in the war and do something herself for the war effort.

She wrote about joining Cecil in London. Cecil described her struggle to live in London with bombing raids and food shortages and advised Shirley against returning to England, 'But gosh, how I'd love to see you, you are the only one of my friends who really knows me . . .'[23] When Shirley was undeterred, Cecil suggested she live with her and join the AFTS or WAFTS. 'You would undoubtedly be wiser to stay where you were, but what the hell, what is the use of unlimited wisdom. . . . I've got a bit tucked away for emergencies, and a flat which would hold two as easily as one.'[24]

While working part-time at Victoria University College, Shirley trained as a Red Cross Voluntary Aid Detachment (VAD) nurse with view to a foreign posting. After she completed her training in September, she attended evening drills and practices and worked at Wellington Hospital in weekends and over the summer vacation.[25]

In January 1942 she wrote to her family at Taupō that the Sutches had taken her in – as she put it, they 'simply forced me to come to stay, they said I couldn't feed myself properly etc. I wasn't v. keen but it has been marvellous for me. Morva cooks wonderful meals and has washed and ironed most of my uniforms.'[26]

BILL AND Morva Sutch had come into Shirley's life again around the time she was regaining her health. She then learnt much more about them.

Bill was nine years older than Shirley, and Morva was older than Bill. She was a school teacher as Bill had been – they both taught at Wanganui Technical College before Bill got a scholarship to do his PhD at Columbia University, New York. (He completed it in just one year, graduating in June 1932.) They had no children. Morva had a degree in Home Science from Otago and had strong views on diet. She followed the School of Radiant Living, whose philosophy was based on a holistic approach to physical, psychological and spiritual health, not

23 Cecil Upton to SHSS, 15 May 1941, SHSS papers.
24 Cecil Upton to SHSS, 21 November 1941, SHSS papers.
25 Notice dated 8 September 1941 stating that SHSS was a member of the New Zealand Red Cross 5th Detachment of the Woman's Voluntary Aid Detachments, section 1.
26 SHSS to family, 30 January 1942, SHSS papers, ATL, MS-Papers-11404-06.

unlike Dr Rollier's sun therapy. Some of this had rubbed off on Bill.

Shirley learnt that Bill had been a sickly child but had transformed his body and health through diet and exercise. He was frugal, austere, a non-drinker, non-smoker; he didn't gamble and didn't swear. Shirley was impressed by what he had made of his life.

Born in England in 1907 to Lancastrian Methodists, Bill was eight months old when he arrived in New Zealand. His father, Ebenezer (Ted) Sutch, had trouble holding down a job and the growing family of eventually five children (Bill was the middle child) depended increasingly on their mother Ellen's earnings as a dressmaker.

More than a working-class-boy-made-good, in Shirley's eyes he was an epic hero. He told her of his lone trek across the Soviet Union in 1932 on his way back to New Zealand after Columbia. He told her he walked around the Arctic Circle, down through Finland, trekked across the USSR to the Afghan border, sleeping rough all the way, then crossed the Hindu Kush ranges to Kabul and on to India. At the time, she didn't doubt his story. Bill Sutch was an exceptional man.

She heard about Bill and Morva's legendary attempt to cross the Tararua Range in Easter 1933. Morva was the only woman in the party, which also included Eric Hill and Bill's Wellington friend, Bert O'Keefe. They left Te Matawai Hut near Levin and set off for Mountain House, below Mt Holdsworth, taking supplies for two days, prepared to sleep out one night if necessary. Delayed when O'Keefe suffered an injury, they were caught by a blizzard, gales, torrential rain and swollen rivers. The search and rescue operation grew into the biggest New Zealand had ever seen. Separate parties of volunteer searchers discovered one another but not the missing trampers who walked out after 15 days.[27]

The remarkable story of their survival was lost in the media furore that followed when they insisted that they had never been lost, and Bill Sutch added that they had not been found.[28] The comment was seen

27 *Evening Post*, 1 May 1933, p.10, https://paperspast.natlib.govt.nz/newspapers/evening-post/1933/5/1/10.

28 Ibid. A statement by Dr Sutch was widely published, e.g. *Horowhenua Chronicle*, 3 May 1933, p.5, https://paperspast.natlib.govt.nz/newspapers/horowhenua-chronicle/1933/5/3/5. Detailed accounts of how they rationed their food and maintained body heat was reported in 'Special to *Northern Advocate*', Masterton, 2 May 1933, p.4, https://paperspast.natlib.govt.nz/newspapers/northern-advocate/1933/5/2/4.

as arrogant and public indignation prompted Bill to write a statement, published in the *Evening Post* on 3 May, 'for and on behalf of the "missing trampers"', thanking the public for their response. This by no means ended the matter.

Shortly afterwards Bill joined the staff of Finance Minister Gordon Coates, who remarked that he knew the new recruit was unpopular throughout the country but as he himself was probably the most unpopular man in the country, maybe they would get on well.[29] Coates became a mentor to Bill and appointed him to his 'brains trust'.

Shirley said that Bill told her that rumour had it the trampers had stayed in the bush so that the men could take turns at 'pleasuring' Morva, and that she insisted Bill marry her to save her reputation.[30]

Both Morva and Bill talked to Shirley about their marriage. Morva observed that Shirley's difficulties with her father were not unlike her own with Bill: both men were autocratic and you couldn't argue with either. Shirley understood how Morva suffered, but saw her attempts to get a reaction from Bill as counter-productive. 'Bill got no joy from an argument; he made up his own mind and that was that: no one was going to influence him to change it. I drew a lot of conclusions as to how I should treat him from what I heard about this unhappy ménage, and faithfully carried them out, at my expense, for, as it turned out, far too long.'[31]

Shirley would meet Bill for coffee at Dick Singleton's café, the French Maid, near Stewart Dawson's on Lambton Quay, where Wellington's intellectual left met to discuss art and politics. 'It was fun, it was the place to go . . . I loved these coffee mornings. I wonder now that Bill was not concerned about being seen with me there, regularly.'[32]

On one occasion, when Morva was away, Bill invited Shirley home to lunch with another female guest. It suddenly struck Shirley that his

29 Brian Easton, *The Nationbuilders*, AUP, 2001, p.129. The comment was made to Dick Campbell. Coates appointed Sutch, Campbell and Horace Belshaw to his 'brains trust'.

30 SHSS memoir, 'WBS meets SHSS', 24 August 1998, SHSS papers.

31 Ibid.

32 SHSS memoir, 'Life with Bill', 3 September 1998, SHSS papers. Photo in Singleton collection, 1940–52. Shirley called the café the California.

other guest, Peggy, and Bill were having an affair.[33] Presumably it was after this that Shirley and Bill became lovers. It was certainly before she moved to Auckland in May 1942.

ONE THING Bill had made up his mind about was politics. According to Shirley, he was introduced to left-wing thought at Columbia University.

At some point he had decided that the Soviet Union was OK, even if they made mistakes. . . . He was committed to the idea that a new world would come through Soviet communism. . . . Bill didn't enjoy sitting around in a group discussing politics and ideas where people might come up with ideas which conflicted with his . . . He told me early in the relationship that he had no need for that kind of discussion because he'd made up his mind.[34]

He told her that he would never do anything wrong; therefore, everything he did was right. 'He would not only *not* accept the opposition's case, but he would behave as if it wasn't there.'[35] She saw early on that in some things he had poor judgment. Seeing Bill in terms of a classic Greek hero, Shirley often referred to this as his 'flaw'. She saw consequences of this in his career.

In 1940, Sutch applied for a five-year University of New Zealand Fellowship of Social Relations in Industry. This new chair in economics was a rare opportunity, financed by businessman and social reformer Henry Valder, whose lifelong passion was to eliminate industrial conflict between employers and employees.[36] There were three overseas applicants and Dr Sutch. The committee set up to make the appointment agreed unanimously that Sutch be offered the chair based on his superior qualifications, experience and local knowledge. They

33 SHSS memoir, 'WBS Meets SHSS', 24 August 1998, SHSS papers. Martyn Finlay married Peggy (his second wife was also called Peggy). They remained friends with Shirley and Bill, staying with the Smiths at Taupō and with Shirley in Auckland when they were househunting soon after they married.

34 SHSS to James McNeish, 4 May 1998, pp.7–8, James McNeish papers. She continues about Khrushchev's Report on the 20th Congress and Bill's response.

35 SHSS to Tim Bollinger, 1991, ATL, MS-Papers-11404-121.

36 Jeff Downs, 'Valder, Henry', Dictionary of New Zealand Biography, first published in 1996. *Te Ara – the Encyclopedia of New Zealand*, https://teara.govt.nz/en/biographies/3v2/valder-henry (accessed 2 March 2018).

changed their decision when reports came back from people who had been associated with Sutch over a number of years. None doubted his ability as a brilliant economist, but they highlighted what they too described as 'flaws' in his character: his impatience, tactlessness, criticism of colleagues and, most seriously, questions of loyalty.

The matter of Sutch's appointment would have come before the Victoria University College Council. David Smith was a member of the Council and a close friend of Professor Thomas Hunter, Vice Chancellor of the University of New Zealand and Principal of Victoria University College. In Hunter's view, Sutch had become 'something of a psychological case' because his ability had been so long overlooked.[37]

Shirley presumably knew something of this and was reassured when Bill's friends told her, 'Bill is like a rubber ball: the harder you hit him, the more he bounces back.'[38] The comment may also have referred to other setbacks. During this time when Shirley first knew him, Bill's criticisms of the government put him offside with both Nash and the new Prime Minister, Peter Fraser. Sutch's authorship was thinly disguised in his articles for left-wing magazine *Tomorrow*, and as its de facto Wellington editor he was responsible for publishing John A. Lee's 'Psycho-pathology in Politics', an attack on dying Prime Minister Michael Joseph Savage.[39] More seriously, Peter Fraser and Nash both read his criticism of the government's financial conservatism in his contribution for the 1940 centennial publications. The editorial committee first rejected it, but accepted a revised version. Peter Fraser, who was trying to unify the country in a wartime situation, insisted the government approve it before publication. It was declined. Sutch developed the texts into two

37 'Dr W. B. Sutch', Report by Sgt 170, Security Intelligence Bureau, 27 August 1941, NZSIS. (That the source, Professor Thomas Hunter, was Sgt 170's father-in-law reflects the small world of Wellington at the time.)

38 SHSS, comments on Fred Turnovsky's account of Bill Sutch in his autobiography *Turnovsky: Fifty Years in New Zealand*, Allen & Unwin, 1 August 1990, SHSS papers.

39 Sutch wrote for *Tomorrow* on economic and political issues, under his own name when he supported government policy, and anonymously or under pseudonyms when he didn't. Regarding Lee's 'Psycho-pathology in Politics', Lee's supporters (who included Sutch) insisted that the issue was democracy within the party, but his enemies saw it as an issue of loyalty. The Labour Party expelled Lee two days before Savage died. Keith Sinclair, *Walter Nash*, AUP/OUP, 1976, kindle edition, loc 6487; Brian Easton, *The Nationbuilders*, AUP, 2001, p.130.

books: Modern Books published *Poverty and Progress in New Zealand* in 1941; he sent *The Quest for Security in New Zealand* to England – in Peter Fraser's luggage by courtesy of his secretary, thereby avoiding the New Zealand censor. In 1942 it came out as a Penguin Special and it sold very well.[40] Shirley thought it 'terrific'.

Fraser had other concerns about Sutch – security concerns. Most serious was the suspicion that he had leaked classified defence information to a left-wing paper during the Imperial Conference in London in 1937.

On 23 June 1937 *The Week* published an article, 'The Dominions Against Britain', reporting on discussions from a secret meeting of the Committee of Imperial Defence about the security of the Pacific in the face of Japanese militarism. The security breach was taken up at the highest level of British Government and suspicion fell on Sutch. An inquiry found that he had clandestine contacts with leading members of the Communist Party. The evidence of his having been the channel of communication was inconclusive, but having a foot in both camps placed him 'under grave suspicion'. The British Government regarded him as a security risk.[41]

When Nash was appointed New Zealand's resident minister in the United States in 1942, Sutch expected to accompany him to Washington. Instead, he was called up into the army and the government didn't appeal. As Keith Sinclair noted, 'Many of those who earned Fraser's displeasure found themselves not in Siberia but in a military camp.'[42]

In May 1942, Shirley moved to Auckland to a full-time job as a junior lecturer in classics at Auckland University College. It was a temporary position to replace Peter Crawley while he was in the army, and could possibly be extended for the duration of the war. She told her father that most people encouraged her to accept, but Bill Sutch had raised points

40 Keith Sinclair, *Walter Nash*, AUP/OUP, 1976, kindle edition, loc 6487 of 15006.

41 Ibid. Russell Campbell, *Codename Intelligentsia: The Life and Times of the Honourable Ivor Montagu, Filmmaker, Communist, Spy*, The History Press UK, 2018, Chapt.13, 'Moscow and Madrid' (notes published online); M. P. A. Hankey to Colonel Sir Vernon Kell, 5 July 1937, MI5 files, National Archives, Kew, UK, KV2/3929-30, P1011172, P1011173, P1011174.

42 Keith Sinclair, *Walter Nash*, AUP/OUP, 1996, kindle edition loc 6498.

that worried her: Did she want an academic career teaching Latin? (She was not offered Greek classes.) Were the salary (£400 per annum) and prestige worth more than living in the capital city, at home, with a pleasant if light job and a considerable amount of time for extra activities that really interested her?

One of those activities was the task of organising an exhibition of Russian Art and Life for the Society for Closer Relations with Russia (SCR).[43] After the Nazis invaded the Soviet Union in June 1941, groups had set up with the aim of sending aid to Russia. (Friends of the Soviet Union was set up in Auckland.) On 6 December 1941, the day Soviet troops routed the Nazi armies outside Moscow, Wellington held the first conference of the Society for Closer Relations with Russia. Bill was closely involved.[44]

So, when Shirley heard that Auckland wanted her, she was in two minds. She telegrammed her father in Taupō, asking his advice. He replied with a reference to Shakespeare's tide ('There is a tide in the affairs of men, Which, taken at the flood, leads on to fortune . . .').[45] This decided the matter. 'I daresay really why I'm going is because I'll always be unhappy to think I'd wilfully missed an opportunity.'[46]

Professor Rankine Brown warned her that she would find life difficult in the department at Auckland. With youthful confidence, she thought she could cope with whatever the problem might be.[47]

43 SHSS to DSS, 19 February 1942, SHSS papers, ATL, MS-Papers-11404-05.

44 Russian Community website, http://www.zelandia.com/eng/history.php; SHSS to MHS, 1994, referred to Box 18, Sutch papers in ATL as having 'quite a bit about the setting up of the Society for Closer Relations'.

45 *There is a tide in the affairs of men*
Which, taken at the flood, leads on to fortune;
Omitted, all the voyage of their life
Is bound in shallows and in miseries.
On such a full sea are we now afloat
And we must take the current when it serves,
Or lose our ventures. – Julius Caesar, IV.iii.216–222.

46 SHSS to parents, 8 April 1942, SHSS papers, ATL, MS-Papers-11404-06. Shirley didn't mention a third path that would have taken her overseas to Egypt as a VAD nurse. She expected to depart within weeks.

47 SHSS to L. W. A. Crawley (Peter), 11 March 1979, SHSS papers, ATL, MS-Papers-11404-70.

10

Auckland

In Auckland Shirley rented a one-bedroom unfurnished flat at 3 O'Rorke Street, close to the university. It was sunny and modern. She loved it.

And she loved her room up in the clock tower in the Classics Department. 'The view, the sun, the spaciousness, the distance from hustle and bustle, the consequent peace in the ivory tower (even if it was made of concrete lace) made it a constant joy to me: . . . I always ran up all the flights of stairs two at a time . . .'[1]

She had heard that her professor, Charles Gordon Cooper (MA, St Andrews), was an ogre, but she found him kind and friendly. She couldn't understand why he was so disliked. His senior students held him in high regard and Shirley came to see him as a scholar of the first order.

She was thrilled that she would be teaching Lucretius at Honours level, as she had read Lucretius as one of her special books under Professor Cyril Bailey at Oxford, but she was disappointed that the professor wouldn't give her at least one Greek class.

He explained that the department was divided between him and Mr Blaiklock, and that he preferred me to assist him on the Latin side and not have any involvement with Mr Blaiklock's sphere. Later I attempted a friendly conversation with Mr Blaiklock, without any success. Somebody told me . . . that he did not like women who wore lipstick.[2]

The schism between the Latin and Greek sub-departments grew out of historical antipathy between Cooper and Edward Musgrave Blaiklock.

1 SHSS to L. W. A. Crawley (Peter), 11 March 1979, SHSS papers, ATL, MS-Papers-11404-70.

2 Ibid.

Instead of scholarly collaboration, there was such backbiting and distrust as to put a strain on the whole department. Shirley experienced this antagonism as soon as she arrived. Blaiklock had friends in high places, leading lawyers who knew Shirley through her father, who made it clear they wanted Cooper gone. She didn't like their attempt to prejudice her against her professor before she had had time to form her own opinion. 'The anti-Cooper faction rather seriously misjudged me. I may have been young and female but I have always had a mind of my own and been a fighter,' she wrote in 1979 to L. W. A. Crawley (called Peter), the lecturer she had replaced in 1942 when he departed for military service, who was writing a history of the Classics Department.[3]

An episode that occurred soon after she arrived had a decisive effect on Cooper's attitude towards Shirley. When a leading Auckland lawyer made a complaint that Cooper had unfairly failed his son, and other fathers of law students associated themselves with the complaint, she spoke to the Professorial Board, explaining how the papers had been marked and why there was no case to be made for those who had failed. That disposed of the matter. When the professor expressed his gratitude for what he called her loyalty, she told him she was only giving her honest opinion. From then on, he accepted her completely. He invited her to his home to meet his wife Alice and son Robin; she often went to dinner there and sometimes stayed overnight. 'There must have been a good deal of dismay when it was found that I was getting on famously with Cooper and that I supported him wholeheartedly on standards,' Shirley reflected. The intrigue and underhand methods of his opponents disgusted her.[4]

When she herself fell victim to their methods, again, they underestimated her.

Peter Crawley later remarked in his history that Shirley brought a 'certain novelty' to the department. As well as being female, young and attractive, she was liberated. 'Report had it that she actually wore slacks in the lecture room, and she had been known to smoke cigarettes

3 Ibid.
4 Ibid. The Smiths' visitor's book in Taupō shows Robin Cooper stayed for nearly two weeks in January 1944.

there too. . . . In spite of these practices of hers, Miss Smith's ability in the more austere business of teaching classics was all that could be desired.'[5]

Everyone knew Shirley was a communist. David Dunningham, one of her Honours students, said they all thought that was exciting. Pamela Key-Jones, another Honours student who thought herself liberal, had her eyes opened far wider by Shirley, especially on feminist ideas. Shirley really challenged their thinking and they loved it.[6]

But some students in her Latin I classes weren't so happy. The subject was compulsory for law students and many of them hated it. When Shirley marked Latin papers for matric the following summer, she realised how badly they had been taught in school but she thought that any intelligent, conscientious student could get through with the help she offered. What she refused to do was to read them a translation of a set book. This led to a complaint against her in her second year.

In 1978, when Peter Crawley wrote to Shirley requesting she provide a memoir of her time at Auckland University College for his history of the Classics Department, she replied:

I could write you an account of the two years I was at the Department which would probably inject more life into your history than you would like. Your remark that [the] *Departmental atmosphere was 'inclined to be strained' is the understatement of the decade. I also see that you have a responsibility 'to exercise the utmost discretion', and that causes me another problem, a moral one. If my contribution to your history is to present an incomplete picture of how things were from 1943–1944 (which I realize is probably unavoidable if I am to contribute at all), should I contribute at all? The question is, is there an alternative between silence and telling the whole truth?*[7]

5 L. W. A. Crawley (co-author, W. F. Richardson), *Classics in Auckland: A Centennial History of the Department of Classics and Ancient History in the University of Auckland*, Auckland, 1983, pp.73–74.

6 David Dunningham to author, interview, 8 September 2004. The references to Pamela Key-Jones are from her letters to Shirley after Shirley left Auckland.

7 SHSS to Crawley, 11 July 1978, SHSS papers, ATL, MS-Papers-11404-70.

She eventually wrote her account the following year, too late for publication. Crawley wrote to Shirley on 15 March 1979 that it was a revelation to him that she experienced any personal unpleasantness in Auckland. 'No-one ever mentioned it to me, and there is no record of it in the official documents to which I have had access.' (The author also could find no records in the University archives and has not seen the account Shirley wrote in her memoirs in 1998.) This official erasure of the whole episode, including Shirley's correspondence with the college council, suggests that things were not above board. From Shirley's copies of the correspondence, combined with her account for Crawley, the following saga emerges.

Towards the end of September 1943, Professor Cooper called her to say that students had made grave allegations that she was unfit to teach. What on earth had she been up to? She could think of nothing. The matter was considered extremely serious and there was talk of an appeal for Mr Crawley's release from military service, but the charges were not put on paper and were never made precise.

Cooper supported her to the hilt and, on behalf of them both, repeatedly requested a conference of those concerned to settle the matter. Shirley later explained to the Acting Registrar on 9 December:

In this situation it was clearly impossible for anyone to make any judgment either acquitting me or otherwise. To me this was intolerable. I thought it most unjust. I do not wish to stress what I suffered during this time; but it will, I think, be understood that it was not easy to carry on with my end-of-term work and subsequent examining under the strain which I inevitably felt. It was under these circumstances that I went to the President, Mr Cocker, and told him what had happened.[8]

On 13 October, two weeks after the allegations were made, she saw Hollis Cocker. It helped that the President of the University College Council was an old and close family friend. On 17 November, the Council resolved to reappoint her for 1944 and not to take the matter any further, but the allegations weren't withdrawn. Shirley and Cooper

8 SHSS to Acting Registrar, Mrs Munn, AUC, 9 December 1943, SHSS papers.

asked that they be either withdrawn or substantiated. At their insistence that a tribunal be set up to deal with them, a committee of Council, with Cocker as chair, heard the case on 29 November.

As requested, Dr Anschutz, who had presented the allegations, submitted a written summary for the meeting and a copy was sent to Shirley before the meeting. Shirley objected to the fact that the allegations differed substantially from those first put to her. In the end, only one stood – lateness at beginning of lectures.[9]

Only one student's name had been mentioned. Dr Anschutz insisted that the enquiry should not include 'the circumstances under which, or the persons to whom, this opinion might have been expressed'. Before the committee met, Shirley gave notice that if the committee accepted this stipulation, she would take the matter further.[10] The committee then acquitted her of all charges, but they did accept Anschutz's condition. Shirley asked for a further enquiry. She wanted to know who first put the allegations against her, what precisely was first alleged, and why the original allegations were put forward.[11]

After considering her letter, College Council passed the following resolution: 'That Miss Smith be informed that having regard to the fact that the Committee of Enquiry had acquitted her of all allegations against her, Council is of the opinion that no good purpose could be served by taking the matter any further.'[12]

There were other aspects of the case Shirley hoped to bring into the open by a further enquiry. When that possibility was closed, she wrote one more letter, at Cooper's request, on 18 December. She referred to her association with Professor Cooper, explaining that it had been 'closer than that of a junior lecturer with the Professor usually is, for the reason that in this College the senior lecturer alone teaches Greek, while the Professor and his junior collaborate in teaching Latin.' She briefly referred to her case, dealing more with wider issues of the departmental relationships that lay at the heart of the troubles.

9 SHSS to Acting Registrar, Mrs Munn, AUC, 26 November 1943, SHSS papers.
10 Ibid.
11 SHSS to Acting Registrar, Mrs Munn, AUC, 9 December 1943, SHSS papers.
12 Acting Registrar, AUC, to SHSS, 14 December 1943, SHSS papers.

I am convinced . . . that Professor Cooper would always be found an extremely pleasant and considerate colleague by reasonably normal people. It is because, in my opinion, he has not always had the good fortune in this College to meet with such colleagues, that I am now writing this letter. My own deep gratitude to him for his generous treatment of an inexperienced lecturer prompts me urgently to put on record my independent opinion.[13]

After elaboration as to why she and his senior students held him in such high regard, and how he invariably put first the good of the students and the department as a whole, she continued:

Of his loyalty to me as a lecturer in his department, and the complete propriety of his behaviour in very unpleasant and difficult circumstances, I cannot speak too highly, or with sufficient gratitude. Of our social relationship, I should like to say that since I first arrived in Auckland, Professor and Mrs Cooper could not have been kinder or more charming to me than they have been.[14]

In its entirety, this letter says much about Shirley herself. Cooper wrote, 'It was only when I read what you had written that I realized what a thoroughly unpleasant thing I had asked of you. But you have done it supremely well, as if it were the most natural thing in the world.'[15]

When Shirley eventually left, Professor Cooper reported to the College Council, 'I cannot speak too highly of the co-operation which Miss Smith gave me during her two years in the department. She was all one could wish a colleague to be – original, independent-minded, enthusiastic, responsive, trustworthy, sincere. We differed on almost every point and worked together in perfect harmony.'[16]

Shirley believed that the main reason for the attack on her was the hostility between the two sides of the department, and that the trail went back to Blaiklock. She was perplexed about the involvement of

13 SHSS, for the attention of Council or the Professorial Board, 18 December 1943, SHSS papers.
14 Ibid.
15 Professor Cooper to SHSS, 29 December 1943, SHSS papers.
16 Cooper's annual report to the AUC Council on staff changes in 1944, SHSS papers,

Dickie Anschutz. He wasn't in her department, and she had considered him a friend. It's unlikely he would have objected to her politics, being on the left himself. Crawley thought it wouldn't have been personal, whereas he wasn't surprised about Blaiklock's part.

There are gaps in this story, and obviously Shirley's account is not the whole account. She does not mention, for example, that they tried to get rid of her on political grounds. Her former Honours student, David Dunningham, recalled being called to the home of Arthur Sewell, Professor of English. (Sewell was a friend of Shirley's, and a radical himself. He was probably on the tribunal.) 'He said, "I have to ask you this question: is Shirley Smith trying to influence you politically?"' At the time they were studying Lucretius, which provoked radical thinking in many respects. David explained that she made them think.[17]

Later, Special Branch's security file on Shirley Smith included a report by A. E. V. Lane, Act-Detective, 12 May 1953, that she was well known for her communist sympathies at Auckland University College, where she used to distribute literature among the students. The report doesn't identify the source. Although Police Special Branch and the Security Intelligence Bureau infiltrated the Communist Party in Auckland, a search of their files found no record of her during her time in Auckland other than the 1953 report.[18]

By Shirley's account, she belonged to the Parnell branch of the Party and their main work was to get Labour re-elected at the end of 1943.

KEITH MATTHEWS, who later employed Shirley as a law clerk, recalled first meeting her when she knocked on his door distributing election pamphlets. He invited her in and soon found they shared views on domestic and international politics, and they also talked about the law. Shirley was very interested in the law. Keith was finishing his law

ATL, MS-Papers-11404-06.

17 David Dunningham to author, interview, 8 September 2004.

18 While public attitudes had softened towards the Soviet Union since it joined the war in June 1941, and especially after the Red Army's heroic resistance during the Siege of Stalingrad in 1942, the Police Special Branch (PSB) and the Security Intelligence Bureau (SIB) kept up their reports on communists. (The SIB operated between 1942 and 1945 as part of the Ministry of Defence.) NZSIS has no record of either organisation reporting on Shirley Smith until September 1944, when she had returned to Wellington.

degree in Auckland while working part-time for David Smith's friend and former associate, Arthur Fair. She told Keith how her father had discouraged her from doing law, but she was still keen on the idea. He thought her very like her father – 'bustling, on-the-go, earnest, easy to talk to.'[19]

An exchange of letters between Shirley and her father shows that they had set aside their political differences. After both reflected on a happy day spent together on one of David's visits to Auckland, he wrote that on such occasions he simply felt her nearness:

. . . the nearness of one who is of myself and of the girl who long ago first really evoked in me feelings of love and wonder and desire. And nearness implies affectionate sympathy and I love it. So I hope some day you will get happily married in New Zealand though I have been guessing you plan to go abroad and you know the last thing I would like to be would be to be a drag or to be thought to be a drag upon you.

Lots of love and all good wishes from
your Daddy.[20]

In another letter to her, David remarked that 'in the minds of the Romans, the chief characteristic of a human being was the capacity to err.'[21] He wasn't referring to Shirley, but it was clearly something they had discussed. It draws attention to a softer side of the Smiths. It sometimes took a long time, but Shirley had the humility to acknowledge her own errors. By nature she was generous and forgiving.

For her twenty-seventh birthday, her father sent her a pendant with little pearls and a green stone that he gave her mother when Shirley was born. 'It's a bit old-fashioned but she liked it. . . . with my love and all the best wishes for the life of my grown-up daughter.'[22] Shirley was thrilled.

19 Keith Matthews to author, interview, 8 April 2011, Track 2.
20 DSS to SHSS, 15 March 1943, SHSS papers.
21 DSS to SHSS, 2 July 1943, SHSS papers.
22 DSS to SHSS, 8 October 1943, SHSS papers.

How can I tell you how much I love and appreciate what you have sent me for my birthday? . . . I love to have my mother's things because they were hers, particularly the pendant because you gave it to her and on such an occasion, but I do as well most truly love the things themselves. . . . Goodnight, my dear Daddy. I love you very much.[23]

'Your letter made me feel very warmly about the past and about my daughter in the present,' he replied, and described the brooch he gave her mother on their marriage. 'Shall I give you that at Christmas? It's time that you got these things, now that you're a 'growed up' person – although I must say I have felt that you never cared for jewellery.'[24]

In fact, he gave it to Shirley for her next birthday. There was an auburn hair across it, which he said was Eva's.[25]

SHIRLEY AND ALLAN had also grown closer. When he flunked his first year at Victoria University College and spent all his money on 'riotous living', Shirley helped mollify their father. Allan then joined the Air Force, trained in the radar section based at Whenuapai and often stayed with Shirley. He recalled her 'marvellous' flat decorated with the Gauguin prints she had continued to collect since her twenty-first birthday. She kept the flat neat and orderly but things would go missing. 'She had this thing about poltergeists . . . She would say she definitely put something down here, and it wasn't there any more, it was somewhere else, so she'd say, the poltergeists have been in. She was on about poltergeists for many decades as an explanation for things she couldn't explain.'[26]

ANOTHER GUEST was Gabrielle Mulgan, John Mulgan's wife. Shirley first met Gabrielle at Oxford. 'She was like a goddess of spring . . . Frank [Harley] introduced her to John. Frank was madly in love with her but had never told her so . . . and it was all over for Frank. John fell for her.'[27] John later sent Gabrielle and their baby son Richard to

23 SHSS to DSS, 11 October 1943, SHSS papers, ATL, MS-Papers-11404-06.
24 DSS to SHSS, 28 October 1943, SHSS papers.
25 DSS to SHSS, 10 October 1944, SHSS papers.
26 AGS to author, interview, 21 March 2011, Track 6.
27 SHSS to James McNeish, telephone interview, 15 January 1999, p.4 of transcript,

his parents in New Zealand to be safe from the war. Gabrielle was lonely, bored with New Zealand, homesick and missing her husband and family. Shirley was glad to find someone she had known at Oxford, who knew her friends.

Shirley wrote regularly to Frank Harley. She loved Frank (so she told James McNeish in her old age), but didn't realise that he was in love with her. Shirley wrote to him about Gabrielle and reminisced nostalgically about Oxford. He replied that Oxford seemed hardly real to him. He had been a soldier so long it made a noise to think.

In the world of academia and classics, Shirley's war was still the internal politics of the department. Otherwise she had the same pressures of work that other academics had. When Gabrielle stayed with her in Auckland, Shirley discovered what husbands experienced as a matter of course – what it was to come home from work at the end of the day to find housework all done and a meal prepared. It was wonderful! She understood why men would want to keep their wives in the home.

She had the same welcome when Bill Sutch came to stay.

BILL SPENT all his army leave with Shirley. He met her friend Cecil Algie, formerly Upton. In London Cecil had married Don Algie, who served with the Royal New Zealand Navy, and had come home to Auckland. (Shirley became godmother to their daughter Elizabeth.) Cecil and another Auckland friend, Loris Chilwell, frankly expressed their admiration for Bill (Shirley explained that he was strong and bronzed) and he liked them.

But mostly Shirley and Bill kept to themselves. 'The time we had was precious, and as much of it as possible we spent making love.'[28]

When Shirley had a late lecture, she came home to a roast dinner Bill had cooked. Sometimes they ate out. Shirley's preference for a basic place with wooden surroundings that served plate-sized whitebait fritters showed the difference in their views of what mattered, she said. She was not what Bill expected of a judge's daughter.

McNeish papers.
28 SHSS memoir, 'Life with Bill', 3 September 1998, p.2, SHSS papers.

Sometimes they rented a secluded cottage Bill found in the Waitākere Ranges. Shirley recalled one occasion when Bill realised he'd be late returning to camp. 'He rang his doctor, a friend in Wellington, and asked him to write him a certificate that he had been delayed by an attack of some sort. His doctor friend was naturally reluctant, but Bill succeeded in getting the certificate, which he duly presented on his return . . . It was this episode, and others like it, that awakened me to the fact that Bill took risks, trusting in his capacity to avoid any unhappy (even if deserved) consequences.'[29]

Another thing that happened at this time bothered her all her life. She recounted in 1998 how Bill was injured:

The way Bill put it was 'the gun was dropped on my foot'. If his foot had taken the full weight of the gun, the injury would have been much more serious: but it was true, as I have told people, that it was sufficient to get him a very small pension from the army, which was continued until he died. I have told people that he didn't go overseas because the injury to his foot was sufficient to disqualify him from marching any distance . . . At one stage I believe that the Army did take that view, but right near the end of the war, they needed fresh troops, but apparently not officers, so badly that they would take any officers who volunteered to drop their rank and go overseas as simply, men. I have not told anyone that Bill knew that he was in the category that could take up this offer. There was nothing compulsory about it. Bill did tell me about this, and that he would not take up the offer. . . . Who was I, whom no one would invite to go into a battlefield and be shot at, to tell him that honour required him to do just that? I am trying to be honest with my daughter . . . and I shall therefore admit to having an immediate feeling of that sort, which I brushed away in my relief that he would be safe in New Zealand. I feel uncomfortable about both of us. Nothing can alter the past, and if it could, would I do anything different? I could not have told Bill that he should go, whether then or given a second chance.[30]

29 Ibid, p.3.

30 Ibid, p.4. In her interview with James McNeish, 4 May 1998, Shirley said, 'Bill was the world's greatest exaggerator. He told me he dropped a cannon on his foot.'

If the question was where he could make his most valuable contribution to the war effort, Sutch was probably right in deciding it was not on the battlefront abroad. While still a soldier he wrote about the war effort at home – what could be done to increase production and so bring the war against fascism to an end.[31] As his administrative abilities were needed in this area, in November 1943 he was discharged from the army to work for the Prime Minister's department and then returned to the Ministry of Supply.

At this time his divorce was going through. As requested, Morva agreed to divorce Bill on the grounds of his refusal to cohabit.[32] She then changed her mind and asked to delay the divorce. Bill wished to humour her, but Shirley was anxious to get her relationship with Bill into the open and thought the delay served no purpose. Decree absolute was granted in February 1944.

On 24 February Shirley handed in her resignation to Auckland University College in view of her approaching marriage. She was to leave at the end of May.[33] (In fact she stayed until July when her replacements could take over.) There was no formal engagement, no announcement, no wedding date.

She wrote in May to tell Irene Wilson about her impending marriage and to ask for advice about getting work as a teacher in Wellington, possibly even at her old college, Queen Margaret's, where Miss Wilson was still principal. Irene Wilson replied:

Well! I hope you won't mind my saying that I can't help wishing it could be otherwise; that you might have married someone more your own generation; but perhaps I think of you as younger than your actual age and of Dr Sutch as older than his. Much more, I wish you could have come to marriage with an even start, without any question of hurt or hardship to others. . . .

31 While still a soldier, Sutch wrote *Workers and the War Effort* and *Guilty of Manslaughter*, both published by the Progressive Publishing Society, Wellington.

32 SHSS memoir, 'WBS Meets SHSS', 24 August 1998, SHSS papers. Divorce on this ground was abolished soon after. There was no specific waiting period before one could apply.

33 Acting Registrar, AUC, to SHSS, 21 March 1944, SHSS papers.

For you – I know you to be true and honest, and must respect whatever way you take, believing it is the right way for you.

She mentioned that she had heard Dr Sutch lecture on his return from Russia years earlier, and the previous year they had been fellow judges at a JC debate.

I can only remember how he reduced me to a state of complete dumb-doggishness . . . I can't see anyone making a dumb dog out of you, fortunately! And I do see how much you will have in common in interests and outlook. You must feel very proud to be linked with one of his intellectual courage and integrity and though sparks will sometimes fly between two such quick and ardent spirits, there will never be a dull moment. I trust and hope you will both find great happiness together.

There would be a lot of talk – yes, a lot of it. But I think you are right in going straight ahead once your mind is made up . . . 'to thine own self' etc.

And now to the real question of your letter – advice about a job – there I'm afraid I am a broken reed, for I don't know what to advise. I think I would try something other than teaching, in a secondary school, that is. There is no calling in which it is so impossible to make any line of demarcation between your official and your private life, and so matters which in any adult surroundings are regarded as purely your personal concern do overflow into your influence and 'force of example', that two-edged sword to the teacher. At the university you are presumably dealing with adults, and this consideration is not so strong. I have been trying to think of any teacher I know of whose circumstances are similar to yours in this regard, but I know of none. . . .

. . . And when it comes down to the issue, 'but what about Q.M.C. itself, and Shirley Smith, one of the brightest, best and dearest of her children?' Well, even so, I don't see Dr Mazengarb (Chairman) welcoming you with open arms – do you? Not yet at any rate. . . . And for Irene Wilson herself as Head? I think she, weak creature, as Head would feel she must stand by that view of life to which the school is committed. As a person she would want to take into account her knowledge of the people concerned, and to say, 'But this is one whom I trust and honour. I know that the good she would

do would far, far outweigh this hindrance.' But I think that is wrong. The matter must be judged on principle and not on personal considerations.

She concluded that that it would be wise for Shirley to seek some work wherein her private life could remain her own concern.

I would have liked you for the teaching world. We have too few people like you in it. But your real work will lie in the home you build, and the family you bring up, and the ripples that flow out from that centre: for you will always matter very much to the people who are close to you. Very Victorian, I know, but I belong to that age.

I suppose this has been a bit of a blow to the family, their being of my generation, too.

For all the defects of my advice, this brings to you my love, and all good wishes for both the near and distant future,

Irene Wilson[34]

Irene was relieved to receive Shirley's reply eventually. 'I thought my letter must have hurt you, and was so sorry that it had, and wondered how else I should or could have written. It was such a comfort, then, to have your long and full letter, and to know that somehow your trust in me was unimpaired.'[35]

She was right in guessing that Shirley's parents were unhappy about the match. Shirley wrote in 1998 that Bill was uncomfortable at Sefton Street and apt to say the wrong thing and, while Meta was always kind, it was obvious that her father didn't take to him.

In fact, her father strongly disliked Bill and opposed the marriage.

34 Irene Wilson to SHSS, 19 May 1944, WBS papers, ATL, MS-Papers-2002-012-17/6.
35 Irene Wilson to SHSS, 2 July 1944, WBS papers, ATL, MS-Papers-2002-012-17/6.

11

Wife and Mother

META OFFERED to put on a small wedding party in Wellington, but Bill insisted on a quiet wedding in Auckland with just their witnesses Loris Chilwell and Cecil Algie present. Shirley had not yet met Bill's parents.

She wrote to her parents on 30 May 1944 to tell them the wedding was to take place on 2 June:

Well, the news is that the vac begins on Saturday, Bill can take some leave from the end of this week, and so we are going to visit the Registrar and get married on Friday morning. This was only fixed yesterday afternoon, when I had a wire from Bill saying he could get away . . .

I can't imagine why people should want to come to a Registry office, but the Coopers have said they'd love to come, please, if they may, and Auntie Annie Mayer, who is up here at present, wants to come and bring Duncan; and Nannie too, and Loris and Cecil. So we'll be duly witnessed. I expect we'd take Nannie to lunch afterwards, or something like that. At night there's Graduation, which I'm still expecting to go to, seats and so on all being arranged. Then there's Grad Ball, but that sounds a bit too exhausting. However, we'll see. Oh and my Honours students had asked me to dinner before the Capping, so now they are going to take us both!

That's about all, I think, except that of course Allan arrived on my doorstep at 9 p.m. this evening . . . I believe he'll still be here for the weekend, and he's delighted to have timed his visit so well for a Grad Ball![1]

Bill travelled up overnight on the Limited Express, arriving on the morning of their wedding. He was strangely distant towards Shirley – she didn't understand why – and at the registrar's office things got worse when he found there were so many people they couldn't all fit in.

1 SHSS to parents, 30 May 1944, SHSS papers.

Uncle Willie had arranged a wedding breakfast at the Station Hotel, at his expense. This also was not part of Bill's plan.

Shirley and Bill didn't attend the 'Grad Ball'. Shirley loved to dance, but Bill didn't. He remained cold and distant. Back at her flat, when he called her 'Morva', she broke down in tears.

On their honeymoon on Kawau Island, Bill was still distant. Writing of this in 1998 in what Shirley called 'Life with Bill', she continued:

Bill couldn't stand the implications and social significance of 'honeymoon', couldn't stand the word; and while I was not so repulsed by the whole idea, to me the only importance of getting married was that it made us acceptable in the eyes of the world, so that we would no longer have the anxieties of keeping our relationship secret. Otherwise it meant nothing. I was to discover Bill's understanding was quite different.[2]

When he asked her to marry him, he said that she was never to put him 'under compulsion'. Whether this meant she was never to make demands of him, hold him to account or put him in the wrong, she gave him her word. He was to do as he pleased.[3]

Shirley expected that she too would remain her own person. 'What never occurred to me at the time was that he would put me under compulsion and I would suffer.'[4]

When his coldness towards Shirley on their honeymoon led her again to tears, Bill finally comforted her. She thought it was probably then that he told her that Morva had been on the train to Auckland, sitting beside him all the way. Shirley thought that Morva told Bill things about her that nearly wrecked the marriage from the beginning.

Shirley saw no reason to change her surname on account of being married, and good reasons not to, to avoid confusion with both Bill's sister, Margaret Shirley, usually called Shirley, and with 'the Mrs Sutch there already is' – meaning Morva. It was also a matter of principle. 'We believe a woman has a right to her own name as much as a man,' she

2 SHSS memoir, 'Life with Bill', 3 September 1998, SHSS papers.
3 This now archaic phrase was used repeatedly by Falstaff in Shakespeare's *Henry IV, Part I.*
4 SHSS memoir, 'Life with Bill', 3 September 1998, SHSS papers.

explained to her Aunt Fiona.[5]

Her reason for using 'Miss' was to demonstrate solidarity with unmarried women. She never forgot how her distinguished headmistress, Irene Wilson, had to enter the dining room at her parents' home *after* the youngest woman there. Shirley often explained that Mrs, Miss and, later, Ms (which she never used) were all derivatives from Mistress, the feminine of Mister which once was Master. There was no legal requirement that married women use Mrs and unmarried ones Miss.[6]

Shirley believed she was the first woman in New Zealand (apart from artists and performers) to keep her own name.[7] She fought for it. Two months before her marriage, a District Manpower Officer interviewed her about her termination of employment with Auckland University College. On 9 June she received a letter from the National Department, noting that she had been loath to disclose her married name and explaining that her termination couldn't be approved until she did. She replied:

I have never 'been loath to disclose my married name.' On the contrary, I repeatedly told your officer, Mr Hopper, that my married name would be Shirley Smith. That is what it now is. Certainly this was also my unmarried name, but according to my legal advice, there is no reason in law for a married woman to take her husband's name. I have not taken my husband's name. Therefore I have given you the only possible truthful answer to your request for my married name.[8]

5 SHSS to Auntie Fiona and Mac (McLean Smith), 25 June 1944, from O'Rorke St. Shirley Sutch, called Margaret by some and Shirley by others including family, is here referred to as Margaret Shirley, or as Bill called her, Sister Shirley, to avoid confusion with Shirley Smith.

6 SHSS to Dr Penny Griffin, undated (1986), SHSS papers. SHSS wrote to correct the reference to her as Mrs Shirley Sutch in St Hugh's Chronicle. 'My research also turned up the fascinating news that if you weren't either a Master of a trade or Mistress of a household, you should properly be addressed as Goodman or Goodwoman.'

7 In a letter to the editor, *New Zealand Listener*, 1985, SHSS enquired if any woman of her generation, apart from artists and performers, was known to use her maiden name after marriage. In a follow-up letter she acknowledged that Dr Muriel Bell, a generation before, had done so, that Dr Bell was a pioneer in more fields than one and that Shirley was proud to follow in her footsteps: SHSS to Editor, *New Zealand Listener*, 3 June 1985.

8 SHSS to District Manpower Officer, 19 June 1944, SHSS papers.

It was incomprehensible to most people that a woman wouldn't take her husband's name. Her father wouldn't accept it; nor would Nannie.

After their holiday on Kawau Island, Bill returned to Wellington, leaving Shirley to pack up her Auckland flat. Her departure was delayed until August as she continued teaching until the university had confirmed her replacement. Meanwhile she wrote to friends to tell them of her marriage.

Her old friend from Oxford, Donald Shepherd, one of the Yorkshire men, wrote from a German prisoner-of-war camp:

10 March 1944:
Your letters – which, incidentally, I read through so many times and so carefully that I most certainly read a great deal of meaning into the most ordinary of phrases, seemed very different. In the first the old frightening comforting-small-child element was present, but in the second you were very human, giving a most vivid impression of bustle, worry and the old fighting Smith strain. And I await the photo with impatience. . . . One of the few reasonable things I've done in the last three years is to hear, time and again, the Beethoven posthumous quartets and now inwardly know them. And the other is to crystallize out the realization that I loved you and didn't understand. And still do, and understand: belatedly: and in vain. But it helps to know. Love, Donald.[9]

30 April 1944:
Maybe my sense of values is a bit warped, but, though we are reputed to be living in the shadow of great events, the last month has for me been chiefly momentous because I have had three letters and your photograph. The letters being one of January and 2 of February. The last being your testament. . . . Concerning your photograph, I feel pencil-tied. I rank with those who like it, emphasizing as it does that clear-eyed glance, seeing life steadily etc. The gaze which used to make me curl up a little inside. In fact it is so like you, as I remember you, that it almost made me weep. It was perhaps with an essential rightness that I received at the same time your

9 Donald Shepherd to SHSS, 10 March 1944, SHSS papers.

letter of 18 Feb. Ἰβρις *&* νέμεσις. *It was bitter news to hear but softened by your obvious happiness.*[10]

11 July 1944:
Your letters have been the most human written to me, being just you on paper. This last one was rather a momentous affair. . . . It means a great deal to me that you have worked out your happiness. That it is not bound together with mine, means, naturally, that it doesn't 'partake of that most pleasant'.

But I am speaking sooth when I say I am glad. He must be a very reasonable person to have achieved your love and I look forward to meeting him. . . . Deepest love, Donald.[11]

Like Donald, Frank Harley didn't overtly express his feelings for her until the end and Shirley apparently didn't pick up the subtle signals in his letters, of which some twenty survive. Still with the Royal Norfolk Regiment in England, he wrote on 28 February 1944:

Your photograph came today. I was half afraid when I saw it was Photograph Only that it might be a wedding group; perhaps by the time you read this letter some time in May you may have had that taken – if not, remember that it still won't be too late to take ship home and marry me.

I wish there had been a letter with it: as it is, I have nothing to answer but your somewhat startled look, which tells me very little. At the moment you are looking rather sternly at your old self in her rather battered leather frame (being carried up and down England in a haversack hasn't done that very much good) as if you couldn't see what she has to be so pensive about. I thought for a while about superseding the old Shirley by the new, but I don't like things to change, and on the whole I think I like your 1939 version better. At all events, not only do you not look a day older, but you actually look younger.[12]

10 Donald Shepherd to SHSS, 30 April 1944, SHSS papers. The Greek here translates to 'hubris & nemesis', the elements of Greek tragedy.

11 Donald Shepherd to SHSS, 11 July 1944, SHSS papers.

12 Frank Harley to SHSS, 28 February 1944, SHSS papers.

From the front in Europe on 15 July he wrote:

I am there at last, as you can see. . . . I still have your photograph in my knapsack along with a Field Marshall's baton and a few other odds and ends. By the way, I sent my mother your address so she'll probably let you know if anything goes wrong. . . . Shirley my love, as dear as ever, Frank.[13]

When he received Shirley's letter telling him she was married, he felt not only his own loss but also the differences now between them. He replied:

5 November 1944:
Your letter written some time in August reached me yesterday. It's no use pretending it did me an awful lot of good, though I must have known it would be coming along sooner or later. . . .

By the time this reaches you wishes for your health and happiness will be a bit musty. Pretend they are as fresh as though I had been there to dance at your wedding – not that dancing at weddings seems to be among the things you approve of.

I rather wonder what we should think if we were to meet each other now: I have given up worrying about anything but my job, and the safety, comfort, food and success in battle of a hundred men: and you, I think, take a lot of things a bit seriously. . . . Perhaps you are a bit too grown-up for me, and so perhaps it is all just as well: but you have the distinction of being the Only Woman but One I ever imagined I loved – a word, by the way, that I cannot recall has ever cropped up between us before.

As for my affairs, they are as they are. I have been here in foreign parts for rather more than four months, and have seen my share of sudden death. . . . worst of all it is to see your friends killed . . . It puts tremendous emphasis on personal relationships and personal values, and politics and principles are all rather beside the point. I value a man for what he can do, and not

13 Frank Harley to SHSS, 15 July 1944, SHSS papers. Promoted to Major, Frank Harley transferred to the Hampshire Regiment in order to take part in the Normandy Landing on 6 June. According to Gabriel Mulgan, he was an expert in signalling and weather surveillance, and played an important role in the timing of the 'D-day' landing: Vincent O'Sullivan to author, email, 10 August 2017.

at all for what he thinks, and the man who is on my side is my friend. It is all delightfully simple – and I know five hundred times more about people than I would ever have learned in five hundred years as a Civilian.

I have just read that again. It sounds horribly smug and pompous, but I am too idle to tear it up and start again (I have done that once already) and I leave it to your well-tried understanding.

I don't think I shall forget you very soon. But I suppose it will become a Christmas Card job as time goes by. It is all a very great pity, and I feel very sorry for myself.

My love, as ever,

Frank.[14]

Bill's letters to Shirley were of quite a different style, dealing with practicalities, but he did state his need and love for her. Writing from Wellington in July when she was still in Auckland, he concluded, 'I feel that part of me is missing when you are away. I don't live at any sort of a level when I'm alone. I'm just a working machine. And I don't want to be just that. I want to love you – always.'[15]

When she joined him in Wellington to start their married life together, however, she felt he neither loved nor cared for her.

Bill had taken a room on the ground floor of an old boarding house on The Terrace, which shared a communal bathroom and kitchen facilities. The room was large and sunless. Their single beds were against opposite walls. Shirley arrived in Wellington with a nasty cough. She felt abandoned as Bill left her alone, coughing through the nights.

During their courtship she had enjoyed going out with him for dinner. When she asked him why that had stopped, he said, 'We're married now.'[16] She was to do all the cooking and household chores. She was to starch his collars. That was the last straw.

14 Frank Harley to SHSS, 5 November 1944, WBS papers, ATL, MS-Papers-11364-18. Shirley wrote in 1998 that he was killed in the Normandy invasion but she received a letter from him (only the first page survives) written when he was home on leave in March 1945, two months before Germany surrendered.

15 WBS to SHSS, 13 July 1944, WBS papers, ATL, Record ID 2002-021-17/6.

16 AGS to author, interview, 28 February 2011, Track 3.

I had thought he was in favour of equality for women. I had never seen why men couldn't do the same things for themselves that women did for themselves. Maybe my father took the old-fashioned view, but Bill was, I thought, a man for the future, who took equality seriously. . . . He'd given no sign that the mere fact of marriage, so insignificant, except for social acceptance, to me, was going to make a difference.[17]

It was of no matter that she also worked outside the home in full-time employment and unpaid work.

SOON AFTER returning to Wellington Shirley was recruited to the new Vocational Guidance Service as Assistant Girls' Vocational Guidance Officer. She was in charge of the Junior Female Manpower for the Wellington area and tasked with editing booklets for boys and girls aged fourteen to seventeen. For the six months she worked as a public servant she was on the women's committee of the Public Service Association.[18]

She had collaborated with Bill and two others on a booklet, *Goodbye to Gold: A Guide to the International Monetary Fund*, published in Wellington in September 1944 by Progressive Publishing Society, and she helped edit Bill's subsequent publications.

On her own, she attended weekly meetings of the Communist Party's Wellington Central branch and attracted the attention of Special Branch who opened a file on her, recording her attendance. 'It will be noted that SS is evidently well versed in the doctrine of Communism and she gave a lecture on Fundamentals of Dialectical Materialism which was much too advanced for most of the members present.'[19] According to this source, she went on to conduct a course of classes on Dialectical Materialism that ran over several weeks.

She tried to get Bill to join the Party but he said that he would never be told by anyone what to think and never follow any party line.[20]

17 SHSS, memoir, 'Life with Bill', 3 September 1998, SHSS papers.

18 Warm letter on behalf of the Public Service Association women's committee, 21 May 1945, WBS papers, ATL, MS Papers-11364-18; Correspondence with Mollie Molloy, Sandringham, Auckland, March and April 1945.

19 SHSS PF, 5 November 1944, NZSIS.

20 SHSS to ATL Librarian, 14 November 1989, as quoted by Brian Easton in *The Nationbuilders*, AUP, 2001, p.126.

Shirley gradually came to understand that many of the contradictions in Bill's personality went back to his early childhood and upbringing. His parents lived in Dorking Road, Brooklyn, in the house where Bill grew up and which his mother Ellen had eventually bought. She had paid for it and it was *her* house. Ted was an alcoholic and, when Shirley met them, he lived in his bedroom where meals were served to him. He never did anything social with the family. Shirley found this quite shocking.

If Shirley had any romantic ideas of Bill's working-class background, she had a lot to learn. Bill's mother was petite but beneath her delicate exterior Shirley saw pure steel. 'She knew what was right and she knew that she was right (not always in such a good cause).'[21]

Ellen managed the family finances and with her treadle sewing machine she earned a regular income, which her husband did not. 'Ted was a good worker but he had an abrasive personality and a short temper: this led, alas, to his frequently losing his job. Bill told me how the children would watch, as Father came through the garden gate, to see whether he had his bag of tools or not. If he had his tools with him, he had lost his job again.'[22]

Young Bill's childhood was the antithesis of Shirley's. In some respects the Smiths with their Scottish Presbyterian stoicism, frugality and matriarchal figures were not dissimilar to the Lancastrian Methodist Sutches, but the Smiths were affectionate, and the daughter of David Smith never went hungry or without the best available medical care. Bill was sometimes very ill as a child, but his mother wouldn't call the doctor if she couldn't pay the full fee on the spot. It was a matter of pride. Over the course of time she managed to save enough money to buy the house which, as mentioned, she kept securely in her name.

Bill's father was a Labour man in the English north-country blue-collar tradition: there were workers and bosses and you knew which side you were on. He was very anti-boss and was often sacked for that

21 SHSS, 'Sutch Family History', Washington 1992, SHSS papers.
22 Ibid.

reason.[23] He dreamed of running a firm called Sutch & Sons. When his eldest son Tom left Brooklyn Primary School he was apprenticed to the building trade. Nellie, the elder daughter, was a seamstress until she married. Bill was to be a carpenter, but his headmaster persuaded his mother that since he was exceptionally bright he should continue his education.

'The battle royal broke out between Ellen and Ted and there was no doubt that Ellen would win. She always did,' Shirley continued. So Bill went to Wellington College. Bill's younger brother Ted followed in Bill's footsteps, attending Wellington College and Victoria University College and graduating with a BCom. When Bill arrived back in New Zealand after his study in New York, and found his younger sister Margaret Shirley had been put into a commercial shorthand–typing course at Wellington Girls' College, he arranged that she be moved to an academic course.

Margaret Shirley went on to have a notable career as a clinical psychologist and it was with her help that Shirley came to understand Bill. Where others saw arrogance, for example, she saw that he was 'always the little weak boy at Brooklyn Primary School whose father drank and whose family had no money and who would have to grow up to be a carpenter.'[24]

Shirley also had to learn Lancashire ways. Praise was not to be expected. If Bill criticised some minor aspect of dinner, it meant he approved all the rest.[25]

Shirley and Bill absented themselves from both their families for their first married Christmas and took to the hills. For a Christmas surprise, Bill produced a packet of chocolate biscuits. This and all Shirley's accounts of tramping with Bill are happy memories. Sometimes Margaret Shirley joined them and she came to regard the flat they had moved to as her other home. She wrote to Shirley some months later to

23 'This is from Bill and has to be taken with a grain of salt. Bill could magnify one sacking into ten.' SHSS to Brian Easton, 22 August 2000, Brian Easton papers.

24 SHSS to Christine Cole Catley (as dictated to Margaret Hayward), 1 April 1980, Margaret Hayward papers, ATL, Ref. 81-048. Here Shirley referred to his longing for recognition from the establishment he despised.

25 SHSS, Sutch family history, 1992, p.28, SHSS papers.

say how much she had enjoyed getting to know her. 'Bill has always had the capacity to wake me up to realities and now with you in partnership the tonic is double strength.'[26]

In March 1945, Bill moved to Sydney to take charge of the United Nations Relief and Rehabilitation Administration (UNRRA) in the south-west Pacific.[27] Shirley was to follow in May after packing up and sub-letting their flat. Meanwhile she learnt she was pregnant. He replied to this news:

I've read your letter about the coming baby several times. . . . I shall be glad when it arrives. I prefer that we have children. I think you regard the baby and me as part of the same thing – our loving each other. I do too. That's how I want it to be. But you are more important to me than anything else.

. . .

I love you,
Bill.[28]

Their Sydney flat was in an apartment building at 87 Ocean Street in the suburb of Woollahra. Bill's job involved a lot of travelling over the next months, including several weeks back in New Zealand, raising money, food, clothing and blankets to send to the destitute populations in Eastern Europe. Besides setting up home, sewing and preparing for the baby, Shirley caught up with her correspondence and reading. She recalled in later years that she read all Ibsen's plays, remembering especially *The Wild Duck*, which posed the dilemma about relationships she always had and could never resolve, about truth-telling, how much to tell and when to suppress part of it.[29]

26 MSS to SHSS, 22 April 1945, WBS papers, ATL, Record ID 2002-012-45/02.

27 Sutch had the dual roles of Deputy Director, South-West Pacific Area Office, Sydney, and Director of Supply and Requirements Division in that office: copy of record of service from Director of Personnel, UNRRA, London regional office, DSS Papers, ATL, MS-Papers-11404-06.

28 WBS to SHSS, 11 April 1945 (from UNRRA office in Melbourne), WBS papers, ATL, MS Papers-11364-18.

29 SHSS to MHS, 9 March 1994, pp.4–5, MHS papers.

SHIRLEY ENTERED King George V Memorial Hospital in Sydney and on 15 November, with great difficulty, gave birth to a daughter. 'You can imagine a little what it was like when the specialist worked an hour and a half with instruments to rescue the child in one piece,' Bill wrote to Shirley's family when he recovered from the shock of seeing the bruised infant covered in bandages and his exhausted wife needing a hefty blood transfusion. 'At this stage I would guess that the infant is a Smith.'[30] (Shirley later recounted how Bill was known in the hospital as Mr Smith. 'They simply would not call me "Miss Smith": they said firmly, "Everyone in here who has a baby is 'Mrs.'". So the husband of Mrs. Smith was obviously Mr. Smith.')[31]

She explained to her parents that friction in the office had 'worn Bill to a frazzle – you know what his nerves are like.' With the strain of the birth on top of that, he was suffering from exhaustion and ordered off work. While she and baby were recovering in hospital, he escaped the sweltering heat and humidity of Sydney for a holiday in Tasmania. Shirley stressed how necessary the trip was and that she had insisted he went:

And I'd also like to tell you how good he's been over these months. He's done all he could to help me, from shopping to washing, and planned all sorts of pleasant things from the trip to the Blue Mountains, to little parties just for us, dinner at some new restaurant, Chinese or Austrian or so on, that he's discovered, with theatre or pictures after. And he has had my room full of flowers and fruit, and was waiting for me when I first came in after the event; and he's so thrilled with our baby. He couldn't have done more or been more thoughtful. Truly, the things that worry you are superficial – he's all good inside.[32]

At the time of writing, nine days after the birth, Shirley was in fact miserable. She still didn't have her baby with her, not even to feed her. The baby was losing weight and everyone was worried. But things came

30 WBS to Smith family, 19 November 1945, DSS papers, ATL, MS-Papers-11404-02.
31 SHSS to editor, *Eve Magazine*, 10 August 1973.
32 SHSS to family, 24 November 1945, SHSS papers, ATL, MS-Papers-11404-06. Bill was to go to Tasmania for five days or more.

right when they moved to a Karitane home for nursing mothers to learn mothercraft, in Sydney.

Bill was back in Tasmania when Shirley came home on 12 December. A coal miners' strike meant power restrictions – use of one electric light until 9 pm, then none. Writing to Meta by a hurricane lamp, Shirley explained they had no power for hot water for washing themselves or clothes, but power and gas could be used for children under the age of four. Cooking hours were restricted, as were trams and trains.

Meanwhile Shirley's father, whose appointment as Chancellor of Victoria University College earlier in the year added to his responsibilities, was himself off work recovering from exhaustion. He wrote to Bill on 23 December, explaining why he hadn't acknowledged his letter about the baby, adding:

You must have had a very anxious time but I should like to tell you that we feel you did everything you could for Shirley. You could not have done more in arranging for the medical, hospital and after-care treatment. Shirley has written most appreciatively about it. It seems that if the arrangements had not been as good, the consequences might have been serious. It is not surprising that with the strain of the event and your office work, you have not felt well. I trust you are better now, after a spell.[33]

Shirley was delighted. 'I think it was very nice of you to write [to Bill], darling. Here's a special kiss.' The baby now had a name – Margaret Helen, to be called Helen. 'Bill liked Helen above other names . . . he chose Shirley Sutch's name which is Margaret Shirley . . .'[34]

Bill was about to depart for Washington, where he had been summoned for 'conversation and orientation'. They didn't know what that meant, but hoped it wouldn't be for longer than six weeks. He left in mid-January. From San Francisco he wrote: 'Everywhere are things I want to share with you and my thoughts take the form of noting them in the language I'd use in speaking to you. But it is all a waste. I've got

33 DSS to WBS, 23 December 1945, ATL, Shirley Smith papers, MS-Papers-11404-64.

34 SHSS to DSS, 7 January 1946. Helen explained that making 'Helen' her second rather than first name was to avoid the initials HMS.

to take this in on my own and you will inevitably share a little of it. . . . But I do wish this separation of ours didn't have to happen. Separation is a waste of two people.'[35]

It was seven months before they were reunited. After organising commodity accounting and shipping records at UNRRA headquarters in Washington, Bill went on to inspect and review procedures in UNRRA missions in Europe. Shirley packed up the Sydney flat and moved back to her family in New Zealand. In June Bill was appointed chief economist to the European Regional Office and later, director of UNRRA's operational analysis division for Europe.[36] After three months in Europe and having settled in London, he cabled Shirley to join him.

35 WBS to SHSS, 25 January 1946, WBS papers, ATL, Record ID 2002-012-43/11.

36 Copy of record of service from Director of Personnel, UNRRA, London regional office, DSS papers, ATL, MS-Papers-11404-06.

12

London and New York

In August 1946, Shirley and Helen departed on the *Ruahine* for England, accompanied by Bill's sister, Margaret Shirley, who was to live with them and study child development at London University.

On the voyage Shirley befriended Margaret Herrick, known to Hawke's Bay gossips as 'the Bolter', a reference to Nancy Mitford's 'Bolter' in her recently published *The Pursuit of Love*. Shirley, who had recently read Ibsen's play *The Doll's House*, thought Margie was courageous for leaving an unhappy marriage. She understood, too, why Margie left her young son.[1] Shirley and Margie saw a lot of each other over the next year in London.

Bill had rented a modern flat on the top floor of a house at 5 Cochrane Street, St John's Wood – a good central location close to Regent's Park and the Zoo. Shirley was thrilled to be back in London. She picked up with her old St Hugh's friend, Phoebe Llewellyn Smith. She found Norman Davis had married and was lecturing in English at the University of London. Shirley invited him and his wife Lena to dinner and learnt about his intelligence work during the war, how he was condemned to death by a military court in Bulgaria for alleged conspiracy against the state, and about his escape with Lena.

Unbeknown to Shirley, she herself came to the attention of British intelligence. On 6 December 1946, Director of Security Intelligence in Wellington, J. Cummings, informed MI5 Director General Sir Percy Sillitoe of her London address and provided a biographical profile. 'She is a person well-versed in Communist phraseology and doctrine and for

1 SHSS to DSS, 13 June 1947, ATL, MS-Papers-11404-07. David Smith had been the judge in Margie's divorce case. According to Shirley, Margie had been persuaded that it would be better for her son if she left. Margie gave her half-custody of him to her sister Rosamund, who was married to Bill's friend Ormond Wilson, Labour MP for Palmerston North.

a period she was engaged in lecturing other members of the Communist Party on "Dialectical Materialism".' Cummings noted that she was 'in close association with other members of the Communist Party up until the time of her departure for England'. The letter included a profile of her husband.[2]

Since she was brought to their attention, MI5 probably would have noted any sign of Shirley's involvement in communist activities in London. They recorded nothing. According to Shirley, soon after arriving she went to the Party headquarters in King Street, intending to rejoin, but when they told her they wouldn't accept her back just because she had been a Party member in New Zealand – she could expect a grilling – she decided they could do without her.

As in Sydney, Bill's work involved long hours and often took him away from home. He hadn't recovered from the poor health he'd had in Sydney and was often exhausted. His job with UNRRA was due to finish in May 1947 and he didn't know what the future held.

In Wellington, Prime Minister Peter Fraser intended to appoint Bill Sutch as New Zealand's representative to the United Nations in New York. Carl Berendsen, New Zealand's representative in Washington, wrote to Alister McIntosh, head of the Department of External Affairs in Wellington, that Sutch had the ability, 'but I don't think the judgment and I would not take the risk.'[3] McIntosh agreed, but it wasn't his decision to make.

In April Shirley wrote to her father that on Walter Nash's recent visit to London, Shirley and Bill had taken him and his secretary, Nancy Bowden, to a play and to dinner

and finally home for a brief look at the sleeping Helen, whom Walter professed himself anxious to see in order to report to you. . . . It was all most successful and Nancy confided to me in the ladies' cloakroom that she hadn't seen Walter so cheerful and expansive for weeks. Finally he wrote me a very

2 MI5, KV2 3929 (Sutch) P1011165, National Archives, UK.

3 Carl Berendsen to Alister McIntosh, 21 January 1947, *Undiplomatic Dialogue: Letters between Carl Berendsen and Alister McIntosh, 1943–52*, ed. Ian McGibbon, AUP, 1993, p.119, note 1.

nice letter saying thank you. So we're hoping for the best. I found him very easy to get on with.[4]

At Easter Shirley and Bill left Helen with Margaret Shirley and went to Oxford for a brief holiday, their first since before Helen was born. 'It did us both a lot of good,' Shirley wrote home. 'My first real holiday away from Helen too. . . . We wandered round Oxford and a bit of the nearer Cotswolds. We didn't look up anyone as we just wanted to be with ourselves.'[5]

The job came through. Sutch was appointed to be the New Zealand Government's representative on the Economic and Social Council (EcoSoc) of the United Nations Organisation (as it was then called) and Secretary to the New Zealand Delegation, which meant running the New York office. He flew back to New Zealand early in June to be briefed. Shirley once again had to pack up their London flat before the lease expired and find alternative accommodation for herself and Helen until she joined Bill in New York.

Shirley spent what she recalled as a 'glorious summer' in Oxford, where she leased a flat at 94 Woodstock Road until the beginning of September. Phoebe Llewellyn Smith was there, and Gabrielle Day (John Mulgan's widow who had remarried after John's death in Cairo in 1945), and Dan and Winnie Davin. Shirley knew Dan from when they were both at Oxford before the war. Now her friendship with the Davins blossomed. Every day she and Helen visited them and their three small daughters. On sunny afternoons Winnie and Shirley took the children over Port Meadow to the bathing place on the Isis. Dan, a writer and editor at Oxford University Press (later Academic Publisher), described what was probably a typical evening in Shirley's company: 'Last night Shirley brought 3 bottles of Algerian plonk and a tin of tongue: so we had a talkative supper.' Later they all (except Winnie) adjourned to the pub up Walton Street. Then home again and talked until after two in the morning.[6]

4 SHSS to family, 20 April 1947, SHSS papers, ATL, MS-Papers-11404-02.
5 Ibid.
6 From Dan Davin's diary, 1947, 30 July, 13 and 26 August 1947, copied for author by KWO. SHSS to Delia Davin, 8 April 1995, SHSS papers.

Dan sometimes went punting with Shirley. He wrote that she cheered him out of idleness and depression. They discussed his just-published novel, *For the Rest of Our Lives*, based on his wartime experiences, and he noted that her points were 'ingenuous but shrewd'.[7]

Shirley wrote to Donald Shepherd, now married, hoping he and his wife would be back in Oxford before she left.[8] She also reconnected with Kenneth Wright. She kept in touch with Donald and Kenneth, and Norman Davis and other friends from Oxford who had survived the war, all their lives.

BACK IN NEW ZEALAND, Bill's onward travel to New York was delayed because he was ill. Where specialists in Sydney, Washington and London had failed, Wellington doctors at once diagnosed amoebic dysentery. He was treated and cured in Wellington Hospital, but remained weak and on medication.

Shirley learnt from Meta that he was out of hospital early in August. It wasn't until 29 August that he wrote to Shirley, when he informed her of his pending departure. He left for the United States early in September.

At the beginning of October 1947, Shirley and Helen sailed for the United States to stay in Philadelphia with her friend Loris Holway (née Chilwell) and her American husband and their small daughter. Shirley arrived to find Loris ill in hospital with a difficult pregnancy and it fell to Shirley to run the house and look after the children. Bill visited them once, found the situation a nightmare, stayed one night and returned to New York in the morning. Shirley and Helen stayed on until late November, by which time Bill had organised their accommodation in New York.

THE UN HOUSING DIVISION had leased a new housing estate, Parkway Village, near Jamaica on Long Island. Comprised of 685 apartments, the estate was bounded on two sides by Grand Central Parkway and another large freeway in a dreary suburban area. The UN sublet about

7 Dan Davin, diary, 1947, 30 July, 13 and 26 August 1947, copied for author by KWO.
8 SHSS to Donald Shepherd, from 94 Woodstock Rd, Oxford, 25 July 1947, SHSS papers.

630 apartments to staff, who then represented 60 nations, and the rest to mostly American families not related to the UN.

The apartments were in blocks of about a dozen, connected by miles of sidewalks in a barren-looking landscape. The grounds were being planted in shrubs and lawns but it was never a garden to play in – that was not allowed. Shirley would have loved a dog but pets were not allowed (and Bill wouldn't allow her to have one). These and other things about Parkway Village reflected her dislike of New York, where she found life was not on a human scale. She disliked 'American bigness, and the continental climate that went with it, muggy heat in summer that is hardly bearable, and savage cold in winter . . . air damp all year round . . . The NY sun seems to come to you through layers of cotton wool – it was stifling, not invigorating. I haven't forgotten the central-heating and air-cooling systems . . . but I feel it's kinder not to mention them.'[9]

But she enjoyed the international community that lived in Parkway Village. They got to know one another at the Parkway Village Association: festivals, clubs, language classes and especially through their children. The Village was swarming with babies – it was the post-war baby boom. They formed their own nursery school, a co-operative run by an elected committee, which Shirley chaired for two terms. The philosophy reflected the ideals of the United Nations:

The Nursery School Children
of the
United Nations Staff
Work and play together
as they
Grow toward better understanding
for
World Citizenship

Among their New Zealand friends were Charles Craw and his wife Evelyn. Their son Richard was about the same age as Helen. Jim Weir,

9 SHSS, radio broadcast, 1951, SHSS papers.

third secretary in the New Zealand Delegation, arrived with his wife Mollie in 1949. He found Shirley and Bill to be good, kind friends. Bill, he recalled, was 'an extremely good boss – he was a charming man. And my wife and I thoroughly enjoyed Shirley, she was so lively and witty.'[10]

George and Ailsa Barton, another younger New Zealand couple, arrived at Parkway when George joined the Human Rights Division of the United Nations. Shirley and George got to know each other later at Victoria University College and became firm friends. Ian Milner joined the UN Secretariat in 1947. Shirley and Bill had seen something of him and his wife Margot in Sydney when he was with the Australian Department of Internal Affairs, and now again they picked up the friendship. They saw a lot of one another until 1950 when the Milners left for Prague, which was by then behind the Iron Curtain, and stayed.[11]

Jim Weir recalled that Shirley and Bill's different names on their door drew some comment in the community. And much as he liked Bill, Weir reflected that he was something of a Walter Mitty character. 'Consider, for instance, that he was a strict teetotaller but, rather oddly, took pride in being a connoisseur of wine although not a drop ever passed his lips. He claimed to judge the quality of wine and where it came from, simply by the bouquet. Others smiled and raised their eyes disbelievingly, as they did, too, when he bought 2,000-year-old Eqyptian antiquities in New York.'[12] Weir may have been thinking of the small Chinese horse from the Han dynasty and a bigger horse from the T'ang dynasty that Shirley herself believed to be originals. If their friends were skeptical, Bill was undoubtedly building up a significant collection of ancient and modern artworks. On the other hand, he wouldn't have a television or even a radio in the house, let alone own a car, which he saw as breaking up the fabric of society.

Not surprisingly, Helen was a little different from other children. Shirley describes coming downstairs early one morning to find Bill

10 Jim Weir to author, interview, 3 August 2011.

11 SHSS described their friendship with the Milners to James McNeish, 3 May 1998, James McNeish papers.

12 Jim Weir, *Eat, Drink and be Wary: A New Zealand diplomat looks back*, Dunmore Publishing Ltd, Wellington, 2011, p.45.

had sat his daughter on a bar stool and they were eating blue cheese and olives. He was probably engaging her in sophisticated conversation – something Helen learnt to avoid. Her father's extensive knowledge overwhelmed the child.

Helen remembered being enchanted by the blue lights her mother hung on their Christmas tree, and her mother making stacks of pancakes on Sunday mornings, which became a family tradition. Shirley often told the story of a big snowstorm their first winter, how she and Bill and Helen cleared a path from their door with pots and pans – 'the New Zealand way' – while their neighbours remained marooned until they were rescued.

WHILE SHIRLEY'S LIFE was largely confined to Parkway Village, Bill lived in a different world. Shirley wrote in 1993 that he had a wonderful time during those three years; that he was in his element, lobbying, debating, persuading people to his way of thinking. As for how he ran his office, a subject of complaint early on, Shirley said she didn't know and had no way of judging.

Occasionally Shirley went into Manhattan, but the subway station was a considerable distance from Parkway Village and the trip took over an hour. Sometimes she attended evening cocktail and dinner parties with Bill in Manhattan. Babysitting was never a problem at Parkway, as mothers sat for one another's children.

Bill's close friendship from his student days at Columbia University with journalist and leading American socialist Leo Huberman now included their wives. Sunday afternoon gatherings at Leo and Gert's home in Greenwich Village brought together radical intellectuals passionate about their beliefs. On New Year's Day, 1948, Leo gave Bill a copy of his book on American history, *We the People* (1932), with the inscription: 'For Bill, frontline fighter for We the People'.[13]

In 1968, when he had news of Leo's untimely death and perhaps with intimations of his own mortality after suffering a serious heart attack, Bill explained the significance of Leo's regard for him in a letter to his daughter Helen: 'I have few really warm friends and most of them

13 Inscription dated 1 January 1948 in book Leo Huberman gave WBS.

are not in New Zealand. Among them Leo was my greatest friend and there was a bond between us despite the fact that we did not correspond much. In fact we both understood that what we each were doing was so important that communication was unnecessary.'[14]

One of their mutual friends was Otto Nathan, a German-Jewish scholar and a refugee from Nazi Germany, a friend of Einstein who later made him the executor of his estate. A third was Paul Sweezy, previously a Harvard University economist who would become the country's leading Marxist intellectual and publisher. Bill told Helen that he helped the three men set up *Monthly Review*, a magazine that was Marxist but independent of the Communist Party, that became one of the most influential radical forums during the McCarthy era. To what extent he helped is open to question, but he contributed to the editorial notes and wrote several articles, using a pseudonym because of his job. Shirley thought it risky, but added that risk never put Bill off.

As the Cold War gathered momentum, so did McCarthyism. Early in 1948, the FBI received intelligence about Sutch's association with Leo Huberman and his circle, prompting a flurry of 'Top Secret' communications with British and New Zealand intelligence:

The F.B.I. have received a report from a reliable and confidential source which shows that a certain BILL SUTCH is a close personal associate of LEO and GERT HUBERMAN, PHILIP M. and OLGA FIELD, and ISADORE GIBBY NEEDLEMAN. The HUBERMANS and FIELDS are pro-Communists, while Needleman is an attorney for the AMTONG TRADING CORPORATION in New York. All are intimate associates of AUBE TZERKO, who is suspected of being implicated in soviet espionage.[15]

The FBI decided not to investigate Sutch, but reported to R. Thistlethwaite at the British Embassy in Washington DC, who passed it on to the head of MI5 in London, who in turn sent it to

14 WBS to MHS, 22 November 1968, MHS papers.

15 R. Thistlethwaite, British Embassy, Washington to Sir Percy Sillitoe, Director-General of the Security Service, London, memo, 10 February 1948, ref. PF 45774, Dr William Sutch, KV2/3929, MI5 Security Service files, UK National Archives.

J. Cummings, head of Security Intelligence in Wellington.[16] MI5 also sent Thistlethwaite a copy of the letter that they had received from New Zealand in December 1946 about Sutch and his wife, adding that apart from that they had little information about Sutch.

In March, 1937, he was described as 'another socialist more or less guiding the destinies of the New Zealand Government', and in the summer of the same year, it was suspected that he was connected with misrepresentation in the leftist paper 'the Week' (23.6.37) of statements made at a secret meeting of Principal Delegates at the Imperial Conference at Geneva at that time.

You will note that Mrs SUTCH is stated as living in London last year, and we will instigate inquiries as to her present whereabouts.[17]

On investigation, the Deputy Commander, Special Branch, New Scotland Yard, found the rationing organisation CNRO still recorded her as living at Cochrane Street, but the tenth series of ration documents had not been issued to her. They found no trace of her having made contact with the Communist Party in the UK. They noted her date of departure from the country and that she had apparently not returned.[18]

At the same time, early in 1948, just after Bill Sutch became Secretary General (with the newly constituted Office of the Permanent Delegation of New Zealand to the UN), his 'titular head', Jim Thorn, who represented New Zealand at the UN, reported to Alister McIntosh his misgivings about Sutch's management of staff and his advice, judgment and behaviour, especially his pro-Russian views and friends. McIntosh had warned Sutch when he was in Wellington that this appointment was a last chance and that if he made any mistakes or fell under suspicion he was definitely and irrevocably out. Now McIntosh wrote to Berendsen that if Thorn's account of Sutch consorting with Russians was correct, he

16 Ibid.; Sir Percy Sillitoe, Director General of MI5, to J. Cummings, Director of Security Intelligence, Wellington, 16 March 1948, PF.54774/B.2b/PS, KV2 3929 (Sutch) P1011161.

17 K. Morton Evans to R. Thistlethwaite, British Embassy, Washington DC, 16 March 1948, PF.54774/B.2b/PMS KV2 3929 (Sutch) P1011159, MS papers, National Archives, UK.

18 H. M. Gee, PF.54774/B1a/HMG, KV2 3929 (Sutch) P1011155, MS papers, National Archives, UK.

was all for pulling him out on the spot. But Prime Minister Peter Fraser wanted substantial proof and sent McIntosh to New York to investigate in person. McIntosh found no evidence of any breach of security.[19]

Bill and Shirley and others (Keith Sinclair, Michael Parker, Sir John Marshall, Sir Robert Muldoon) later asserted that the FBI closely monitored his activities in New York. The official FBI line was that they never ran an investigation. A secret memorandum by J. Edgar Hoover, 24 April 1957, confirmed FBI reports in 1949 that they had not investigated Sutch and that the bureau was 'not in possession of additional pertinent information concerning his activities in the United States.'[20]

Sutch nevertheless riled the Americans, not to mention his New Zealand masters, when he disobeyed instructions (he claimed he didn't receive any) and voted with the Soviet bloc for the repatriation of Yugoslav gold that had been held in the New York Federal Reserve since the war.

Bill continued to make friends where he was inclined and Shirley said she herself was questioned by a US security man about her friendship with a communist, Erika Spitzer, a Sudeten German who escaped from Czechoslovakia before the German invasion.

She recalled that they laughed at McCarthy and his allegations until the night of a dinner with their friends Bill and Martha Jovanovich in Parkway Village. Bill Jovanovich, of Yugoslav descent but born in Denver, Colorado, was a promising young executive in the publishing firm Harcourt Brace. Shirley and Bill had always talked freely with Bill and Martha until Shirley referred to something in the *Star*. A silence fell upon the gathering. Someone asked, 'Who admits to reading the *Star*?' This made an impression on Shirley. Did the Jovanoviches assume that their house was bugged?

19 Berendsen to McIntosh, 30 March 1948, *Undiplomatic Dialogue: Letters between Carl Berendsen and Alister McIntosh, 1943–52*, ed. Ian McGibbon, AUP, 1993, pp.159–61.

20 Military Intelligence Department, War Department, Washington DC, Summary of Information on Dr W. B. Sutch, UNO Representative of New Zealand in the USA, 13/10/1947, in FBI File 100-HQ-353048, Volume 1, William Ball Sutch; J. E. Hoover, Washington DC, Secret Memorandum to [name withheld]. Subject: DR WILLIAM BALL SUTCH. INTERNAL SECURITY – NEW ZEALAND, 24/4/1957, in FBI 100-HQ-353048; Aaron Fox, http://www.kiwispies.com/pdfs/PedigreeofTruthWebVersion2013.pdf (accessed 5 March 2018).

Our friend, Howard Daniel, an Australian in the Human Rights section of the UN, who lived nearby in Parkway Village, told us that he was sure his phone was bugged. We decided that the safest thing to do was to assume that ours was too, so we then fell into the habit of never saying anything important or sensitive on the telephone. . . .

A dreadful miasma grew up, so that you didn't know whom you could trust. Someone told us that Howard was a spy. I remember that Bill and I sat down to consider seriously whether we could believe this and what we should do about it. We decided that Howard was our friend and that we should simply behave normally and disregard the rumour. I told Howard this years later and he laughed and said, 'Oh I wasn't suspected of being an FBI spy but an MI5 one!'[21]

According to Bill and Shirley's friend Fred Turnovsky, who visited them from Wellington, Bill warned him that their phone was probably bugged. Fred thought Bill was rattled. Shirley said Bill was never rattled.

But she herself was rattled on one occasion. She went alone during the day to see the film *Battleship Potemkin*, based on the mutiny of Russian sailors in 1905. It stirred her to sing along with *The Internationale* at the end, whereupon a man sat down at the end of her row.

There were no people in the seats between. I thought, it doesn't matter, I'm diplomatic, he can't do anything to me. And then I thought, but that's worse, I could lose Bill his job. . . . Obviously with such a wife, he must be not only undesirable but a threat to the stability of the United States. . . .

So . . . before the lights went up, I got out of the other end of the row . . . and went upstairs to what the Americans call the restroom, and here I hid, safe in the Ladies, until I began to worry that they might shut the theatre and I'd be trapped inside . . . so I cautiously emerged and went downstairs and out and was not challenged.[22]

21 SHSS, 'Some Notes on the Beginning of the McCarthy Era as perceived by someone who lived in New York', Washington August 1992. Howard Daniel, an advocate for human rights, had assisted refugees to escape from Nazi Germany, and so met Judith, who became his wife. He was also an avid art collector.

22 Ibid.

Over two successive summers, Shirley and Helen spent a month at a university enclave in Vermont in a pleasant boarding house beside the Caspian Pond. After her stay there in 1948, Shirley left Helen in the care of Jeanie Priestman, the resident child-minder in Parkway, while she joined Bill for a month in London and Europe. Her father was in London to receive a knighthood, having in July received an Honorary Doctorate of Civil Law at Oxford for his work as Chancellor of the University of New Zealand. He wrote to Meta that he found Shirley more composed than she used to be.

Jeanie looked after Helen again in January 1950 when Shirley and Bill went to Mexico, their only holiday together during their time in New York; and Jeanie lived with them between jobs for other families. Shirley obviously valued her help and company. Later Jeanie thanked Shirley for her love and friendship, adding that theirs was the first real home she ever had.[23]

A big issue for Shirley was that, from the time they moved to New York, she was desperate to have a second child. Bill made it clear Helen was enough. Shirley was very unhappy that he wouldn't talk about it. She had always wanted and expected to have a bigger family, but he wasn't child-oriented. He disliked any mess or misbehaviour and Shirley found his attitude to bringing up children was quite different from hers. He more or less left Helen to her.[24]

Shirley said he would never admit it but she thought it was her near-fatal haemorrhage at Helen's birth that made him afraid to have another baby. That was her explanation when the subject came up, as it often did down the years.[25]

In her last year at Parkway, Shirley had more of a life of her own. She was one of three people on the executive committee of the Community Association, and was also involved in setting up and running the United Nations International School, which opened at the beginning of 1950

23 Jeanie Priestman to SHSS, 11 April 1951, SHSS papers.

24 This is from the oral history of Shirley Smith with Hugo Manson on 4 November 1988 commissioned by the New Zealand Law Society, Wellington Branch, side 5, ATL, OHInt-0082-02.

25 Ibid; SHSS to Donald Shepherd, 25 July 1947, SHSS papers; Shirley spoke of this to many others.

in an old farmhouse in open fields near the UN at Lake Success. The school absorbed the nursery school and at the age of four-and-a-half, children graduated to kindergarten.

With Helen there, Shirley had time to attend United Nations sessions as an observer for the International Federation of University Women. The IFUW sent accredited observers to all organs of the United Nations and had official consultative status with EcoSoc and UNESCO. It must have been stimulating, but only two sessions stand out in Shirley's accounts. One was Bill's address on the future of UNICEF. Shirley recalled in 1993:

When poor Eleanor Roosevelt, who was the US representative, put up (as she had to) the US proposal that the very successful Unicef operation be ended, each country to try to do the job itself, with minimum of help from the UN, Bill engineered things so that the only vote for the US proposal was the US vote. A few countries abstained, the rest voted against. . . . It was said that the US did not want to provide, through UNICEF, aid for the children of the eastern European countries, which had been devastated in the war, and were now communist. I need to say that Bill, and the others who voted with him, were concerned only for the children. It was clear where he stood, as he made a two-hour speech, at the meeting where the votes were taken, against the US proposal, which was listened to in absolute silence. . . . I know, I was there.[26]

Shirley thought it was Bill's worst crime as far as the American establishment was concerned, and his finest hour. Her pride and admiration surely fired up their marriage. 'I was very glad to hear everything was going so well with Bill,' wrote Phoebe Llewellyn Smith

26 SHSS to Josh Webber, 7 July 1993, SHSS papers. Shirley gave other versions later that vary in some respects. Though the author has not found an official record of the address (the delegate from Pakistan, Ahmed Shah Bokhari, is credited with persuading the General Assembly to vote unanimously to extend UNICEF's charter for another three years), one can safely say that Bill played a major part, both in lobbying delegates and in speaking persuasively in the assembly. Shirley's view that it was Bill's finest hour speaks volumes. For UNICEF's official history, see http://www.fundinguniverse.com/company-histories/united-nations-international-children-s-emergency-fund-unicef-history (accessed 7 October 2016).

from London. 'It looks as though you've passed those rapids all right.'[27]

The second United Nations session that stood out in Shirley's memory involved an elegant woman lawyer in a black dress from the Status of Women Commission. Shirley thought she could be that woman.

SUTCH WAS RECALLED from New York after the New Zealand government changed in December 1949 and the political climate under the Holland government veered right. In May 1950, McIntosh wrote to Berendsen:

So far as Sutch is concerned, all that I have been able to do is to put off the eventual time of his withdrawal for a variety of reasons. . . . no job for him here . . . no suitable replacement in New York, thirdly, I have been trying to use the period to persuade him to get himself another job. So far he has no success, mainly for the reason, I am afraid, that when a United Nations opening comes up he is pushed aside because he is not liked or trusted.[28]

Bill considered work he might do in London – Shirley hoped they would go there. Her letters to family and friends referred to the uncertainty about their future, which must have been a strain on them both. Sutch applied in 1950 for the economics chair at Victoria University College but, for the second time, was unsuccessful.[29]

THE DECISION for the family to return to New Zealand was reached through Bill's discussions with Leo Huberman. He wrote to Helen on 22 November 1968:

[Leo], *of course, was sure of my political position and also admired my ability to write without jargon and to speak without being a demagogue. His personal appreciation of my judgment was also very flattering to me and when Otto for some reason would not cooperate any more in MR* [*Monthly Review*], *it was more necessary to broaden the theoretical base and that obviously pointed to me. By 1950 several countries had asked that I be sent on missions to help them with their economic and social legislation and the*

27 Phoebe Llewellyn Smith to SHSS, September (1950), SHSS papers.
28 McIntosh to Berendsen, 12 May 1950, *Undiplomatic Dialogue*, p.227.
29 WBS sent a copy of his application to DSS, SHSS papers, ATL MS-Papers-11404-06.

choice had to be made among such requests; returning to N.Z.; working with MR; or going to Britain to be a growing point there.

In Britain I knew pretty well Harry Pollitt, Secretary of the C.P. and Palme Dutt, Editor of the Labour Monthly, Strachey . . . Laski, Zilliacus, and his group of like-minded M.Ps., Gaitskell, Harold Wilson, the Hungarian economists, Del Vayo, and several leaders from Catalonia. There were also others, some of whom had been expelled from the U.N. under the McCarthy hysteria. There was no doubt that there would be a place for me, probably on the journalistic left, for I also knew Kingsley Martin, but there was no base and I didn't come from Oxbridge and it looked as though any influence I could have in the U.K. would be peripheral.

I had my own reasons for wanting to go back to N.Z., first to give you a healthy upbringing and education, secondly to give Mummy a better chance for development, and thirdly to take my share of supporting my parents which had been carried by the others of the family. I also had, I must admit, a nostalgia for N.Z.

But it was Leo who put it all into perspective, who said 'Revolutions are made in your own country. They are seldom imported.' I replied that N.Z. was the last country where there would be a revolution and Leo dryly remarked that that was all the more reason for me to be in N.Z. It would be a contribution if I could even make them realise their colonial status. So though it meant leaving Leo, Otto, and several others whom I may one day tell you about, the decision was made to come back to N.Z. and this was before Mummy's grandmother died and before the National Government had decided that I was to return anyway.[30]

In 2014 evidence emerged in the newly opened Mitrokhin Archive in Cambridge, England, that Dr Sutch was recruited to the Soviet intelligence service in 1950.

The Mitrokhin Archive comprises notes of KGB foreign intelligence files hand-copied secretly by archivist Vasili Mitrokhin, who had spent most of his working life in the KGB foreign intelligence archives. Disillusioned by the Soviet system and sympathetic towards dissidents, his chance came to do something when KGB foreign intelligence

30 WBS to MHS, 22 November 1968, MHS papers.

archives were moved to new headquarters. In 1972 he was given the job of overseeing the transfer. He personally catalogued the files, signed them out before they left the old premises and signed them in again on their arrival at the new building. Under this cover he copied summaries of the files into notebooks, which he smuggled out of the building and hid under the floor in his villa. After the ten years it took to complete the transfer, he had accumulated six trunks of material.

In 1992 Mitrokhin approached British Secret Intelligence, who then arranged for him, his family and his archive to be brought to the United Kingdom. As copies of original documents, the files have no direct evidential value, but their value in terms of intelligence proved immense.

The entry believed to refer to Sutch is brief:

'Maori' – Englishman, born 1907, New Zealand citizen, doctor of philosophy, former high-level bureaucrat in government service, retired in 1965, recruited in 1950, contact with him via Drozhzhin.[31]

The NZSIS did an exhaustive analysis to see if the biographical details fitted anyone other than Dr Sutch. They found they described Sutch uniquely. With his identity established, the significant information is 'recruited in 1950'. The Russian word translated as 'recruited' has a specific meaning in Soviet intelligence, signifying the subject is 'knowing, tasked and will respond'.[32] (Mitrokhin later published a KGB dictionary in which 'recruitment' is defined as 'secret co-operation with [Soviet] intelligence'. 'Agent recruitment' is defined as 'the covert involvement as agents of individuals who have opportunities to carry out intelligence tasks at the present time or in the future'.)

There is no indication that Shirley knew Bill was working for Soviet intelligence and much to suggest she was completely unaware. Knowing or not, she shared her husband's belief in a better world as they saw it.

31 MITN 1/7, Britain, Ireland, Australia, New Zealand [Box 33], p.173 (translation by Oksana Yurchyshyn-Smith). Drozhzhin was the KGB officer who operated in Wellington in the 1960s and early 1970s until Razgovorov replaced him in 1974.

32 Director of NZSIS Warren Tucker to author, 3 February 2014. Being 'in contact' with the KGB (or its predecessor before 1954) didn't make one a recruit.

13

1951

WHEN SHE heard Nannie was dying in November 1950, Shirley returned to New Zealand with Helen on the first available flight. She didn't make it in time, not even for the funeral. She deeply mourned her grandmother.

But she was glad to be back in New Zealand. She remembered her first morning in Auckland: 'everything seemed new and strange – and wonderful, in the way the world seems wonderful to a child . . .' She marvelled at the way the sun shone and the air sparkled, the taste of honest bread and the flavour of a real tomato. She marvelled too at the kindness of strangers. 'I fell head over heels in love with New Zealand and New Zealanders.'[1]

Bill, who was to arrive at the end of the year, wrote from New York:

There's one thing I didn't mention to weigh in the balance about our being in New Zealand, and that is, that we shall be together oftener, and will be able to do things together. These last five years have been a strain on both of us, and quite unfair to you. That should be remedied when I get back, for I ought to be able to keep normal working hours, daily and weekly. I am missing you.[2]

David and Meta invited Shirley to make their house in Wellington her home until she decided what to do. They hoped she and Helen would join them at Taupō for the summer holidays.

Her brother Allan was engaged. Having decided during the war to do medicine, he was in the first intake of 'rehabs' at Otago Medical School, where he met home science student Helen Paine. They were

1 SHSS, 'It's Nice to be Home Again', radio talk on the Women's Session, 2YA, 21 November 1951, SHSS papers.

2 WBS to SHSS, 28 November 1950, SHSS papers.

married on 2 February at Helen's parents' farm at Piopio in the King Country. Her new sister-in-law won Shirley's heart when her Helen unexpectedly appeared with the wedding party as a flower girl.

Bill and Shirley moved back into their two-bedroom flat under the hillside at 359 The Terrace (later renumbered 365).

As well as accommodating everything they brought home from New York, they had to find room in the small flat for the belongings their families had stored for them while they were away. The bedrooms were so full of boxes that there was little room for people.[3] Helen's room was piled high to the ceiling with packing cases. At the head of her bed was a case on top of which stood a cathedral-shaped wooden box with the T'ang horse they had bought in New York.

Shirley liked the flat no better than when they had lived there six years earlier. She and Bill started looking at sections with the idea of building a new house. Nannie's bequest of her house to Shirley made this possible.

Wellington was then facing the biggest industrial confrontation in New Zealand's history, the waterside workers' dispute ('lockout' or 'strike', depending on the point of view) that lasted 151 days. Thinking in Cold War terms and the context of New Zealand's entry into the Korean War alongside its ANZUS allies, the National Government branded the strikers as traitors and enemies, declared a state of emergency, refused to call Parliament to debate the issue and announced the country was 'at war'. Emergency regulations made it an offence for citizens to assist strikers. Giving food to watersiders and their families could get someone three months in jail. Shirley remembered Bill ducking into an alleyway to give money to a union officer. She supposed he did that regularly.

The government deregulated the watersiders' union and seized all its assets. It imposed rigid censorship to prevent their story being told and police had powers to search and arrest without warrants. Bill and Shirley's friends, Rona and Chip Bailey, to whom they had sub-leased their flat while they were overseas and who now lived close by, ran

3 SHSS, memoir, 'Life with Bill – No.2', undated (1998), SHSS papers.

an underground press to produce newsletters. Special Branch searched their home for the 'Gestetner' but never found it. Shirley recalled in 1998 that at one point Chippy brought round the 'typewriter' and she hid it in a wardrobe covered in clothes.[4] The risks of it being found were even greater than she realised.

Special Branch intercepted a package of the illegal bulletins Bill sent to a woman at the United Nations.[5] And they re-opened their file on Shirley. They recorded that soon after her return to New Zealand, she had met with the leaders of the New Zealand Communist Party in Auckland with a view to renewing her membership but had been advised not to rejoin. She later wrote about this meeting, adding that they told her she'd be more use to the Party as a non-card member, doing whatever she thought would be good for New Zealand.[6]

Special Branch also learnt 'on reliable authority' that she spoke of her connections with the Communist Party in the USA.[7]

A MORE pressing problem for Shirley was what to do with her life now that Helen was starting school. She thought of enrolling in Law School. She talked it over with her father, but he still thought the law wasn't for women and Bill was dead against it, so she dropped the idea.[8]

She thought of opening an omelette restaurant but didn't act on it. 'I did nothing. I was a housewife, but I wasn't a housewife. I was hopeless. If I had washed up breakfast and made the beds by lunchtime, I thought I'd done well. . . . I sank deeper and deeper into depression.'[9] The worst of it was feeling diminished. 'I thought, someone is going to

4 David Grant, 'Never a Backward Step', Trade Union History Project Newsletter No. 38, December 2005, p.3; SHSS, memoir, 'The Human Rights Organisation', 1998, SHSS papers. Whether or not it was the typewriter Dick Scott used to type the bulletins, or the 'Gestetner', its discovery in Shirley and Bill's house would have been serious for both their future careers.

5 WBS PF, Target Assessment, 30 May 1974, NZSIS. http://www.nzsis.govt.nz/assets/media/1974-05-30-Sutch-TA.pdf.

6 SHSS, memoir, 'NZ Council of Civil Liberties', undated (1998), SHSS papers.

7 H. J. McLeod, W. B. Sutch, Target Assessment, NZSIS, 30 May 1974, p.16.

8 This is an excerpt from the oral history of Shirley Smith with Hugo Manson on 4 November 1988 commissioned by the New Zealand Law Society, Wellington Branch, side 4, ATL, OHInt-0082-02. In another account she recalled discussing it with Nigel Taylor. He encouraged her when she eventually decided to do Law.

9 SHSS, memoir, 'Life with Bill', undated (1998), SHSS papers.

walk into this room and look around and I'll be there and they'll say, "Where is Shirley?" because I will have become so insubstantial. I will have faded into the wallpaper.'[10]

She joined the film society, expecting Bill to look after Helen on those nights since she was often at home alone with Helen. It was something she wanted to do on her own, without having to organise and pay for a babysitter. It didn't work out that way and after six months, when Bill suggested they take out a double subscription, Shirley let her membership lapse.

Yet her life was quite social. She saw a lot of her brother and sister-in-law, Allan and Helen. Allan was a house surgeon at Wellington Hospital. Helen Smith was teaching maths at Queen Margaret's College and was also very involved in Wellington's left-wing Unity Theatre. And Shirley made new friends, including the mother of her daughter's best friend at school, broadcaster and journalist Christine Cole. Chris brought Shirley into radio, starting with a panel discussion, and so she met one of the panellists, artist and writer Peggy Garland, who became another close friend. Bill renewed his old friendship with Bert O'Keefe, who was now Public Service Commissioner. Bert's wife Madge became Shirley's closest confidant. With the perception of a child who saw and heard more than the adults intended, Helen thought her mother confided too much in Madge. Shirley also advised Madge on her volatile marriage and later helped her leave Bert.

But Shirley still felt very much alone. When she was unhappy in New York, Shirley's old teacher from Nga Tawa, Miss Young, suggested she keep a diary – at least 15 minutes a day – to see where it led. Now she started a journal. To start with, as the following extracts show, it was an outlet for her feelings.

Wednesday 18 April
Spent £6.6.0 on woollies (own money). . . . Tidied fiercely but before done Bill arrived from Chch just as Helen spilt oceans of green 'magic paint'. Allan and Helen came in response to S.O.S. so I could go with Bill to

10 SHSS to Neville Glasgow, interview, broadcast on National Radio, 18 January 1989, published in *Directions: New Zealanders Explore the Meaning of Life*, Shoal Bay Press, Christchurch, 1995, pp.197–98.

Horace's inaugural. [Horace Belshaw's inaugural lecture as Macarthy chair of economics at Victoria University College.] *Good evening but later Bill froze me by needling about litter. I can no longer swallow it and smile.*

Why do I so resent Bill's saying 'Where shall I put your five pound note?' Why doesn't he just give it to me or say 'I've put it on the table' – or whatever? It always reminds me of his saying to Morva as he left the house . . . 'Do you want any money?' It is so bloody patronising, it so underlies one's economic dependence. . . .

p.m. Bill's lecture. . . . Bill started slowly but when he hit his stride gave a brilliant lecture, an organic interpretation of U.N. with emphasis on economic and social factors and endeavours. He said the sight of my drawn face exhausted him. I couldn't help it – but he didn't sound exhausted.

Thursday 19 April
. . . The effort of maintaining my identity drains me of energy for anything else. I find rather to my horror that I now could be rude to and regardless of Bill without giving a damn for the consequences – rather roles reversed from when we lived here before. So far I keep it in and remain silent and stony. Seeing I still feel the cost of asserting myself in this way isn't worth it, I shall have to find some other way of keeping my head above the water of the deadly pressure from Bill, as the stoniness is bad for me as well as Bill. Hence my use (at last) of the diary. Ibsen's Nora chose an easier way to find herself. To seek the same end while staying in the house is harder. I remember Morva's 'How you keep so cheerful while living under the same roof is what I can't understand'. Then it was Dad for me and Bill for her. I seem to have chosen a husband according to Freud all right.

Friday 27 April
Tom, Gladys and Barry [Sutch] *invited for tea. Rush of a day – shopping, washing, cleaning, cooking – roast forequarter and onions and pots, and carrots and beans, apple pudding, served at 6.30, not too bad after aiming at six. . . . Madge* [O'Keefe] *and Maureen Audley, Bert's niece, came in*

about 9 p.m. After all had gone, Bill and I stayed up till about 2.30 a.m. discussing why I'm a failure – promise but no achievement. When Bill said I was still at Oxford, I gave up. My troubles are not those of the eternal undergraduate, nor are they caused by the tie of a child. No more of these talks – I only plummet deeper. I can do better on my own. Fundamentally (I think) anything but political action seems to me piffling.

Saturday 28 April

. . . Very bad night. Felt desperate for depression and lack of sleep. . . .

Sunday 29 April

Slept in. Bill brought tea and toast to bed. Stayed in bed all morning. No headache and felt much better. Madge [O'Keefe] *came in as I was cooking lunch – around 2 p.m. She drove us up to Wadestown where we inspected section. Then to Sefton St and afternoon tea with Wilson (Sec. of Board of Trade), wife and children. . . . Helen behaved quite well. . . . Dad drove us home. Bill cooked chips. Working evening (Bill writing I ironing).*[11]

Contrary to Shirley's recollections that she did nothing all year, her journal shows that apart from running the house and looking after Helen, she and Bill entertained a good deal. She wrote book reviews, talked to mothers' clubs and other groups (Special Branch noted that she talked to the radical Progressive Youth League), and gave radio talks for the 2YA Women's Session.

Far from being tired and depressed, Shirley's talks on radio were lively and upbeat. Her subjects included Mexico, New York, the UN, life at Parkway Village, urban development, the New Zealand novel and women writers, women's magazines, relationships between men and women and more. In her talk 'It's Nice to be Home Again' she measured life in New Zealand against New York. Those who found New Zealand a backwater and New Zealanders dull and smug all missed one thing, she said, 'that we're human, really truly honest-to-god human beings and we live on a human scale.'[12]

11 SHSS, journal, SHSS papers.

12 SHSS, 'It's Nice to be Home Again', radio talk on the Women's Session, 2YA, 21 November 1951, SHSS papers.

She stopped her daily entries in her journal after just a month. When she started again on 30 October, it was with a fresh purpose. She resolved not to use the demands of housekeeping and a child as an excuse to let life drift by. 'I still don't know how the problem is to be met, but met it must be. After all, the recognition of the necessity is psychologically the main thing. If I were left in the position of providing for Helen and me I would organize the physical basis of life somehow.'

She saw that housework was justifiable only if it facilitated her proper work. 'I can live and work in an atmosphere of domestic disorder and culinary crudeness.' That was one side of the problem.

But what if one's domestic happiness is jeopardized by such an attitude – if one's husband is made really unhappy by domestic disorder – if his ability to work at home is almost destroyed by his feeling of discomfort. It is easy to say 'let him do it himself' but it really won't do. For one thing he works far harder than I all day (at least while I just moon around the flat deploring the need to do the ironing) and then he is deeply soaked into the old feeling that his domestic comfort should be secured by his wife – far more deeply than I think he knows. He thinks a woman should be able to handle the domestic setup – by second nature – and have plenty of time – if she is efficient – for occupations of the mind. It is all very well to think he is wrong – asserting one's own position proves nothing and alters no feeling.

Myself, I think it is a betrayal of womankind to make oneself so efficient in domestic affairs that one can manage another life as well and leave one's husband unconscious of the physical claim of family living – perhaps mechanical would be a better word. It is quite wonderful to do one's own job and come home to a pleasant fireside and a cooked dinner and a tidy house. I KNOW – it happened to me on rare occasions when I was lecturing at A.U.C. either when Bill was in Auckland or when I had Gabrielle staying with me. I know *how wonderful it is. I also know how pleasant it is to arise from a dinner and go out leaving the maid to clean up, wash up and put away.*

But if one has come to believe, as Bill has – and I (I think) that such an organization of society involves an injustice to individuals – e.g.

He wants no servants under him
And no boss over his head
how can we avoid the conclusion that to live so off one's wife's work is at least equally unjust?

. . .

When however a wife feels as I do that her work in the world should be work of her brain – whether in freelance writing or paid professional work or whatever – I feel there is no justification for a husband's profiting from his wife's ability to carry on two separate and different kinds of work. For one thing she will probably be putting in at least 80 hours of work a week . . . (Christine Cole reckons her work at least 100 h.p.w.) for another – and I think this is more important – her resentment of the housework is likely to weigh on her spirit and reduce her power of attack on her other work. Bill doesn't feel she should feel resentment. But then I feel husbands shouldn't expect their wives to be unpaid housekeepers. . . . In the first place the thing to do is to remove the cause of resentment, either by paying someone else to do the housework or by persuading one's husband (and family) to share it with one.[13]

She considered different attitudes towards people one might employ, patterns of living in other societies – the large family in Sāmoa, communal living in the Jewish Kibbutz, widespread provision of crèches, nurseries and kindergartens as in the USSR combined with the sort of janitorial service for flats, or the Swedish system of flats with communal services. While New Zealand men attended to such things as carpentry, mending gadgets and mowing lawns, she objected to the assignment of activities according to gender, 'For why shouldn't a professional wife sometimes have a domesticated husband as well as vice versa – without ridicule and shame for the man?' She totally rejected the idea that she should like cooking and mending because she was a woman and that her husband should be spared them because he was a man.

This was her theme for a talk for the Women's Session on Radio New Zealand's 2YA, hosted by Christine Cole, 'Can Women Do Better?'

13 SHSS, journal, SHSS papers.

After an erudite outline of the customary arguments that women are not as capable of good work as men, she gave her well-considered exposition of an ideal equal partnership:

For the first time in civilized history, men are being asked to face up to the problem of standing on their own feet – living on their own resources – facing up to their own real natures; instead of building their self-respect on the homage done them by women, they will have to build it on a cold and honest appraisal of themselves.

Virginia Woolf says, 'women have served all these centuries as looking glasses possessing the power of reflecting the figure of man at twice his natural size.' And she goes on 'For if she' – woman – 'begins to tell the truth, the figure in the looking-glass shrinks; his fitness for life is diminished. How is he to go on giving judgment, civilising natives, making laws, writing books, dressing up and speechifying at banquets, unless he can see himself at breakfast and at dinner at least twice the size he really is?'

So if women are 'to tell the truth' – and I believe they must – if they are to refuse any longer to spend their best energies in cushioning men and giving nourishment to their self-respect – some might say their self-importance – men too will have their first chance of showing that they can be human beings in their own right, too. It is both an opportunity and a challenge to men. Can the parasite rata develop into a free-standing trunk?

On the material side there is no less challenge to men . . . To ask men to take over their share of the housework and cooking and looking after the children is to ask a very great deal – the giving up of age-old privileges, a more than three-quarters share of the ease and comfort available in the world at any given moment.

But this new movement of women can never succeed as a WOMEN'S movement – it must be a MEN'S AND *WOMEN'S movement. MEN, as such, are not an exploiting class to be fought, overcome and replaced; they too, are people who are capable of becoming HUMAN-BEINGS. Men can only be partially-realised human-beings while they live on the subjugation of women; just as women can only be partially-realised human-beings while they are subject to men.*

So what, practically, does this lead up to? As I see it, a family home where father and mother both take part in affairs outside the home – in their work, in local politics, national politics, perhaps, in committee work of useful kinds – and both, preferably, in some kind of money-winning activity, for nothing so raises one's status, and that of one's activities, as to be capable of making money; and of course as far as possible, that activity should be one which uses one's best gifts and talents; for nothing is so good for the self-respect as to feel that the work one is doing is what one can do best, and that it's worthwhile – WELL. And both husband and wife should help in doing those household tasks which are essential to ordinary life . . .

A rounded life, with both public and private satisfactions, for both man and woman; a true companionship, where man and wife can discuss impersonal topics together and also the truly personal questions of their own home. How much happier marriages should be; how much more loving than is usual should be the atmosphere of the home for the children in it, how much greater the background of security from which they will go out into the world. Why should we not have this equal partnership?[14]

She noted a reaction in her journal on 5 November: 'Enraged technicians and [radio host] Selwyn Toogood by my ideas for men and women sharing each other's work.'

Continuing her journal, she moved on to the problem she still had: What was to be her work in the world? One problem was her 'advanced age' – thirty-five. She assessed her qualifications and work record. Reading the philosophical discussions in the early part of the Keynes biography by Roy Harrod re-stimulated her interest in those questions.

Resolved *to read more – starting with* [Alfred North] *Whitehead.*

Resolved *to go back to classical reading – notably Thomson.*
To read a little Vergil every day.
Possibly to draw on this material for articles or broadcasts – but primarily to keep my mind working.

14 See p.201 for details. SHSS papers.

Economics *This book makes me realize one must know more about it. First book to read* Das Kapital.

Literature *Attempt to make up one's deficiencies.*

Resolved *to read what is in the house first, notably* The Waves [by Virginia Woolf].

The most important thing is to get the wheels turning again. Discussion is also necessary – problem – with whom to discuss?

Resolved *to deal promptly with requests for reviews e.g. 'Happiness' etc. request from F. L. Combs.*

It is also possible that if I get going like this I shall begin to feel physically better.

Resolved *to* write *something every day – even if it is only this diary.*

And for God's sake let me resolve to get all outstanding affairs, like letters, photograph distraction etc. acknowledgements, cleared off and KEPT cleared off.

. . .

What shall I concentrate on finally? Choice will become essential. What of this idea of LAW *that I had? This must be thought out.*[15]

Shirley was particularly interested in constitutional and international law. She joined the Anti-Japanese Rearmament League, which was part of the international protest against pressure from the United States on Japan to abandon its post-war declaration to renounce war. The League, along with the whole peace movement, was regarded by political right-wingers as a front for communism, and Shirley's role on the committee and the public platform were duly noted on her security file, as was her association with other 'subversives'.

15 SHSS, journal, SHSS papers.

The chairman of the League was lawyer Nigel Taylor, who had defended union workers during the 1951 waterfront dispute and he attracted liberal-minded clients. Shirley spent a lot of time over the next months talking about the law to Nigel and his partner Keith Matthews, whom she had met in 1943 in Auckland when she was distributing election pamphlets. Keith and his wife Jackie had recently returned from Paris, where they worked for the World Peace Council.

The events of 1951 had shored up political support for the National Government. After a landslide electoral victory in September, it introduced draconian legislation that swept away human rights and liberties. Shirley recalled that, on the night of 26 October, Nigel Taylor burst into a League meeting with the news that the Police Offences Amendment Bill had been introduced. This called for action – the League morphed into the Human Rights Organisation with Shirley as its elected chairman (she spurned gender-neutral language) and her sister-in-law Helen Smith as secretary.[16] They set up in a small office on Lambton Quay.

On 15 November the Human Rights Organisation held a protest meeting against the Bill. Special Branch noted: 'Addressing the meeting, SS remarked that while in the USA she could not help being concerned with the Red Bogey hysteria sweeping through that country. She herself had been called a "Red" whilst there, and she thought the same fear complex was being fostered in New Zealand.'[17]

Shirley and Nigel Taylor prepared submissions to the Statutes Revision Committee, protesting that the Bill was contrary to the long-established practices of British justice, explicitly contrary to specific provisions of the Universal Declaration of Human Rights and would 'paralyse the normal working of democracy'. Shirley drew on her knowledge of the great philosophers to support her case – a feature of the many submissions she made throughout her life.

The Bill was returned to the House with 50 amendments. It was

16 SHSS, memoir, 'The Human Rights Organisation', 18 August 1998, SHSS papers. Shirley wrote that she and Helen Smith founded the organisation and they were chairman and secretary throughout. However, Margaret Brand was secretary by 1954.

17 Annex, 'Incidental references to Shirley Hilda Stanley Smith/Sutch (SS)', 15 November 1951', SHSS PF, NZSIS.

passed late on the night of 3 December. Though they had failed to have it withdrawn, Shirley saw that the expression of public opinion was the most important force leading towards the amendments. Furthermore, the battle had educated the public in ways of effective protest, and success encouraged further participation.[18]

She drew up a Draft Constitution on 16 March, defining the HRO as a non-party, non-sectarian group whose purpose was to uphold rights and freedoms set down in the Universal Declaration of Human Rights.

In the process, talking to Nigel and Keith over the summer, she had become fascinated with constitutional law.

18 SHSS, 'History of the Police Offences Bill (from its introduction in the House until its passing', undated, SHSS papers, ATL, MS-Papers-11404-41.

14
Law School

On New Year's Day 1952, acting on one of her resolutions, Shirley wrote to George Fraser, editor of the left-wing intellectual journal *Here & Now*, offering to send him something on the Police Offences Amendment Bill. She included a letter for publication defending the Washington correspondent William McChesney Martin, who was in fact Bill Sutch writing under a pseudonym, against criticism in the November issue. 'Bill doesn't think W. McChesney Martin will deign to take notice of such rubbish and also thought it beneath his notice, so the way seems clear for me, lowly as I am, to have a shot. I must say, I enjoyed it.'[1]

George Fraser invited her to be *Here & Now*'s 'friend' in Wellington. She took this on for a while. (*Here & Now* became referred to as 'Now and Then' until it ceased publication in November 1957.)

A big change in Shirley's life came with Bill's concession towards owning a car. They also purchased two adjoining quarter-acre sections on Brooklyn hill, but Shirley didn't suggest this as a reason. She explained that he had always been against owning a car, believing one should walk or use public transport, but she had grown up with a car in the family and she wanted one. 'Surprisingly Bill did not put up much resistance. He just made conditions. I was to drive the car, wash and polish it, get it serviced and so on. All he would do would be to allow me to drive him. With all of which I gladly agreed. . . . It was of course a great benefit to me because, although at times I had to go out of my way to drive him . . . the car was always available to me.'[2]

1 SHSS to George Fraser, 1 January 1952, SHSS papers, ATL, MS-Papers-11369-217. Dr Northey criticised the Washington Newsletter published in *Here & Now*, November issue, about United States constitutional procedures regarding her ability to declare war.

2 SHSS memoir, 'Life with Bill – No.2', undated (1998), p.6, SHSS papers; Wellington

Over the next summers, the family and Margaret Shirley Sutch (who now lived in Christchurch, working in the Education Department's psychology division) crammed into the tiny pea-green Austin A40 packed with a tent, sleeping bags, billies, provisions and suitcases, and set off to explore New Zealand, starting with the South Island. The idea was to see as much of the country as possible. It wasn't much fun for Helen, squashed in the back. She pleaded to stay at nice camping grounds where she might play with other children, but there wasn't time for that. Shirley enjoyed camping but it wasn't a restful holiday. Having driven all day and helped put up the tent, she wondered why neither Bill nor his sister ever gave her a night off cooking. What's more, she never suggested they should.[3]

For several summers the family took off on road trips around the country. At other times of the year, Shirley and Helen took holidays at Taupō, just the two of them, where they had a real rest and, in Helen's case, recovered from regular bouts of tonsillitis. Shirley completely relaxed in Taupō. They played cards, sat in front of the fire, talked and read. Shirley read detective stories – Georgette Heyer and Margery Allingham were favourites – and imagined being a criminal lawyer.

AT THE BEGINNING of 1952 Shirley had quietly enrolled at Victoria University College Law School. Only when it was settled did she tell anyone. Despite his earlier opposition, her father was delighted. The law brought them together and remained a close bond between them always.

Bill's reaction was quite different and things again became very difficult. 'He really found it hard to understand that I wanted to be more than a wife and mother. He was really puzzled. . . . on his death bed, he asked me why I had wanted to have my own profession?'[4]

At one point he suggested he should take a law degree too and they could practice together.

City Archives, Subdivision Dr W. B. Sutch, Reference No. 00001:1429:36/2592, 1951–55; 00009:1195:36/2594, 1952–55.

3 SHSS memoir, 'Life with Bill – No.2', undated (1998), p.6, SHSS papers.

4 Ibid, p.4. Shirley recalled that fees were no more than 4 guineas a unit per annum.

Shirley Smith, Wellington, about 1927. *Photographer Hal Collidge, David Smith collection*

The Cumming family; standing from left: Kathleen (Kitty), Duncan, Annie, William (Willie), Eva in the middle; sitting: Emma née White, Duncan. *Cumming family collection*

The Smith family at 84 Hill Street in 1913 or early 1914; back row from left: James (Jim), Annie Ethelwyn (Wynnie), George, Fiona (Woey); front row from left: David, Ann née Gibb, John, Lorna (Tom); child in middle: Alison. *Shirley Smith collection*

David Smith and Eva Cumming in the Wellington Botanic Garden. *Shirley Smith collection*

From left: Kathleen (Kitty) Cumming, Emma Cumming, Eva Cumming, David Smith. *Shirley Smith collection*

From left: Kitty Cumming, Lorna Smith, Fiona Smith, Eva Cumming. *Shirley Smith collection*

Shirley's father, David Smith.
Shirley Smith collection

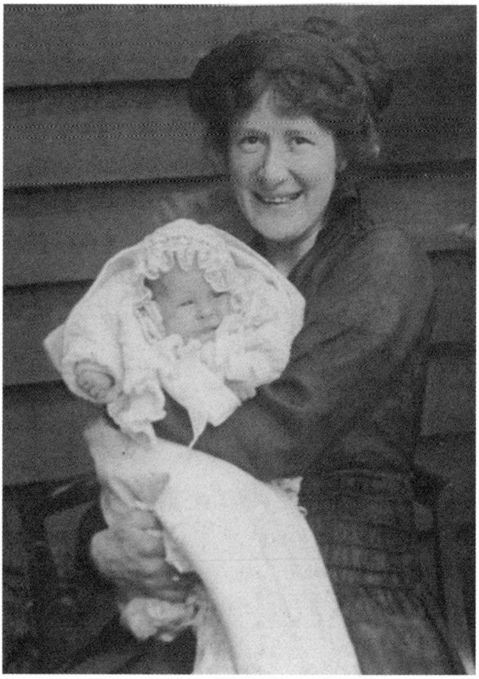

Shirley's mother, Eva, with Shirley.
Shirley Smith collection

Shirley's grandmother Emma White (Nannie), with Shirley. *Shirley Smith collection*

Shirley's grandmother Ann Smith (Gran'ma), with Shirley. *Shirley Smith collection*

Eva, David and Nannie with baby Shirley. *Shirley Smith collection*

David with Shirley. *Shirley Smith collection*

First steps, with Nannie, Hill Street. *Shirley Smith collection*

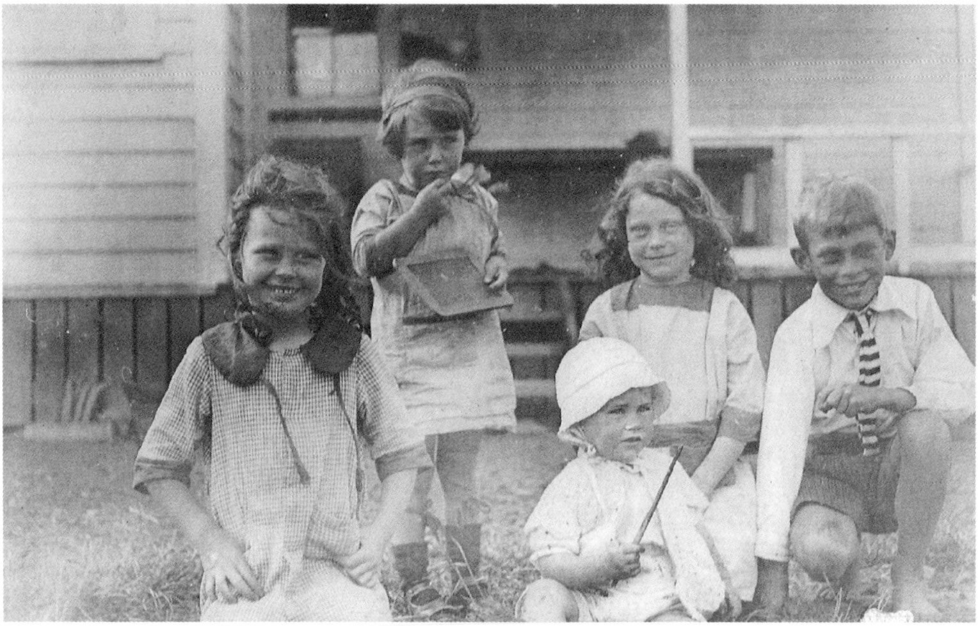

Shirley with step-cousins in the Waikato; from left: Shirley, Isobel Cumming, Barbara Mayer, Duncan Mayer, Betty Cumming (in front in hat). *Cumming family album*

Sister Kathleen Cumming, New Zealand Army Nursing Service (NZANS), World War I. *Collection of Auckland Museum Tāmaki Paenga Hira, 2002.114.8*

Shirley with David. *Cumming family collection*

Shirley's stepmother Margaret Elizabeth Smith, née Gibbs, called Meta. *Photographer S. P. Andrew, David Smith collection*

Mr Justice Smith. *Photographer S. P. Andrew, David Smith collection*

Shirley. *Photographer Elizabeth Greenwood, David Smith collection*

Shirley with her half-brother Allan. *Photographer Elizabeth Greenwood, David Smith collection*

David Smith, Richard Gibbs (Meta's father), Shirley and Allan at Taupō. *David Smith collection*

Shirley's stepmother Meta at Taupō, about 1928. *Shirley Smith collection*

Shirley, Wellington, 1935, shortly before her departure for Oxford.
Photographer S. P. Andrew, David Smith collection

Shirley, Wellington, 1935, in her debutante ballgown.
Photographer S. P. Andrew, David Smith collection

Shirley, Oxford, about 1937.
Photographer Ramsey & Muspratt, Shirley Smith collection

A postcard to Allan Smith from Munich, 1937.
Shirley Smith papers

Wendelstein, Munich, on Shirley's European tour, summer 1937; below: Shirley third from left, leaning against Martin Watkin. *Shirley Smith album, William Ball Sutch Collection, Alexander Turnbull Library, PA1-o-1176-002, PA1-o-1176-003*

Hungarian State Wine Cellars, Budafok, Budapest; above: Shirley second from left; left: Shirley back row, centre.
Shirley Smith album, William Ball Sutch Collection, Alexander Turnbull Library, PA1-o-1176-005, PA1-o-1176-004

Vienna, with Roland Towers. *Shirley Smith album, William Ball Sutch Collection, Alexander Turnbull Library, PA1-o-1176-001*

Paris, with Martin Watkin. *Shirley Smith album, William Ball Sutch Collection, Alexander Turnbull Library, PA1-o-1176-006*

Wooden head of Shirley by sculptor Alec Miller, 1938. *Photographer Sarah Gaitanos*

Shirley with her father, Geneva, 1938. *David Smith collection*

David and Meta Smith, Grisons, Switzerland, 1938.
Shirley Smith album, William Ball Sutch Collection, Alexander Turnbull Library, PA1-o-1176-007

Shirley, about 1943.
David Smith papers, Alexander Turnbull Library

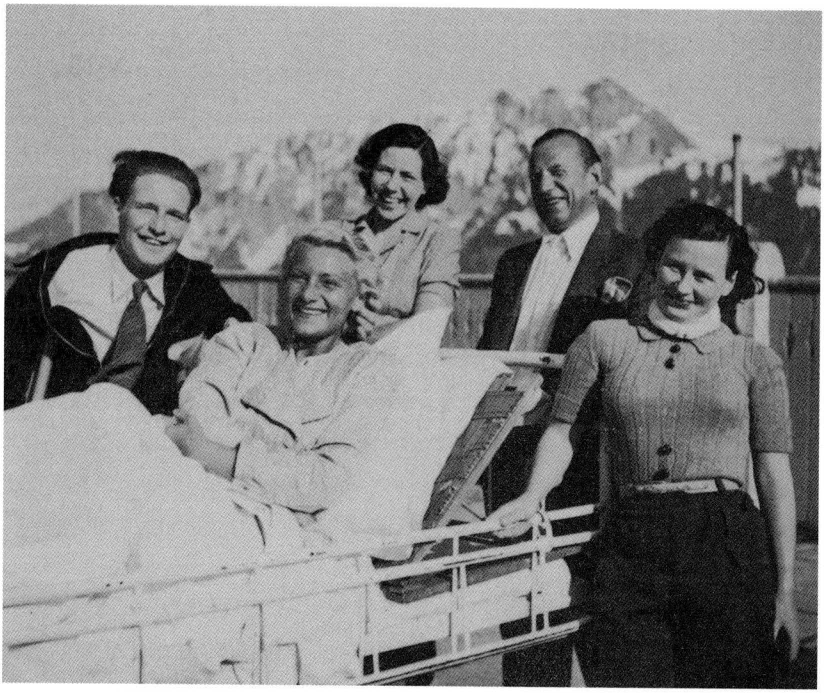

Leysin, 1939; Shirley on right, probably Dr Rollier behind her. *Shirley Smith album, William Ball Sutch Collection, Alexander Turnbull Library, PA1-o-1176-008*

Shirley with Bill, Sydney, May 1945. *William Ball Sutch Collection, Alexander Turnbull Library, PAColl-7591-1-53-1*

Shirley with her daughter Margaret Helen Sutch, called Helen, 1946.
William Ball Sutch Collection, Alexander Turnbull Library, PAColl-7933-2-2

Shirley, Helen and Margaret Shirley Sutch departing for England on the *Ruahine*, August 1946. *William Ball Sutch Collection, Alexander Turnbull Library, PAColl-7933-2-01*

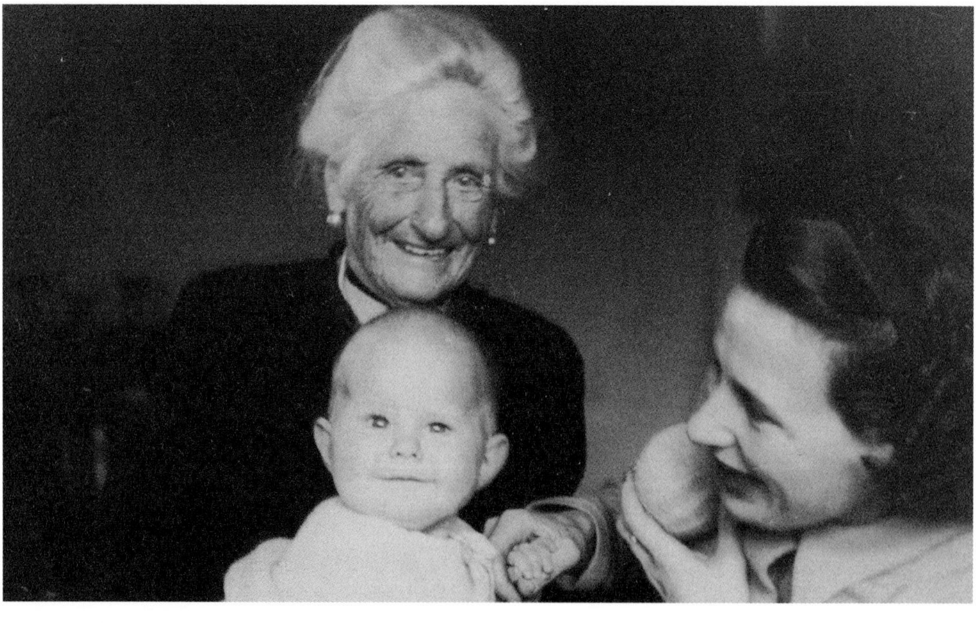

Shirley with Nannie and Helen, 1946.
William Ball Sutch Collection, Alexander Turnbull Library, PAColl-7933-04-2

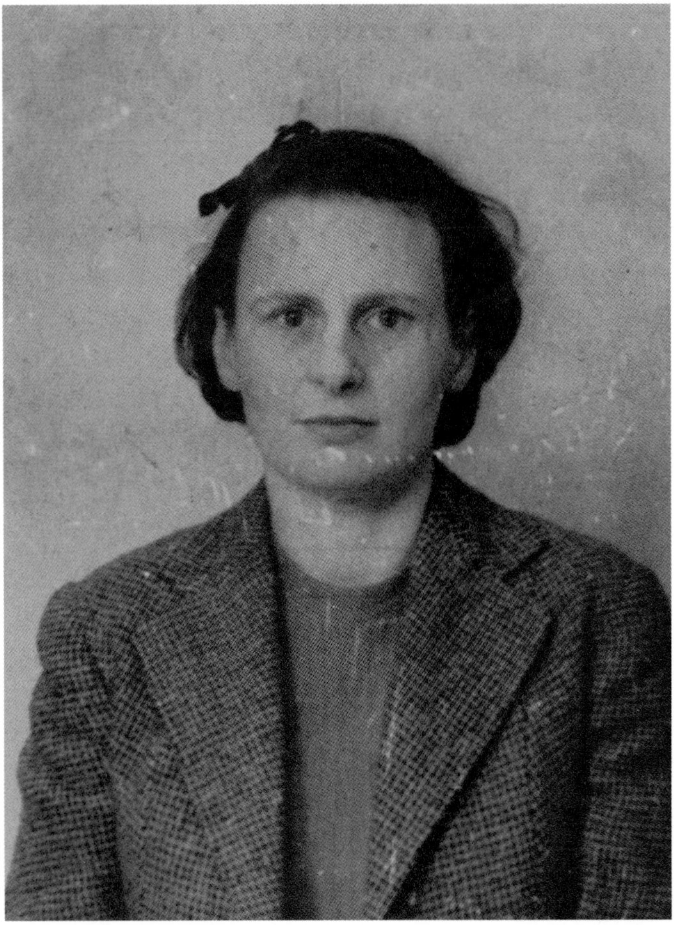

Identity photo of Shirley Smith attached to a Special Branch profile on her in 1953, probably taken before she left for England in 1946.
NZSIS archives

NZUSA Congress, Curious Cove: Shirley, Bill and Helen centre, second row, about 1955. *Dennis Rose collection*

The Sutch–Smith house designed by Ernst Plischke, Todman Street, Brooklyn, 1962. *Photographer John Ashton, Alexander Turnbull Library, 1/2-199947-F*

Bill Sutch, Shirley Smith and Mike Bungay arrive at the Wellington Magistrate's Court, October 1974, after Sutch was charged under the Official Secrets Act 1951. Dominion Post *Collection, Alexander Turnbull Library, EP/1974/6745a/8a*

From left: Mike Bungay, Bill Sutch, Shirley Smith, Michael Houston (behind), Ian Greig, arriving at the Supreme Court, Wellington, 17 February 1975. *Alexander Turnbull Library, EP/1975/0659/8*

Shirley with Bill and Helen after the trial, 1975. Evening Post, *Shirley Smith papers*

David holding his great-grandson Crispin, with Helen and Shirley, and Piers climbing the bookcase in the background, Todman Street, 1978. *Shirley Smith papers*

Shirley Smith ponders a point of discussion with Mongrel Mob members outside the courthouse. Shirley represented fifteen gang members charged with unlawful assembly. Evening Post, Stuff, *626551295*

Shirley in her law office, 1982. Evening Post, *Alexander Turnbull Library, EP/1982/1586*

Shirley outside the Wellington High Court, 1993.
Evening Post, *Alexander Turnbull Library, EP/1993/4642*

Luckily he did nothing about it. The idea appalled me. . . . Bill's personality was so powerful that I felt insignificant in his shadow. I had to exist in my own right. I needed to score off my own bat, so to speak. What he had no idea of, was that it was necessary for our marriage to succeed that I should have my own role. His unrecognized urge to take me over, and his resentment that he hadn't, showed in some curious ways. He never asked himself why he reacted in any particular way, he just reacted.[5]

On the issue of her doing law, Shirley held her ground. She recalled much later Helen asking in distress if they were going to divorce. Shirley reassured her, 'No of course not, darling.'[6]

Once university started, things improved. She loved studying law and, being happier, she was more energetic and got through the household chores more easily. Lectures were mostly first thing in the morning or early evening, to accommodate students and part-time lecturers who had full-time jobs in the city. Various friends minded Helen at the end of the day, or Shirley brought her to university and left her curled up with a book in the women's common room, where other women students kept an eye on her.

The women law students in Shirley's time included Shirley Robson (later Parr), who was finishing her degree in 1952; Shirley Sunley; Alison Alexander (later Quentin-Baxter), who became a lifelong friend; and Paddy West-Walker, who enrolled later. In most of her lectures, Shirley Smith was the only woman.

A number of the students were public servants. Among them was Bill's friend in Industries and Commerce, Jack Lewin. Jack and Shirley often shared a bench and they were both vocal. Jack saw no reason to be deferential to his lecturer. Sir Edmund Thomas (Ted), who had been a fellow student, recalled, '[Jack Lewin] would sit in the front row right in the middle with his arms crossed – so he didn't take notes – and was therefore quite intimidating to some lecturers. If a lecturer didn't measure up or had not done his homework, Jack would put his hand up and chide him for it. . . . This was unprecedented behaviour.'[7]

5 Ibid, p.5.
6 Ibid.
7 Hon. Sir Edmund Thomas to author, interview, 11 March 2013, track 2.

Shirley in her less aggressive way argued fine points of law. She brought the house down in a Legal Ethics lecture when, warned not to chat about their cases over dinner with 'the little woman', she rose and asked if this stricture applied equally to 'the little man'.[8]

One of her lecturers was George Barton. He recalled her in his Torts class in 1953 and they worked together editing *Law Review*.[9] George appreciated her independence of judgment and her willingness to question and debate legal principles. He became one of Shirley's most valued friends in the law. Throughout her career she had many dealings with him, often related to human rights, when she instructed him as Counsel.

Her knowledge of Latin and Roman history gave her a great advantage in Roman Law. A fellow student recalled, 'After an examination Professor Braybrooke announced to the class that he would never give anyone 100 per cent for an examination paper, not even to himself. But he was pleased to announce that he had given one of the class 99 per cent – Shirley Smith.'[10]

While she looked forward to studying Constitutional Law, Jurisprudence, Conflict of Laws and International Law, she found the subjects covered in her first years very interesting, especially Professor Ian Campbell's lectures on crimes. He worked from case studies, asking questions and interacting with students, rather than giving straight lectures. Shirley soon found herself studying her father's cases.[11] She doesn't say so but Campbell was known to discourage women from doing law for the same reason as her father had discouraged her. His lectures on rape were explicit at a time when sex still wasn't spoken about.[12]

Shirley apparently took it all in her stride. She won the Mackay

8 SHSS, 'My Life in the Law', *Claiming the Law: Essays by New Zealand Women in Celebration of the 1993 Suffrage Centennial*, eds. Elisabeth McDonald and Graeme Austin, VUW Law Review & VUP, May 1993, p.1.

9 Dean of the Faculty of Law Professor Robert Orr McGechan to SHSS, 23 February 1954, SHSS papers.

10 Hon. Sir Edmund Thomas to author, quoting a friend, email, 13 March 2013.

11 SHSS to DSS, 2 April 1952, SHSS papers. This was the Socratic Method, which Shirley herself had used as a classics lecturer, now adopted at Victoria University College.

12 Associate Judge Jim Thomson to author, interview, 16 November 2013.

Memorial Prize for Criminal Law and Law of Contract, and the Butterworth Prize for Roman Law, at the end of her first year.[13]

She said that she didn't experience any sexual discrimination in her classes, but the Law Faculty's annual dinner, held on the night of the last exam, was another matter. Women were customarily excluded. An exception was made in Shirley Robson's last year because it was the first time a woman had graduated for years, but their pre-dinner drinks were to be separate. Objecting to segregation on principle, Shirley Smith joined the men. She was appalled: 'People got drunk, they fell under tables, all the speeches were as blue as blue as blue, including those given by senior members of the profession.'[14] She decided never again to attend a law dinner.

But the next year, when everyone was swotting for finals, a notice went up to the effect that women students were not to be admitted to the dinner. Shirley burst into Professor Campbell's study with the idea of taking out an injunction. He laughed, and said that she might try milder remedies first. He suggested calling a Special General Meeting of the Law Faculty Club. Shirley then put out her notice and talked to other students to get a following. At the meeting she made a light-hearted speech. 'I said, I know there are quite a few Bible Class students who wear Bible Class badges on their lapels. They probably don't go to your dinners because they don't like them but you don't put out a notice saying Bible Class boys are prohibited. That's all we're asking you to do, not to put up signs saying women are prohibited.' The motion was passed that the dinners should be open to all students.[15]

13 Professor Ian Campbell to SHSS, March 1953; VUC Calendar 1954, p. 189. The Rupert Fred Mackay Memorial Prize was awarded to the student who had done the best year's work in any two of four prescribed subjects.

14 This is from the oral history of Shirley Smith with Hugo Manson on 4 November 1988, commissioned by the New Zealand Law Society, Wellington Branch, side 4, ATL, OHInt-0082-02. Shirley deplored the New Zealand custom of segregating men and women, which she didn't experience elsewhere. She wrote to the editor, *Dominion*, 3 December 1953, about the suggestion that women should be legally banned from bars to protect them from the deplorable conditions. She called for civilised conditions for drinking for all: SHSS papers, ATL, MS-Papers-11369-217.

15 This is from the oral history of Shirley Smith with Hugo Manson on 4 November 1988, commissioned by the New Zealand Law Society, Wellington Branch, side 4, ATL OHInt-0082-02. Shirley thought this was in 1953 and that Professor Campbell was the dean. Her memory might be correct in other respects, but R. O. McGechan was then still

After her last exam, just as she was settling down to relax for the evening, she remembered it was the night of the law dinner. Having made an issue of it, she thought she had better turn up to support other women who might be there. She arrived to find there were none. It didn't bother her. She realised it was less daunting for her, being older and more experienced.[16]

WHILE SHIRLEY was starting law, her research for the Human Rights Organisation highlighted the need for another organisation that would focus specifically on civil liberties. The New Zealand Communist Party's general secretary, Sid Scot, had planted the idea when he suggested she could be useful working outside the Party, doing what she thought good for New Zealand. She had first thought of setting up a town hall meeting, but Bill told her she would have to organise the debates so that she got the results she wanted. 'Such an idea being anathema to me, I did not argue, as I knew I'd have Bill against me, but gave it up.' She decided to go ahead with her second idea, a Council for Civil Liberties.[17]

She talked to Walter Scott, deputy principal at Wellington's Teachers' College, who helped her draw up a list of people to invite to an initial meeting. They set up a provisional committee on 12 June (she was a member), held a constitutional convention and adopted a constitution.[18] Recognising that 'the price of liberty is eternal vigilance' and that 'the more insidious restrictions on liberty and the less spectacular abuses of power may pass unobserved', they determined to detect such abuses and rally popular opinion against them. Professor John Beaglehole, a

Dean of the Law Faculty. He was killed in a plane crash in Singapore, March 1954.

16 SHSS, 'My life in the law', *Claiming the Law: Essays by New Zealand Women in Celebration of the 1993 Suffrage Centennial*, eds. Elisabeth McDonald and Graeme Austin, VUW Law Review & VUP, May 1993, p.2.

17 SHSS memoir, 'NZ Council of Civil Liberties', undated (1998), SHSS papers. Shirley repeatedly used 'of', not 'for', in the title. The error is notable, as she was usually meticulous about accuracy.

18 SHSS PF, Annex: Incidental references to Shirley Hilda Stanley Smith/Sutch, p.2, NZSIS. 'The object of the Council shall be to assist in the maintenance of civil liberties, including freedom of speech and assembly; to advance measures for the recovery and enlargement of such liberties; and to take such steps as it may deem necessary to attain these ends. The Council shall be non-party and non-denominational.'

strong opponent of the Police Offences Amendment Bill, was elected president and Walter Scott chairman. Shirley withdrew – for the time being.

Special Branch regarded the Council as a potential threat. Their spies recorded Shirley's attendance at its meetings, including one on 4 November 1952, held jointly by the Human Rights Organisation and the Council for Civil Liberties to discuss South Africa's racial policy. (It was noted that she spoke in favour of the motion but not what the motion was.)

Her attendance at a public meeting organised by the Peace Council drew comment that she was 'well known to Special Branch. She was a member of the CP and has been associated with many organisations that are sympathetic towards said Party.'[19] Even her attendance at a Theosophical Society meeting was recorded, though the address, 'India – key to the world's future', was acknowledged to be of no security interest. Her election as a vice-president of the university Socialist Club in April 1952 passed unobserved but her re-election in 1954 was noted.

Shirley became aware of Special Branch reporting on her activity when someone told her they knew she had purchased a copy of *People's Voice*. She was 'deeply vexed'.[20]

The Police Commissioner's office requested an update of her particulars when, as chairman of the Human Rights Organisation, she took up the Save the Rosenbergs campaign, which was part of an international protest against the death sentence on Ethel and Julius Rosenberg in the United States for conspiring to pass atomic secrets to the Soviet Union in World War II. The protesters argued that the verdict was based on spurious evidence, that their real crime was being communists.

A. E. V. Lane, Acting Detective, OC Special Branch, Wellington, reported that Shirley Smith was 'well known to this office for pro-Communist activity', and that her activities clearly indicated she was still very much pro-Communist. 'Perhaps another indication as to the

19 SHSS PF, Annex: Incidental references to SHSS p.2, 30 December 1952, NZSIS.
20 Hector MacNeill to author, interview, 13 November 2011; SHSS PF, Annex 24 February 1954, NZSIS, report with details of Shirley's car and registration.

subject's political outlook is the fact that she is an agnostic,' he added, concluding:

She is not referred to in the Police Gazettes. Her description is already on record in Special Branch but in addition it could be stated that she now wears horn-rimmed glasses. Her hair nearly always bears a scraggy appearance. She has a rapid and crisp manner of speech but is nevertheless quite a good clear speaker. Photographs of the subject have been previously submitted by me.[21]

Julius and Ethel Rosenberg were executed on 19 June 1953.[22] Shirley's next campaign, also related to capital punishment, was closer to home and successful. It involved three young Niue Islanders who, in August 1953, were condemned to death by hanging for killing their Resident Commissioner, C. H. W. Larsen. Once the circumstances that provoked their action became known in New Zealand, there was widespread sympathy for the three young men, whose mental ages were said to be between ten and twelve years. (They had received heavy sentences for petty offences, and as prisoners were forced to work long hours for Larsen who starved and beat them. The case then came before a presiding judge and assessors on the island.)

The New Zealand Government was seen to endorse an abusive colonial rule over its protectorate and the condemned men were looked on by fellow Niueans as liberators.

The three men appealed their convictions in New Zealand. The Supreme Court dismissed their appeals. Representations to the government followed and these too were dismissed, but on the same day the Executive Council commuted the death sentence on a woman,

21 SHSS PF, A. E. V. Lane, Acting Detective, No. 3992, New Zealand Police, Special Branch, Wellington, 12 May 1953, NZSIS.

22 The Venona files, the US counter-intelligence programme to decrypt cables sent by agents of the Soviet intelligence agency, identified Julius Rosenberg as head of a spy ring involved in atomic espionage, and showed Ethel was a minor participant. The Venona operation was revealed to historians and the public in 1995: *Venona: Decoding Soviet Espionage in America*, by John Earl Haynes and Harvey Khelr, Yale University Press, 1999, Chapter One. http://www.nytimes.com/books/first/h/haynes-venona.html (accessed 19 June 2018).

Edna May Wilson, who had been found guilty of a double murder in Napier. The reason later given was that the jury in Napier had recommended mercy. The fact that the Niue Islanders weren't tried by a jury wasn't lost on their supporters.

When the Howard League for Penal Reform applied for leave to appeal to the Privy Council, the Prime Minister announced a stay of execution pending a decision as to whether the appeal would proceed.

In February 1954 the failure of yet another appeal to government saw forty organisations come together in Auckland to form the United Committee to Save the Niue Islanders. Shirley and Margaret Brand, who was now Shirley's secretary on the Human Rights Organisation, immediately responded to the call for help. On 24 February 1954 they called a meeting of concerned citizens in Wellington at which they formed the Wellington Citizens' Niue Islanders Committee, with Shirley as chair and Margaret as secretary. This led to a deputation to the Prime Minister on 2 April.

Expecting a decision from the Privy Council to be announced any day and that execution could follow within a week, Margaret and Shirley organised a meeting on 12 April in Wellington Town Hall's Concert Chamber in association with the Society of Friends, the Christian Pacifist Society, the Human Rights Organisation and the New Zealand Howard League. About 200 attended.

Shirley released a statement on 23 April on behalf of the Wellington Citizens' Niue Islanders Committee. It did not question the legality of the trial under the Cook Island Act 1915, which provided a criminal code and procedure for the islands. But she wrote, 'It does suggest that those provisions be re-examined with a view to bringing them more into line with those under which New Zealanders are tried. The Official Report for 1953 says Niue Islanders are "New Zealand citizens"; do we want to have first- and second-class citizens?'[23]

As well as suggesting Niue Islanders should have the benefit of trial by jury, the committee questioned 'the advisability of administrative, legislative and judicial functions being combined in any one man, who,

23 SHSS on behalf of Wellington Citizens' Niue Islanders Committee, 23 April 1954, SHSS papers.

in addition in this case, supervised the daily duties of prisoners.'

Public opinion was so hot that Prime Minister Sidney Holland, with an election approaching, at last softened his stand. He saw a final deputation of three that included Shirley.

After the Executive Council had twice turned down requests for clemency, the sentence was changed to life imprisonment.[24] It was a triumph for the campaigners and demonstrated that in a democracy, when people were motivated to act, they could influence government at the highest level.

STALIN'S DEATH on 5 March 1953 saw a relaxation of Cold War tensions, but things stirred up when news of Soviet agent Vladimir Petrov's defection in Canberra hit the papers in April 1954. Australia's Prime Minister, Robert Menzies, informed Holland that the Russians had a 'contact' in his department. Holland confided in his two departmental heads, Alister McIntosh and Foss Shanahan, and with the department's Head of Security, Reuel Lochore. When their investigation cleared everyone in the Prime Minister's department, suspicion fell on Sutch, who had some access to the department.[25] He dismissed the Petrov Affair as a 'bogus American plot',[26] but found himself blocked in his career.

Special Branch kept Sutch under passive surveillance, which included cross-references to their file on his wife, whom they consistently referred to as Shirley Sutch. It appears that her 'subversive' activities, which were overt, were of interest to them on account of her relationship to Sutch. They noted in his file in 1954 that she was working as a law clerk at the Gleneagles office of Duncan, Matthews and Taylor. Both she and Bill's sister Margaret Shirley were involved in the Peace Council (the World Peace Council set up at the Second World Peace Congress in Warsaw in 1950 was ultimately directed by the Communist Party of the Soviet

24 Dick Scott, *Would a Good Man Die? Niue Island, New Zealand and the Late Mr Larsen*, Hodder and Stoughton, Auckland, 1993, pp.137–38.

25 Petrov also identified Ian Milner as a Soviet agent, which Milner vigorously denied all his life. (The Venona files confirmed information from Petrov.)

26 WBS PF, 1958, NZSIS; https://www.scribd.com/document/51280260/The-Fuss-About-Sutch (accessed 19 June 2018).

Union) and the Society for Closer Relations with the Soviet Union. In 1953 the American Embassy had refused a visa to Margaret Shirley because she was a member of the Christchurch Executive Committee of the Society for Closer Relations with Russia.[27] It meant that she couldn't take up a research grant awarded to her by the American Association of University Women to study specifically the use of play therapy for emotionally maladjusted children.[28]

While Special Branch regarded the activities of Dr Sutch's wife and his sister as relevant to their suspicions that he was a communist-sympathiser, he had the support of a powerful friend. This was their head of department, Secretary for Justice Sam Barnett, who had been appointed Controller-General of Police to clean up police corruption at the highest level. An outstanding administrator of scrupulous integrity, Sam Barnett set about modernising the police force in every respect, including the security service. On finding that the standards of personnel and records of Special Branch fell far short of professional counter-espionage agencies such as MI5 and ASIO, he determined to create a new dedicated security organisation.

Shirley and Bill both regarded Sam Barnett as a good friend. He had championed Shirley when she joined Vocational Guidance soon after her marriage in 1944, when he put her in charge of preparing vocational booklets. His friendship with Bill was cemented when Sam visited New York on a Fulbright grant in 1950 and Bill went out of his way to help him meet people. They admired, liked and respected one another. Shirley said that Sam was one of the few people Bill looked up to, and he listened to him.

When Sam Barnett examined all that Special Branch had on Sutch, he thought it 'no more than innuendo or unverified rumour'.[29]

27 W. Kling, First Secretary, American Embassy, Wellington, Confidential Foreign Service Despatch to the Department of State, Washington DC, 15 February 1956, in FBI 100-HQ-353048 (refers to Embassy dispatch 40, 22 July 1953).

28 *The Press*, 19 March 1953, as copied for FBI files, 20 May 1953.

29 W. Kling, First Secretary, American Embassy, Wellington, Confidential Foreign Service Despatch to the Department of State, Washington DC, 15 February 1956, in FBI 100-HQ-353048.

As Special Branch noted, Shirley had started work for Duncan, Matthews and Taylor. She wanted office experience. Nigel Taylor and Keith Matthews gave her work on an hourly basis, allowing time off for school holidays or to look after Helen if she was ill. Jim Thomson, who also worked there as a law clerk, noticed that Nigel and Keith went out of their way to support Shirley. They didn't need her. The office was small, they were young and struggling to get the firm back on its feet (the third partner was losing his memory), but they gave her a space and created work for her. Later they gave her facilities to set up her own practice. Shirley acknowledged that she owed Nigel and Keith a great deal.

The ambience at Duncan, Matthews and Taylor was convivial, with June Lewin – Jack Lewin's wife – presiding graciously over the main office. The conviviality included an unusual feature for a law firm – a co-operative for wholesale vegetables. On the pretext of collecting their weekly produce, the Vegetable Club, as it was called, brought people together on Friday evenings after work to have a beer and to talk about politics and sport. Shirley enjoyed all this when she could stay. Bill sometimes met her there and stayed on after she left to collect Helen. Jim Thomson was one of several people who observed that Shirley was afraid of her husband.[30]

Special Branch thought the Vegetable Club was a communist cell. Their mole recorded occasional references to Shirley.

Over this period Shirley suffered two sad losses. In September 1953, her dear friend Phoebe Llewellyn Smith, aged 36, drowned in a sailing accident in the Thames Estuary. Shirley was devastated.

Soon after, it became apparent that Meta was dying of what was eventually diagnosed as pancreatic cancer. After weeks of suffering, the end came on 24 May 1954. Shirley's loss can be understood in a response from her aunt Annie Mayer, who, thinking of her own stepmother (Shirley's Nannie), replied to Shirley's letter, 'I have been in much the same position. Granny and I grew nearer and nearer as time passed.'[31]

30 Jim Thomson to author, interview, 16 November 2013.
31 Annie Mayer to SHSS, 4 June 1954, SHSS papers. 'Granny' was 'Nannie' to Shirley.

Among letters of condolence was one from Helen Garrett, now living in Christchurch where John Garrett was Professor of English at Canterbury University College. Helen had known Meta since the 1920s, before Shirley went to Nga Tawa. 'I always remember her as so kind and cheerful – a model stepmother.'[32]

May Ives, who had been housekeeper for the Smiths since the war, stayed on with Sir David. She was a good cook and Sir David, who enjoyed entertaining, continued to give dinner parties, some of them very formal affairs. Shirley often acted as his hostess. She was most attentive to her father.

She was also a devoted aunt to Allan and Helen Smith's children, David and Jenni, and to Hugh and Ian when they came along. They moved to Tītahi Bay, where Allan began practice as a general practitioner.

A third death must also have badly shaken Shirley at the time. In August 1954 she had a car accident that resulted in a man dying of his injuries. She told the coroner at the inquest that she was driving at about 25 mph up Molesworth Street when she neared the Shamrock Hotel (it has since been relocated) and saw an elderly man crossing the street from west to east, with his head down. She tooted her horn and braked, whereupon he ran directly into the path of her car. She swerved but was unable to avoid him. An independent eyewitness told the court that the man did not look in any direction to see if the road was clear.

The coroner found his death was 'purely accidental'.[33]

Apart from Sir David's newspaper clipping of the findings, dated (in his handwriting) Saturday 9 October 1954, the author found no reference to the accident among Shirley's papers. Allan Smith remembered it when asked, but not that the man had died. He couldn't recall any discussion about it. Neither her daughter nor her son-in-law knew about it. This silence speaks volumes but still leaves big questions. Did she fear, during the weeks of waiting for the coroner's decision, that she might be tried for manslaughter? Her future law career was in the balance, but more disturbing surely was the knowledge that she had

32 Helen Garrett to SHSS, 6 June 1954, SHSS papers.

33 Inquest on the body of Thomas William Proctor of the Public Works Camp in Trentham, Archives NZ, J46 1426. The accident occurred at about 3.20 pm on Saturday 28 August 1954. Press clipping, 9 October 1954.

killed a man called Thomas Proctor. Was she haunted by the memory of the actual event?

Was it possible she blocked it out of her memory? Shirley subsequently had many minor accidents, but she loved driving. One of her fantasies about herself was that she could have been a good racing driver. Her son-in-law Keith Ovenden described at her funeral how she told him this in all seriousness when they were driving from Napier to Taupō. 'Happily, I was at the wheel at the time. Briefly I imagined her on the starting grid, circa 1953, with Juan Fangio to one side and Sterling Moss to the other, and all the havoc of the track ahead of them.'[34]

On top of these troubles, Bill's parents, now in their seventies, were both suffering from dementia. Shirley recalled that Ellen 'lost her acerbity and became sweet and gentle, but not quite all there.' Ted, on the other hand, became increasingly aggressive.

They were cared for in Dorking Road by a very capable housekeeper, but she couldn't deal alone with the crises. Bill's older sister Nellie was herself in Porirua Hospital (for reasons described below), his younger brother Ted was overseas and Margaret Shirley was in Christchurch. Tom, the eldest, lived in Wellington, but apparently didn't help. (His niece Shirley Hope said he was like his father.) So the burden fell to Bill and Shirley. Margaret Shirley felt guilty, but Bill and Shirley both insisted she should put her career first. After setting up a psychology clinic for the Department of Education in Christchurch, she moved to Dunedin to open another clinic.

Later in the year, after Ted attacked Ellen, the family had him committed to Porirua Hospital. Dr Ernst Philipp said that his behaviour was pathological: he was suffering from atheroma of the brain and was not responsible for his actions.[35]

Shirley rose to the occasion. Margaret Shirley wrote, after an earlier crisis in September, that she had been 'magnificent'. In response to Shirley's letter explaining the latest situation and the decision to have

34 Keith Ovenden, eulogy for Shirley Smith, 7 January 2008.

35 MSS to SHSS, 25 November 1954, SHSS papers, ATL, MS-Papers-1609783; Shirley Hope Evans to author, interview, 20 February 2015; SHSS, Sutch family history, 1992, p.29, SHSS papers.

him committed, Margaret Shirley again expressed her gratitude and gave her own analysis of her father:

I feel so very remote and useless down here but while it may seem strange comfort I confess your letter relieved my mind rather than increasing my anxiety for if his condition is pathological it explains my inability to get through – and for that matter the failure of all of us in this respect and because it explains, it may be that the personal guilt and sense of failure lessens. Do you understand? Of course the question still arises as to the precipitating causes of the pathological condition. Bill and I are perhaps over-conscious of our association with Mother in past isolation of Father from participation in family affairs. Mother was so strong a personality that even had we wished to support Father . . . we didn't feel secure enough to do so but that is perhaps only a small part of the story and while undoubtedly a contributing factor one would have to go back further to constitutional predisposition for example. A letter is not the best place to express what I feel except to once again assure you that I am deeply grateful for all you have done on our behalf.

Even my job takes on more purpose, for if I can help a few children and quite a few parents towards a more satisfactory adjustment to each other and to people outside the family it may well be because I have been made aware of the damage that can be done to human personality, and while fully aware that I haven't escaped damage myself and realise that my own defences are brittle and could well crack under pressure perhaps it may be possible to use such awareness for the advantage of others. This is popularly known as sublimation but for me it is perhaps the only possible compromise.

Thank you for being you. We seldom tell our friends how much they are appreciated and less so those we love and yet the telling should not be one for embarrassment, which it so often is, because of our Anglo Saxon distrust of over-statement. Believe me Shirley I am not overstating when I say I both respect and like you very much – it is a combination to be treasured.[36]

Not one to restrain her appreciation out of embarrassment, Shirley replied:

36 MSS to SHSS, 25 November 1954, SHSS papers, ATL, MS-Papers-1609783.

I have never told you how much help you have been to me at various difficult times, notably in London and later in New York, and then again over my law, making clear to me the roots of conduct in Bill that baffled and worried me. I have often thanked heaven – or luck or whatever – that I came by you as a sister-in-law, and more important, as a most valued friend. I realise too how much you have had to put up with from the hangovers of my past in me, and with what understanding you have done so; thereby incidentally helping me more (possibly?) than you know. So here are my thanks now, and with love.[37]

As far as she knew, Shirley was the only person to visit Ted Sutch in Porirua Hospital. He died there in 1956.

In fact, Ted Sutch's grandchildren, Hope and Gavin Evans, used to visit him when they went to see their mother in Porirua Hospital. According to Hope (who now calls herself Shirley), her mother Nellie suffered some kind of physical (probably sexual) attack when she was aged seventeen or eighteen. She had a mental breakdown then and was always fragile thereafter, breaking down completely when her adored firstborn, William ('Bill', named after his uncle), died suddenly of meningitis in 1948. She spent the rest of her life in Porirua Hospital. Her brothers and sister stopped visiting her because, Bill explained, they 'tended to bring her back to the life that was so cruel to her'. They had not seen her in twenty years when she died in 1969 of pneumonia.[38]

It would be surprising if Shirley didn't visit Nellie during her many visits to the psychiatric hospital. These family tragedies and her own memories of her father's sister, Auntie Lorna, gave her personal experiences of mental health, which became a particular concern in her work with the New Zealand Council for Civil Liberties and later in her law practice. In 1956 Shirley founded a group called Stepping Stones to help mental patients make the transition when they were discharged

37 SHSS to MSS, 1 December 1954, MSS papers, ATL, MS-Papers-9268-015. This was in response to MSS expressing gratitude for her help in crises with her parents Ellen and Ted Sutch. (She had stayed with Bill and Shirley in New York in 1948 on her way back to New Zealand.)

38 Shirley Hope Evans to author, interview, 20 February 2015; SHSS to MHS, 21 November 1969. Ellen died in 1959, Tom Sutch in 1961. WBS to MHS, 25 November 1969.

into the community. She incorporated Stepping Stones in 1961 and was honorary secretary for many years.

Among the happier family times in these years were tramping holidays on Mount Egmont (now Taranaki). One that stands out in Helen's memory was when her mother sprained her ankle crossing a dry riverbed. Realising they couldn't get back to the hut that night, they had to find suitable spot to sleep. They crossed the river to an island in the middle, her father supporting her mother. By the time they got there it was dusk. Helen recalled:

We poured the water out of our boots and put them on again so we wouldn't get cold. . . . My father gathered bracken, pulled out undergrowth and made beds for us and bracken to pull over us and we all lay down in a sort of spoon-shape with me in the middle, my mother and me and my father curling round both of us to look after us. And it was lovely. It was also clear that everyone was very happy, in spite of my poor mother's sprained ankle. . . . And then in the morning my father managed to help my mother back. They hadn't sent out a search party yet.[39]

These holidays were combined with Worker's Education Association (WEA) summer schools, usually held at New Plymouth Boys' High School but sometimes at Nelson College. Helen was proud of her parents. Her father was a star. He held his audiences spellbound as he spoke about economics in ways they could relate to. It was all about people.

From their first summer back in New Zealand, Bill and Shirley had taken part in the New Zealand University Students Association's annual summer Congress. This was a week-long talkfest at Curious Cove in the Marlborough Sounds. Here again, Bill had a big following, and Shirley too. Some of her new friends joined her human rights and civil liberties groups. Among them were Hector MacNeill, a law student; Dennis Rose, who recalls her giving a talk on feminist issues; Conrad Bollinger, who later started the Socialist Forum; and many of Bill and Shirley's

39 MHS to author, interview, 1 September 2011.

friends, there with their children who were Helen's friends. It was a sociable time for all.

Back in Wellington, Bill roped in teams of helpers – students, family, young men in his department – to work in the weekends excavating and clearing the land he and Shirley bought at 79a Todman Street in Brooklyn. The site was steep, scrubby and covered with gorse, broom and bracken. Shirley did her bit with grubber and slasher, leaving to Bill the finer aspects of landscape design, creating a setting for what would be an architectural masterpiece with panoramic views over Cook Strait, the city, Wellington Harbour, the valley and mountain ranges beyond.

Bill was a prominent member of the Wellington Architectural Centre and a champion of modernism in architecture and furniture design. He chose as architect Viennese Ernst Plischke, a world-renowned leader of modernism and the International Style. Since emigrating to New Zealand to escape anti-Semitism (his wife was Jewish), Plischke had revolutionised architecture and design in his adopted country. He designed the first glass-faced high-rise building in Lambton Quay, Massey House, and developed the idea of pedestrian shopping malls. But he became best known for his private houses. The house Plischke designed for Bill and Shirley would be regarded as his masterpiece.

Plischke conceived a way to place the house on the difficult site to gain maximum advantage of sun and views, while aesthetically relating his design to the landscape. In 1984 Shirley wrote, 'We all three worked on the architectural conception and the detailed plans: and we accepted it with enthusiasm. It was a very harmonious cooperation.' Asked how she viewed the architectural style, she replied, 'We thought it was beautiful and appropriate to the site and us.'[40]

She also privately and widely aired her dissatisfaction. After enthusiastically accepting the concept, while Bill worked closely with the architect, Shirley was largely excluded from the design process and her objections as time and cost grew were brushed aside. Allan Smith recalled her saying she was fed up with making do in the poky flat, she didn't care for this 'high falutin' architecture' and wished Bill

40 SHSS to Linda Tyler, School of Fine Arts, University of Canterbury, 29 May 1984.

would 'get rid of this wretched Plischke. All I want is a kitchen and a bed.'[41]

But when she learnt there was to be no open fireplace, she put her foot down, and she prevailed. Built of Sydney bluestone to match the terrace outside, it became a key feature of the living room, along with Bill's art collection. In pride of place was a bespoke glass showcase for the T'ang horse Bill had bought in New York.

Shirley said that Bill was responsible for the other change to the building plans. 'In his passion to have as much storage space as possible, he began to dig into the hillside from the stackroom . . . which was, in effect, a tunnel under the house. When Ernst Plischke discovered this, he was appalled. He told Bill that he was undermining the house, and I was told he brought tram rails from the Council . . . to hold up the floor above. . . . Bill had this lined with shelves, and it is to this day [in 1998] full of stuff which has hardly been touched for over twenty years.'[42]

41 AGS to author, interview, 28 February 2011.
42 SHSS memoir, 'Life with Bill – 3', undated (1998), pp.3–4, SHSS papers.

15

Hungary

AFTER SIX YEARS of making do in the flat on The Terrace, the move to the new house in Todman Street in September 1956 was a momentous event. Settling in would have been easier for Shirley had she not also been working towards her final law exams. Then came a bombshell that shattered her political faith.

While not a Party member, Shirley had not yet broken with the communists. Like other liberal communists, she hoped that Stalin's death in 1953 would open the way to a more democratic leadership under his successor Nikita Khrushchev. Instead, the New Zealand Communist Party allied itself with the Maoists, who adhered to hard-line Stalinist principles.[1]

The conflict came to a head with the publication of Khrushchev's secret speech at the 20th Party Congress on 25 February 1956. His 26,000-word report denounced Stalin, exposing evidence of his monstrous despotism. It said he was responsible for the murder of thousands of loyal Party members in purges between 1936 and 1938, the deportation of whole nations from their countries of origin, violent anti-Semitism, the use of torture to obtain 'confessions', shooting Soviet generals on false charges of treason, and – in Party terms his greatest crime – for carrying the 'cult of the individual' to extreme lengths to raise himself above the Party and all else.

Shirley told James McNeish in 1998 that she saw the report when it first came out in New Zealand. 'When Bill came home he said, "Well, so you've read it. I suppose it's a lot of old cobblers." I said no, I think

1 Kerry Taylor, 'Scott, Sidney Wilfred', from *Dictionary of New Zealand Biography*. Te Ara – the Encyclopedia of New Zealand, updated 11 February 2014, http://www.TeAra.govt.nz/en/biographies/4s15/scott-sidney-wilfred; George Fraser, *Seeing Red: Undercover in 1950s New Zealand*, Dunmore Press, 1995. Former Party Secretary Sid Scott bitterly opposed leaders Vic Wilcox, Hugh McLeod and Bill Anderson on this issue.

one must take it seriously.' She presumably said much more, provoking Bill to say he couldn't discuss it with her, she was too emotional, and he 'swept out of the room'. It became a taboo subject between them. 'Of course it hurt him so much to discover his god had feet of clay.' McNeish recorded her as saying that Bill was 'a Moscow right-or-wrong Marxist'.[2]

She herself didn't doubt that the revelations were true. She said later that she hadn't believed that Marshal Tukhachevsky (executed just before the war) was guilty; nor the old Bolsheviks, or Slánsky in Czechoslovakia and the other post-war victims (Dimitrov, the Reichstag fire man in Bulgaria); nor that the Yugoslavs became 'running dogs of capitalism' when they refused to join the USSR. She was nevertheless shocked at the breadth and depth of Stalin's tyranny.

She read the warning by Howard Fast, Stalin Peace Prize winner for 1953, who wrote that Khrushchev's report gave no assurance that the last execution had taken place on Soviet soil, nor pledges on civil rights, the sacred right of *habeas corpus*, public appeal to higher courts, or final judgments of one's peers rather than by professional judges.[3] Shirley hoped these things could still come.

Her optimism was shared, even by her father. Sir David Smith, in his capacity as Chancellor of the University of New Zealand, joined a New Zealand delegation to Russia in September 1956. He wrote to

2 SHSS to James McNeish, interview, 4 May 1998, transcript pp.7–8, James McNeish papers. Shirley said in the same interview, 'He wasn't a communist. He never joined the communist party. I know that because I was a member up to 1956. I was, yes.' Other records, including Shirley's accounts, state that she was in contact with the Communist Party and sympathetic until 1956 but that she left the Party in 1945. She apparently didn't consider that Bill could have been a 'crypto communist'. Economist Brian Easton, who has written extensively about Sutch, concluded Sutch was not a Marxist but was 'very pro-Soviet': to author, email, 8 January 2018. Easton explains his thinking in his essay, 'Trying to Understand Dr Sutch', September 1998. He adds, 'Some of my attempts to nail Sutch have their humorous side. I went through his book case at home, and yes there are texts by Marx in it, but some had the name of his father-in-law, Sir David Smith, on the fly leaf. Sir David, a judge of the high court, was unlikely to be a Marxist. More probably he was an intelligent concerned intellectual, interested in important ideas of the day.' https://www.eastonbh.ac.nz/1998/09/trying_to_understand_dr_sutch/ (accessed 9 October 2018).

3 Howard Fast, *New York Daily Worker*, quoted in London Letter, *Here & Now*, July 1956, p.24.

Shirley that the Russians had to be judged in many matters by the improvements they had made.

The enthusiasm in university circles for greater freedom is immense. Since 1953, there has been more food and more freedom . . . We could go everywhere and photograph anything. We saw some terrible dwellings but I didn't photograph them. It wouldn't have been fair. They have done so much to replace their slums with modern buildings. They are on their way to better things – I'm sure they don't want war. . . . their fundamental attitude must, I believe, be one of as friendly coexistence as practicable.[4]

All hopes for an enlightened Kremlin were shattered when the Red Army crushed the people's uprising in Hungary.

What started in Budapest in the last week of October as a peaceful student rally for reform erupted into a bloody street battle with Soviet troops firing on unarmed protesters. This in turn provoked a nationwide people's uprising against Soviet rule. Initially Russian troops backed off, but on 4 November, after newly elected Prime Minister Imre Nagy announced Hungary's withdrawal from the Warsaw Pact, the Soviet army invaded. Their tanks rolled into Budapest before dawn and attacked. Thousands were killed or wounded, tens of thousands were jailed or sent to the Soviet Union and the leaders were executed. Some 200,000 refugees fled the country.

That, Shirley said, is when she clearly split with the Communist Party.[5]

Over the next weeks and months, the Party in New Zealand saw its

4 DSS to SHSS, 25 September 1956, DSS papers.

5 SHSS to Brian Easton, 5 July 1997, Brian Easton papers. Dist. Off. Wgtn, 19 March 1957, SHSS PF, Relative to William [Willis] Thomas Goodwin Airey, SHSS, WBS and Harold Winton Rhodes (copied 27 February 1958, received 20 March 1958), p.2: *to William Thomas Goodwin Airey, SHSS, WBS and Harold Winton Rhodes allied with the Communist movement until the revelations of the 20th Congress of the CPSU were made, and the cleavage occurred in the NZ Communist Party through Soviet policy in Hungary. Report of Senior Detective A. R. Grant, Superintendent of Police, Special Branch, Christchurch, 4 April 1957, relative to Shirley Smith 'on adverse record', quotes a letter from SHSS, details withheld: 'You may be interested to know that I do not accept the Soviet line on Hungary and have been reviewing my views. Not that this was the beginning of doubt – it was the end. Shirley.'*

membership decimated. Rallying the dissidents, former Party secretary Sid Scott called for a new kind of socialist party that allowed free expression. It was to be founded on 'respect for and faith in people' and based in New Zealand. This last, he said, would mean the end of the 'Soviet Union – right or wrong' attitude.[6]

This gave something to dissidents who were struggling not only with disillusionment but also bitter antipathy between themselves and their former comrades, who saw them as traitors. Friendships ended, marriages were strained or broke down completely. Detective Sergeant David Paterson of Special Branch in Wellington wrote in Shirley Smith's security file that the dissidents maintained 'friendship and personal contact with one another and all appear to have suffered emotionally since breaking with the Communist Party.'[7]

He referred specifically to Elsie Locke's 'clandestine and intimate correspondence' with Shirley Smith, which had been intercepted in a post office in Christchurch 'under delicate circumstances'. (It was then illegal under the Post Office Act for anyone to open another person's mail.) Elsie wrote that she was writing 'under the nose of the enemy, as it were' – referring to her husband Jack. She feared 'her home would be shattered and her family divided' if she allied herself with Sid Scott. She intended to stand by Jack personally.[8]

For both Elsie and Shirley, Hungary was a breaking point. Immediately after the Soviets invaded, Shirley went down to Christchurch to be with Elsie. They worked out their positions, prepared a manifesto and supported each other.

Between Shirley and Bill, the subject of the Soviet Union remained almost taboo, but Shirley warned Bill of the risks of airing his pro-Soviet views with others.[9] He had that year been promoted to Deputy Secretary of Industries and Commerce and desperately wanted the top job.

6 S. W. Scott, 'Where Do We Go From Here?', *Here & Now*, December 1956, pp.18–19.

7 Special Branch spy George Fraser, who reported to Paterson, was tasked to find out the impact of Soviet action in Hungary on the dissident group. SHSS PF, NZSIS.

8 Elsie Locke to SHSS, 'Friday' (11 November 1956, date of enclosed authorisation to Shirley to append her signature to the Statement on Hungary), copy, SHSS PF, NZSIS.

9 SHSS to WBS during his absence overseas in 1958, quoted in letter to MHS, 28 November 1994.

While Shirley feared Bill's pro-Soviet views would harm his ambitions, Jack Locke feared Elsie's anti-Soviet views would damage his as the Communist Party candidate in the Municipal elections. And he intended to stand for Parliament in 1957. Elsie was sure he was under pressure from the Party to cast her off. Things were very difficult between them for a while. 'Fancy you remembering us having the double bed cut in half – one half on either side of the room, against the walls,' she wrote to Shirley in 1999. 'That was my initiative, not Jack's. I had hurt my back quite badly (it still wasn't strong after my long illness) and I was very restless and we agreed I'd do better sleeping alone. We bought a new bed after a while and snuggled up happily – keeping clear of divisive topics. As you perceived, it paid off. We were together emotionally with the family intact.'[10]

Elsie recalled that Shirley was the only one of her friends with any understanding of these things.[11] They both felt terribly alone at times.

After Shirley's visit to Christchurch, Elsie decided that, having resigned from the Communist Party, she had to let it be known that she and Jack had honest differences of opinion. She gave Shirley permission to append her signature to her 'Statement on Hungary', the manifesto they had written together, addressed to the Government of the USSR.[12]

The statement declared that the signatories could not accept the official line from Moscow, that the Hungarian People's Government had asked the Soviet Union to repress a fascist attempt at counter-revolution.

For many years, we as friends of the Soviet Union, have accepted official statements at their face value, only to find, as a result of the truths revealed at the 20th Congress, that we have spent much time sincerely and earnestly justifying what could not be justified, and for whatever share our uncritical acceptance has had in the strengthening and perpetration of error, we are responsible. We can now, therefore, only discharge our responsibility as friends by basing our judgment on the facts as we see them.

10 Elsie Locke to SHSS, 8 July 1999, SHSS papers, ATL, MS-Papers-11369-039.
11 Elsie Locke to SHSS, 24 July 1999, SHSS papers, ATL, MS-Papers-11369-039.
12 Elsie Locke to SHSS, 'Friday' (11 November 1956), copy, SHSS PF, NZSIS.

Far away as we are and few and prejudiced as are our sources of information, we are convinced that the uprising in Hungary was a national popular movement to protest against the admitted excesses of the secret police and other mistakes of the Rakosi Government. . . .

The Soviet Union has, by its action in Hungary, struck such a blow at its own declared policy of peaceful co-existence and the self-determination of peoples, and done such damage to the cause of socialism as could never have been done by the setting up even of an unfriendly government in Hungary. . . .

We urge the leaders and people of the Soviet Union to do all that can be done to repair the results of this terrible mistake; to allow the entry of relief supplies, to withdraw their armed forces, to help actively in healing the ravages caused by the fighting; finally, to reaffirm and act upon their policy of peace and five principles which have been made the basis of agreements with the Indian and other peoples.

Shirley's friend Professor Willis (Bill) Airey returned a signed copy of the statement.[13] He sent her copies of letters and statements he had written as Deputy Chairman of the New Zealand Peace Council. The general reaction of the World Peace Council to Hungary was much the same as that of the New Zealand Communist Party, 'to regard the Soviet action in Hungary as a mistake'.[14]

Wellington's Special Branch intercepted this letter and his signed copy of the Statement on Hungary, and submitted them with a report to Wellington Headquarters dated 19 March 1957. Director of the new Security Service Brigadier H. E. Gilbert commented on the naïvety of the authors, but he was interested in the views expressed, especially as they were the views of Shirley Smith. Another copy of the statement had come into his hands some days earlier, from Sam Barnett.

13 'Statement on Hungary' to the Government of the USSR, 12 November 1956. SHSS PF, NZSIS. There are two copies of the statement, one that Shirley provided via Sam Barnett, the other signed by Willis Airey. Airey told Shirley that Sid Scott would sign it, and Shirley probably collected many other signatures, as she recalled distributing it widely.

14 Airey wrote on 31 October – before the British and French had struck at Suez, creating another major crisis.

Sam Barnett had by then set up the new Security Service and was overseeing its transitional period (28 November 1956 to 1 August 1957) after which it would take over full operations under Gilbert. The timing coincided with Sutch's bid for promotion.

Earlier in 1956, when Bill Sutch was being considered for the position of Deputy Secretary of Industries and Commerce, Barnett visited the American Embassy in Wellington to ask whether they had any reason to consider Sutch a poor security risk and whether, if he got the post, the Embassy would issue him with a visa. He explained that he thought Sutch was 'probably the best economist in New Zealand' and he didn't want 'to condemn a man of Dr Sutch's great ability to lose out on a promotion to which he seemed eminently deserving from a professional viewpoint merely on the basis of unsubstantiated rumour and "bar-room chatter"'.[15]

The embassy's files on Sutch revealed only that he was suspected of 'pro-Communist leanings'. Their main concern was a lecture he gave in July 1952 about the Korean War 'that went right down the Communist line'. After Sam Barnett's enquiries, the reporting officer made his own enquiries of a Special Branch officer who advised that Sutch was a 'full-scale security risk' – backing up his view with the information on his security file, which Barnett had considered low-grade. The FBI files then carried that assessment, including references to both Sutch's wife and sister having associations with communist-front organisations. (As an example of intelligence files getting things doubly wrong, they note that 'Shirley Hilda STANLEY, as she usually calls herself (having gotten special dispensation to be known by her maiden name) . . .'[16]

Based on reports in the Embassy's files, plus the above information, the Embassy recommended against issuing Dr Sutch a visa to the United States if he were to apply for it in either a private or public capacity.

Sutch was appointed one of three Assistant Secretaries of Industries and Commerce. When it was known that Secretary P. B. Marshall was to resign on 10 April 1957, Sutch was considered the most suitable

15 W. Kling, First Secretary, American Embassy, Wellington, Confidential Foreign Service Despatch to the Department of State, Washington DC, 15 February 1956, in FBI 100-HQ-353048.

16 Ibid.

applicant to replace him, but for his poor security status. According to Shirley, National Party Minister Tom Shand leaked to Sutch that *she* was the snag in his promotion because of her communist background. (She was sworn to secrecy never to disclose who this was, or what followed, but in 1976, after Shand's death, she spoke of it in an interview with Chief Parliamentary Correspondent Alistair Rowe.) Sam Barnett then arranged a private interview between her and Brigadier Gilbert, so that she could explain her past and present relationship with the Communist Party.[17]

The interview took place on 15 March 1957, just three days after Gilbert's appointment was announced. In his handwritten summary of the interview, Gilbert wrote that Shirley spoke frankly about having been a Communist Party member while in Wellington in 1944–45. She said that she had made no contact with any persons known to her as communists while in the United States, that back in New Zealand in 1951 she had approached Hugh McLeod (Sid Scott's successor as Party Secretary) with the idea of rejoining the Party but was advised against it and that, although she had supported various causes, such as the protest against the Niue Islanders' death sentence, she had become increasingly disillusioned with Communism and taken no part knowingly with any Communist Party or communist-inspired activities since 1951. She described her revulsion against the Soviet State arising from Khrushchev's speech and the Hungarian affair.[18]

She explained that the Statement on Hungary represented her views on the Hungarian issue, except that it was deliberately slanted in the direction of friendship towards Russia (coming from the New Zealand Society for Closer Relations with Russia) with the intention of making it more acceptable to the Russian Government and so possibly leading to a change of Russian policy towards Hungary. Brigadier Gilbert thought this naïve, but he accepted the statement as genuine.

17 SHSS PF, NZSIS.

18 Gilbert's report of the interview, SHSS PF, NZSIS. Shirley recalled that she submitted a letter from her to Elsie Locke at the time of her interview, to support her case. Gilbert recorded that she spoke about her correspondence. She may have shown him her letter of 12 March, if she had not posted it then. This letter came into the Security Service's hands later 'in delicate circumstances'.

Following her interview, Reuel Lochore, head of security in the Prime Minister's department, wrote a new report on Sutch. Regarding the 'Communist-inspired' organisations and causes with which Shirley had been associated since 1951, he wrote:

These activities, fairly harmless in themselves, may show that Mrs SUTCH'S aloofness from the Communist Party is due to grounds of expediency rather than to any radical change of view, and that she continues to support the Communist cause in general. While she is in other respect frank in conveying her views, there was a marked disingenuousness in her address of November 1951 in which, speaking of McCarthyism in the United States, she is quoted thus:–

She could not help being concerned with the Red Bogey hysteria sweeping throughout the country. She herself had been called a Red whilst there.

He knew that she had been in contact with communists in the United States and also that, on her return to New Zealand, she had agreed to help the Communist Party. Regarding the Statement on Hungary, Lochore continued:

The document implies a fundamental challenge to the previously accepted infallibility of Soviet Russia, and if it is accepted as a genuine expression of Mrs SUTCH'S views, it will do much to remove security suspicion from her. The document is known to be genuine as it is identical word for word with another copy signed by 'WILLIS AIREY' which came into our possession some days ago. It is known that some leading dissidents who are close friends of Mrs SUTCH (S. SCOTT, W. AIREY, E. LOCKE) support this statement, and if Mrs SUTCH claims also to support it, there is every reason to accept her word in this respect. The effects of the Hungarian dissident movement have yet to be determined in detail, but they will undoubtedly lessen greatly the subversive element in the political activities of this whole group of left-wing intellectuals. (This concerns Mrs SUTCH only and not her husband, whose attitude to events in Hungary is unknown.)[19]

19 Lochore, Annex, 19 March 1957, SHSS PF, NZSIS.

As to whether her former Communist Party membership and present Party associations represented a security danger, he concluded that it was safe to take a much more lenient view in consideration of her attitude to the Hungarian question, '. . . and the political views of husband and wife are so similar that Mrs SUTCH probably adds little to whatever risk is inherent in the views of her husband.'[20]

But ten days later, Detective Sergeant D. S. Paterson, Special Branch, Wellington, referred to a letter to Shirley from Sid Scott, found in a rubbish tin in the street outside her office. (Shirley used her office address for all her correspondence with dissidents.) The letter implied that her husband held the view that Soviet intervention was justified and necessary.[21]

An assessment in a report for Prime Minister Sid Holland on 14 March – the day before Shirley's interview – concluded:

Dr W. B. Sutch is believed not to be, nor ever to have been, a member of any Communist Party or subservient organisation. He is not known ever to have propounded subversive doctrines such as the establishment of a dictatorship of the proletariat. Nevertheless, his Marxist-Leninist approach to problems, coupled with his independence of mind and his acceptance of the infallible rectitude of the policies of the Soviet State, have led him in his official work into judgments and actions which have been unacceptable to his employers and have generally been interpreted by them as indicating disloyalty to themselves and as the denial of their policies. There is no indication that such incidents will not recur. He is not considered a person to whom highly classified information can be safely entrusted.[22]

This last point referred to the British Government's proviso since 1937 (when MI5 suspected Sutch of a security breach) that Sutch not have

20 Ibid.

21 Detective Sergeant D. S. Paterson, 29 March 1957, copied on 14 October 1957, relative to William Ball Sutch, Shirley Hilda Stanley Sutch and Sidney Wilfred Scott, SHSS PF, NZSIS. The letter, thought to have been written in 1957, was considered important because the comment 'Unfortunately, [Tom Crawford] is rather on Bill's line as far as the Soviet Union is concerned, and Hungary' appeared to place Scott's friend Tom Crawford (known to Special Branch) and Sutch in the communist camp, at least ideologically.

22 Report, 14 March 1957, SHSS PF, NZSIS.

access to secret information they provided. Also, the United States now informed the New Zealand Government that they would 'regard New Zealand's security as suspect' if Sutch were appointed Secretary to Industry and Commerce.[23]

As Shirley said later, she knew nothing of this at the time. She believed that by showing she was not a security risk, she had cleared the way for Bill's promotion. But that was a way off yet.[24] Meanwhile the position remained vacant.

SHIRLEY FELL SICK immediately after the interview. Elsie invited her to stay for Easter, but she was too ill to travel. She fretted about being off work for so long, 'just when I wanted to buy new winter under- and outer-wear for Helen and me. *And* I owe bills for car maintenance and books.' She added in the margin that all Bill's money was tied up in the house.[25]

With time to read, think and write, Shirley continued to re-examine what she had earlier accepted as facts, trying to distinguish political reality from myth. She discussed these things with a friend, Max Wilkinson, who had been a revolutionary in China. He was a member of the Communist Party but he questioned the Party line, especially on Hungary. In his doubt, he wrote to a British journalist in China called Nan Green, a staunch Communist Party woman, asking for her views. He showed her reply to Shirley. She thought it a dreadful letter, 'written from *inside* un-reality – right inside.' Bringing Elsie into the discussion, she sent her copies of both Nan Green's letter and her own exposition of it, point-by-point. She saw the need to 'uncover the facts from the mist of myth-making. For . . . if we do not start from a clear-eyed facing of the actual facts we cannot do or think anything right.'[26]

23 The Security Service informed Nash of this when he became Prime Minister at the end of 1957. Keith Sinclair, *Walter Nash*, AUP/OUP, 1976, kindle edition loc 10567 of 15006.

24 SHSS to Alistair Rowe as quoted in his article, 'University Faces Order by SIS for cuts from Nash Story', publication and date unidentified (1976), SHSS PF, NZSIS. The suggestion that her husband was blocked from becoming head of Industries and Commerce in 1958 surprised Shirley. She explained how she was officially cleared of being a security risk herself.

25 SHSS to Elsie Locke, 14 April 1957, SHSS papers, ATL, MS-Papers-1609784.

26 Ibid.

At the heart of the matter were the questions related to truth, reality and falsehood, the great ponderables that confronted Shirley in her studies at Oxford and were re-examined throughout her life:

So-called truths need constant re-examination, measuring against reality, and revision in the light of new facts. The one unchanging truth of Marxism is that truth is always relative; what was genuinely 'true' for Newton is imperfectly so for Einstein, who had to enlarge his concepts to cover factors of which Newton did not know and could not have known. 'Truth' is not a thing-in-itself . . . it is the most complete and accurate synthesis that can be made at any given time of all the then known opposing and conflicting factors relevant to the particular enquiry, i.e. factors in whatever field is under discussion, politics, economics, science etc. Why should the formulations made by Marx at one particular point in time and space, or by Lenin at another, be exempt from this rule? Are not the present Facts *of politics and economics different from what they were at either of those times? Marxism has always taken pride in being* Scientific *Socialism; but a scientist measures his theories against the facts and if the theories don't cover the facts, he reverses his theories. What so-called Marxists have been doing is to say that the theories can't be wrong, therefore the facts are. This leads to a descent into unreality and consequently to weakness. Those who insist on dealing with this method of facts do more harm to Socialism than all the capitalists in Wall St. and the City.*[27]

Seeing both Americans and Stalinists as self-deluded victims of their own propaganda brought to her mind lines from Meredith, which Shirley misquoted, tellingly, for Elsie as 'No villain need be when passion spins the plot . . . we are betrayed by what is false within.'

'Though of course,' she added, 'there might be a few villains about too.'[28]

27 SHSS, 'Comments on Nan Green's letter', 1957, pp.1–2, SHSS papers, ATL, MS-Papers-1609784.

28 SHSS to Elsie Locke, 14 April 1957, SHSS papers, ATL, MS-Papers-1609784.

16

Love from Bill

In 1957 Shirley graduated with a Bachelor of Laws. Her father, as Chancellor of the University of New Zealand, capped her in the town hall. Helen wore a dress Shirley made for the occasion and presented her mother with a bouquet of flowers as she came down from the stage. David Smith and Bill later saw her admitted to the Bar by her father's old friend, Mr Justice Stanton.

Shirley continued working part-time for Duncan, Matthews and Taylor, and she returned to Victoria to teach Roman Law, the first woman in New Zealand to be appointed to a Law faculty. As when she taught Latin at Auckland University College during the war, she had a large unruly class of over100 predominantly male adolescents who would rather have been elsewhere.

In the first year after moving to Brooklyn, Shirley and Bill gave a series of dinner parties in their new house. While Bill showed his guests around, Shirley struggled in the badly designed kitchen, which had not received the attention given the rest of the house. Not only was it inferior to kitchens in state houses being built at the time, but she also complained that it was designed for tall people. In other respects the house was beautiful, especially with the ceramics, paintings, rugs and furniture Bill had collected, but as a home it didn't function as she wished.

Even the fireplace that she had insisted on wasn't effective initially. Margaret Long (formerly Brand) recalled that when she went to dinner there, if Bill was dining with them the table would be set and everything was beautiful, but when he was away, Shirley would put a rug on the floor and they'd eat by the fire, sitting up close to it because it didn't throw out the heat. To solve this, she fitted a wooden baffle board, which her father replaced with one of corrugated iron. She recalled that when Plischke saw it while showing someone over 'his masterpiece' he pulled it out in a fury. She understood how he felt because it looked awful, but it worked.[1]

She was nevertheless indignant that their home came to be known as the Sutch House. She said she put up half the money – the sale of her grandmother's house in Auckland had made it possible.[2] But she apparently never knew the total cost. 'My husband was his own contractor, employing sub-contractors, and he always said he never added up what it cost,' she explained to Linda Tyler.[3]

This begs further questions, considering Shirley's feminist views. Regardless of what she contributed, it was their joint family home.

After a year or so the parties stopped. Helen recalls their flat on The Terrace as 'a place of light and laughter and people dropping in', but while Shirley liked to talk and laugh and have a beer, Bill didn't, and now their social life just fell away as he devoted himself to work, writing and the garden.[4]

Things relaxed when he was away. During his six-month trip in 1958, Shirley entertained a great deal, providing teas and high teas for her friends and Helen's, all with apparent ease.

Bill's big trip in 1958 was with the New Zealand Trade Delegation to London to review the Ottawa Agreement with the United Kingdom. This was an anxious time, waiting to hear whether he would be appointed Secretary of Industries and Commerce. The Labour Government had come to power at the end of 1957 and Walter Nash, now Prime Minister, favoured his former economic advisor, but nothing was certain. While Bill was overseas Shirley sent him what news she could get from Sam

1 SHSS to MHS, 26 November 1994, MHS papers. Allan Smith thought Shirley never really appreciated the house. Others commented that it was like a museum. Margaret Long told the author Bill wanted the loveliest house, but he didn't want it for Shirley, he wanted it for himself.

2 Decades after Bill had died and Shirley had lived in the house for over forty years, she protested, 'His modernist house! – riles me – I put up half the money . . .' SHSS to Brian Easton, 2 November 1998, Brian Easton papers.

3 SHSS to Linda Tyler, School of Fine Arts, University of Canterbury, 29 May 1984, SHSS papers.

4 MHS to author, interview, 1 September 2011.

Barnett and Allan Atkinson, who was Acting Secretary, and from Jack Lewin. Bill instructed his office to pass on all letters and cables to Shirley during his absence.[5]

Bill's letters to Shirley over the next months show him winning back Shirley's love. The background isn't clear but it may well have related to an affair Bill had around this time. Shirley knew he had affairs and that others also knew. Later she would shrug off his philandering as something to be expected of men in that era (adding that she herself was too busy to have affairs). In this case Bill wanted to make amends.[6]

There were other things that troubled Shirley. Bill still considered that whatever he did was right. She wrote to Brian Easton in 2000, 'He was *very* wilful, he did exactly what he wanted to do . . . But he got very good at understanding what I would object to, so he never told me in advance. I doubt if he'd have listened, anyway, but at least I'd have been forewarned.'[7]

Before Bill left in April, they had some kind of reconciliation, which led Shirley to address other aspects of their relationship, including their domestic roles, surprisingly for the first time. Bill took this on board and her response then encouraged him to express himself more freely.

His first letter was written late at night on Tuesday 8 April from his hotel in Auckland before flying out the next day. Shirley had dropped him off at his office the previous Thursday, then left with Helen to spend Easter at Taupō with her father. After describing how he spent Easter, Bill continued:

I find I was most of the time thinking solely of you this Easter, wanting to talk to you, wanting to write to you, wanting to be with you. When Helen turned round in the car on Thursday morning and said 'Daddy, you look

5 WBS PF, p.14, NZSIS.

6 NZSIS PFs; Julie Grenfell to author, interview, 9 April 2014; Margaret Long to author, interview, 27 May 2011; other sources. One affair noted in 1958 was with his secretary, Aileen Finucane. Because of her 'subversive' activities, notably her involvement with SCR and the Peace Council, the Security Service had a file on her. Shirley subsequently had a long friendship with Aileen and Aileen's partner Max Wilkinson.

7 SHSS to Brian Easton, 22 August 2000, Brian Easton papers. This was in relation to Bill's meetings with a Russian KGB agent in 1974, but it was something she struggled with throughout their marriage.

happy' she had insight. I was happy. You had put your arm round me coming up the drive. It was that that made the difference and it has meant that I leave on this trip feeling much more light-hearted and secure.

He continued carefully:

I told you on Wednesday night that I needed you. I do. I don't want to sound selfish at a very difficult time for you, [a reference in part to her law class] *nor do I want to be selfish. I know that because of my approach to life I often am, that is, from another person's point of view. I know too that sometimes my methods of helping you may be irritating. I've just got to try to do better. I think I understand a little better than I used to. And while I've always said I believed in a cooperative partnership I'm beginning to get a better realisation of what it means. You can well say that I've taken a long time over it. I can only agree, and hope that your deep generosity will stretch a little further.*

. . .

Thank you and Helen for your telegram. It was good to be shown to this room and find your message there. . . .

Goodnight darling,

Bill.[8]

From Honolulu, after reading the Bible by his bed, he wrote her a postcard with a list of verses from the Old Testament.[9] He explained later how they applied to her.

In New York, the Hubermans organised a party for him. After writing about their affection for Shirley and Helen he continued:

You know how I discussed with you whether I should see the Hubys. It was impossible not to. I just feel it would be the last straw. So instead of confining myself to New Zealanders, I decided that my friends were my friends. And towards the end of the afternoon I called on Otto Nathan and

8 WBS to SHSS, 8 April 1958, pp.4–6, SHSS papers, ATL, MS-Papers-11404-15.

9 WBS to SHSS, 9 April 1958, SHSS papers, ATL, MS-Papers-11404-15. Solomon I, 15 & 16, Solomon VI 9 & 10, Solomon VII especially 10, Psalms 119, 5, 7, 59, 68, 96, 173, Psalms 138, 1, Proverbs III, 15.

spent a long time with him. . . .

Otto was, of course, full of you and Helen. It fills me with wonderment – and I feel very humble – when a man like Otto can include me in his affections. I can understand you for you are good and fine. And I can understand Helen, but not me. And it is not my economics they like me for. The warmth of our New York friends is very touching and encouraging. Otto, the Hubys and Sybil [May] *are such genuine people that I feel ashamed that I had so far compromised as to consider not seeing them. You may say that this is romantic and unreal of me. Probably it is. But I'm sure I was right.*[10]

Shirley replied:

I am concerned about what seems to be a misconception of my attitude e.g. re. seeing the Hubys etc. I always put it conditionally; if *you want advancement,* then *such and such actions are necessary. Conversely, I always told you that if you decided to do exactly what you wanted and be damned to the consequences, I would back you all the way. Of course, humanly speaking, it was right to see the Hubys; I only ask that you be clear about the risk and accept it – and I mean, accept truly inwardly. I did object about the Soviet party because I was involved and it looked like throwing away the effort I had made on your behalf. It was one of the most distasteful things I have ever done and I would never have done it for myself.*[11]

Finding this letter in 1994, Shirley didn't know what she had meant by the 'Soviet party', or what could have been so distasteful to her. The party may have been at the Soviet Embassy in Wellington, and it's likely that the effort she had made on Bill's behalf referred to her interview with Brigadier Gilbert, particularly giving the assurance that she had no contact with communists in New York, which she knew to be untrue. Her final remark makes sense in that light.

10 WBS to SHSS, 14 April 1958, pp.8–11, SHSS papers, ATL, MS-Papers-11404-15.

11 SHSS to MHS, 26 (sic. 28) November 1994, p.4. MHS papers. Shirley copied this from her original letter (not including the date). The author has not seen any of her original letters in this 1958 correspondence.

Bill replied from the Savoy Hotel in London on 30 April:

Tomorrow is May Day. I've been thinking how much this means to me and how sorry and uneasy I am that its celebration at least in the capitalist world seems to be more and more perfunctory and carried out by fewer people. Of course, it is but a sign of the difference between the thirties and the fifties and it also means that I haven't changed. I don't believe in capitalism, no matter how well developed its so-called welfare aspects may be. And I do believe in positive socialist alternatives which are evolutionary and enthusiastically striven for.

Maybe my sadness about May Day is an extension of my own sadness about myself. Whenever I lectured in the U.N. on international affairs or the Children's Fund or the history of anything I felt integrated, happy and honest. To stop this activity has hurt me even though I know I can continue and will continue to express myself and make a contribution to the present and the future.

He continued about his promotion:

Yes, I do want it and much more too. What I don't want is that the sacrifices you have made bring a final result that stultifies both you and me. It is hard to write about this, and perhaps harder to talk about it. But, and I'm reminded of this by your comment on my comments about visiting Huby, I don't want you to think that I feel you were advising me not to see him. I knew your qualification to this and you had said it clearly and I loved you for saying it (though I knew it was your position) that you would back me up all the way if I felt that my path was openly with the [handwriting unclear, possibly 'I&C', meaning Department of Industries and Commerce]. *My remarks about seeing Huby were rather meant as an answer to myself – that I could go too far in paying service to McCarthyism. But again I'm getting into deep water – I need* [handwriting unclear, possibly 'balance'] *to write all this down. But there's no need. We can talk about it later. But I did inwardly accept the risk of seeing Huby.*[12]

12 WBS to SHSS 30 April 1958, SHSS papers, ATL, MS-Papers-11404-15.

In his absence, Shirley bought a radio. (In fact, she bought two – one for Taupō as well.) When she confessed to this, Bill replied that he was going to bring one back for her, and he was glad that she had spent the money.

He wanted a photo of her. 'When I picture you it is sometimes with your hair done in your usual way and sometimes with your hair washed, either wet and dripping or dry and electric. So you can see that it is a picture of you that I would like. Could you send me one – even a little one! And I'd also like a recent one of Helen.'[13] He asked for Shirley's measurements to buy her a suit or frock, but before he had received her answer, he went shopping with Shirley's friend Margie Herrick ('the Bolter'), found a shop assistant Shirley's size and bought her a grey suit.

He was still apprehensive about his promotion. 'From that point of view I wish I were back in Wellington. And from my inner personal view I want to be back to be with you. From the long term career view I should stay here longer and get as much new experience as I can.' He wondered if Sam Barnett knew anything. Would she ring Sam and tell him that Bill still hadn't received his measurements or his tailor's address? Bill was to get Sam a suit.[14]

He finished his letter with thoughts about her difficult Roman Law class:

I suppose that there must be some compromises with a class of over 100. But I'd look to see the kind of compromise that takes less meaning out of the subject. In fact, it's not the kind of compromise that you would or could make, I'm glad to say. But there must be some allowance for the inadequate preparation that 90 per cent of your class have had.

I haven't put that very well. I've been thinking a lot about your Roman Law class, but I'm still not articulate enough to write it down. But I'm very pleased you are doing it.

Dear, I must go to bed. I do wish it were with you.

Love, Bill[15]

13 WBS to SHSS, 20 April 1958, SHSS papers, ATL, MS-Papers-11404-15.
14 WBS to SHSS, 15 May 1958, SHSS papers, ATL, MS-Papers-11404-15.
15 Ibid.

Four days later he wrote again:

And – at this late hour – a page boy bearing a silver salver has just brought me an air letter from you – dated 12th May – a week ago. In it were your measurements . . . and the answer to the request I made to you in my letter of the 15th – to find out from Sam what was going on.

Thank you, dear, for so promptly sending me the news from those who have good will towards us. I'm glad I received it so soon. But like you, I'll believe it when I see it in print and when they pay me the first month's salary.

. . .

Whether you are 35" or 36", 26" or 27", 37" or 38" my arms will still go round you. Love, Bill[16]

On their wedding anniversary he cabled her: 'June 2 is the most important date in my life'. On 12 June he wrote that he expected to stay on until the end of the month because the Ottawa talks would continue after the economic talks finished.

I've been re-reading your letter of May 29 in which you gave me reports of Sam, the mortgage, Tingeys, the [unclear, possibly A.C. for Architectural Centre] *Gallery and several successes with fines. I liked that letter. For some reason that I can't nail down I felt direct communication with you. I suppose it was a bit like our swapping news of the day as we came home from town in the car. I can see that our daily homecoming – you, Helen and me – has become a part of me which I value.*

. . .

I am enjoying the discussions in the various trade and finance committees. This has been very valuable to me. It could presage my accompanying the Minister (Nordmeyer) to Montreal in September. But the future is too fluid and uncertain to be certain of anything.[17]

16 WBS to SHSS, 19 May 1958, SHSS papers, ATL, MS-Papers-11404-15.
17 WBS to SHSS, 12 June 1958, SHSS papers, ATL, MS-Papers-11404-15.

17 June
Your letter discussed your emotional attitude to things, including me. My reaction to this was one of happiness. This letter, despite its bad tidings in other places, is, of those I've received from you, the one which gave me the most pleasure (or is it relief?). . . . I hope we shall be able to discuss it amiably and at length when we return. I shall genuinely try. I know I've tried before and I've got angry or gone silent, but I think I've been slowly changing and I believe I can do slowly better at examining my share of our life.

I have been conscious, of course, of your numbness and I've several times wondered, while I've been away, whether I should refrain from sending you enthusiastic communications – I mean those that show I'm enthusiastic about you – or even sending you clippings which would distract you and make you feel you had to read them. I realised that my actions in this were putting compulsions on you, but nevertheless, they were something positive and I felt it better to do what I did than to refrain.

But I know that these are minor compulsions compared with my major unfairness, that of not realising the damage I had done by my own compulsions on you. You may think this strange, but it has taken me a long time to realize that people feel the weight of my personality.

. . . and when I consciously try not to put pressure on you, it often consists, as you say, in self-abnegation which again is a pressure, though I do not intend it as such. But I hope you will regard this self-abnegation of mine as an almost frantic attempt to repair the damage I have done and also as a beginning of something better.

I am very dissatisfied with myself and these last 18 months of the difficulties associated with the [Industries and Commerce] *job have caused me to examine again my shortcomings. The result is a further lack of confidence in myself. This is the kind of thing I have always felt might happen if ever I went through a course of psycho-analysis.*

However, I only write this to show that I'm at the bottom of the trough and will take a lot of trial and error to get out of it. In effect it means an attempt to become emotionally mature, I suppose. But even this judgment may be wrong.

I know, too, that you are at the bottom of the trough. And there is not necessarily much difference between our reactions to political developments. I think perhaps that my adjustments were made over a very long period, rather than suddenly. Nevertheless I was glad I could recapture some of the old enthusiasm. It made me feel cleaner.

I can understand that my postcard sent from the Pacific must have been hard to take, but it was meant to express how I felt.

'I thought on my ways and have turned my feet unto thy testimony.'

You see, I wanted to tell you, and as my sister Shirley will tell you, I'm not very articulate, that I understood, at least a little, how you feel, and that I wanted your guidance. Do you recall:

'Thou art good and doest good; teach me thy statutes.'

and

'Let thine hand help me, for I have chosen thy precepts.'

and

'I have seen an end of all perfection; but thy commandment is exceeding broad.'

In my indirect way I was trying to tell you that the scales had been gradually falling from my eyes and that I didn't think that my arrogance would again stand in our way.

Those Biblical quotations said other things – mainly in worship of you. I felt that they might jar on you, but I wanted to say them. If there was still too much self-abnegation in them, they nevertheless expressed my feelings. And as I suggested earlier, I think you can grow out of self-abnegation.

And it's my hope that you will continue to be like Alice, growing upwards. Anyway, I'll try to lift the weight off your shoulders.

There's a lot unsaid. But maybe we can say it one day.

Goodnight dear,

Bill.[18]

Shirley cabled Bill when she received this letter, and again for his birthday. He replied that he was glad she sent them.

They were positive and warming. Your letter written before the cables made me a bit sad – for you were in the midst of your Roman Law and had

18 WBS to SHSS, 17 June 1958, pp.10–18, SHSS papers, ATL, MS-Papers-11404-15.

reported on your appearance before the Supreme Court. I was sad because of the nervous exhaustion of more work than you can handle and because of the emotional depression that your relations with D.M. & T. [Duncan, Matthews & Taylor] *is bringing you. And I was sad that I couldn't be with you at such a time. If I can be of any help to you at all I feel that it is now – this year. And I am in London.*

I know so well how a person can be continuously apprehensive, self-doubting and drained of energy because of relationships with the job. I have been like this for years and in recent times, as you know, it has been worse.

It is no comfort to know that you also are familiar with such feelings which could lead to despair.

I wonder whether it is partly because we set ourselves a standard of achievement which others don't have and how much we project our own doubts and shortcomings into the minds of others.

If we looked at ourselves objectively we would, while recognising whatever human shortcomings we have, know that our achievement is a reasonable one. Yours is. The fact that you were chosen to lecture in R.L. is a sign of achievement. The fact that you can take a case in the Supreme Court is an achievement at this early stage in your career. There are many in the profession who have been there many years and cannot do as well. . . .

And above all, of course, is a burden greater than any one person should ever bear – a day time job, your and my parents, housework, outside activity, entertaining and a husband who could be a greater help than he has been. We know all these things, but your burden continues.

The essential we agree on is help in the house, at a time when the supply of appropriate help seems to have dried up. We must solve the help problem.

But above all, dear, don't think that you can't be good in the law. You are good. And, given some health and an easing of the work load you will yourself be reassured on the quality of your thinking and performance.

. . .

Goodnight darling. I want to give you all the support I can and I'm sorry I am away from you. I want you to be able to rely on me to help you take the strain.[19]

19 WBS to SHSS, 7 July 1958, SHSS papers, ATL, MS-Papers-11404-15.

Bill expected to be home by the end of July, after a visit to Cairo to discuss a trade deal with the Egyptian authorities, but he had difficulties, first in getting a visa, then a flight. He explained that Egypt was one of the pet projects of Minister of Industries and Commerce Phil Holloway, who hoped he (Bill) would pull off a big trade coup. 'The trouble is that my visit to Egypt has by now quite important political overtones. If I go it is a gesture by my government. If I don't go it is similarly a gesture but in the opposite sense.'[20]

In the event he did go at the end of July, on his way home.

BACK IN WELLINGTON Bill's appointment to Permanent Secretary of Industries and Commerce finally went through on 4 September – just before he departed again for the Commonwealth Economic Conference in Montreal.

He wrote to Shirley on 9 September, after a sleepless night:

Occasionally I would think of the job but always my mind (and probably my body) brought me back to you. I composed love letters to you, even though I realised that the third term in Roman Law was bogging you down. It was wonderful to feel so close to you and it was good to be kept awake by thoughts of you. I felt how wasteful it is to spend a day away from you.[21]

20 WBS to SHSS, 18 July 1958, SHSS papers, ATL, MS-Papers-11404-15.
21 WBS to SHSS, 9 September 1958, SHSS papers, ATL, MS-Papers-11404-15.

17

Going solo

In 1959 Shirley added Constitutional Law to the subjects she taught and, together with tutorials and editing Victoria's *Law Review*, it all added up to a full-time position. For the first time in her life she was earning decent money and could put some aside in savings.

Roman Law was dropped from the curriculum at the end of 1959. To mark its passing she threw a toga party, but she was sorry to see it go. She explained to Hugo Manson:

Roman Law is the basis of the Civil Law which they have in most of Europe and in Scotland and in many ways it's a much more rational approach than the Common Law, which is severely pragmatic and not always worked out on the best intellectual grounds. The Common Law tradition is terribly proud of itself. You'll find judges in England and here, or certainly in England, panegyrising Common Law and what a wonderful heritage it is, and so on, and young students who came straight to it from school kind of swallow all this uncritically. . . . I think it has impoverished the degree to take Roman Law out of it.[1]

As a lecturer at Victoria, Shirley found none of the sexual discrimination she had experienced at Auckland in the 1940s, with the exception of the law faculty dinner. The ban on women had been re-imposed. Once again she fought that and had the rule reversed.

Later, running her own practice as a barrister and solicitor in an almost wholly male domain, Shirley would find it much harder to get the Wellington District Law Society to include women at their dinners. As her colleague Jim Thomson saw it, the law dinner wasn't just a

1 This is from the oral history of Shirley Smith with Hugo Manson on 4 November 1988, commissioned by the New Zealand Law Society, Wellington Branch, side 3, ATL, OHInt-0082-02.

question of sexism for Shirley. She was asserting the kind of lawyer she was, not just a wallflower but 'one of you guys'.[2] Her tenacity paid off, but it took years.

Meanwhile her father kept telling her to 'come down from the ivory tower', that she was getting old and she had to find out before it was too late what it really was to be a lawyer. 'He told me that I should "earn my spurs in the heat and dust of the forum", a mixed metaphor which I understood to mean that I should return to the practice of the law, particularly in the courts.'[3] She thought he was right and decided to give up the security of her university work and set up her own law practice. Sir David explained in his memoir: '. . . she wanted to show that a woman could practise law on her own account and employ others to assist her instead of simply being employed as a law lecturer by a University or as a lawyer by a Government Department or large legal firm with the consequent advantage of a regular salary cheque.'[4]

But she didn't want to be stereotyped as a women's lawyer. As a student she had excelled at writing opinions in international and constitutional law and she loved the analytical thinking involved. 'I wanted to be a high flyer and do things that would take me to the Privy Council . . .'[5]

Keith Matthews and Nigel Taylor gave her a room in their office in the old T. G. McCarthy Trust Building on Lambton Quay for £1 a week. It had what she saw as Dickensian charm. In April 1961 she sent out cards announcing her new practice.

It was difficult for anyone, let alone a woman, to set up as a sole barrister and solicitor.[6] Her first year was extremely slow. She had to

2 Associate Judge Jim Thomson to author, 16 November 2013.

3 SHSS, 'My life in the law', *Claiming the Law: Essays by New Zealand Women in Celebration of the 1993 Suffrage Centennial*, eds. Elisabeth McDonald and Graeme Austin, VUW Law Review & VUP, May 1993, p.3.

4 DSS memoir, p.293.

5 This is from the oral history of Shirley Smith with Hugo Manson on 4 November 1988, commissioned by the New Zealand Law Society, Wellington Branch, side 5, ATL, OHInt-0082-02.

6 Others were Miss Ongley, who practised on her own; Miss Julia Dunn, who was a partner in her family firm; Mrs Marjorie Taylor, who was a partner in her husband's firm in Petone; and Olive Smuts-Kennedy. Shirley wrote that for some years she was the only woman principal. At that time, qualified women were rare and seldom seen outside their offices.

send monthly audit reports to the Law Society, advising them what she had in her trust account – 'nil, nil, nil . . . I would rather have kept it quiet. I survived . . . because I did not have to pay my own living expenses, and could pay practising fees, printing, rent . . . from my university salary savings. I also had a very small private income.'[7]

She took whatever work came her way. One of her first cases was an Italian law student, Renato Amato, who came to her about a dispute with the Public Service Commission regarding his student bond. Besides studying law, he was a published writer. Shirley offered him more than legal advice. After reading a story of his in *Landfall*, she suggested that his mind was 'possibly too creative for the law, which requires a coldly analytical, positively destructive bent. I don't mean that you should give up the law, but I feel that it is not creative enough to be your metier.'[8]

She was not alone in thinking him gifted. James K. Baxter, Maurice Shadbolt and other writers regarded him as an emerging talent when just three years later he died suddenly of a brain haemorrhage, aged thirty-five. A collection of Amato's short stories, *The Full Circle of the Travelling Cuckoo*, edited by Maurice Shadbolt, was published posthumously.

During her second year, Shirley looked after the practice of her colleague Olive Smuts-Kennedy. It was awful work, collecting debts for the College Debt Collecting Agency, but it kept her afloat.[9] Things looked up when a former extramural student, Byron O'Keefe, grateful to Shirley and Don Inglis for their support as lecturers, sent them clients related to his work at the Crown Lands Department in Napier. Shirley and Don worked together on these referrals for years, as solicitor on the record and counsel in court respectively.

Byron O'Keefe also sent Shirley clients for solicitor's work. Among them was a Napier farmer, Frank Steiner, who wanted to set up a

7 SHSS, 'My life in the law', *Claiming the Law: Essays by New Zealand Women in Celebration of the 1993 Suffrage Centennial*, eds. Elisabeth McDonald and Graeme Austin, VUW Law Review & VUP, May 1993, p.4.

8 SHSS to Renato Amato, 12 October 1961, SHSS papers, ATL, 2013-045-05.

9 This is from the oral history of Shirley Smith with Hugo Manson on 4 November 1988, commissioned by the New Zealand Law Society, Wellington Branch, side 5, ATL, OHInt-0082-02.

company to get around regulations preventing him from buying more land. Shirley was delighted. 'My father had specialised in company law, and I thought, "I'm away".'[10] She proposed setting up a company of ten; fortunately, the client had nine obliging relatives willing to hold one share each.

This job involved driving up to Napier, meeting my unusual and interesting client and his relations, and brought me a good deal more work, more visits to Napier and some acquaintance with the profession there, who did not appear to resent my poaching on their territory. This may have resulted from the known character of the clients sent me by Byron.[11]

After about three years, clients brought more clients and her practice grew exponentially. She undertook a wide range of work: cases on contract, tort, building disputes, immigration, conveyancing, tenancy, paternity, divorce and general domestic law and, later, matrimonial property and crime. Many cases related to traffic accidents (her clients were usually uninsured). She drafted wills, wound up estates, incorporated societies and continued to form small companies.

Despite not wanting to be typecast, she heard from both men and women that they wanted a woman lawyer. Some male clients told her they chose her because they thought that a woman would be more sympathetic.

Other writers and artists followed Renato Amato to her door. One satisfying case came via her friend Ray Grover, who asked her to defend artist and book collector David Cheer of Christchurch against the charge of importing indecent literature. Ray felt responsible. On a trip to Paris, he had come across two classics, *Justine* by the Marquis de Sade and another by Guillaume Apollinaire, bought them for David and had the bookseller post them. Customs picked them up and, though a police search found David had no pornography in his house, the case proceeded. Shirley took it pro bono and won.[12]

10 SHSS, 'My life in the law', *Claiming the Law: Essays by New Zealand Women in Celebration of the 1993 Suffrage Centennial*, May 1993, pp.4–5.

11 Ibid.

12 Ray Grover to author, interview, 24 February 2012. This probably occurred just before

She did a lot of pro bono work, sometimes simply because she felt strongly about an issue. On occasion it was enough to threaten court action, as when a client complained that her landlord insinuated she had to be 'rather nice' to him. After speaking to him, Shirley assured her client that if she had any more problems with that man, she'd take him to court for nothing.[13]

There was then no legal aid other than the little that came from the District Law Society. (In 1969 the Legal Aid Act established a Legal Aid Board, but even that didn't cover all costs.) Shirley thought it important to represent people who wouldn't otherwise be represented and, as a sole practitioner with no responsibility for the income of a legal partner, she had the freedom to take on cases, whether or not they paid. She was particularly keen to help young families. The following case is characteristic of how far she would go.

On 18 June 1962, house painter Ron Fackney fell off a ladder in the course of his employment, leaving him with serious head and spinal injuries. He was told he would never walk again. His head injury left him mentally unstable and this was aggravated by deep frustration and anger. Bob Adams, secretary of the Wellington Painters' Union and an old friend of Shirley's, sent Ron's wife Betty to her. Shirley not only took on the case but also became an advocate for Betty and their four young children.

Addressing their financial situation, Shirley found Ron had no grounds to sue his employer, since there was no evidence of negligence – the ladder remained tied to the railing on the top storey balcony after he fell. She looked at how he could get better value from his weekly payments of £10 5s in compensation plus £3, the total allowances for his five dependents. Paid out all together as a lump sum, calculated over a period of six years, this money could be invested to provide income on an ongoing basis. She went to the Compensation Court with a case for including his dependents' allowances in the lump sum to which he was entitled.[14] She argued that a discrepancy in the law showed it did

the new Indecent Publications Tribunal was established in 1964.

13 Joan Wooler to author, 4 June 2011.

14 Ron Fackney was entitled if it were to be assessed under s. 17 (6) of the Workers'

not reflect the intention behind it. However, the judge saw no room for doubt as to the legislature's intentions and they lost the case.

The case was reported and was the subject of an editorial in the *New Zealand Law Journal.* The editorial was sympathetic to Shirley's argument but added, 'This type of argument, however, is more a plea for the amendment of the legislation in the normal manner rather than the straining by the Court of the language used in the existing legislation.'[15]

Though the compensation Ron received didn't include his dependents' allowances, it enabled him to buy a rental property.[16] As he was mentally unstable and Betty had no experience of financial matters, Shirley was closely involved at every stage of finding and purchasing a suitable property. And she helped them sell their family home in Aro Valley and buy a sunny house on Brooklyn Terrace with a view of the harbour. She thought that was the best they could do for Ron. He was a former seaman – he could sit and watch the ships come and go.

Shirley helped Betty manage her volatile husband while caring for their four children. Ron gradually recovered his mental health and he was determined to walk again. Not only that, Shirley recalled, 'He said to me, I shan't be satisfied until I can walk up and down Brooklyn Hill without sticks. And I shall never forget the morning when, driving down . . . I saw Ron F. striding down the hill stickless.'[17] He eventually returned to work, not to a sedentary job but as a painter.

SHIRLEY'S OWN family life centred around Helen, now at Wellington Girls' College, where she was shining in all fields. Helen's best friend Denise Almao gives an insight into the Sutch household in comparison to her own family life in their house above her parents' shop where her

Compensation Act 1956. Considering discrepancies between s. 17 and ss. 13 and 20, Shirley submitted that the legislature would not have intended to make it more difficult for the most badly incapacitated workers. Doctors agreed that Ron had suffered a permanent injury, which, if it were assessed under s. 17, would be equal to not less than 100 per cent of total incapacity, and Mr Eichelbaum, counsel for the defendant, accepted this, but he argued that this did not mean the plaintiff was totally incapacitated for work for the full six-year period.

15 C. N. Irvine, New Zealand Law Journal, 7 April 1964, p.122.

16 New Zealand Law Reports/1964/Fackney v John Henderson (Wellington) Limited [1964] NZLR 422–11, February 1964.

17 SHSS, draft of eulogy for Ronald William Fackney, undated, SHSS papers.

mother worked 18 hours a day. Her father, a self-made businessman, was often away from home.

What Denise found in the Sutch–Smith family opened her eyes to another life. It was a revelation to see that a mother would do so much for a child. She was astonished that Shirley cooked them breakfast, ran them to school, took them to hockey and other out-of-school activities. She had never experienced family dinners sitting around the table talking. She was introduced to goulash, salami, olives and other foods she had never encountered in her 'meat-and-two-veg' family. Shirley talked about Latin and the poetry of Catullus. Denise recalled an idyllic holiday with Shirley and Helen in Taupō: honeysuckle on the veranda, hot pools and honeycomb.

When she thanked Shirley for all she did for her and asked how she could ever repay her, Shirley said there was no need to repay her, 'just do it for the next generation'.[18]

It was clear to everyone that Bill and Shirley were extremely proud of Helen. She was good at sport, loved drama, won speech competitions, joined the International Club and started a junior Campaign for Nuclear Disarmament (CND) group. She was beautiful, bright and fulfilled her parents' expectations. While other parents struggled with troublesome teenagers, Helen was a dream. That's how it seemed, but when Shirley made some remark about this years later she was devastated when Helen told her she had never had any adolescence, that her parents had been too powerful and implied that they possessed her and excluded normality.[19]

What Helen missed as time went on was normal family life. It was partly that she was an only child with two excessively hard-working parents. When they came together at dinner, her father would talk about his work, her mother about hers, and Helen might say something about school, but she was aware that these weren't conversations. After dinner, they went to their separate work areas – Helen to her room, Bill to his corner of the living room, and Shirley would drive back to her office. Helen's birthday wish one year was simply that they spend an

18 Denise Almao to author, interview, 8 May 2012.

19 SHSS to MHS, 9 March 1994, MHS papers. Shirley pointed out in defence that Helen started the CND on her own initiative and only then did Shirley join the movement.

evening together as a family.[20]

Several children of Shirley and Bill's friends boarded with them in the 1960s. Cecilia Wilson (later Johnson) joined the family as a student boarder in her first year at university in 1961. Cecilia's father was Ormond Wilson, a former Labour MP who had known Bill since the 1930s. Cecilia's stepmother, Rosamund, was the sister of Shirley's friend, Margie Herrick. An unspoken bond between Shirley and Cecilia was that both had lost their mothers as babies. Shirley was very kind to Cecilia, but, apart from mealtimes, there was little socialising with everyone working so hard.

SHIRLEY'S SOCIAL LIFE was in the city. She got on well with colleagues, clients became friends, and she befriended experts in whatever field she sought advice. It helped that she was seen as her father's daughter, though she preferred to be taken on her own account.

The café at Parsons' Bookshop was a meeting place. One of the regulars was Aileen Finucane, who was a useful sounding board for Shirley on many subjects. Shirley, and sometimes Helen, attended Socialist Forum meetings held at various homes, including that of Aileen and her partner Max Wilkinson in Thorndon.

Shirley and Helen were very close. Helen would later wonder if their intimate relationship had hindered her development. It made their eventual separation – both physical and psychological – more painful for them both. Shirley was convinced she knew who and what was good for Helen.

That included boyfriends. First was Martin O'Keefe, Bert and Madge's handsome son, who came to live at Todman Street in 1962 in his first year at Victoria University. Helen was sixteen, in her last year at Wellington Girls' College.

Shirley had kept in touch with Madge after supporting her through her divorce and helping her settle in Hamilton. She helped Martin, who had taken the brunt of his parents' violent relationship. He trusted Shirley. He wrote to her during his last year at school that it was a pity she didn't have a son as well as a daughter – 'He would appreciate you

20 MHS to author, interview, 29 September 2011.

very much – and would be a big help . . .', to which she replied that for the first time in her life she missed having a son. 'There's a lot of things that I'd like to say to that,' he responded, 'but they'd probably only lead to misunderstanding. I only hope you realise a little of what I feel.'[21]

Things came to grief at Todman Street. Martin lied and deceived, threatened violence, stole items from the house and a car and ended up in court. Shirley thought he was psychotic or psychopathic, but, when tests in Porirua showed him to be neither, Martin was sent to borstal.[22]

While Shirley thought Helen came through the whole experience steady and integrated, she herself was badly shaken. The experience may have been useful in later dealings with troubled young men, especially gang members for whom she developed great empathy, but though she did her utmost for Martin, she found that she couldn't cope with him on a personal level. As she reflected years later, 'Martin was a nightmare.'[23]

HELEN CONTINUED to fulfil her parents' hopes. Dux of Wellington Girls' in 1962, she went on to do a BA, then an MA (with first class Honours) in English Language and Literature at Victoria University. She represented the university at women's hockey, belonged to the drama club, was still active in CND and the Committee on Vietnam (CoV), organising a teach-in on Vietnam in 1966, and in May that year she represented NZUSA at the Fourth Asian Regional Co-operation Seminar in Manila. She held office on the Victoria University of Wellington Students' Association Executive, was chairman of the International Affairs Committee and vice-president of NZUSA (1965–66), whose president was Alister Taylor. Helen and Alister were soon seen as a 'hot' couple. Alister was regarded as a future National Party leader, until Helen and her parents changed his thinking. He recalls:

Both Bill and Shirley . . . expanded my horizons politically (as did Helen) but also made me aware of social and cultural issues of which I was then

21 Martin O'Keefe to SHSS, undated, SHSS papers.

22 Bert O'Keefe to SHSS, 19 October 1962, SHSS papers.

23 SHSS to MHS, 13 July 2002, MHS papers. Shirley wrote this after Martin's brother Gavin died, explaining why she had not visited Gavin after his father died; Peggy Garland to SHSS, 8 January 1963, SHSS papers.

ignorant. They invited me to cultural performances (Russian, Mexican) to which I would not otherwise have considered going (nor could I afford) and they helped expand my mind. They were both generous hosts and interesting people to be around. I helped Bill with research on a new edition of one of his books, The Quest for Security in New Zealand [published 1966].

I often accompanied Shirley, Bill and Helen for meals at Monde Marie, a popular 'coffee bar' or café of the time, run by Mary Seddon, a grand-daughter of the Right Honourable Richard John Seddon, Premier 1893–1906. Dr Sutch always paid and rebuffed me when I tried to contribute. They invited me to plays, cultural performances and frequently to their home.[24]

By then, Bill had been forced into early retirement. The news became public in November 1964. Shirley reflected that it was inevitable with National back in government. In 1983 she explained:

It was an uneasy situation. It had been widely said that Bill would be for the chop if National got in. He believed strongly in import control and a managed economy, and at that stage, National and its backers, big business, were pressing for economic freedom and no controls. It was obvious Bill would fight for the retention of controls. Labour's philosophy was in line with his.

In fact he lasted three years with Marshall, and got on very well with him and ran a very successful Economic Development Conference [sic. Export Development Conference] *for him.*

But we learned from an unimpeachable source that the people who held the purse strings – big business – were the ones who wanted him to go. The final straw was the NAFTA agreement, which Bill opposed. He was inclined to go on arguing for his own point of view, even when he knew it wouldn't be accepted.[25]

Shirley later rejected John Marshall's account of Bill's departure in his autobiography (where she also learnt that Marshall didn't think he

24 Alister Taylor, memoir of Shirley Smith for author, May 2012.

25 SHSS to Rosemary Vincent, 'Mongrels lawyer takes it quietly', *New Zealand Times*, 27 November 1983, p.9.

and Sutch worked well together).[26] But there was more to the matter.

MI5 records show that early in 1962 Prime Minister Keith Holyoake stormed into Alister McIntosh's office demanding Sutch be found a post overseas: 'He must be got out of New Zealand immediately.' The records don't say exactly what provoked this outburst, but Deputy Prime Minister Marshall showed his exasperation months later in July when he asked the British High Commissioner in Wellington if they had 'a sinecure in an area suitably near to one of the Polar Regions' where they could send him. Unable to find an alternative position for him, they considered him a candidate for the purge procedure they had established in December 1962, probably with Sutch in mind.

Since December 1961 the New Zealand Security Service had run a 'very delicate' long-term operation on Sutch that involved MI5, FBI and CIA, but apart from showing he had been 'completely disloyal to his Government', it yielded too little adverse up-to-date security information to make a case.[27] The government then passed legislation to make it discretionary whether a person should retire after 40 years' service.[28] Shirley knew about this.

They counted up everything they could think of to get Bill's service to 40 years – holiday jobs with the Post Office, a period as a probationary teacher, everything. They gave him the opportunity to resign and he refused. So he was told his service would terminate in March, 1965.

But he had a lot of support from manufacturers, whose interests he'd promoted. Eventually Sam Barnett, then Secretary of Justice, organised a group of important people to try to press for the Government to keep him on, or make sure he had reasonably prestigious jobs to do.[29]

26 John Marshall, *Memoirs: Volume II*, 1960 to 1968, Collins, New Zealand, 1989.

27 MI5 archives, KV 39-30, PF.45, 774/E2A/JLJ, J. L. Jones to K. A. S. Woolverton, Commonwealth Relations Office, 5 September 1963, P1011199. The operation started in 1961.

28 As a permanent head of department, Sutch couldn't be sacked. Provisions for the retirement of public servants were laid down in regulations in Section 72 of the New Zealand State Services Act of 1962. The State Services Commission had the power to oblige a public servant to retire, even if he was under 60. Sutch was 57. When this became public, allegations were made that the Government had put pressure on the State Services Commission, which it certainly had done.

29 SHSS to Rosemary Vincent, 'Mongrels lawyer takes it quietly', *New Zealand Times*, 27

There was a big public protest. The Council for Civil Liberties objected to the absence of the normal appeal procedure in preventing any improper political influence and wrote to the Prime Minister asking for an inquiry by a special parliamentary committee. The PSA printed a leaflet headed 'What the Newspapers Wouldn't Print' that pointed to signs of political interference, which the Commission Chairman Allan Atkinson denied, explaining that the commission's prime concern was 'to obtain the most efficient administration in each department to carry out the functions required of it by the Government.'[30]

A public statement on 15 January 1965 announced that Sutch had 'resigned' as from 31 March to take up consultant positions with the Reserve Bank and the Iron and Steel Corporation. (He later set up on his own as an economic consultant, working from the office of the NZ Woollen Mills Association, who employed him as a consultant.)

Shirley remembered either Holyoake or Marshall saying at his farewell that of course Dr Sutch had always been controversial, and that in his reply he said, 'It's not I who am controversial, it's the people who disagree with me who are controversial.'[31] She thought he never understood that it was a natural consequence of his own actions that he was not accepted. He would 'challenge and affront the establishment, conventions and accepted ways of thought and behaviour, but he still wanted to be accepted by the establishment, he wanted recognition.'[32] As noted earlier, she saw Bill as a Greek tragic hero whose 'internal flaw' – his total belief in his own rightness – would bring him down.

BILL SUTCH still had a strong following in the country at large, including the new generation of students at Congress at Curious Cove, and Shirley was still making new friends there. In 1962 Bill gave a paper and departed, leaving Helen and Shirley to stay on for the week. Brian Easton recalls being part of the group that formed around Shirley. Talk about nuclear disarmament persuaded him and other students to take part in CND's Easter march.

November 1983, p.9.
30 *Dominion*, 15 January 1965, p.1.
31 SHSS, 'WBS – Departure from I and C', undated [1998], SHSS papers.
32 Ibid.

He recalls that on the first day of the march, from Featherston to Upper Hutt, when they reached the summit of Remutaka Hill, a big car stopped and out stepped Prime Minister Keith Holyoake, who had decided to take that route to his farm in Pahīatua for Easter so he could meet the marchers. As others crowded around Holyoake and began haranguing him, Shirley stayed in the background seeking to avoid attention that might have rebounded on Bill who was then still head of Industries and Commerce. She and Brian got talking – the beginning of another friendship.[33]

This was the second year of the three-day march from the Wairarapa town of Featherston to the capital, drawing attention to their cause in ways that would mark the protest movement of the 1960s. They stayed in youth hostels and camps, waving banners and singing, and finally marching on Parliament. One year they marched down the Kāpiti Coast, ending at the marae in Porirua. Another time they distributed pamphlets in Palmerston North. The nuclear threat was about their future existence. It inspired a sense of urgency, solidarity and camaraderie as they chanted and waved their banners, proclaiming 'Make Love, Not War', 'Ban the Bomb' and many other slogans.

In 1965, after Bill left Industries and Commerce, Shirley took over from Mary Woodward as national secretary of CND with Aileen Finucane as her assistant. The headquarters moved to Wellington from Christchurch, where Mary Woodward and Elsie Locke had built up the organisation. By then, CND was losing momentum. Elsie considered it had done its dash and could hand over to the Committee on Vietnam, but, if it continued, it needed to change. A new person at the helm, based in Wellington where he or she could pressure government more effectively in a crisis, would help, she thought. And so it proved during the French nuclear testing in the Pacific in 1966.[34]

Shirley certainly brought a change in style. NZSIS noted, 'Rona Bailey described Smith in 1965 as one of the Party's most bitter opponents, who would like every communist out of the CND.'[35] (Rona Bailey,

33 Brian Easton to author, interview, 15 December 2011.
34 Elsie Lock to SHSS, 13 May and 17 June 1965, SHSS papers, ATL, MS-Papers-11369-191.
35 WBS PF, p.16, NZSIS.

Shirley's old friend and comrade, remained a staunch Party member.) Shirley didn't succeed – any protest movement in the 1960s was bound to include communist radicals and when overly zealous members were apprehended, she represented them – but she was not going to lead an organisation that was a communist front. For one thing, she wanted support from mainstream New Zealanders. (That mainstream support grew eventually, in the 1980s, and led to the government's nuclear-free policy.)

As CND's media spokesperson, Shirley gave television interviews and arranged television coverage of their activities, including one of their camps. She organised the youth camps and marches. As always, the last day's march along the Hutt Road finished with speeches on the steps of Parliament.

As the anti-Vietnam War protest movement grew stronger, she did her bit there too. When US President Johnson made his 24-hour visit to New Zealand in 1966, Shirley was among the chanting protesters who lined the route on the way from the airport. The following year, when US Defense Secretary Clark Clifford and General Maxwell Taylor came, she was again part of the protest that helped prompt Clark Clifford to question US policy in Southeast Asia.[36]

Some of Shirley's other causes fell under the umbrella of the New Zealand Council for Civil Liberties. Throughout the sixties and into the seventies, she continued this work. The campaign against Capital Punishment ended with the abolition of the Death Penalty in 1961. Jury reform took longer. Shirley made submissions to the Statutes Revision Committee every time it came up. Minister of Justice Ralph Hanan, who introduced the Crimes Bill 1961, was in favour of equality

36 Patrick Anderson, Clark Clifford 'Sounds the Alarm', *New York Times*, 8 August 1971. 'As Clifford looks back, he says his first doubts about U.S. policy in Vietnam came in the summer of 1967 when President Johnson sent him and General Maxwell Taylor to urge several of this country's Pacific allies to increase their support of the war effort. To Clifford's surprise, the leaders of Thailand, South Korea, Australia and New Zealand – the very dominoes that were supposed to be in danger of falling – had little enthusiasm for the defense of South Vietnam.' https://www.nytimes.com/1971/08/08/archives/clark-clifford-sounds-the-alarm-clifford-sounds-the-alarm-clifford.html (accessed 28 May 2018).

for women jurors, but he faced a lot of opposition in his own ranks and had to go slowly.

The Women Jurors Act (1942) had provided for women between the ages of twenty-five and sixty to have their names placed on the jury list on the same basis as men – if they so desired. While the names of men were automatically listed, women were obliged to enrol personally.

When the Minister had got nearly there, but not quite, and I was defending my submissions before the Statutes Revision Committee, and indignantly asked why, if the Government would go so far, they would not go the whole way, Mr Hanan smiled at me and said it was better to go as far as possible, although the final goal was not reached, than not to proceed at all. This I understood and felt sorry I had been so impatient. I was sure that, even if it was little by little, Mr Hanan would get there in the end. And he did. He was one of the best, if not the best Minister of Justice that we have ever had.[37]

In Christchurch, Helen Garrett (née Coates) had also been agitating for a change. In February 1960, she became the first woman to serve on a jury in a criminal case in the High Court. On another jury the same week, she was elected the first woman foreman of a jury in New Zealand.[38] But there was still much to do to break down patriarchal assumptions about the propriety of women in the public arena and the misconception that women were unwilling to go on juries, and that their occupations as housewives and mothers prevented them from doing so.

Shirley and Elizabeth Orr, another leading campaigner for equality for women, appeared before the final select committee in 1962. Their call for compulsory jury service for women as well as men was achieved at last by the Juries Amendment Act in 1963. The legislation went further, making provision for gender-neutral language, but gender distinction continued with a proviso that presumed a domestic occupation allowed

37 SHSS, 'Jury service for women', August 1998, SHSS papers.

38 Helen Garrett to Jim Sullivan, recorded 7 July 1994 for 'History Repeated', broadcast 30 December 1994. http://collections.soundarchives.co.nz/search.do?view=detail&id=109603&db=object

women an exemption without giving any reason. It wasn't until 1976 that this part of the legislation was removed.

Shirley usually avoided women's organisations for the same reason that she opposed those that excluded women, but she joined the Joint Committee on Women and Employment to campaign for equal pay and opportunities.[39] Bill too was exceptionally active in this campaign, and he was also very supportive of the Society for Research on Women (SROW), an organisation Margaret Shields and Mary Mowbray co-founded in 1966. On his suggestion, they asked Shirley to be their honorary solicitor. She declined at first but changed her mind, recognising the value of their work. Over the next years SROW carried out research on topics such as childcare, professional women, maternity services, doctor–patient relationships, immigrant women, sole mothers, older mothers, family violence and women in unusual jobs.

Mental health issues were still near to her heart and relevant to her work. In 1961 Shirley incorporated Stepping Stones, the organisation she had set up five years earlier, and she served as its honorary secretary.

Her clients, especially victims of abuse, found Shirley provided more than legal help. One such client was Bill's niece Hope (now Shirley Evans), daughter of his older sister Nellie. Hope was suffering from her husband's cruelty. She recalls Shirley saying emphatically, 'You are a *whole person*!' and arranging psychiatric help to restore her sense of self.[40]

39 Elizabeth Orr to author, 22 March 2012. An outcome of a conference at Victoria University in November 1964 on 'Women's Contribution in a Changing Society', its members were drawn from the New Zealand Federation of Business and Professional Women's Clubs, the New Zealand Federation of University Women, the National Council of Women and other organisations. Their lobbying led to an official body, the National Advisory Council on the Employment of Women, being formed in 1967.

40 Shirley Hope Evans to author, 20 February 2015.

18

Apron strings

SHIRLEY CONSIDERED her four years at St Hugh's College, Oxford, a wonderful transforming experience and wanted the same for her daughter. Her former moral tutor, Dorothea Gray, remembered Shirley as one of her most satisfactory undergraduates: 'I think this is good blood, and promising', she wrote when Helen applied for a place at St Hugh's.[1] With an MA First Class Honours degree in English Language and Literature, and a scholarship, Helen departed for St Hugh's in October 1967. She was to read Philosophy, Politics and Economics (PPE).

Bereft at losing her, Shirley took comfort in writing her long letters, usually from the office after midnight or over the weekend.

Dear sweet precious girl, I must stop and do some work. I just love chattering on to you, feeling so close and conscious of you. It was truly wonderful to hear your voice when you rang up, and we are both so *glad you did. Truly we are not really separated, and even so far as we are physically, it will not be for long, I am sure. I am just* pining *to come to see you at Oxford.*[2]

Bill and Shirley spent Christmas at Taupō, just the two of them. They both found it strained without Helen and on Boxing Day things really fell to pieces. 'Daddy got awfully anti-Smith, it seemed, and appeared to be madly uncomfortable in a Smith stronghold,' Shirley wrote to Helen. '. . . I only tremble about the effect of the Smith invasion [Allan and family] tomorrow. I didn't intend to overlap a whole day . . .'[3] After more about her difficulties with Bill, Shirley paused to wonder whether she should write such things to her daughter. 'I don't like entirely to

1 Dorothea Gray to Theodora Cooper, undated, St Hugh's Archive, Oxford.
2 SHSS to MHS, 10 November 1967, MHS papers.
3 SHSS to MHS, 29 December 1967, MHS papers.

paint a rosy picture when it's not true – and I've become too used to confiding in you.'[4]

Shirley hated leaving Taupō for Mount Egmont, but wrote ecstatically days later from Stratford Mountain Hut. They had achieved their old ambition of seeing Bell's Falls. Bill wrote, 'It was a very long tramp, and the track was terrible for several hours with bog and leatherwood together. We, of course, thought about you a great deal, and recalled that day and night in the upper reaches of the Stony River when we failed to get any objective. . . . Mummy did very well indeed. She is strong.'[5]

Back in Wellington, Shirley moved into a new office in Gleneagles Flats at 69 The Terrace. Alister Taylor and Max Wilkinson helped transform the rooms on the ground floor into a light, modern law office. Amidst the chaos of renovations, she tried to make a start on her work.

About then, Alister and Helen broke up. Alister turned to Shirley, who became intensely caught up in the fallout until she realised how that must seem to Helen.

This is your life, and Alister's, and you could rightly be disturbed by feeling that I seem to be running it. But I feel sure you won't mind Alister's turning to me in his distress, and you wouldn't have wanted me not to respond. I shall try to fade out now . . . And above all, be very sure that what I want for you is to be free and independent in your developing life and I am not committed to influencing you into my [any?] *direction in your personal life or otherwise.*'[6]

But for all the talk about wanting Helen to be free and independent, Shirley couldn't let go.

Shirley remained close to Alister, as did Bill, who was his landlord. Bill had some years earlier bought a cottage at 39 Glenbervie Terrace, next door to Aileen Finucane and Max Wilkinson. They all worked closely together with other residents to oppose the new motorway that threatened to destroy Thorndon and, in the long term, to find ways to

4 SHSS to MHS, 12 January 1968, MHS papers.
5 WBS to MHS, 15 January 1968, MHS papers.
6 SHSS to MHS, 21 January 1968, MHS papers.

preserve its historic buildings and character.

In 1968 Shirley and Alister worked together on the Committee of Vietnam (CoV). Related to this was the Peace Power and Politics in Asia (PPPA) conference, planned to coincide with the South East Asia Treaty Organisation (SEATO) conference in Wellington at the end of March 1968. Alister was chair of the organising committee.

The PPPA conference was a great success. Bill and Shirley hosted their old friends the Aireys, trade unionist and peace activist Sonja Davies, and their star guest, Conor Cruise O'Brien, later described in his *Guardian* obituary as 'the most pugnacious Irish intellectual since George Bernard Shaw'.[7] Shirley was run off her feet providing meals and a dinner party but she managed to attend O'Brien's address, which Bill chaired. When news came through that President Johnson wouldn't run for re-election and would partially stop the bombing in South Vietnam, O'Brien threw aside his prepared speech. 'I think we are in the presence of the beginning of the end of the war in Vietnam. This is the turning point,' he declared. The audience was ecstatic. It was the high point of the conference.[8]

Alister earned considerable kudos in Shirley's eyes for the way he ran the conference, but she found his judgment not always sound in other respects. She represented him in an employment dispute with the New Zealand Broadcasting Corporation and in a number of other legal cases. Though she was frustrated when he didn't take her advice, they remained good friends. She told Helen she would always love Alister.[9]

On 10 April 1968, the Wahine storm, named after the ferry that sank in Wellington Harbour with tragic loss of life, left the city reeling in shock and chaos. Shirley and Bill suffered relatively lightly. A window

7 The epithet comes from his *Guardian* obituary in 1991: https://www.theguardian.com/media/2008/dec/19/conor-cruise-brien (accessed 12 October 2018).

8 SHSS to MHS, 8 April 1968, MHS papers; Redmer Yska, 'Give Peace a Chance', *New Zealand Listener*, 5 April 2008: 'The final PPP communiqué of April 2, urging New Zealand's withdrawal from military alliances like Seato (and presumably Anzus), said "non-alignment does not mean neutrality, but by avoidance of the Cold War and its rival ideologies, an independence of policy". It was a message that would embolden a cautious Labour Party to begin moving out of Uncle Sam's shadow.'

9 SHSS to Alister Taylor, 3 February 1973, SHSS papers. 'I told Helen, "Well, anyway, I shall always love Alister": and I've never felt any differently.'

blew in at Shirley's office and, while she was dealing with the mess that created, a plank fell on her car. At home, she and Bill had no power for a week. 'Mummy is at last doing housework she enjoys – cooking on an open fire with candlelight and no telephone,' Bill wrote to Helen.[10] But most of the time she was sick in bed with flu. She was ill for weeks.

Shirley got up to attend CoV meetings, where she was subject to in-fighting. She had earlier influenced a decision not to have a CoV demonstration during the PPPA conference, so as not to distract media attention from the more important messages. She strongly opposed attempts to turn CND into anti-Vietnam, arguing that it was wrong to use one movement with a specific aim for another purpose. People on the left accused her of being a traitor to the cause. She was angry and hurt and wanted to opt out altogether.[11]

She worried about Helen, who had a new boyfriend, Keith Ovenden. Shirley, echoing her father's concern when she was at Oxford, saw it as necessary for Helen's development that she remain unattached at this stage. Thinking that Helen equated her parents with Alister, Shirley explained that they had 'no feelings against Keith, because he is Keith and not Alister . . . our criterion is *your* good, in terms of your independence and fulfilment.'[12] She hoped that Helen would do something and be someone as herself, in her own right.[13]

Shirley worried that she and Bill had over-protected their daughter. Margie Philips (née Herrick, now remarried to a Harley Street psychoanalyst in London), wrote that they shouldn't persecute themselves with ideas of what they should or shouldn't have done, 'for from the moment a child is born he or she is an individual and develops according to his capacity . . .' Margie suggested that two years away from parental protection could have a salutary effect.[14]

She assured Shirley that Helen's new boyfriend was intelligent, sensitive and thoughtful. He came from a 'solid but intellectually stifling middle class . . . background from which he has made his escape.' His

10 WBS to MHS, 11 April 1968, MHS papers.
11 SHSS to MHS, 30 April 1968, MHS papers.
12 SHSS to MHS, 23 April 1968, MHS papers.
13 SHSS to MHS, 1968, MHS papers.
14 Margie Philips to SHSS, 20 June 1968, SHSS papers.

father, a surveyor, was 'a very decent man'.[15]

Keith was a graduate (Double Honours) in English Literature and Politics from the University of Keele; he had an MA in Political Science from the University of Michigan and was now on a Social Science Research Council scholarship at Nuffield College, Oxford, studying British politics for a DPhil. Shirley might have compared him with her own friends, those from Yorkshire grammar schools and New Zealanders like Dan Davin, who got to Oxford on their own merits; or with Bill, who came even further from his beginnings; but some residual class prejudice surfaced in her regard for Keith. That became apparent later, however.

Bill made disparaging remarks about political scientists, but David Smith remembered meeting Keith when he came to New Zealand in a university debating team and thought him an 'estimable young man'.

Shirley fretted. She was disappointed that Helen wasn't enchanted with Oxford and wasn't making the most of it. She told herself that she couldn't expect it to be the same for Helen as it had been for her. Struggling with her course, tired of student life and impatient to get into the real world and 'do something', Helen was considering switching from the DPhil her parents expected to an MPhil in Economics.

This became more likely when she agreed to accompany Keith around the United States over the summer vacation. He was to report on the Democratic Party's presidential election primaries. Shirley, who loved Europe and not America, thought the trip met Keith's interests and questioned how it fitted Helen's. 'In brief, does it serve the development of your independence and self-realisation? I am genuinely asking questions, darling, I am not deciding that it doesn't.'[16]

Helen went with Keith. After receiving her enthusiastic travel accounts, Shirley wrote to him warmly:

We are feeling particularly friendly to you . . . because [Helen] *is obviously so happy, and this is what matters more to her doting parents than almost anything else. These marvellous travels in the States, too, are a wonderful*

15 Margie Philips to SHSS, 8 May and 20 June 1968, SHSS papers.
16 SHSS to MHS, 7 May 1968, MHS papers.

experience which you have provided; and we realise we were wrong in thinking a summer in Europe would have been better. The laugh (if you could call it that, under the circumstances) is clearly on us, in suggesting that the US would be more dangerous than Europe. She could easily have been in Prague.[17]

This was a reference to the Soviet (Warsaw Pact) invasion of Czechoslovakia on 20 August 1968. Shirley and Bill described to Helen their different views of the Prague Spring that began on 5 April when Dubček announced his programme to reform the constitution of Czechoslovakia to make it more democratic. Shirley wrote on 23 August, two days after the invasion, 'I think the Russians' action is stupid and wrong and in the long run will harm Russia more than anyone', adding, 'but their fears of world capitalism – U.S. and W. Germany in particular are very real and far from unjustified.'[18] (Bill had earlier written that, as the future lay with the Communist Party and the Soviet Union, as well as with the Chinese and revolutionary parties, 'the events in Czechoslovakia must be watched carefully.'[19])

Ted and Judy Sutch wrote from New York, where Ted was New Zealand Trade Commissioner, expressing cautious approval of Keith, having first met him before he and Helen set off around the country.

On their return to New York, Keith and Helen stayed quietly together at Jule and Chris Beeby's apartment. When Helen eventually contacted her uncle and aunt they exploded: where had she been? Ted had been frantically trying to contact her. Her father had had a coronary thrombosis.

Bill's heart attack on 20 September 1968 came at an extremely stressful time for Shirley. Over the previous weeks, she had struggled with a complicated marital case that came to a crisis with a hearing in late August. She felt she was on the brink of disaster and would have mishandled the case without her father's help. 'His 80 years don't seem to have any effect on his legal acumen, he is quite fantastic . . .' she

17 SHSS to KWO, 28 August 1968, KWO papers.
18 SHSS to MHS, 23 August 1968, MHS papers.
19 WBS to MHS, 27 May 1968, MHS papers.

wrote to Helen.[20] But he kept telling her that she couldn't practise law properly while trying to do so many other things.[21] She knew that he was right, that she had been too much distracted from 'pure' law and was very rusty.[22]

Bill was in hospital for a month. After he came home, Shirley cared for him while dealing with more clients than she could manage. She needed a law clerk, but had no money to spend on wages. She confided in Helen, asking her not to tell Bill, that she now had a 'massive' overdraft.[23]

Bill wrote to Helen that he was less concerned with his own health than he was with her mother's. 'In some way we will have to cut down the amount she does and her retirement from the Secretaryship of CND has been one of the necessary steps, but her compassion and her knowledge are so great that it will be difficult for her to reduce activities.'[24]

Her resignation from CND was a relief to her, but it marked the end of the organisation as a national coordinated body. An information centre was kept going in Christchurch but, except in Auckland, branch after branch fell away as its members were absorbed into the protest movement against the war in Vietnam.

WHEN HE CAME out of hospital, Shirley persuaded Bill to get a television set and together they watched several programmes in which she appeared. One was a *Gallery* panel on whether a single act of adultery should no longer be sufficient grounds for divorce.

I took the view that adultery shouldn't be a ground for divorce at all – cruelty, as in England, should be, and adultery could be part of that; but that adultery was in fact used *– either to get an unfair advantage in not*

20 SHSS to MHS, 28 August 1968. '. . . what I didn't realize was that I had to prove the previous case and that I couldn't even prove the facts unless I had pleaded them in the Statement of Claim (which I hadn't). . . . It has been a sheer nightmare': SHSS to MHS, 23 August 1968, MHS papers.

21 SHSS to MHS, 6 July 1968, MHS papers.

22 SHSS to MHS, 3 September 1968, MHS papers.

23 SHSS to MHS, 31 October 1968, MHS papers.

24 WBS to MHS, 22 October 1968, MHS papers.

paying maintenance or in custody of children (Mary Bryan helped here) or in order to get a quick and easy divorce when the marriage was over anyway. . . . even strangers in the street spoke to me – and I didn't get any outraged letters![25]

Bill reported on another 'triumph', when Shirley spoke on the subject of what Christ would be like if he came to earth today.

She said in effect that whatever person arrived today (man or woman), s/he would be a subversive, would fight against war, finance and capitalism and inevitably be unpopular. She praised the action of the Seamen's Union in refusing to service the U.S. Aircraft Carrier when it visited Wellington and said all this was the kind of action that the new Christ would have advocated.[26]

Bill and Shirley had recently heard from Helen that Leo Huberman had died suddenly. Helen had met him when she was in New York. Bill wrote to Helen of their close friendship and the inscription Huby had written for him in *We the People* – 'frontline fighter for We the People' – and explained his thinking behind the Kobi Bosshard necklace he gave her for her birthday: 'When I was assisting in the designing of it I had at the back of my mind that I hoped it would be a symbol of some kind of link between me and you. In my own way I have tried not to say what you should do or think but I had wanted you to carry on the fight wherever it leads you, hence the necklace.'[27]

While declaring their wish for Helen to find her own path, her parents both expected her to 'fight the good fight'. But Shirley saw contradictions in Bill's positions.

She had always wrestled with the problems of being a socialist in a capitalist world. She thought it fair enough to use the system but she was concerned about Bill's growing obsession with money and his

25 SHSS to MHS, 31 October 1968, MHS papers. The Law Society gave Shirley permission to speak as a lawyer.

26 WBS to MHS, 23 December 1968, MHS papers.

27 WBS to MHS, 22 November 1968, MHS papers. This is the letter referred to earlier on pp.182 and 189.

secrecy around his financial dealings (overlooking that she also had financial secrets from him). She wrote to Helen:

I do wish he would relax about money – we've got quite enough, although the capital is largely tied up at present in real estate and so on. Not that I've been informed about any details by Daddy, but people (especially other solicitors) assumed I know or am acting and tell me things before I can put them off. Embarrassing for me as well as them. I have given him opportunities to open up, but he hastily changes the subject. But he said since his attack, with a satisfied smi*le, 'If I die, you'll be a very wealthy woman.' To which what is the answer? – 'Oh how lovely, darling!'? . . . He seems to be getting more obsessed with money rather than less . . .*[28]

The problem as she saw it was what to do with the surplus, but as her practice brought in 'chicken feed', she herself had no great difficulty. 'I give money to Catacombs and Godfrey Wilson's paper, and Corso and a host of other good causes who send me appeals and I don't really see what else I *can* do at present.'[29]

Shirley wanted her practice to pay for itself, but she depended on Bill for her costs of living while she wasn't drawing any salary. In this sense, at least, he subsidised her work. Her friend Julie Grenfell (formerly Cook) recalled, 'She didn't know where the money was coming from that supported her work . . . This brought her to the edge of anxiety. She couldn't get past Bill's defences – he wouldn't talk about things.'[30]

By 1969 clients were flooding to her. Most of them were penniless, but there was a move towards enacting civil legal aid. She began a long association with Cook Islanders when she represented a Cook Island woman, a mother of eight children, from Porirua. The woman's brother-in-law, Mr Karati, then brought a procession of clients. The Cook Islands Society made her their honorary solicitor and for some twenty years she served them in this capacity. The relationship meant a great deal to them and to her.

She could now employ a typist and a law clerk. Conveyancing paid

28 SHSS to MHS, 12 January 1969, MHS papers.
29 Ibid.
30 Julie Grenfell to author, interview, 9 April 2014.

well and helped pay wages, but the economic squeeze saw several jobs fall through. She remained slightly in the red.

When Helen came home on a visit in July 1969 she was shocked at how hard her mother worked. 'It's frightening,' she wrote to Keith. '. . . She now has a clerk and a typist which is some improvement, but seems to spend most of the time doing their work for them, or unravelling their mistakes.'[31]

Helen persuaded her one evening to retire to bed early. Since his heart attack Bill usually had dinner in bed, but she considered it a major success with her mother. After dinner Helen talked to her father in his room.

. . . all the while I thought my mother was asleep and it turned out she had got up and was doing the washing-up. It's so frustrating trying to help! I'm really worried, more about my mother's, at present, than my father's health. She has been looking after him for so long, and hasn't been well herself; simultaneously she has been working far too hard at the office . . . And neither of them (my parents) manage to have any life of their own, to speak of – they hardly ever go out, my mother works most evenings and when they stop they are usually too exhausted to do anything.[32]

But this had long been the pattern of Bill and Shirley's lives, and to a large extent it was Shirley's choice. Shirley looked to Helen for intimacy and affection, but Helen loved her father as well as her mother.

Before Helen came home, Shirley proposed a holiday in Taupō, just her and Helen. She was dismayed when Bill said he wanted to join them. 'Taupo is so very much your and my place, and I have been so looking forward to having you there to myself, to be able to talk absolutely freely about everything,' she wrote to Helen.[33] In the event, they reached a compromise: Bill and Helen went to Taupō ahead of Shirley, who joined them two days later, they had a couple of days as a family, then Bill left and Shirley had two days alone with Helen.

While it was apparent that her parents' lifestyle wasn't what Helen

31 Helen to KWO, 18 July 1969, KWO papers.
32 Helen to KWO, 31 July 1969, KWO papers.
33 SHSS to MHS, 3 June 1969, MHS papers.

wanted for herself, Bill and Shirley were at one in their high expectations for her. Failure wasn't an option. Shirley wrote on Helen's return to Oxford:

My beloved girl, I love you so much but because I love you . . . I want you to live fully and face your challenges; and as I know *this is so much more of a strain for you than for most because you are so much more sensitive and finely tuned than most, but I am sure it is worth it in the long run, and in truth necessary if one is to be a whole person, a free and sovereign individual. . . .*

I must seem to you to have a very harsh and granitic approach to life, but I do also want you to be happy, my most lovely gifted and beautiful girl. Above all, precious, do have confidence in yourself . . .[34]

Meanwhile Shirley's relationship with Keith was developing tentatively. Replying to a letter in which he acknowledged the confidence she must have placed in him (relating to Helen), she was circumspect.

It doesn't seem to me that I'm entitled to have confidence or not have confidence in you. I can hope that Helen's relationship with you will make for Helen's happiness, as of course I do, and of course Helen's happiness is very important to me. But loving and trusting Helen, as I do, I can only accept her decisions at this stage and in this area of her life . . . I offer my friendship to you without reservation; how it develops depends upon ourselves, what we are and what we do; and upon circumstances – what chance we have of getting to know each other at some nearer distance than half the world's circumference away. I am very eager to come to England next July . . .[35]

About Helen she added:

I hope she'll be happy; but it is really a long time since I thought of happiness as an end in itself. The old bromide of whose truth I am entirely sure, is

34 SHSS to MHS, 2 September 1969, addressed to Oxford, MHS papers.
35 SHSS to KWO, 1 October 1969, KWO papers.

that happiness is a by-product. I am nothing but an old Presbyterian at heart . . . I believe one must do what appears to be one's work in the world, and do it with all one's might, and do whatever one can, however little, against the world's evils; and to spend time worrying about one's personal happiness is not only sheer self-indulgence (and therefore bad; generations of Presbyterian ministers speak through me) but also futile.[36]

She was anxious that Keith didn't take this in any way amiss. One of the reasons she wanted to go to England was to meet him. Bill had gone off the idea of going but she would go anyway; in fact, she preferred to go alone.

She didn't know until she heard from Helen that Victoria University had invited Bill to give a course of lectures the following year on New Zealand history. Neither Helen nor Shirley thought it a good idea. It was difficult to tell him, Shirley explained to Helen, because he had always pined for academic recognition and an academic job.

So I said it was splendid but could he do both that and the Woollen Mills – would he give up the Woollen Mills for it? This startled him and he said certainly not. So I said – well he just had to consider his health and the demands of the two jobs, and then I did the difficult bit, saying straight out that he couldn't afford any criticism of the academic quality of his work in the V.U.W. job. He bristled a bit but I stuck to it, as straight as I could, because I thought it was absolutely vital. He subsided much sooner than I thought he would and talked without resentment of what he'd have to do and how he'd have to plan the course and so on, and I did get the impression my warning had sunk in.[37]

She thought the appointment hadn't been finalised and hoped for the best, but read the announcement in the press confirming it soon after.

She resolved definitely to go to England for Helen's graduation. Apart from Oxford, she wanted to see London and to go to Europe, to see friends and to meet Keith, but she wanted to spend most of her

36 Ibid.
37 SHSS to MHS, 29 October 1969, p.5, MHS papers.

time with her daughter. She hoped Helen would postpone her planned holiday with Keith in northern Italy and join him there later, after she herself had left. Then a letter came from Keith wanting to know her plans. Time was running out, he and Helen needed to book their car on the ferry – or should they cancel their trip to Aulla? Unhappy about the way he had taken over, Shirley replied briefly that they should go ahead and make their ferry booking and not trouble Helen, who was anxious about her exams.

On her way to England Shirley stayed a night with Ted and Judy Sutch. They conveyed their opinion that Keith wasn't good enough for Helen. Then Shirley met Keith and disliked him on sight. She later explained to Helen that her reaction was '*not* a thing I could alter by taking thought. It was spontaneous and in the technical sense, immediate.'[38] She made no pretence of her dislike. She wasn't interested in getting to know him, what he thought, what he did. Keith was bewildered. 'I must confess for my part that I am not proud of the way I behaved to Keith,' Shirley continued. 'I should have been capable of being more civilised, and I am sorry.'[39]

At the same time, Shirley thought she had to be honest with her daughter. Instead of being happy that Helen had found love, she saw her as besotted and she couldn't understand it. She thought that she was under an influence that prevented her being her true self.

Peggy Garland, who had known Helen as a child in Wellington in the 1950s when their families were close, and who now lived near Oxford, offered sensible advice:

I feel sure that you must make greater efforts to understand and to even like him. Also to recognise his efforts at friendship even if they seem to you who do not like him to be impertinences. One asks oneself what he could possibly do short of vanishing into thin air that would please you. I think that from what you tell me, he has been trying to please you and do what is helpful.

Anyway Helen loves him – that really is the important bit. In fact it is the only important bit, for if she didn't you would never have had to cope with

38 SHSS to MHS, 20 July 1970, MHS papers.
39 Ibid.

your feelings about the pair of them. It is quite on the cards that she will stick with him – two years is a long time for two youngsters to be together and I think it looks serious. He is not a lame duck – so that is not Helen's reason for choosing him – and Oxford is bristling with beautiful, gifted, attractive young men, so she can hardly have been short of the opportunity of meeting anybody else.

We have to face it then. Helen has chosen K. and if you want to be friends with Helen you mustn't blackguard him to her or even tell her you don't like him. Remember what it's like to be gone on a man and consider what she would feel: it would alienate her from you *perhaps for ever, and* nothing *can be as bad as that.*

So my advice is – relax. There is nothing in the world you can do about it and what you propose to do can do nothing but harm. You are all steamed up at the moment and can easily make mistakes – irretrievable ones. It is far better to do and say nothing and to try and play it all down to Bill so that he doesn't do anything that Helen can't forgive.[40]

But egged on by Bill, and feeling that she had to be honest with Helen about how she felt, Shirley continued to express her opposition to Keith. Predictably, this backfired. Helen determined to marry Keith.

IN 1971 HELEN had a lectureship in the Economics Department at Victoria University of Wellington and Keith, having just completed his doctorate, was also working at the university on a post-doctoral fellowship. They took a flat by the university. Shirley was no more taken with Keith than before. Helen told the author that she appealed to her mother, reminding her how she felt when her father opposed her marriage, and Shirley replied that *now* she knew how he felt.

Despite the unpleasantness, Keith and Helen had dinner with her parents every Sunday evening. As Keith recalls, there was no conversation, no attempt to include him and get to know what he thought or did. He felt he couldn't speak and just listened while Bill held forth, talking about himself. Keith found all situations when Bill was present were tense.

40 Peggy Garland to SHSS, 14 July (1970), SHSS papers.

Bill's sister Margaret Shirley was often there. She lived almost next door at 103 Mitchell Street (one of the houses Bill bought years earlier to acquire driveway access). Recently retired as chief psychologist with the Education Department, Margaret Shirley was enthralled with her older brother but she irritated him. The sisters-in-law, once close, now rubbed each other the wrong way.

To get through these occasions, Helen and Keith took Valium. And they took it to get through their wedding.

Keith's mother Dolf came out from England for the wedding. It must have been awkward, considering Shirley and Bill's opposition to the marriage, but Shirley invited Dolf to stay at Todman Street and lent her and Keith her car to tour the North Island.

Bill offered to host an afternoon tea after the wedding. Allan and Helen Smith, who were appalled at Shirley and Bill's attitude towards the marriage, suggested a real celebration at their place, which Helen and Keith gratefully accepted, so after the civic ceremony the wedding party headed for Tītahi Bay – all except Shirley and Bill. According to Shirley's friends, she wanted to go but thought she should stay with Bill.[41]

After Helen and Keith went back to England, Shirley wrote to her cousin, Dr Ruth Oakley (née Milne – Sally and Charles Milne's daughter who had been a missionary in China when Shirley was at Oxford), that things were worse than ever between her and Helen. Ruth suggested 'love treatment':

I think in a situation like this the only thing to do is to cast oneself at the Lord's feet and to plead forgiveness for one's own lack of love and not to think at all of the other person's faults. . . . It isn't our job to try to change others . . . our job is just to love them and keep on loving them as they are . . . Do they have retreat houses in N.Z.? Or some quiet place where you can go to wrestle with this problem on your own, and seek forgiveness for anything in you that is contributing to the problem? Then you may get that outpouring of love . . . that enables you to see the situation afresh and give

41 KWO to author, 7 December 2017; Amanda Rosenberg to author, 20 June 2017; Julie Grenfell to author, 29 April 2014.

you courage to go on. I can see that the situation is destroying you and you must find an answer – and really the way of utter self giving in love to Helen (and so inevitably to Keith) is the only answer.[42]

However Shirley responded to being told that it wasn't her job to change people and the gentle suggestion that something in herself might contribute to the problem, she found neither peace nor answers. Two years later, alone at Taupō, she wrote to Margie Philips:

Somehow my mind hasn't been as peaceful and quiet as I should have liked it to be. . . . When we go away at Christmas I spend the first week in an agony over Helen – can't sleep, or if I do, I dream horrible dreams. This time I've been beset as well by thoughts of all the awful things I've done to people at one time or another and the ghastly mistakes I've made. The short-term remedy is work! Escapism, you'd say – the long-term psycho-analysis?

Helen. I think there is a lot of truth in what you say about seeing what one wants to see in a child. . . . and it is true that I imposed my conception of what she should be with much certainty. Part of my conception was that she should do things. Spread her wings, use her abilities, make her own decisions. So that I never thought that I was holding her back or smothering her with possessiveness. . . .

But it seems that now she thinks that everything was predetermined by us, by our being the sort of people we are. Basically, how can one ever get away from that? I know I was always very clear about what was right and wrong, what was the right way to live. Psychiatrists say now, don't they, that it's better that a child has a firm framework to grow up in, whether they accept it or rebel against it.[43]

And so she continued, struggling with things all mothers have to face but which Shirley, whose obsessive attachment to her only child grew out of her own need, failed to accept.

42 Ruth Oakley to SHSS, 24 February 1972, SHSS papers, ATL, MS-Papers-11369-196.
43 SHSS to Margie Philips, 22 April 1974, SHSS papers.

19

Crusader

THE NEXT YEARS saw Shirley's practice expand and her reputation grow. Though it was always a struggle to keep her head above water, she would look back with pride on what she achieved. It was during this time that her colleagues, those who understood the nature of the work she was doing, started to see her as an icon.

Before her trip to England in 1970, Shirley made some changes to her staff. The mechanic who looked after her car, on learning she was in a fix, suggested his wife could help for a week. This was Helen Edwards, who eventually became Shirley's long-term secretary. Initially she just had to answer the telephone, make appointments and look after the office while Shirley was in court. One week became two and more. Helen learnt how to use the dictaphone and follow precise instructions regarding punctuation. Everything had to be perfect. Born in Shanghai to Russian émigrés, she was multilingual but had to learn the refinements of English grammar and the language of law. And everything in Shirley's office had to be recycled: envelopes were cut up so the backs could be used for notes and files, used stamps were saved for collectors, rubber bands for who knows what – Shirley wore them on her wrist. Newspaper clippings on all manner of subjects sat in piles: all had to be filed.

Shirley asked her to stay. They agreed she would start on a weekly wage of $26.50, but it immediately increased when Bill said it was too little. That was the only time he had anything to do with the practice as far as Helen was aware. 'Her practice was her practice and if it went down, it went down; if it went up, it went up . . . Nothing came from Dr Sutch. Nothing.'[1]

Cathy Shaw, Shirley's first and very competent secretary, had moved

1 Helen Edwards to author, interview, 8 April 2011.

to Waikanae. She now came to the office once a week to manage the trust and office accounts. As the firm was so busy and she was going overseas, Shirley decided to replace her law clerk with a qualified solicitor who could run the office while she was away. She advertised that the position could potentially become a partnership. One of two applicants suggested they set up a branch together where he lived in Wainuiomata, a fast-growing 'dormitory' suburb where there would be plenty of conveyancing work. She entertained the idea, but their paths parted soon after her return from Europe when she found her office had ground to a standstill while he was away doing a second job.

Fortuitously she heard that George Rosenberg, the son of her friends Wolf and Ann Rosenberg, had just qualified as barrister and solicitor and needed office and courtroom experience. George recalls there wasn't even an interview – she asked him to start at once.

Despite their longstanding family connections, Shirley hadn't known George previously. As a young boy he had accompanied his father to visit Bill Sutch at Todman Street, but he never met Shirley on those occasions. His first memory of her was in a set-to outside the Duke of Edinburgh hotel in Willis Street where students regularly got arrested for disorderly behaviour. Shirley had been called to the scene. 'Shirley Smith was a big name – and there was this tiny woman which didn't fit my picture of her at all, arguing with the policeman.'[2]

George found her office chaotic, but she seemed to know where everything was. She had good basic practices. She supervised his work initially, scrutinising drafts of letters and affidavits and correcting his English. Participles and gerunds had to be right and she was a stickler for Latin maxims. Her command of English was a distinguishing quality of her practice and it gave her a strong presence in court. Above all, she exemplified principles of fairness and justice, and the right everyone had to the best defence she could offer, and this had a huge influence on George. Like her, he became known as a champion of the underdog.

The practice grew and in 1972 Shirley advertised for a part-time law clerk. Gordon Webb, a third-year law student, saw her notice, met her that afternoon and she offered him the job there and then. He found

2 George Rosenberg to author, interview, 15 February 2012.

Shirley a kind, considerate boss. She lived at a frenetic pace, always busy but never too busy to stop and say something or help if he had a problem.

In 1973 she moved to a bigger office on the first floor of the Dunbar Sloane building on the corner of Maginnity and Waring Taylor streets. Her office retained its friendly informal atmosphere with everyone now on first-name terms. Amanda Russell (later Rosenberg), the daughter of a client, joined her staff, initially as a typist, and became a close friend. Amanda found Shirley charmingly eccentric and her office was unlike any she had worked in. 'It was her world where she was boss, and a nice boss, and that was her escape as well as her work; and she felt she was with people who weren't being super-critical of her and she had her own status, which she lost when she went home.'[3] In the corner was a space where she did yoga and where sometimes, late at night, she curled up among her files on the floor and slept.

SHE SHARED the floor with Bungay, Greig & Co. Mike Bungay was a cockney, hard drinking and hard fighting, a big, tough, rough, successful but not yet famous defence lawyer. Shirley wasn't part of his macho scene but they were friends. She had known him since he was in the army and studying law at Victoria, where he distinguished himself in her Constitutional Law class. Now they saw each other almost daily and in court she crossed swords with him in matrimonial cases, which comprised a large part of her caseload.

Another opponent was Bill Gazley, a brilliant barrister whose firm, Gazley and Black, had a substantial practice for family and matrimonial law, as well as criminal law. Shirley knew him well and liked him.

Shirley held her own in this male domain. Sir David Smith, who still kept a file on his daughter, recorded her jury trial for a criminal law case in August 1971. It was, he noted, the second time a woman barrister appeared before a jury, 'this time a win, even after police grilled Maori for 2 hrs – confession, then withdrawn. Judge praised her address (as

3 Amanda Rosenberg to author, interview, 15 February 2012. Amanda added on 29 February 2012 that Shirley 'hero-worshipped her husband but was afraid of him.' Others also observed that Shirley felt Bill's lack of respect.

thorough and painstaking). I rang Jack Young for his Caucus column.'[4] The *Evening Post* columnist slipped in an expanded version some weeks later: 'Shirley Smith . . . recently distinguished herself as the first woman barrister in New Zealand to take a criminal case on her own through all the proceedings to the trial in the Supreme Court and incidentally to be able to persuade the jury to acquit her client . . .'[5]

Her colleagues, who also saw the difficult work she was doing as part of her mainstream practice, and knew just how hard it was, held her in high esteem. In court, she addressed judges with utmost propriety, but she was also fearless in the protection of her clients. Recalling her appearances before him, one of New Zealand's most distinguished jurists, Sir Owen Woodhouse, reflected that she was 'a very strong woman prepared to battle to the last gasp on behalf of people, meticulous in trying to get to the bottom of all the things she tried to do. In that sense she inherited that side of her father's strengths.'[6]

A contemporary of Shirley's, Woodhouse had as a young barrister appeared on several occasions before her father. 'He was a very courteous man, unlike some judges who imagined the office turned them into something powerful. He never had delusions of grandeur of that kind.' And Woodhouse found Smith knew his own mind. 'Smith was clear about what he thought about all various kind of cases.'[7]

As an aside, Woodhouse was the architect of New Zealand's world-leading no-fault accident compensation scheme, based on the Woodhouse Report (1967). In 1969 at the New Zealand Law Society's conference in Rotorua, on the Matrimonial Property Act 1963 and its 1968 amendment, Shirley argued that marital conduct had no place in what was essentially a property question and called for a Woodhouse Commission in this field of law.[8]

4 DSS, note, 4 August 1971, file 'Shirley 1967–72', SHSS papers, ATL, MS-Papers-11369-255.

5 *Evening Post*, 22 September 1971, p.34. The main topic was a constitutional issue Shirley Smith had raised in a letter to the editor about the doctrine of Cabinet responsibility having been abandoned.

6 Rt. Hon. Sir Owen Woodhouse to author, interview, 14 September 2011.

7 Ibid.

8 SHSS, 'Comment on Mr D. B. Inglis's paper', NZ Law Society Conference, Rotorua, 11 April 1969, SHSS papers, ATL, MS-Papers-11404-136.

That jurists compared Shirley favourably with her father did her no harm. It helped, too, that she had grown up with the legal establishment. Among those whose friendship she enjoyed was Robin Cooke QC (later Lord Cooke of Thorndon and considered by many to be New Zealand's greatest jurist). Their fathers had served on the bench together and been close friends. Robin Cooke helped and advised Shirley. Though he was in the highest demand, he acted as her Counsel in the Supreme Court on a marital case.[9]

Roy Stacey was another older barrister who had a lot of time for Shirley, and for her father. A charming, colourful character who defended the downtrodden, he was seen as the closest New Zealand had to a real-life Rumpole of the Bailey. (Later, lawyer Bill Sheat and writer Peter Coates conceived the idea of a television series about a female Rumpole of the Bailey, modelled on Shirley.) Roy Stacey represented Carmen Rupe, Wellington's first iconic drag queen, and Shirley represented some of Carmen's girls.

Shirley's criminal work was largely defending social outcasts charged with petty crime. The right to legal representation that had long been her concern was now an issue for a new questioning generation. The civil rights movement in the United States caused people to look closely at New Zealand society and see that it wasn't the land of equal opportunities that they had believed it to be. To young idealists, Shirley became an inspirational figure. Social worker Tina Reid, who worked in areas of addiction, says she and her colleagues saw Shirley Smith as a great role model. 'What Shirley was doing was awesome and we were in awe of her.'[10] Another in awe of her was Geoff Lewington, who worked with Denis O'Reilly running homes for Black Power. He remembers Shirley in and around the courtroom, talking to guys in leather jackets and taking notes. He saw nothing but respect for her. She made him think about civil rights, especially the role of the police at a time when police interviews weren't recorded and lawyers seldom challenged police accounts. Charging police with bad conduct was almost unthinkable.

9 DSS file 'Shirley 1967–72', SHSS papers, ATL, MS-Papers-11369-255. The case was a matter of legal aid. This was shortly before Cooke was called to the bench in 1972.

10 Tina Reid to author, 13 May 2015.

Generally, Shirley had good relationships with the police. As well as her connections with police officers in her court activities, she had the ear of Police Commissioner Angus Sharp, who invited her to have a chat over a cup of tea whenever she had something she wanted to discuss, sometimes under the auspices of the Council for Civil Liberties, which she now chaired. She had talks with several high-ranking police officers over the case of Gilfedder, a Christchurch policeman who beat up a fourteen-year-old gang member in the back of his van (1973). Shirley spoke about this on the radio on *Checkpoint* and put out a statement for the Council for Civil Liberties. While she supported the police prosecution of Gilfedder, a vocal section of the public strongly supported him. 'It is utterly clear that the "law and order" crowd are not concerned with the law being upheld at all, but with bashing the kids,' she wrote to Elsie Lock, adding that she found the attitude of the police at inspector level encouraging:

I had a Maori lad of about 18 who rang me in a great state the other day about police walking in and searching and abusing people, and when asked, saying they didn't need a warrant: as a result, we had a meeting with Det. Inspector Duncan on Friday evening – 4 kids, 2 policemen and me. I kept as quiet as possible. He was very good, gave them a fair hearing, and eventually after sending the policemen out, told the kids he would deal with their complaint on the basis that their version of the facts was correct and would discipline the p.c.s. There are still a number of things I want to talk to Mr Duncan about, but it was a remarkable event in my experience. My little Maori lad spoke up as we moved downstairs 'He seems to be an honest man'. But I shall have to warn the lads to keep mighty clear of those p.c.s in future, and not to mock them if they see them.[11]

She wasn't always so encouraged. Shirley spent nearly ten years seeking justice for a young Māori transvestite, Paula Konia (referred to in court records as male and by her birth name, Hiritana Te Amohaere Konia). Tragically, Konia's life would be cut short before the case ended, but her friends, Dana de Milo and Jennifer Edwards, who were also

11 SHSS to Elsie Locke, 5 August 1973, SHSS papers, ATL, MS-Papers-11369-197.

clients of Shirley's, tell her story.

Dana (who started life as Darryl Pickering) left home in Auckland at the age of thirteen in order to live openly as the female she had always felt was her true identity. There was no law against a boy wearing women's clothing and she was never charged, but her six feet three inches made her an easy target for police harassment. She left Auckland when she heard things were easier in Wellington. Unable to get work, she started soliciting on the streets and supplementing her irregular income with petty crime. She served a month in Mt Crawford prison, on remand, for being idle and disorderly. The first time she had legal representation was when Shirley approached her in court and offered help. (The charge was what Dana called 'snow dropping' – stealing clothing off washing lines.) Dana recalls:

She was the first person I met in that system . . . that actually treated me with a bit of respect as a human being. . . . She knew . . . who I was . . . that I was female and that all I wanted to do was get on with life and live. I didn't want to be in trouble with the police. I didn't want to steal. . . . it was about survival.[12]

Shirley heard from Dana and her friends how the police humiliated them in the cells, making them undress repeatedly through the night to show their genitalia, having their hair cut or wigs removed. Jennifer Edwards said that Shirley was the only person who believed their complaint that the police bashed them with sandbags during interrogation. Shirley would go down to the lockup to get them out in the small hours of the morning, and instructed her clients as well as police that any warrant for their arrest should be brought to her first.

Konia v. Morley related to events on the night of Saturday 28 and Sunday 29 January 1967. Late in the evening at the Sorrento Coffee Bar in Ghuznee Street, Vice Squad Detective Constable Trevor Morley asked Paula Konia to go outside and get into a police car to be interviewed. She agreed. He then got into the car where another policeman was at the wheel and, without Paula's consent, they drove off, heading up the

12 Dana de Milo to author, interview, 15 April 2015.

Ngauranga Gorge.

According to Jennifer and Dana, it was common practice for police to pick them up, scare them by driving fast and abuse them. If this failed to provoke a chargeable response – bad language at least – they dumped them wherever they were and left them to find their own way home. On this occasion, they left Paula at a remote spot off the Old Porirua Road, near Arohata Borstal. In the small hours of the morning, in her nightclub attire, Paula had to walk some considerable distance to Tawa before she caught a taxi. Unable to pay the fare, she gave the taxi driver the name and address of her lawyer, Shirley Smith.

Acting in the first instance for the taxi driver, Shirley made enquiries about the incident and was told the taxi fare would be reimbursed. She said she was obliged to inform her client, Paula Konia, that she would have a case against the police for unlawful detention. Later, having heard Paula's story, Shirley advised police that she was indeed bringing such an action. This led to a departmental investigation and a disciplinary tribunal in which Detective Morley was charged with a breach of the Police Regulations 1959, being guilty of conduct tending to bring discredit to the police. Shirley was not allowed to attend the hearing, but Paula was called as a witness and, as she was underage, her grandmother accompanied her. Morley was found guilty and fined $5 for a breach of the regulations.

Shirley then proceeded with her action, claiming $2,002 damages for deprivation of personal liberty, false imprisonment and assault.

At an early stage, the Attorney-General was added as a second defendant. He agreed that Morley was a member of the police force but denied every other allegation. Shirley needed to see the transcript of the evidence of the disciplinary hearing. In September 1971 she obtained an order for discovery of documents by the Crown relating to the hearing but, after further proceedings, the Commissioner and the Minister of Police reversed the order based on legal professional privilege and what was commonly (though inaccurately) known as Crown privilege.

There matters lay until Shirley instructed her good friend George Barton to take over the case. The Appeal for discovery was allowed and the case was eventually resolved, but Shirley had lost contact with Paula, who had moved to Australia. In a later effort to find her, Shirley learnt through Paula's friend Jennifer Edwards that Paula had succumbed to heroin addiction and died of an overdose.[13]

AROUND 1973 Shirley started representing members of the recently formed Black Power gang, which came to figure largely in public perceptions of law and order before the end of the decade. Black Power's founder and leader Rei Harris saw the gang as a movement. He brought in non-Māori activists such as Burmese Buddhist refugee and former judge Bill Maung and Pākehā social worker Denis O'Reilly.[14] Denis was a close friend of George Rosenberg. George introduced him to Shirley.

A former seminarian, Denis's mission was to create something along the lines of Baxter's commune for young Māori at Jerusalem. 'Denis's boys', as Shirley called them, were mostly from rural areas. Some had been in borstal, some in state-run boys' homes and mental institutions, others had run away from home. Victims of violence, abuse and neglect in their childhood, lacking education and training, they found a sense of belonging in their gang that they didn't find in society at large.

Denis found Shirley was without prejudice or favour. They both believed that people were essentially good and full of potential; they both wanted a just and inclusive society. Denis invited Shirley to dinner at Walton House, the boys' home he ran in Newtown, to meet members, share ideas and to explain what they were doing. She agreed that a big part of their problem was unemployment and applauded Denis's initiative in starting a work co-operative, Te Kaha Trust.

Geoff Lewington recalls how, after a hard day's work mixing concrete, he and his fellow labourers drank into the night at the Tramway Hotel,

13 Ibid; Jennifer Edwards to author, interview, 6 March 2015; Paula died in 1979, according to Dana de Milo. Shirley tracked down Jennifer Edwards to tell her she had a sum of money to be paid to Paula's next-of-kin.

14 Most of the boys Denis took were Black Power, but, in an attempt to break down hostilities between the rival gangs, he joined forces with Mongrel Mob member Bruce Stewart to set up a boys' home in an 18-bedroom City Mission hostel, Walton House, at 277 Mansfield Street, Newtown. When the gangs found they couldn't live peacefully under one roof, Bruce Stewart left to set up Tapu Te Ranga Marae at Island Bay, leaving Walton House to Black Power. They continued to drink, party and fight together and often ended up in court together. There was a time, before hostilities became more extreme, when Shirley represented members of both gangs.

singing to guitars, living in the moment, cherishing their group energy and camaraderie. 'All these people were able, bright, had fire in them; some had real damaging experiences in their lives, particularly those who had been to prison.' Geoff recalls several times when police came into the bar when it was full. 'Some police were overtly hard-line racist, they talked disparagingly and were grossly offensive in their attitudes.' The patrons would erupt into the Black Power anthem, 'Power to the People', performing it in a haka manner. The pushing and shoving that followed invariably led to arrests and charges of under-age drinking, disorderly conduct, assault or wounding with intent to injure.

In court the next morning the boys were usually told to plead guilty so as to get their sentences reduced by mitigation. (This was a time before duty solicitors.) Shirley and George would not only take on these cases, but they also got Denis and others to make formal complaints about police violence and showed them how to gather evidence.[15]

Shirley was proud of the cases she and George took over a couple of years 'because we won every single one of them – not by any sleight of hand, just by seeing their cases were properly put.'[16] But she was never paid. If they couldn't pay the full fee she asked them to pay what they could afford – five or ten dollars a week. Some of them earned good money in demolition work and so were ineligible for legal aid. One client said, 'But I was found not guilty. What have I got to pay for? I haven't done anything wrong.' No one considered that Shirley was giving full service for nothing.

Her secretary Helen Edwards took things in hand when Denis phoned one day wanting help for one of his boys. She told him that they never paid – go away.[17] Shirley was furious, but it marked the end of her work for Black Power.

She was briefly involved with the gang girls associated with Black Power. They used to sit around Cuba Mall all day and didn't know where they were sleeping from one night to the next until they realised

15 Geoff Lewington to author, interview, 4 May 2015.

16 SHSS to Neville Glasgow, interview for National Radio, broadcast 18 January 1989, published in *Directions: New Zealanders Explore the Meaning of Life*, Shoal Bay Press, Christchurch, 1995, pp.186–201.

17 Ibid.

the possibilities open to them if they earned their own money. They looked at Te Kaha Trust and thought, 'If the boys can do it, we can.' They asked Shirley and Sonja Davies to help them form the Aroha Trust, the only women's work co-operative in the country.

Shirley and Sonja registered the Trust and continued as trustees. 'We needed their skills and respectability but made sure we outnumbered them when it came to making decisions,' Pip Desmond wrote. This, and the fact that the Aroha Trust didn't last much longer than a year, probably explains why it slipped from Shirley's mind in her later accounts, but she would have been proud of having played a critical part, however limited her influence, in its short life. Denis O'Reilly wrote on his blog 'Nga Kupu Aroha' on NZEDGE: 'Aroha Trust was one of the gutsiest, most feisty, courageous and generally unknown expressions of women's liberation that this country has seen. These were the women who challenged the Black Power over our attitudes to rape and who, at the end of the day, were responsible for a change in gang behaviour, nationally.'[18]

Apart from the Aroha Trust, Shirley's work as honorary solicitor for numerous organisations continued through the 1970s. In 1972 the Society for Research on Women (SROW) completed a landmark nationwide study on urban women.

In 1971 Shirley was elected vice-president of the Wellington branch of Abortion Law Reform of New Zealand (ALRANZ), a cause she shared in common with her brother and sister-in-law, Allan and Helen Smith. Allan was involved on the medical front and Helen raised the national profile of abortion and women's health when she stood as Values Party candidate for Porirua against anti-abortionist Dr Gerald Wall. In March 1975 when the national office of ALRANZ was shifted from Auckland to Wellington, Helen was elected vice-president.[19]

Shirley's ongoing work for the Cook Islands Society (mentioned in the previous chapter) and the Council for Civil Liberties continued.

18 Pip Desmond, *Trust: A True Story of Women and Gangs*, Random House, Auckland, 2012, pp.25–26, p.251.

19 Margaret Sparrow, 'Allan Smith's story', *Abortion Then and Now: New Zealand Abortion Stories from 1940 to 1980*, VUP, 2010, pp.193–195.

She drew up the constitution for Wellington's first lesbian club in 1974 and continued to campaign for homosexual law reform.

Also in 1974 she joined the Druids Friendly Society (the Brooklyn Lodge of her father-in-law). This service organisation is like Rotary and Lions but has traditionally welcomed and honoured women members. And it appealed for other reasons. Druids look after families in need, especially children; they follow ancient philosophies with a leaning towards Celtic ideals; and they promote a love of learning, understanding nature and taking care of the natural environment.

Environmental, conservation and heritage organisations were yet another area that claimed Shirley's time, energy and generosity. She campaigned to save Lake Manapōuri against hydroelectric development and generally added her voice to environmental causes, but the cause closest to her heart was the preservation of Wellington's historic Thorndon. She had previously campaigned at the end of the sixties for the preservation of the Bolton Street Cemetery against the encroaching motorway. The construction of the motorway saw part of the Hill Street ridge excavated. She saw it as an urban tragedy that the residential area she described as 'a little bit of paradise in Wellington' should be sacrificed for the motorway. She and others raised public awareness of the cultural value of Thorndon. Instead of demolishing the old houses, they recommended they should be restored. This was a novel idea – restoration wasn't something people usually thought about in the early 1970s.

In 1972 Shirley, together with local architect Martin Hill and journalist Gillian McGregor, formed the Thorndon Trust to buy the 1860s Granny Cooper's cottage at 30 Ascot Street to save it from demolition. The Trust proceeded to buy and restore other cottages to save the historic area from commercial redevelopment. They then leased or sold the buildings as residential dwellings. The next step was to set up the Thorndon Society as an action group to support the Trust. The society succeeded in persuading Wellington City Council to create a new historic Residential E zone. Any future changes within the zone had to be in character with the existing fabric and required Council consent. This was radical. Previously in New Zealand single buildings had been identified for historic preservation, but this was a whole district. And the campaigners not only sought to preserve Thorndon's historic buildings, but they also aimed to preserve the sense of place and community. From 1973, community activities brought residents together in fundraising events. Though Shirley wasn't a resident, she knew many who were, including Aileen Finucane and Max Wilkinson, and Bill owned the cottage next door to them in Glenbervie Terrace. As well as chairing the Thorndon Trust (1972–93) and doing the conveyancing, she was proactive in fundraising. She spoke at public meetings, on radio and television and wrote letters to the paper, raising public awareness.[20]

In this, as in many of her causes, Bill and Shirley were at one. They both made submissions to the Royal Commission on Social Policy (1970). Shirley said she had to call on her better nature as Bill expounded ideas that were originally hers 'as if they were hitherto unthought of by anyone. When first I told him of them, he thought they were too way out. I have to tell myself the only thing that matters is the ideas.'[21]

Sutch's submission was seen as the most outstanding contribution, with Sir Thaddeus McCarthy saying he had proposed 'a minor revolution'. Sutch developed his plan and published it in *The Responsible Society in New Zealand* (published by Whitcombe and Tombs Ltd in 1971).

In 1973 he published *Women with a Cause.* He thanked Shirley for providing the section on matrimonial property law and for her contributions to his first chapter. At one point – the moment stuck in her memory clearly – when he told her he had decided who he would dedicate his book to, for a moment she expected it would be to her, until he went on to say it was to his mother. Her telling of the story years later showed how hurt Shirley still felt that Bill never dedicated any of his books to her. (He had dedicated books to Helen.)[22]

20 Ben Schrader, 'Residential E and the "Saving" of Thorndon', Research Roundup Seminar Series, Stout Research Centre, 18 October 2017 (forthcoming book, *Won + Lost: A History of Historic Preservation in New Zealand*); SHSS papers on Thorndon Trust, ATL, MS-Papers-11369-254; SHSS memoirs, 'The Rita Angus Residency', 23 August 1998; 'The Thorndon Trust' and 'Achieving the E-Zone', 28 August 1998, SHSS papers.

21 SHSS to MHS, 17 December 1970, MHS papers.

22 Brian Easton to author, confirmed 14 January 2018. Sutch dedicated *The Quest for*

While Bill and Shirley were both leading exponents of feminist ideals, in terms of their own arrangements, despite long hours of work in her profession, Shirley remained the housewife, with most of the chores that that entailed. Shirley thought that Bill saw her law work as a hobby and felt demeaned by this.[23] He never really appreciated the difficulty of being responsible for running a law practice and a house, as well as looking after a husband.

Shirley drew an amusing picture of herself as seen by her guests on one occasion. As soon as the Chinese set up an embassy in Wellington, Bill invited the Ambassador, his wife and an interpreter to a Saturday lunch, which Shirley had to prepare. After a hard week's work, it nearly killed her. As she carried the dishes in and out of the kitchen on her own, it dawned on the guests that there were no servants at all in the house. The Ambassador said, through his interpreter, 'You are the best proletarian of us all!'[24]

In fact, Bill and Shirley were both working themselves into the ground. Their friend Ormond Wilson wrote to Peggy Garland in England (March 1974), 'Bill and Shirley grow more, not less, overwhelmed by the pressure of their affairs. Shirley is surely killing herself by her efforts to right injustices and take up lost causes.' After commenting on Bill's new appointment by the Labour Government (elected in December 1972) as chair of the New Zealand Queen Elizabeth II Arts Council and what that involved, he added he was 'also trying to write a biography of his early hero, Gordon Coates [Prime Minister 1925–28, who later, as Minister of Finance, employed Sutch as an economic advisor] . . . Bill is trying to write his book at the weekends. It can't be done like that.'[25]

Security (1966) and *The Responsible Society in New Zealand* (1971) to Helen. As mentioned in Chapter 11, Shirley jointly wrote a booklet with Bill in 1944.

23 Several people close to her at the time, Amanda Russell, Julie Grenfell, Deirdre Macken and others, spoke of this.

24 SHSS to Brian Easton, notes on chapter on WBS in *The Nationbuilders*, 22 August 2000, Brian Easton papers. NZ officially recognised the People's Republic of China on 23 December 1972. By July 1973 China had established an embassy in Wellington and trade talks were underway. Kirk reopened an embassy in Moscow and the USSR upgraded its office in Wellington from legation to embassy status.

25 Ormond Wilson to Peggy Garland, 17 March 1974, published in *Dear Peggy: Letters to Margaret Garland from her New Zealand friends*, eds. Peter and Dianne Beatson, Sociology Department, Massey University, Palmerston North, 1997, p.129.

Later in the year, Shirley's father wrote to his former colleague Ralph Grey, now in England:

Shirley tries to combine a legal practice with various activities aimed at reforming the world. She is probably the only woman lawyer in the country who runs her own office, employing several staff, appears regularly in the Magistrates court and sometimes in the Supreme Court – jury trials with some success – but it's a hard life and the overheads are so high that she doesn't make much money. She also seems to have no recreation except so far as a bit of housework now and then provides it.[26]

After describing Allan's full family life, he concluded, 'Shirley and her husband simply go their own ways in New Zealand . . .'[27]

ON 2 JUNE 1974 Shirley and Bill celebrated their thirtieth wedding anniversary with a family dinner party at home. Their guests included Shirley's step-cousin, Meta's niece Betty Batham, who had recently moved to Wellington. Bill commented that she was 'more than a little odd'.

Betty – renowned marine biologist Dr Elizabeth Batham – had resigned from her associate professorship at Portobello biological station in Dunedin and come to Victoria University to carry out research in Wellington Harbour.[28] On 7 July her unlocked car was found near Fort Dorset army base in Seatoun and items identified as hers were found on the beach. The police sent out teams of divers and, a week or so later, scuba divers meeting for a conference in Wellington carried out a search, but her body was never found. A mystery phone call and reported sightings of her from three reliable people raised rumour and conjecture.

Shirley helped police and devoted a lot of time to trying to solve the mystery. She took a Zoology Honours student with her to check over the diving equipment found in Betty's car to explain its significance. Her scuba diving gear was there, but Shirley learnt that Betty had duplicate

26 DSS to Lord Ralph Grey, 25 October 1974, DSS papers.
27 Ibid.
28 *Dominion*, 8 July 1975, 'Inquest sought on lost scientist'.

diving equipment. Her fins, belt and knife were missing. None of her bottles for samples were in the car. Her purse, bankbook and traveller's cheques were found there, which ruled out murder motivated by theft.

Betty's sister Esperance Anderson sent Shirley a letter she'd received from Betty, dated 3 July 1974, telling her what she intended to do – that she would swim out into really deep water. They already knew that Betty had suicidal thoughts – she had not been well for some time – but reported sightings of her after her disappearance meant that Shirley couldn't exclude the possibility that she had gone elsewhere, probably to Australia (for which in those days she didn't need her passport, which was in Dunedin). The police were making enquiries there.

'What are we to do about Betty's letter to you?' Shirley asked Esperance. 'Do you authorise me to tell the Police? I suppose I cannot tell a lie, but I do not have to volunteer information. Please let me know what you want me to do.'[29]

The letter, which Shirley did give to the police, added to many accounts that showed Betty was very unwell. As more came to light, Shirley agreed with the police's assumption (and eventually the coroner's finding) that Betty had drowned.[30] At the end of August, Betty's cousin Dick Skinner and his father came up from Dunedin and stayed at Todman Street. Having earlier emptied Betty's university office, Shirley now had the mournful task of helping Dick pack up her flat.[31]

Preoccupied, Shirley didn't see that another, very different crisis was fast approaching.

29 SHSS to Esperance Anderson, 7 August 1974, SHSS papers, ATL, MS-Papers-11369-195.

30 Detective Inspector Craig Scott, National Criminal Investigations Group, Police National Headquarters, Wellington, to author, 26 March 2018. The finding of Coroner Andrew David McGregor, 27 May 1977, was that 'she died on or about 8.7.74 in the waters of Wellington Harbour off Seatoun, Wellington, her death being self-inflicted but from causes unknown, her body not having been recovered.'

31 Ibid; SHSS to MHS, 20 August 1974, MHS papers; Gordon Webb to author, interview, 26 April 2011.

20

Smoke and mirrors

In the early hours of 27 September 1974, Dr W. B. Sutch was arrested on the charge of espionage. For Shirley, this came out of the blue and, like a rogue wave, it crashed over her life.

Twelve months earlier, when New Zealand was setting up a new embassy in Moscow, an officer of the KGB, Dimitri Aleksandrovich Razgovorov, applied for a New Zealand entry visa to join the Soviet Embassy in Wellington as First Secretary. The Foreign Affairs Ministry knew he worked for Soviet intelligence but didn't want to provoke Moscow to reject New Zealand diplomats, so granted the visa. NZSIS identified him as successor to Yuri Drozhzhin, the KGB *rezident* (station chief) in New Zealand between 1968 and 1973. NZSIS spies could never follow Drozhzhin to a rendezvous with an agent – he was what they described as 'a consummate practitioner of trade-craft' – a master-spy – but Razgovorov was another matter. From the time he arrived in January 1974 they had him under surveillance. They soon learnt that at 8.30 on Thursday nights 'something happened', usually a contact between him and another agent or a prospect 'under cultivation'.

The two security officers on duty on the night of Thursday 18 April 1974 expected to observe a meeting between Razgovorov and a prospect they code-named 'Hyderabad'. At 7.30 pm NZSIS agent Kit Bennetts and his colleague (identified respectively as 'S' and 'T' when they gave evidence in court) saw Razgovorov leave the Russian Embassy in Messines Road, Karori, in a maroon Mercedes-Benz driven by KGB agent Vitaly Pertsev. They followed the car downtown where the Russians went through standard counter-surveillance manoeuvres before returning to Karori where Bennetts and his colleague lost sight of the Soviet car. Bennetts dropped his colleague off at the Karori Mall to search on foot. Driving on, Bennetts saw the Russian car again, noticed its driver was now alone and followed him along the dimly lit Lewer Street. At the entrance to the Karori Bowling Club, Bennetts saw, in the shadows, two men dressed in dark clothing talking. Bennetts recognised Razgovorov but not the other man. He'd never seen him before.

According to his evidence in court, the two men were still standing together as if talking when he drove past a second time to get a closer look. He then returned to his colleague, parked the car and together they walked down Lewer Street, where they saw Razgovorov and, shortly after, the man he had been talking to.

They had no doubt what they had seen. 'It was a clandestine meeting by the book, "Moscow Rules": it was near a well-populated place, but private and seemingly safe from prying eyes and the chance of being overheard. . . . The site gave both men the opportunity to escape in opposite directions.'[1]

Bennetts's colleague followed the unidentified man on foot along Karori Road while Bennetts followed in the car at a distance. When their target hailed a taxi, Bennetts picked up his colleague and they followed the taxi to Brooklyn where the passenger got out at the top of a long driveway in Mitchell Street. They returned sometime later to note the street numbers: 91–111.

'Alex', a long-serving intelligence officer, in an interview with the author, recalled SIS Deputy Director John Maling's look of horror when he realised who Razgovorov had met. Maling had been head of counter-espionage since 1964, during which time the SIS had collected and added information to Sutch's file (as they had with Shirley's), but he hadn't been under surveillance. No one imagined he might have been spying for the Russians. Young Bennetts had never heard of him and neither he nor his colleague could positively identify him from the old photos they were shown.[2]

Bennetts and his colleague formally identified Sutch on the morning of 30 April when, from an observation post the SIS set up opposite his

1 C. H. Kit Bennetts, *Spy: A Former SIS Officer Unmasks New Zealand's Sensational Cold War Spy Affair*, Random House, 2006, p.18.

2 'Alex', NZSIS, to author, 17 December 2013. John Maling retired in 1974, but returned to assess files.

office, they recognised the man they had seen talking to Razgovorov get out of a yellow Mazda and enter the ANZ Bank building. The car was driven by a woman who was identified after further checks as Miss Shirley Smith.

From then, the SIS kept surveillance on both Sutch and Razgovorov. They discovered that Sutch paid for his taxi fares by chits, which he charged to New Zealand Textiles. By a clandestine operation code-named 'Andromeda', Bennetts intercepted and photocopied the chits before the taxi firm sent them to Sutch's office. These chits, combined with their surveillance, strongly suggested a pattern of meetings taking place around 8.30 pm on the penultimate Thursdays of the month, or on Thursdays in the penultimate week of the month.

The SIS had observed one meeting in Karori, missed another that they believed had occurred in Kelburn, and seen another in Karori aborted. They anticipated that the next meeting would be on 25 July. To avoid detection, they used static observation posts to track the embassy car from Karori. Two mobile officers followed Sutch from his office to Upland Road via the cable car. They saw him approaching Razgovorov (who had parked his car in Kelburn village and was on foot). The two men passed one another on the footpath without giving signs of recognition. Sutch was carrying a newspaper under his left arm, which the SIS officers identified as a pre-arranged signal that it was all clear to meet. (If it was under his right arm, it was not.) He continued along Upland Road almost to Kelburn village, then turned, backtracked and turned down a small footpath into Glen Road, where Razgovorov was waiting further down the hill. At exactly 8.30 they met, stepped back into the shadows of an open carport and talked quietly for a few minutes. Bennetts and his colleague watched from the shortcut footpath between Upland Road and Glen Road, while a third colleague covered Upland Road. They then saw Sutch walk slowly down and turn into Rimu Road. Razgovorov headed up Glen Road to Upland Road. The consul from the Soviet Embassy, KGB agent Boris Belousov, pulled up in a yellow Toyota Crown (not the car Razgovorov had parked in Kelburn Village). Razgovorov leant in through the open passenger window; Belousov then sped back to the Embassy and

Razgovorov returned to continue his meeting with Sutch, now waiting in Rimu Road.[3]

The SIS agents had no doubt that Razgovorov had passed something to Belousov. Their superiors concluded that Sutch was a controlled KGB asset acting as an agent of influence, and that he was passing information to the KGB. They didn't know what the information was or where he got it, but, considering the possible damage, they decided to brief Prime Minister Norman Kirk and Solicitor-General Richard Savage. Norman Kirk, who suffered from heart problems exacerbated by operations on both legs for varicose veins, was by then seriously ill.

In his written submission to them, Brigadier Gilbert related the sequence of events since 18 April. He suggested three courses of action: that they should continue to observe further meetings in order to obtain further and more decisive evidence; that they should arrest Sutch and Razgovorov at the next meeting; that Sutch should be invited to offer an explanation and, subsequently, Razgovorov, Pertsev and Belousov could be expelled. Sutch was to be given immunity from prosecution and public exposure in exchange for his cooperation.

Gilbert recommended the third course, as did Solicitor-General Richard Savage QC. On 2 August, when the briefing took place, Gilbert and Savage stressed their wish to get Sutch's cooperation to give them an idea of past and present KGB activities in New Zealand so they could assess the damage.[4]

Norman Kirk distrusted Brigadier Gilbert. He had previously warned him that the SIS must stick to its business, to respect civil liberties and not concern itself with people whose views on foreign

3 Kit Bennetts, *Spy*, pp.63–67; depositions and trial transcriptions; former senior SIS officer involved in the operation to author, 2 February 2018.

4 Solicitor-General Richard Savage to Attorney-General Martyn Finlay, 8 October 1974, 'SECRET': *At that stage I suggested that Dr Sutch might be confronted with the information that he had been seen meeting Razgovorov with an indication that the Government was considering declaring Razgovorov and another Soviet official* persona non grata *and that part of the reason for this was the clandestine meetings that had been occurring between Razgovorov and himself. He should be asked to indicate precisely what it was they discussed, and why, with an intimation that if he was not prepared to disclose it then the only conclusion that could be drawn was that there was an ulterior purpose which was contrary to the interests of this country.*

policy differed from those of the government.[5] He was unhappy that they tapped phones while denying to him that they did so, and that they rarely briefed him although, as minister in charge of the SIS, he was responsible for their actions. He was angry that Gilbert had rejected his idea of appointing someone to oversee the Service to protect the rights of individuals. (The post of Inspector-General responsible for reviewing issues of legality and propriety was established in 1996.) He was disinclined to believe whatever 'the Brig' told him.

Yet he was totally convinced and visibly shaken by what Gilbert showed him about Sutch. Kirk's secretary Margaret Hayward wrote in her *Diary of the Kirk Years*, 'Mr K used to be gentle with Dr Sutch. When I'd asked why he was so patient with him he had explained that he was an elderly man "who can't have much money, no future but an old age pension, and has only his reputation to cling to". He had excused Dr Sutch's arrogance by saying that he wore it like a threadbare cloak. Now he is furious.'[6]

Kirk wanted to know what was being passed to the Soviets and instructed the SIS to continue their surveillance. He realised they would have to use clandestine methods. He told them, 'Get a cleaner.'[7]

The SIS set up a top-secret annex which Kit Bennetts in his book code-named 'Vulcan'. The operation involved searching Sutch's office on a regular basis, bugging it and installing a tap on his phone. Nothing came of the tap and bugs, but the search produced a diary in which

5 Clipping, unidentified, 9 April 1973:
PM TAPES N.Z. SPY SERVICE
The Security Intelligence Service has been warned by the Prime Minister, Mr Norman Kirk, that it must stick strictly to its own business and give due regard to civil rights.
Mr Kirk revealed in an exclusive interview with the Sunday Herald *that he has told the director of the service, Brigadier H. E. Gilbert, precisely what he may or may not do.*
Mr Kirk said, for instance, that there was no need for the service to concern itself with people whose views on foreign policy differed from those of the Government.

6 Margaret Hayward, *Diary of the Kirk Years*, Cape Catley Ltd, Queen Charlotte Sound, and A. H. and A. W. Reed Ltd, Wellington, 1981, p.282; Margaret Hayward to author, interview, 4 August 2014. What offended Kirk more than what Gilbert told him about Sutch being a spy was what he said about his activities in UNRRA and the means by which he and another New Zealander had allegedly acquired substantial assets.

7 Paragraph 26, Chief Ombudsman Sir Guy Powles' Top Secret Report, NZSIS, 16 July 1976, http://www.nzsis.govt.nz/assets/media/SutchOmbudsmanReport.pdf (accessed 20 June 2018).

Sutch had written the dates and cryptic references to his clandestine meetings with Razgovorov. The cryptic annotations lined up with the meetings the SIS had observed, missed and seen abandoned.

'Vulcan' reported a new entry in the diary for 28 August: '8.30 Webb and Hopper'. With their knowledge of the kind of locations chosen (just off but close to main roads), the SIS anticipated where the meeting would occur and set up static observation posts in strategic places. On 28 August, from opposite a telephone booth in Hopper Street, they saw Sutch and Razgovorov meet, speak briefly, then step back into a darkened doorway where Sutch lifted his briefcase onto his knee and opened it. Razgovorov stood between him and any possible passer-by. The low light further obscured the view from the observation point. The two men then went in their separate directions, Razgovorov to his car, driven by his wife on this occasion.

On the day of the Hopper Street meeting, Prime Minister Norman Kirk was admitted to Our Lady's Home of Compassion Hospital in Island Bay. He died three days later, on 31 August. The country was in shock.

When he was confirmed as Kirk's successor, Prime Minister Bill Rowling approved the course proposed regarding Sutch. 'Vulcan' reported that a new note in Sutch's diary next to Thursday 26 September was '8.30 Holloway'. For this meeting, the SIS brought the police into the picture, briefing the head of their team, Detective Chief Inspector A. W. (Wally) Baker and his 'oppo', Detective Senior Sergeant Colin Lines.

The plan was to apprehend Sutch during his meeting with Razgovorov, and a senior SIS officer was to take him aside to an unmarked car around the corner and deliver him discreetly to the Central Police Station to be interviewed. The SIS was to offer him immunity from prosecution in exchange for his cooperation. They expected him to talk to them and to cooperate when he learnt what they knew. Baker and Lines, whose role was to intercept Sutch, knew that the first priority was to gain his cooperation, but they were not fully briefed on what the SIS would offer him, nor did they have enough information about what was already known of previous meetings between Sutch and Razgovorov.

On the evening of 26 September, SIS officers monitored both Razgovorov's departure from the Soviet Embassy and Sutch's departure from his office. They saw Pertsev drop Razgovorov off at Entrance Street, near the small war memorial park, and estimated the time Sutch would arrive. They didn't see that some 500 metres before the arranged meeting place, in a brief lull between heavy showers of rain, he hailed a passing taxi and so passed unseen through the cordon of stationed officers. Neither SIS nor police (some of whom were hiding in the public toilet in Holloway Road) observed Sutch meeting Razgovorov at this point, but they saw Razgovorov walk across the glade from the top of Aro Street and cross Raroa Road into Entrance Street, where the big maroon Mercedes-Benz was parked. According to testimony from witness 'X', Razgovorov approached the passenger's side and appeared to lean in through the car window for about twenty seconds. After Razgovorov left the car, it took off up Raroa Road in the direction of the Embassy. Razgovorov returned in the direction he had come from, crossed Aro Street and entered a pathway that led back to Holloway Road. From a different perspective, according to their evidence in court, Colin Lines and Wally Baker saw two people briefly together. Soon after, Lines approached one of the men, Razgovorov, who then suddenly changed direction, ran down towards the path into Aro Street, crossed Aro Street and sprinted in the pouring rain down the road until he was stopped by an SIS officer (witness 'W').[8] The two men talked as they walked on down Aro Street towards a phone box, where the SIS officer called the Soviet Embassy for a car to pick up Razgovorov. (He had diplomatic immunity.) They were in each other's company for about 90 minutes, which later gave rise to further speculation about collusion

8 Sir Guy Powles: 'Dr Sutch was apprehended after the two men had met and Razgovorov had had the opportunity to go to his car and talk to his driver who then left the area.' Powles Report, 16 July 1976, Paragraph 15.

Detective Senior Sergeant Lines, giving evidence in the trial, said he saw a person near where the paths intersect 'and as I approached this person another person stopped beside him. I approached the first person I had seen, whom I recognized as Mr Razgovorov . . . I stopped in front of him, identified myself, he made no comment. He stepped around me, and walked quickly down the path towards Aro Street. As he approached the road he started running down Aro Street . . .': trial transcript, p.58.

between the SIS and the Soviets to trap Sutch. The car eventually arrived and took him back to the embassy.

Meanwhile Colin Lines, after walking back along the footpath behind the memorial towards Holloway Road, saw Sutch step out from under a tree near a driveway. (For some weeks afterwards, Shirley knew only that he had stood under dripping trees in Holloway Road, waiting to meet Razgovorov. Photos show Sutch was again carrying a newspaper under his left arm – all clear to meet.) Lines approached Sutch, spoke to him by name, identified himself and asked him what he was doing in the area. Sutch said he was out for a walk because he had a heart condition, and asked several times what was going on. Lines told him that a member of the Russian Embassy was also in the area. Sutch wanted to know where this man was. He then repeated his explanation that he was out walking for his health, and was in Holloway Road because he was interested in historic buildings. He protested at the 'preposterous' suggestion that he had met any Russian on this or any other occasion.

At that point Detective Chief Inspector Wally Baker joined them. Baker told Sutch it was alleged he had met with a member of the Russian staff on three occasions in Karori, Kelburn, and Hopper Street in Central Wellington. Sutch continued to protest and became increasingly excitable at seeing officers appear from out of nowhere, cameras flash and what he thought was a tape recorder pushed towards him. He refused to speak to the SIS officer and would have nothing to do with the security service.

Sutch later explained to Attorney-General Martyn Finlay, 'I was told by Mr Baker that I could be arrested under the Official Secrets Act, but if I could explain my presence satisfactorily he would not arrest me. He said "I might be on the hook to the Russians" and if I could explain what this "hook" was I might not be arrested.'[9] Baker mentioned other occasions when Sutch had been seen meeting with Razgovorov, but he was wrong in some respects. Sutch persisted in his total denial.

At about 10 pm the police took Sutch to the Central Police Station for further questioning. When shown a photo of the First Secretary of

9 WBS to Attorney-General, 17 October 1974, Martyn Finlay papers.

the Soviet Embassy and asked if he had ever seen him, Sutch replied that maybe he had, once, at a big function to do with the United Nations in the Overseas Terminal. He denied meeting him anywhere else and continued to protest that the whole thing was preposterous. He would have understood from their questions that the SIS had seen him in Karori at the same time as Razgovorov, but not on two occasions. He didn't know that on one occasion he and Razgovorov had been seen together. Asked about the meeting in Hopper Street, Sutch said he had never been in that area during 1974.

Senior Magistrate J. A. Wicks signed a warrant for the police to search Sutch's house and office, but this didn't include the assistance of the SIS officers who knew better what they were looking for. Sutch continued to express hostility and distrust of the SIS, but showed a trusting, cooperative attitude to the police.[10]

On 28 September 1998 – the twentieth anniversary of Bill's death – Shirley wrote her account of the night of his arrest under the heading 'Night of 26.ix.74'. As she recalled, she was at her office as usual that evening, but found she couldn't settle to work. Unable to concentrate, she drove home 'early' – around midnight – to find a police car parked just outside the gate and several police officers waiting there. Detective Senior Sergeant Burgess met her and explained that the police had apprehended her husband and he was at the Central Police Station. Burgess showed her a warrant to search her house. Shirley was too shocked to do more than identify the signature of Magistrate Wicks. The sergeant told her that they had been waiting for hours and were about to break in.

She thought she must cooperate and stay on good terms with the police. She knew them and got on well with them – as she testified in court, they were kind and considerate. She herself was shocked and confused. At some point one of the male sergeants offered her a cigarette. 'I had given up, but stress, and this was the worst I had suffered, drives me, not to drink, but to smoking. He kept me going until they left . . .

10 Interview, CIB, Wellington, 11 am, 27 September 1974; present were Detective Inspector Baker, Detective Senior Sergeant Lyons and M. A. Bungay.

and gave me his packet with the few left . . . I shall always, as long as I live, remember his kindness.'[11]

They started the search upstairs in the living room. On request, Shirley provided a stepladder for one of the policemen to search the top shelves of the bookcase. He checked the books one by one, riffling through the pages, holding them upside down by the spine and shaking them. Another sergeant had gone around the corner to Bill's study. Shirley sat on a stool in the angle of the L-shaped room so that she could keep an eye on both areas to see that no one planted evidence. She watched Sergeant Burgess examine artefacts Bill had collected on his travels, unscrewing the heads off bronze buddhas and peering inside. She asked them if they knew what they were looking for. Photographic equipment and microdots, they told her. 'I laughed and said Bill didn't take photos and both my cameras were at the office. . . . I did not even know what microdots were, not being a reader of spy stories.'[12] (In fact neither the police nor the security service were equipped to find microdots, and there was no attempt to carry out the kind of destructive search that would have been necessary.)

Burgess asked Shirley to show him the layout of the house. She took him into the stack rooms and storage places and unlocked doors, including her bedroom cupboard where she kept her jewellery.[13] At one point the woman sergeant opened one of the cupboards next to the fireplace and saw a piece of plywood screwed to the wall at the back. Shirley explained that it provided access to their previous washing machine, brought from New York, which could be repaired only through the back. She provided a screwdriver and the searchers gathered around in anticipation to watch the sergeant, on her knees, unscrew the plywood. It came away, exposing the back of the washing machine.[14]

Soon after this Shirley spoke on the phone to Bill at the police

11 SHSS, 'Night of 26.ix.74', 28 September 1998, SHSS papers. (Shirley dated this 29.ix.98 but further down she noted that she had written it the previous day, on the anniversary of Bill's death.)

12 SHSS to Martyn Finlay, 31 January 1975, Martyn Finlay papers.

13 Ibid.

14 SHSS, 'Night of 26.ix.74', 28 September 1998, p.2, SHSS papers.

station. 'He was very excitable, and said, "It's ridiculous, they're saying that I met some Russian in Holloway Road, it's nonsense." He was in total denial.' A very senior officer – probably Wally Baker – came on the line and asked if she'd like them to bring Bill up to the house.

Shortly afterwards (about 1.30 am according to Baker's deposition), Wally Baker, Colin Lines and Bill arrived. Baker emphatically urged Bill and Shirley to go into a bedroom to talk. Lines strongly objected on the grounds that Bill might commit suicide but Baker was insistent – so much so that Shirley thought they had bugged the room. 'I made Bill lie down, went and made a cup of tea for him, and we talked of nothing but who to get as a lawyer.'[15] She didn't ask him what had happened. She thought it better, in the state he was, that Bill said nothing. (Months later she thought that if only she had got the proper story from him then, she could have prevented all that subsequently happened.[16])

After a while Baker and Lines came down to the bedroom and stood, 'two tall men, against the cupboards at the side'. In January 1975 she wrote to Attorney-General Martyn Finlay, her old friend, and Bill's:

Baker thrust under my nose a duplicated copy of sections of the Act, which I was quite incapable of reading because of the shocked state I was in. Baker kept urging Bill to take this opportunity of 'getting himself off the hook' and Bill kept saying he wasn't on any hook. I however became aware that Bill had been talking to Baker and Lines and I said, 'For heaven's sake, didn't you realize you didn't have to say anything?'[17]

In Warsaw in 1998 she recalled Baker saying that if the Russians did have Bill on the hook, it would be better for him to tell the police now and get off the hook. Bill then asked, 'And what would happen then?' As Shirley recalled, Baker replied, 'The law would have to take its course,' and Bill said, without hesitation, 'There is no hook.'[18]

'I think that Bill probably was on some sort of hook; that they had some sort of information that they held over him that Bill did not want

15 SHSS to Martyn Finlay, 31 January 1975, Martyn Finlay papers.
16 Ibid.
17 Ibid.
18 SHSS, 'Night of 26.ix.74', 28 September 1998, p.3, SHSS papers.

divulged. This simply stems from the conversation, it is implied. I asked no questions, I did not think of asking him.'[19]

The gist of her recollection and what she thought it implied is in line with official records. The differences in their accounts, however, are telling. Colin Lines, giving evidence in the trial in February 1975, said that when initially asked whether he was on the hook, Sutch had said it was 'preposterous', but when the question came up later, they had a discussion:

He said that if he was on the hook about something with the Russians and he told us about it, then he would be on the hook with us. . . . when he put that proposition to me, we had a discussion about if he told us he was on the hook with the Russians and told us about it, that we would pass that information to the appropriate authorities and that it may then have been a different situation than denying he had ever met this Russian or had discussions with him. . . . he thought about that for a while and then he denied that he was ever on the hook with the Russians.[20]

Shirley, assuming Bill was under arrest, thought they were laying traps. She realised that Bill's talking was getting him into deeper trouble and asked if he had been given the usual warning. He hadn't.

Baker had gone out of the room at this stage. I said to Lines 'But you can't arrest anyone without warning them' and Bill said 'No one has said I'm under arrest.' . . . Baker came back and said Bill wasn't under arrest but he wanted him to come with them while they searched the office and he might as well pack a bag as they might keep him all night.[21]

Baker said later in court that Bill had been able to see his wife who was a lawyer. This, she explained to Martyn Finlay, was true but 'as

19 Ibid.

20 The Queen v. William Ball Sutch, trial transcript, p.65. Kit Bennetts in *Spy* wrote: 'Our biggest failing was that Colin Lines had not been comprehensively briefed and was not aware at all of the nature of the offers that might have been made.' 'Alex', a long-serving intelligence officer, gave the author the same explanation.

21 SHSS to Martyn Finlay, 31 January 1975, Martyn Finlay papers.

a lawyer I was a total loss that night except when I thought of asking about the warning. I also had no idea of what had happened, not having asked Bill, and was in no position to advise him.' She thought Bill went on talking to the police down at the station. 'He has never really paid any attention to what I've told him about these things because it is quite outside his sphere.'[22]

On the way back to the police station he was taken to his office, which he unlocked to be searched. At the police station he was formally arrested at 3.25 am.[23] He spent the rest of the night locked up. Out of consideration he was put in one of the women's cells.

Shirley had no sleep that night. She made cups of coffee and tea for the police and the security officers who had now joined the search. They left the house soon after 6 am, taking with them stacks of documents.[24]

Her biggest worry was getting someone to represent Bill. One after another the lawyers she phoned declined to take the case. The third, Bill Gazley, told her that if he ever got into that sort of trouble, he'd go to Mike Bungay, so she rang Mike and he leapt into action. He had everything organised by 10 am when he appeared before the magistrate.[25]

Bungay arranged bail on the basis that his client would give up his passport, that his case would be called first and that he would be in the dock only a few minutes. Asked who would stand bail, without

22 Ibid.

23 According to Chief Ombudsman Guy Powles' report, after Dr Sutch had consistently denied any association with the Russians, the officers of the Service, the police and the Solicitor-General held a meeting. They concluded that the primary objective of apprehending Dr Sutch had not been and would not be achieved, and there was no choice but to charge him. 'He was advised that in the absence of a satisfactory explanation of his conduct he would be charged. The charge was then drawn up and at 3.35 a.m. he was formally charged.'

24 Inventory of property taken from WBS 79b [sic] Todman St Brooklyn between 0015 and 0535 hrs on 27 November 1974, compiled by Detective Sergeant Burgess, witnessed by Sergeant Pickens, included diaries 1950, 1958, 1966, 1937; 15 diaries found in basement storage room; Cabinet Economic Committee minutes dated 1964, all marked 'Confidential and Restricted', in basement storage room; other papers marked Confidential, 'Secret', related to trade and industry; cheque book, Swiss Credit Bank, Zurich: WBS PF, NZSIS.

25 SHSS to Brian Easton, 22 August 2000, Brian Easton papers. In one account Shirley wrote that she first phoned Martyn Finlay. She also phoned Dick Collins.

hesitation Shirley said, 'Jack Lewin.' She was shocked when he refused. She then gave the name of Bill's brother Ted Sutch (living locally in retirement) and he stood bail.[26]

WHILE THIS was going on, Shirley appeared at court to represent her friend Julie Cook (later Grenfell) in her divorce hearing. Shirley arrived late, looking harried. When she explained what had happened, Julie thought her hearing should be deferred, but Shirley insisted it should go ahead.[27]

Back at her office, everyone was in a state of bewilderment. George Rosenberg had just left Shirley's employment to take a break before starting a new job. He came back to help her through the crisis.

Her immediate concern was Helen in London. The magistrate had refused Bungay's request for name suppression and Shirley expected the story would be headline news in London's morning papers.[28] When she spoke to Helen on the phone, Helen said she would come home at once, but Shirley said there was nothing she could do at this stage. Helen offered again the next day and got the impression from both her parents that they didn't want her to return.[29]

THEIR FIRST interview with Sutch that morning left Bungay and his partner Ian Greig in no doubt that he had handed something to the Russians. 'We didn't want to know what the something was, and the less said the better,' Greig told the author, explaining that it would have limited their defence options to have known.[30] Sutch's guilt or

26 SHSS, 'Night of 26.ix.74', 28 October 1998, p.4, SHSS papers.

27 Julie Grenfell to author, interview, 14 January 2012.

28 The news was reported sensationally in London papers: *Guardian*, 28 September 1974, 'Ex-civil servant on spy charge': 'There are now fears that an extensive spy network may be operating inside key departments, feeding sensitive information concerning not only New Zealand Government activities, but also those of friendly nations to a member of the Communist bloc.' 'Already the case is seen as involving the most sensational allegations of espionage New Zealand has known.' *Guardian*, 5 October 1974, p.2, from their correspondent, Wellington, 4 October: 'It is believed that the Russians were seeking to uncover details of a secret agreement which has been under negotiation between New Zealand and Iranian Governments for the last six months.'

29 MHS to MSS, 10 October 1974, MHS papers.

30 Ian Greig to author, interview, 26 October 2011.

innocence had no relevance at all as to how they handled the case.

They also learnt then of Sutch's earlier meetings with Razgovorov in similar questionable circumstances. It was after this first interview that Bungay and Greig decided that Sutch would not give evidence, and that no one besides him and his lawyers was to know this. Sutch was instructed not to talk about the case with anyone. This, Ian Greig said, was their most important decision.[31]

At 11 am Bungay met with Baker and Lines at the CIB. When Shirley later realised that mistakes were made at this stage, she thought that Baker had set a trap. Noting what the police had told him of the meetings the Security Service had observed between Sutch and Razgovorov, Bungay wrote that the first meeting was 'in the vicinity of the Karori Mall at about 8.30 p.m. They were not seen to converse and the security officers believed they became suspicious.' This account is confused with a later occasion in Karori on 20 June when Razgovorov aborted a meeting on Parkvale Road after spotting the SIS during their counter-surveillance in Flers Street and again nearby. Bungay later wrote in the margin of his notes, '*Interview, Confusion* – Lewer St Fluer St'.[32]

Baker showed Bungay the diary taken from Sutch's office by the police during the search, with eleven entries of meetings. Bungay noted that on four of the dates mentioned in the diary, security officers said they had eye-witnessed meetings between Sutch and Razgovorov. It was apparent, however, that nothing was seen to change hands and the search for evidence *after* Sutch's arrest (including chopping down a grove of trees in Holloway Road) indicated that the SIS had no hard evidence. (Bungay noted that it had not been confirmed if photographs had been taken of the meetings, but he decided not to discuss this with the police at this stage.)

Bungay concluded that Baker did not think the meetings alone were grounds to arrest Sutch, but that it was Sutch's denial of knowing Razgovorov that prompted the arrest. That did not prove he 'obtained information' for them, or that he was a spy.

31 Ibid.

32 Also, the account given of the Glen Road meeting was misleading.

Bungay outlined his case: Sutch wasn't clever – leaving diary entries in his office wasn't clever – but stupidity was no crime. It was his own vanity and ego that landed him in dock. 'Is he a spy? *No more despicable label you can give a man.*'[33]

This would be the defence, assuming there was a case to be answered.

SHIRLEY DESCRIBED the weekend as 'sheer hell'. She acted like a dragon with all callers, protecting Bill from the media, phone calls and visitors, many with messages of support. Bill had conferences with Mike Bungay, who also came to dinner. Between seeing her father at his urgent request and preparing dinner, she dashed off a letter to Helen.

I cannot tell you anything much in this, but I must warn you that there is a case to answer, and Daddy made the basic mistake of talking away to the Police instead of saying he would need to see his lawyer first. This does not mean he has admitted anything – quite the contrary. He has denied things which apparently they can prove. You know he has always made his own rules and he has always believed that whatever he does is right, otherwise he wouldn't do it. What it is really all about I do not myself know at all; but it is like living in a nightmare.[34]

She was sure the Security Service had stolen her handbag when it went missing. (It turned up the next morning but that didn't allay her suspicions.)[35] Rumours spread that Bill, and later Shirley also, had taken refuge in the Russian Embassy. She scotched these by having Bill talk on the phone to Radio Windy and NZBC.

Shirley wrote again on 2 October to explain that, under the Official Secrets Act, evidence of associating with 'foreign agents' puts the

33 Mike Bungay's notes of meeting.

34 SHSS to MHS, 29 September 1974, MHS papers.

35 In reply to a written inquiry about this and similar events Shirley attributed to the Security Service, Director of Security Dr Warren Tucker told the author on 3 February 2014 that there was no search of the house after 26/27 September, nor any search of her office and she herself was never under surveillance. None of the family, apart from Dr Sutch, was ever under surveillance by the SIS or the police. Further enquiries of former senior staff and SIS files confirm that the only time SIS officers entered the Sutch–Smith house was on the night of the arrest.

onus on a person charged under the substantive section of proving his innocence.

The charge under that section is (briefly) obtaining *evidence prejudicial to NZ and advantageous to 'an enemy'. Of course, nobody knows who the enemy is. But Daddy as you know freely meets people from many overseas embassies and has done reports for them in his consultative capacity as an economist (notably the Japanese who think he's Christmas). I was worried about this at one stage, but he told me he gives them nothing that doesn't come from published sources. It is just that he knows where to get the information and can collate it whereas they are at sea in a country they don't know.*

Mike Bungay tells us that the brig's people have been shadowing him for years and they have evidence of his meeting such people including Russians and they have apparently decided that he is the King pin of a spy ring . . . I know nothing of the facts and I have not talked to Daddy about it at all because we believe everywhere is bugged, probably even the car. We have been told that great diplomatic disapproval has been expressed to the Government because all foreign reps greatly resent any suggestion they might be classed 'an enemy'. The Attorney General (Marty Finlay) has to authorise a prosecution and it is likely that he has not so far done so . . . Daddy has had tremendous public support and the Government is reported to be gravely embarrassed. (They knew nothing of the Brig's activities.) Mike Bungay is doing a terrific job.[36]

Bill wrote to Helen that Shirley 'seems to be bearing up reasonably well, but I am very worried about the enormous load she is carrying. And though I hate to think of it, she should probably drop some of the outside activities on which she lavishes so much time and emotion.'[37]

The following Saturday Helen phoned to tell her parents that there was no problem at her end if she were to come home. Keith was supportive and her boss in the UK Government Economic Service was understanding and would allow her to leave immediately. She had

36 SHSS to MHS, 2 October 1974, MHS papers.
37 WBS to MHS, 2 October 1974, MHS papers.

intended to return in the new year: it was simply a question of leaving slightly earlier than she would have anyway. Bill brusquely replied that she wouldn't do him or herself any good.

However, Shirley had second thoughts and sought Aileen Finucane's advice which was that Helen should make up her own mind. That evening Shirley wrote again to Helen. She started by saying that she had felt she had been wrong in telling her not to come home when Bill had his heart attack in 1968, which naturally alarmed Helen. She continued:

You will understand I am sure that the basis of our saying to you this morning that you should not come back now is that we want to keep you out of this as much as possible; that we don't want you to be harmed, and we feel very conscious that you have most of your life ahead of you and that you matter infinitely more than we do. But because this has become an international thing, whatever we do, we can't keep you out of it – and of course, even more, because of what you inevitably feel about it.

You are an adult, and – as we have been trying to realize in the marrow of our bones and not just rationally accept (which is easy) – an independent individual: and it is not for us to tell you either to come or to stay away. You should consider everything that seems to you relevant and make your own decision. Whatever it is we shall accept it. I decided to write this without discussing it with Daddy because I think it is better not to involve him. If you decide to stay, he need never know I wrote to you along these lines: if you decide to come, it will be entirely your own decision.

. . . You have to think of the effect on your own future and Keith's. Whatever happens, there is bound to be a smear that will probably never be erased. I cannot see you getting a job in a NZ Govt department. One side issue of this that affects me is that I have got to make my practice profitable, because if it comes to the point of my having to get an independent income, I can't see anyone employing me. . . .

As for how we are bearing up, the initial shock was pretty terrific, and I think I was more or less paralysed to start with: it took some time for my brain to start functioning again. But I think I am pretty solid now, and feeling very hard and pugnacious. . . .

Dearest girl, we are horrified about the repercussion of all this on you, and also on all the others who cannot help but be affected.

You know I love you more than I can say and you are precious beyond anything to both of us.

– Mummy[38]

Despite her stoicism, Shirley was under enormous strain. Helen understood that she wanted her home – 'every line shrieked that she wanted me', she wrote to her aunt Margaret Shirley. But why did her mother not wish to involve her father? Why was he not to know about the letter?

UNDER THE TERMS of the Official Secrets Act, Attorney-General Martyn Finlay had to give his consent for prosecution to proceed. As yet, he had not done so. The Crown still wished to avoid prosecution and hoped to get Sutch to talk. At their first meeting on Friday 27 September, Baker had asked Bungay for a precise explanation of four meetings between Sutch and Razgovorov, stating times and places. Sutch then agreed to admit he had met Razgovorov on several occasions. On Wednesday 2 October, Solicitor-General Richard Savage and his junior Paul Neazor indicated to Bungay that 'this being a somewhat unusual case', if Sutch could provide an acceptable explanation, the Crown was prepared to consider it and a prosecution might not proceed. Savage pointed out that they were 'more concerned to protect the security of the State by closing any places where information was being wrongly disclosed, whether this was deliberate or inadvertent, than in obtaining a conviction.'[39]

38 SHSS to MHS, 5 October 1974, MHS papers.

39 Solicitor-General Richard Savage to the Hon. Attorney-General Martyn Finlay, 3 October 1974, Martyn Finlay papers. Continues:
1. Mr Bungay indicated that Dr Sutch was preparing a lengthy memorandum about the whole matter and made no secret that he had lied when he said he did not know the Russian or that previous meetings had occurred. He said that they would disclose the material at the trial and hinted that there was going to be a good deal of embarrassment for prominent people when the information was disclosed. He said, however, that in light of my intimation he would refer the matter to Dr Sutch and they were faced with a question of disclosing this information and thus disclosing his defence, or keeping it up his sleeve to the trial. I told him that we would not be unduly worried about any embarrassment if it led to closing any leaks of important information. Mr Bungay made a reference to whether prosecutions of others might

Mike Bungay involved Shirley as little as possible (for example, it was not until late January that she saw the transcript of the list of meetings Bill recorded in his diary).[40] And, according to Shirley, she and Bill had had no discussion at all at this stage and were practically not speaking. Nevertheless, when he got the message that Martyn Finlay would consider Bill's explanation, she insisted on being in on the conference with Bill and his lawyers. Shirley wrote to Maurice Shadbolt on 7 May 1975 that she and Mike 'grilled' Bill before sending the letter:

. . . and we told him that the SIS would undoubtedly have had listening devices and would have overheard every word he and R said and that if he told anything but the truth he would be shot. He laughed (not very happily) and said nobody could possibly have overheard anything but what he said he said, because that was what he said: and what the Russians said too.[41]

She qualified this: Bill's letter was based on the four meetings he was asked to explain and he was unhappy about it because some of it didn't seem right to him. In her January 1975 letter to Martyn Finlay she wrote:

Mike said that Baker had asked for an explanation of four meetings precisely, with times and places stated (as in Bill's letter to you). I assumed, without asking, that Mike had these 4 occasions in writing from Baker, and I agreed with Mike that Bill should account for them and not volunteer further information. Bill thought he should explain everything he could remember, although he was still very confused because of the shock he was still suffering from. . . .[42]

follow if material was disclosed . . .

2. Mr Bungay expressly asked that you should consider the question of whether to consent to a continuation of the prosecution only after he had had an opportunity of discussing the matter with Dr Sutch. . . .

3. During the course of the discussion, Mr Bungay said that both he and Dr Sutch accepted that there was a prima facie case and they would now have to accept the burden of displacing it. He also said that there could be no criticism of the Police action in the circumstances as they had developed.

40 SHSS to Martyn Finlay, 31 January 1975, Martyn Finlay papers.

41 SHSS to Maurice Shadbolt, 7 May 1975, ATL, Maurice Shadbolt papers, MS-Group-1280, 91-047-16/14.

42 Ibid.

Dr Sutch's letter of explanation to the Attorney-General was sent off on 17 October. Mike Bungay showed it to Shirley. She recalled in 1998:

As far as I remember, Bill had signed it in his office and brought it over to Mike. Mike showed it to me . . . he was quite proud of it. I read to my horror that Mike had put into Bill's mouth, so to speak, the statement that he had never favoured the Soviet Union. I said to Mike, but this is not true! He was one of the founders of the NZ–USSR Friendship Society. Lots of people will know this. Well, I can't help it, said Mike, I've promised it for today and it is already late – I've got to get it in. I gave him the document. From then on, I suffered: I knew that I should have torn it up. I believed that Mike had put a noose round Bill's neck and I had not stopped him.[43]

The defence team was not told about two of the documents taken in the search of Sutch's office that would influence Martyn Finlay's decision. Paul Neazor informed the Solicitor-General that one was a carbon copy of a memorandum dated 1970 about the personal experience, aptitudes and ambitions of six senior officers of the Foreign Affairs and Industries and Commerce departments and their wives.[44] In particular, in the case of four of the officers, their attitude towards the Soviet Union was indicated. The second document, also thought to be intended for the Russians, was a copy of a memorandum relating to the Japanese fishing industry in New Zealand, with information about a Cabinet decision that had not yet been made public. It named a senior public servant as the source. 'At this stage it has not been revealed to Mr Bungay that we have this information and Police inquiries have so far been kept to a minimum to avoid scaring Sutch off if he is inclined

43 SHSS, memoir, 'Night of 26.ix.74', September 1998, p.10, SHSS papers.
I am not a friend of the Russians or their system, and have never had any strong political affiliation. From time to time I have displayed enthusiasm for certain Government policies and been critical of others. I feel this fact is well known publicly. . . . intrigued . . . nothing sinister . . . under no circumstances would I have been disloyal to New Zealand, and perhaps it can be ascribed to my own vanity that I felt I might find something of use to the New Zealand Government or for my own future writings. I realise now I was naïve and even stupid . . . W. B. Sutch to Attorney-General Martyn Finlay, 17 October 1974, Martyn Finlay papers.

44 The profiles refer to 'External Affairs' which was renamed Foreign Affairs in 1970; Industries and Commerce became Trade and Industries in 1972.

to make a full disclosure. But once we have whatever he offers, further avenues of inquiry suggested by these documents will be followed up by the Police.'[45]

SHIRLEY WENT through a period of agonising doubt about Bill those first weeks, and she was furious with him. Paranoid about bugging and fearing that anything he might say would further incriminate him, they both avoided discussion. They were scarcely talking anyway because of her anger. She thawed a little when Bill gave her a piece of Kobi Bosshard jewellery for her birthday. 'I was still distant: but I did recover, got over my anger, realised that he was still my Bill, and that I loved him, whatever he did. I had never any doubt but that I would do whatever I could to help him, but it was better to do it with love.'[46] By the time of the depositions they were on speaking terms again, although she still had no idea what was going on.

45 D. P. Neazor to Solicitor-General, memorandum, 8 October 1974, Martyn Finlay papers. Bungay wrote to the Attorney-General, 10 October 1974, requesting a frank discussion in the interests of Dr Sutch and of the Nation: 'The Crown has outlined to the writer briefly what is alleged against Dr Sutch and the writer now feels that he is in a position to make certain representations on behalf of his client . . .': Martyn Finlay papers.
46 SHSS, memoir, 'Night of 26.ix.74', September 1998, p.5, SHSS papers.

21

A case to answer

THE DEPOSITIONS were heard before Wellington's Senior Magistrate, J. A. Wicks. The courtroom was packed – people queued for an hour before the courthouse opened and not everyone got in. SIS officers being identified by letters of the alphabet became a joke. Mr Wicks liked all his court sessions to be jolly. Shirley thought he overdid it, 'but his influence during the depositions made them not only quite bearable but quite enjoyable for us. It seemed as if he were hearing a comic farce, quite hilarious at times . . . There was nothing that surprised us in the evidence.'[1]

In fact, there *were* surprises as the prosecution's evidence showed discrepancies with Sutch's account in his letter to Martyn Finlay. When Shirley read the depositions for the first time some three months later, she attributed some of the discrepancies to his state of shock and confusion, and to his legal advice to explain only what was known. Not knowing that Detective Chief Inspector Baker had a limited knowledge of the meetings the SIS had observed, she thought that he had set a trap.[2]

At the time, she must have been shocked, as Sutch was, when it became apparent how much the SIS knew about his meetings with Razgovorov. At one point when Kit Bennetts was giving evidence he looked at Dr Sutch: 'Our eyes met and as I watched I could see his hands shaking – almost imperceptibly, but they were shaking.' One of his colleagues also commented on Sutch's discomfort and pallor. The mood had changed.[3]

The magistrate found there was a case to answer and committed

1 SHSS, memoir, 'Night of 26.ix.74', September 1998, p.5, SHSS papers.

2 Shirley's account of the depositions, even in the short term, was inaccurate in several respects, perhaps an indication of her own state of mind under great stress.

3 C. H. Kit Bennetts, *Spy*, Random House, 2006, p.134.

Sutch to a jury trial in the Supreme Court. It was then up to the Attorney-General to give his decision, which he announced on 21 October. 'What appears on the face of it to be melodrama may turn out to be farce but I cannot assume that it will,' he wrote in his statement. And so 'with a heavy heart and after much reflection', Finlay gave his consent to further proceedings.[4]

On 25 October, Sir David Smith wrote to his colleague and associate, Ralph Grey (now Lord Grey of Naunton in Gloucestershire):

. . . I see you have heard of the Sutch case. He was yesterday committed to the Supreme Court for trial. The whole business is awkward and unhappy for my family. I am particularly sorry for Shirley who knew nothing about the matter and was suddenly faced with detectives who came to search her house at midnight . . . She has forced herself to recover and is being very loyal to her husband.[5]

Over Labour Weekend, four weeks after Bill's arrest, Shirley had her first real conversation with him about his meetings with Razgovorov. She suggested they go to Castlepoint on the Wairarapa coast and talk while walking on the beach where they couldn't be overheard. She needed to ask Bill many questions, but still feared even the car could be bugged. She was sure they were being followed.[6]

The weather at Castlepoint was horrible, so they left and visited Alister Taylor near Martinborough. He recalled that Bill and Shirley were 'like frightened rabbits. They were both tense and aware of being followed everywhere, their phones tapped, their correspondence opened, files and papers removed from their house and offices.'[7] (When questioned about this in 2014, SIS Director Warren Tucker told the

4 Secretary of the Cabinet to Attorney-General, copy to Prime Minister, 21 October 1974, Martyn Finlay papers; Martyn Finlay press statement, 21 October 1974, Martyn Finlay papers.

5 DSS to Lord Ralph Grey, 25 October 1974, DSS papers.

6 SHSS to Martyn Finlay, Jan/Feb 1995, Martyn Finlay papers. Shirley continued: 'We had no conversation about the matter at all until Labour Day Weekend – four weeks later. After trying to get a chance to talk out in the country and having our nerves shot to pieces by the obvious security cars checking us, we finally found refuge in a friend's house out of town and talked for hours.'

7 Alister Taylor, memoir of Shirley Smith for author, May 2012.

author that there were no office break-ins or phone-tappings after the night of the arrest and no SIS officers followed Shirley and Bill to Castlepoint, adding that to have done so would have been pointless and could have compromised the trial.)[8]

Alister showed them to a room with thick concrete walls, which he assured them would block any bugging, and there Shirley put to Bill her questions. 'Bill was down to bedrock and I'm sure he told me the truth,' she wrote to Martyn Finlay. 'There is no doubt that the Glen Rd conversation was as Bill reported it.'[9] But this wasn't the case.

She wrote in 1998 that she accepted what Bill told her and did not ask if that was all. To others, she expressed doubts. Julie Grenfell heard her talk about it on several occasions. 'I would say that from the way in which she would break off and look intellectually perplexed that she never received an explanation to her entire satisfaction that she could accept. . . . She was after all a capable defence lawyer.'[10]

Alister always wondered if Bill was totally frank with Shirley. She was reserved about discussing the case or anything associated with it with Alister. 'She would always say, "Now's not the time Alister, it's too hurtful to talk about now; we'll talk about it later." But that time never came and she appeared to me to force it from her mind.'[11]

Looking back, Alister thought that Shirley began a slow decline from this period.

Shirley told Alister when she and Bill visited him after the trip to Castlepoint that she felt isolated and alone, bereft of personal support. She desperately needed Helen home.[12]

Helen arrived at the beginning of November. Contrary to Shirley's assumption that government jobs would be closed to her, she started at Treasury on 18 November. Keith, who had been appointed senior lecturer in the Political Science Department at Canterbury University, arrived later to take up his job in the new year.

8 NZSIS Director Warren Tucker to author, 3 February 2014.
9 SHSS to Martyn Finlay, 31 January 1975, Martyn Finlay papers.
10 Julie Grenfell to author, interview, 14 January 2012.
11 Alister Taylor, memoir of Shirley Smith for author, May 2012.
12 Ibid.

Shirley wrote warmly to Keith, acknowledging his sacrifice in having to finish his term at Essex University alone. She was feeling more positive about the case:

[Helen] *found us in rather better condition than she expected and indeed, than we had been in the earlier weeks. One learns to live with things, even this sort of thing: also, however, there are a number of reasons for feeling more cheerful, especially a closer study of the law, and a realisation of how non-existent the case against Bill is. One has to be careful about counting chickens but hope keeps trickling through about not only vindicating Bill but turning the tables.*[13]

Support for Sutch had gathered momentum. His supporters believed that he was the victim of dirty dealings; that the law by which he was prosecuted was draconian. Added to this were rumours that the SIS had new bugging devices, all of which prompted renewed calls to curb the powers of the service, or dismantle it completely.

After Sutch's committal, George Rosenberg, Amanda Russell and some others formed a group calling itself the Sutch Defence Committee. Early in December they sent out an appeal stating that the prosecution brought against Dr W. B. Sutch under the Official Secrets Act 1951 was entirely inappropriate in peacetime and should long ago have been repealed. Donations were to go into a trust fund that the committee established to assist Dr Sutch with legal and other expenses involved in his defence. 'It is hoped in this way to encourage discussion of the Official Secrets Act and other aspects of the case.' (Sutch's legal fees were anticipated as being between $30,000 and $40,000. Public contributions solicited by the Sutch Defence Committee amounted to $1,768, of which $781 was allotted to defence costs. The rest was to be assigned to fund opposition to the SIS and the Official Secrets Act.)[14]

13 SHSS to KWO, 5 November 1974, KWO papers.

14 The amount held by the Sutch Defence Committee was, at Sutch's request, to be donated equally to two new organisations, Repeal of the Official Secrets Act (ROSA) and Campaign to Oppose the Security Service (COSS): Sutch Defence Committee to Friends, March 1975, ATL, MS-Papers-11404-143. Figures given in this letter showed at that point the total donations to the Trust Fund were $1,569, of which $581 had been spent on pre-trial assistance and a further $200 allotted for defence expenses.

A Motion to Quash was to be heard in the Supreme Court on 16 December before Chief Justice Sir Richard Wild. Shirley was probably involved in the legal research for this, but her hopes for a successful outcome were dashed when Wild gave his judgment two days later. Dismissing the motion, he set the trial date for 17 February 1975.

Two days later Crown Counsel Paul Neazor gave Mike Bungay preliminary notice of the Crown's intention to call additional evidence and to use photocopies of additional material in the trial. He intimated their intention to call an officer of the Security Service to give expert evidence about the methods and information targets of Soviet intelligence agencies.[15] This related to the carbon copy of a memorandum the SIS had taken from a file labelled 'Foreign Affairs' in Sutch's secretary's office on the morning of his arrest. Headed 'Memo for file' and dated 20.10.70, it appeared to have been written for the Russians.[16]

Before Christmas, Mike Bungay went up to Todman Street with this document. Shirley and Bill both read it. The six senior public servants described in 'the profiles', as they came to be called, were Tom Larkin and Charles Craw in Foreign Affairs, Geoffrey Easterbrook-Smith, G. H. Datson (Geoff) and H. C. Holden (Harry) in Industries and Commerce. The sixth, 'the main left-winger', was Jack Lewin, who in 1970 was Government Statistician. Bill knew them all well and so did Shirley. She would have recognised Bill's views, his voice, his astute observations summed up concisely in his characteristic style. She later wrote to Martyn Finlay that she realised they could be 'damaging if sheeted home to Bill, not so much in themselves as what they might suggest.'[17]

The SIS assessment noted that the writer clearly had a long association

15 D. P. Neazor to Attorney-General, 21 July 1975, Martyn Finlay papers.

16 D. P. Neazor to Solicitor-General, 8 October 1974, Martyn Finlay papers. Neazor referred to one of two documents seized under warrant from his office the morning of Sutch's arrest, which were suspected to have been intended for transmission to the Russians. See p. 318.

17 SHSS to Martyn Finlay, 23 October 1993 (dated 1974 but written the day after she received Finlay's letter of 20 October 1993), SHSS papers. The author has read the profiles.

with the subjects and had their confidence, notably about their attitudes to the Soviet Union. It noted that the descriptions also mentioned each man's interest in international politics, personal ambitions, intelligence, whether he was energetic or lazy, discreet or talkative, and commented on their wives and marriages. The profiles also included past activities and postings and anticipated future appointments. The SIS assessment noted that the memo was intended for a third person who was not a New Zealander. The account of Lewin was an update, assuming past knowledge.

The Security Service assessment concluded that the 'Memo for file' 'was probably prepared by Dr Sutch for a trained Russian Intelligence Officer seeking personality information on leading NZ Govt representatives which could in turn be used by the Soviets for recruitment purposes.'[18] The profiles closely resembled criteria for talent-spotting as revealed by Igor Gouzenko, a cypher clerk with the GRU (Soviet Military Intelligence), who defected to Canada in September 1945.[19]

Bill's first reaction to the memo was that he didn't remember it at all and thought it was a plant. Shirley thought that would sound unlikely and it had to be explained on another basis. Gladys Brown, widow of Bill's brother Tom, now remarried, was his secretary in 1970. She confirmed that the memo was written on the office typewriter (presumably it had been replaced), but later said she hadn't typed it and knew nothing about it.[20]

On 31 January 1975, Shirley wrote to Martyn Finlay that Solicitor-General Richard Savage had advised Mike Bungay that the Crown would after all not present as evidence the additional material they had sent before Christmas. But the profiles continued to worry her. She was shocked when Alister Taylor wrote to her from Martinborough after

18 Assessment of profiles, November 1974, declassified by NZSIS 23 June 2008.

19 Ibid; The Canadian Royal Commission Report, 'The Gouzenko Report', 27 June 1946.

20 SHSS to Martyn Finlay, 30 August 1975, fragment of draft, SHSS papers, ATL, MS-Papers-11404-68: 'We discussed it when we were away on holiday and it was I who persuaded him that that would not sound likely and it had better be explained on a different basis. He then tried to think how it could have been written. I should have told you this when I saw you: I assure you it is true. Mrs Brown who was his secretary confirmed that it was typed on the office typewriter . . .'

the trial and asked her about them. She denied all knowledge of them.[21] When Leader of the Opposition Robert Muldoon asked a question about them in the House, prompting the Attorney-General to make an inquiry as to why they weren't used in the trial, Paul Neazor explained, 'Substantially our approach was that the evidence was relevant (although even that might have been the subject of argument) but that there could be an argument about its probative value not sufficiently outweighing its prejudicial effect, and that it was not of sufficient value to the case as framed to warrant the diversion it would cause.'[22]

Shirley made no reference to the second document seized under warrant during the search of Bill's office the night he was apprehended. This was the copy of a memorandum relating to Japanese fishing industry interests in respect of New Zealand that claimed to contain information about a Cabinet decision that had not then been released, naming a senior public servant as the source.[23]

In Neazor's same memorandum to the Attorney-General, he wrote that there was never any intention that any cabinet ministers should be called as witnesses and none were interviewed.[24] Sutch's diaries, not his current diary but those seized on the night of his arrest that went back years, indicated clandestine meetings with the KGB. (The SIS thought his contact was *rezident* Yuri Drozhzhin, which the Mitrokhin files later confirmed.) These early entries weren't presented as evidence in the trial because the charge against Sutch covered a specific period and they fell outside that timeframe.[25]

From 22 December to 13 January, Shirley and Bill were away on holiday. Baker arranged for Bill to report at various police stations. A friend of Bill's, a baggage handler at the Māngere airport, offered them his beach house at Orere Point, overlooking the Firth of Thames. There they enjoyed what Shirley considered the best Christmas possible under

21 SHSS to Martyn Finlay 23 October 199[3], SHSS papers; SHSS memoir, 'Night of 26.ix.74', September 1998, p.7, SHSS papers.

22 Crown Counsel Paul Neazor to Attorney-General Martyn Finlay, memorandum, 21 July 1975, Martyn Finlay papers.

23 D. P. Neazor to Solicitor-General, memo, 8 October 1974, Martyn Finlay papers.

24 D. P. Neazor, memorandum to Attorney-General, 21 July 1975, Martyn Finlay papers.

25 'Alex', a long-serving SIS officer, to author, firthk-10-17-02.pdf, 11 October 2017.

the circumstances and a peaceful recuperative time.

Bill didn't swim, but he lay, still and silent, sunning himself on the flat top of a rock. I did not know what he was thinking, but it was easy enough to guess, when he had the sure prospect of a trial on a serious charge ahead of him, and the possibility of a long prison sentence. . . . We did not discuss prospects or possibilities. Bill could not have conducted himself better than he did at this tragic time of his life.[26]

For Shirley, it was a reflective time. She wrote letters. To Margaret Shirley, who had given her a book about Katherine Mansfield by Vincent O'Sullivan, Shirley wrote:

The little girl in the hat does indeed remind me of my childhood . . . Perhaps wandering alone in what were then bare Wadestown hills in the wild northerlies (which I have always loved) helped stiffen my back. How difficult to work out what made one the person one is. But I do like your Fairburn quotation, and rather particularly the last line 'which is neither a matter for pride nor a cause for grief.' That is really how I feel about my commitment to Bill. It is a thing in itself. I couldn't leave 'until the game is up and my hand has lost its power' – neither of which events I envisage in the foreseeable future.[27]

The A. R. D. Fairburn quotation was from *To a Friend in the Wilderness* for Sir Douglas Robb, his and Shirley's mutual friend who died during the year. It was Fairburn's response to the imagined call to 'let go the rope, the weight is dead against you'.

Old rebel, what is there left for me to say?
This only: till at length
I reach the end of action, the last of my strength,
I cannot sever the bond,
destroy the documents, cut the cord

26 SHSS, memoir 'Night of 26.ix.74', September 1998, p.11, SHSS papers.
27 SHSS to MSS, 29 December 1974, MHS papers.

of my origin and being. This is my world.
These people are my clansmen, my accomplices.
I share the crime. This guilt is my reprieve:
I am alive, and I do not mean to leave
till the game is up, and my hand has lost its power.
These are my people. Till seventy times seven
I am committed to them,
which is neither a matter for pride nor a cause of grief: . . .

This was the clearest statement of Shirley's commitment to Bill. It was, as she said, 'a thing in itself'.

The same day she wrote to her father.

Dearest Daddy,

This card reminds me of my childhood. Some games are universal. We drew hopscotch patterns on the asphalt and in the gravel, and yesterday on the beach here there were two great mazes drawn on the sand, reminding me of the great figures you drew on the sand for me when I was a little girl, and how we watched the tide devouring them.

One seems to have lived many lives in a lifetime; and the shadow-play goes on. (I am thinking of Plato.) Our present drama is one I could well wish you had been spared. But I am committed to it; and in spite of my initial anger, I am quite sure that it is bad judgment and nothing more that has brought this upon Bill (and us all). When I say 'nothing more', I mean on Bill's part. As for others, I believe a trap was deliberately set. You'll think this fantasy: but this is really a digression. What I really wanted to say is that my attitudes, my loyalty to Bill, my commitment ('for better or worse'), my determination to fight and not be put down is, in the principle of the thing, what I've inherited from you and my stiff-necked Scottish forebears; and not less, I should think, from Nannie and my mother. Where I've gone wrong, over the last 30 years at least, is that I've not asserted myself enough. I should have risked more – you remember Montrose's 'He either fears his fate too much / or his desserts are small / who never puts it to the touch / to win or lose at all.' I feared losing Bill, depriving Helen of a father. I didn't risk rows, I didn't risk confrontations, when (looking back) I know I should have. Women can go too far, suppress too much, in fulfilling the traditional role of keeping the peace. Imagine me being too traditional! But I was. Hence my responsibility. From the end of last September and from now on, I shall be me. *At 58, about time.*

My best love to you now and always, Shirley.[28]

Her father replied:

Many thanks for your note, the hopscotch picture and your reference to the big pictures I drew on the sand at Titahi Bay bring back memories for me too. What a good day we had, at times, at Titahi Bay over 50 years ago! No crowds, just a few scattered houses and the old Titahi Bay pub, sandhills with a grassy growth on top, a large expanse of usable beach, one water tap, good swimming, a walk along to the rocks at the southern end when the tide was out to see the crabs and shellfish etc. in the pools, happy fun, a drive home in the old car along country roads and down the windy Ngahauranga Gorge after a sunny day in unpolluted nature and a dreamless sleep, or am I being too rosily reminiscent? I don't think so.

Your other observations go deep. They would bear comment but not here. I do profoundly hope he will be acquitted.[29]

On New Year's Eve, Bill and Shirley moved on to spend a night with Valerie Davies and Pat Booth in Drury. Pat was assistant editor of the *Auckland Star* and Valerie wrote a column for solo parents in *Women's Weekly*, which is how she met Shirley and Bill. On receiving a letter of congratulations from Shirley for one of her columns, Valerie decided to interview her for a story. In September, shortly before Bill's arrest, Shirley invited her home for lunch. Pat recalled that Valerie came back from her visit quite dazzled. Now it was as though both couples had always known each other.

To Pat's disappointment, they didn't talk about the case at all. Valerie thought Bill and Shirley wanted to be in a bubble and nothing was to spoil this precious time. She saw them totally at one with each other:

28 SHSS to DSS, 29 December 1974, SHSS papers, ATL, MS-Papers-11369-254.
29 DSS to SHSS, 2 January 1975, SHSS papers, ATL, MS-Papers-11369-254.

Shirley seemed to accept that Bill was perfect and he was right, and Bill was tender and gentle towards Shirley. He told Valerie how sad he was that he had put her through all that she was suffering.[30]

When Valerie later published her glowing account of Bill, Shirley wrote:

It is clear to me that Bill's fate derived from Bill's nature. More surprisingly, he knew this too. Surprisingly, because most of the time I knew him, he was out of touch with his feelings, his motives and unconscious of his effect on other people, at least until he got a cold prickly reaction, and then it was always all their fault. From that dreadful night when he was arrested, he changed. He blamed no-one for his predicament but himself – he told me so. He became the person you met, and I can tell you it was a change. The potentiality must have been there, overlaid with all his arrogance (which was a cover for insecurity), defensiveness and will to put over himself and his ideas.[31]

After New Year's Eve with Valerie and Pat, Shirley and Bill drove north to Mahurangi Heads to stay with their old friends and fellow peace campaigners, John and Cathy Male. Shirley wrote in 1998:

We had the best possible time with John and Cathy. The weather was brilliant, John took us out in his launch . . . showed us how to spear flounder, made available his Bert Brecht/Kurt Weill records, which I lay on the floor and listened to over and over again. He had The Threepenny Opera, and a collection of songs, most of them sung by Lotte Lenya: he gave the songs to me.[32]

On the way back to Wellington, Shirley called on former Police Commissioner Sir Angus Sharp in Rotorua. When he was Commissioner, Shirley had on several occasions taken up his invitation to drop in on him for a cup of tea. In reply to her letter on his retirement he wrote:

30 Valerie Davies and Pat Booth to author, interview, 7 September 2011.

31 SHSS to Valerie Davies, 16 September 1989, p.5, SHSS papers, ATL, MS-Papers-11404-82.

32 SHSS, 'Night of 26.ix.74', 29 September 1998, pp.12–13, SHSS papers.

Dear Miss Smith,
Many thanks for your letter of 15 October 1974 and for the kind thoughts expressed therein.

I am sure that you will know better than most people that the police were not responsible for recent events, and that we are only on the fringe, acting for another organization. I do not know any policeman who does not deeply regret the necessity for us to become involved.

Although I agree it would not be wise for us to have a cup of tea together at this time, I see no reason why you and your husband should not join me and my wife for a 'cuppa' in Rotorua sometime, and as an indicator of the sincerity of this invitation I now supply our address:

. . .

Yours sincerely,
Angus Sharp[33]

Shirley visited him without Bill and learnt more about what had been going on, but was no less confused.

As explained, Shirley thought Baker had set a trap for Bill by misleading Mike Bungay about the meetings. She thought that Razgovorov was 'in cahoots' with the police or the SIS, or that the SIS had colluded with the Soviet Embassy, and so had knowledge of where and when meetings were to take place. She thought they had set Bill up, but she realised that didn't explain how the whole thing started. Shirley also knew that Bill had no compunctions about skewing the truth to suit his purposes. She appeared to hold two paradoxical views, that he both was and wasn't the victim of lies and conspiracy.

While Bill apologised to his family and said he took responsibility for what had happened, he and Shirley were keen to use the conspiracy line of defence. Mike Bungay said no, keep it simple.

After their holiday, Shirley was busy with her own practice while still being preoccupied with her husband's impending trial. She drew widespread admiration, especially for her fierce loyalty to her husband, but her determination to do her best for him exasperated Mike Bungay.

33 Angus Sharp to SHSS, 17 October 1974, SHSS papers.

Ian Greig recalled Mike telling her to go away and stop annoying him. Bill told him to calm down. 'Be kind to Shirley,' he instructed.

She then devoted herself to gathering evidence that Bill was in the habit of carrying milk home in his attaché case, so as to verify his story about the night he met Razgovorov in Hopper Street. She got a small private laboratory in Johnsonville to carry out forensic tests to find traces of milk, which they did. She insisted they continued until they found cream, and this too they found. While this evidence didn't 'prove that Bill had not been telling a fairy story', as Shirley suggested, it proved some of his story true.

Mike Bungay had managed to get the jury list long before the defence would normally have seen it, as did the Sutch Defence Committee. The committee organised people to interview prospective jurors by means of a bogus 'market survey' and devised a questionnaire designed to find out how liberal potential jurors were. 'Mike had warned them that no questions should be asked with the remotest connection to Bill or the trial, and they adhered to this,' Shirley later wrote to Maurice Shadbolt.[34] She knew about the survey, though George Rosenberg and Amanda Russell, who organised it, tried to keep her out of it.

When the *Queen v. William Ball Sutch* trial started on 17 February 1975 before Justice David Beattie, Bungay used the information. He challenged six members of the jury and the Crown challenged five, ending with an all-male jury.

During the trial, some women on the list realised that they had been part of a bogus survey to sound out their views about matters that might have a bearing on the trial. They told Solicitor-General Richard Savage on the fifth and last day, but as the information he received didn't suggest men on the jury had been so subjected, nor was there any suggestion of any attempt to influence the jury, he didn't ask the Judge to discharge the jury.[35]

AMONG THE FOURTEEN or so journalists in the press bench was novelist Maurice Shadbolt, who covered the case for the *Listener*, commissioned

34 SHSS to Maurice Shadbolt, 7 November 1979, SHSS papers.

35 Solicitor-General to Attorney-General, 5 March 1975, 'Truth Comments Concerning Jury Panel: R v. Sutch', Martyn Finlay papers.

by editor Ian Cross, who had worked with Sutch and thought highly of him. And (he told the author with a smile) he always had a soft spot for Shirley. In any case, the intense public interest justified the attention. Cross gave Shadbolt an unprecedented twelve pages.

Shadbolt reflected the feeling of Sutch's supporters present:

None – except the backwoodsmen of New Zealand's far right, perhaps – can relish the sight of this 67-year-old retired civil servant, who has given his remarkable administrative talent and distinctive human vision to his country for 40 years, standing uncertainly in the dock, as if still bewildered by it all, and then gripping the rail for support. None can be indifferent either while a man who once spoke for his country at the United Nations is obliged to plead, in a quiet and almost shy voice, 'Not guilty.'

We shall have to hope that we can make the same plea ourselves at the end – as a people, as a society. . . . The penalty for an offence under the Official Secrets Act *is up to 14 years in prison.*[36]

'Shirley just held her own as you do in these things when you face adversity, take a grip and just deal with it,' recalled Gordon Webb.[37] She spent little time in court during the trial. She bought Lands and Survey maps, marked them to show what could or could not be seen from given points and got Gordon to take photographs to give visual support to her version. She asked photographer Tom Shanahan to photograph her house to illustrate her evidence about the night of the arrest. She made these maps and photographs up into albums for the jurors.

Bill had to surrender his bail and was down in the courthouse cells when he wasn't in the dock. (Unusually, he was released at night.) Gordon Webb, who sat at the back of court for much of the Crown evidence, delivered to him the packed lunch Shirley had prepared. He was surprised that Bill was so relaxed. Bill thought it was going well, the witness for the Crown had been very fair really. Shirley would later say they were grateful the SIS officers gave their evidence honestly without slanting it, as they could have done.[38]

36 Maurice Shadbolt, 'The Trial of Dr William Sutch', *NZ Listener*, 26 April 1975, p.38.
37 Gordon Webb to author, interview, 26 April 2011.
38 SHSS to Valerie Davies, 16 September 1989, p.5, SHSS papers, ATL, MS-Papers-11404-82.

Bungay's cross-examination of SIS officers was designed to make them look stupid and appear as unreliable witnesses. Character witnesses for the defence included upstanding prominent New Zealanders who spoke of Sutch's patriotism and achievements. Former Labour Government minister Phil Holloway was brought from Rome where he was New Zealand's ambassador; Sir Guy Powles, who had known Sutch since they were at school together, gave evidence under subpoena, describing Sutch as a 'staunch New Zealand nationalist' whose loyalties were in no doubt; Bruce Alexander, managing director of Alliance Textiles, spoke of Sutch's work as an economic consultant for the wool industry. He described Sutch as the 'most loyal New Zealander' he had ever met. Others testified that Sutch customarily took home the leftover milk from his office and the scientist Shirley had employed gave evidence that he found traces of milk in his briefcase, though he couldn't say when that milk had been spilt. Even Bungay made a joke about that.

Shirley gave evidence on the afternoon of the fourth day. She spoke mostly about the night the SIS searched their house. Was the tea she made for the searchers made with the milk her husband brought back from the office, Shadbolt mused? Someone came up with the idea of a 'sutchel'. But with a fourteen-year jail term in the air, there was nothing funny about any of this for those close to the accused.

At the end of Shirley's testimony, Bungay surprised the court, including Savage, by announcing the conclusion of the evidence for the defence.[39] Sutch's letter to the Attorney-General had been read to the court and it stood as his explanation. Though evidence during the trial had contradicted his account of the meetings, as planned, Sutch did not give evidence, so the prosecution was unable to cross-examine him.

At the beginning of the fifth and final day, Shirley appeared at the Supreme Court to move Gordon Webb, who was admitted to the Bar along with other law graduates. When the ceremony was over, the Sutch case resumed with the final addresses and judge's summing up.

No evidence that written information had changed hands between Sutch and Razgovorov had been presented. But the judge told the jury

39 Ian Greig to author, interview, 26 October 2011. In his view, Savage conducted his prosecution in the belief that Sutch would take the stand and that was the most important single factor in the outcome.

'that there need be no evidence of any information being obtained or communicated'. Shirley expected the worst.

Shadbolt captured the overwhelming sense of relief when the jury announced their 'Not guilty' verdict, 'the only verdict for our sanity'. But like many others he was left wondering what it was really all about. 'But that's another game,' he wrote. 'A truth game. Another danger zone. The real danger zone.'[40]

40 Maurice Shadbolt, 'The Trial of Dr William Sutch', *New Zealand Listener*, 26 April 1975, p.48. Shirley thought his piece a tour de force and wrote to congratulate him.

22

Aftermath

THE SUTCH CASE polarised New Zealanders and left many people confused. Maurice Shadbolt thought it like something out of a novel – Lewis Carroll rather than John Le Carré. Though many questions remained unanswered, family, friends and supporters felt that their faith had been vindicated. Reading later the notes she had written at the time, Shirley reflected on their sense of being carried aloft, 'buoyed up by the wonderful support we got from all over New Zealand, from people we knew and people we did not know. It was as if we were borne up on a cloud of unseen witnesses, to the music of a choir invisible.'[1]

Celebration and congratulations continued with the publication of *Spirit of an Age: New Zealand in the Seventies: Essays in Honour of W. B. Sutch*, edited by John L. Robson and Jack Shallcrass. Three days after the trial ended, Sutch was posing at his desk with copies of his festschrift.[2]

Sutch then told his story in a television interview on *Seven Days* with Ian Fraser on 26 February. Shirley apparently went along with this – she was home during the day when Ian Fraser was there preparing the interview, setting parameters – but, if she hoped that Bill's explanation would convince viewers and put the matter to rest, she was mistaken.

Those who didn't see the nationwide interview read about it in the papers next morning. The *Dominion* recounted it under the heading 'Sutch: Envoy wanted my help to defect'. *NZ Truth* ran an editorial headed 'NONSENSE, DR SUTCH!' and asked, 'Would a jury have believed him if he had told them such stories?'[3] It pointed out

1 SHSS to Margaret Hall, 6 March 1991, SHSS papers, ATL, MS-Papers-11364-20.

2 http://www.nzhistory.net.nz/media/photo/william-sutch (accessed 15 October 2018). Photo taken 24 February 1975. Shirley was closely involved with this publication.

3 *NZ Truth*, 4 March 1975. See also *Dominion*, 27 February 1975. Sutch told Fraser he had not taken the witness box because his solicitor had told him there was no case to answer.

inconsistencies between his explanation on television and his letter to the Attorney-General.

David Smith wrote to Ralph Grey in the UK:

Re the Sutch case, we were all very relieved by the verdict of 'Not Guilty'. Technically, I think it was correct because there wasn't sufficient proof that the meetings were of advantage to an 'enemy'; even though the statute made the meetings evidence of that – but not conclusive evidence. However Dr Sutch did not give evidence and I don't think anyone, except the persons directly concerned, knows what actually happened. Then though he didn't give evidence, he went on T.V. (for a fee) to give his version. I thought this was in extremely bad taste in the circumstances. What he indicated was that the Soviet agent wanted to talk to him about Zionism as a method perhaps of defecting to New Zealand. He thought that there was collusion between the Soviet Embassy and our Security Service and that the Embassy told the Service where to go to watch the meetings of himself and the Soviet agent. Our Security Service denied any contact with the Soviet Embassy. The Sutch version on T.V. has not persuaded me. I am still mystified.[4]

The day after the interview, *Truth* also ran an item about the Sutch Defence Committee's survey of potential jurors and questioned when, and by what authority, the jury panel was made available to the defence. This immediately prompted Attorney-General Martyn Finlay to order a departmental inquiry. The Secretary for Justice assured him that making a copy of the list of jurors available to the defence some two to three weeks prior to the date fixed for the hearing was proper. Solicitor-General Richard Savage thought that the information he had received during the trial, and read from *Truth*, did not amount to an offence of corrupting a juror under s.117 of the Crimes Act. However, he thought it went distinctly beyond the bounds of propriety.

He said that he met Razgovorov to talk about Zionism (as he wrote in his letter to the Attorney-General) and posed the idea that the Soviets must have collaborated with the SIS to set him up and that probably Razgovorov wanted to defect.

4 DSS to Lord Ralph Grey, 14 April 1975, DSS papers.

It seems to me that a fair basis for judgment is presented by the question: what would one's reaction be if the prosecution had done this? Surely the standard of propriety in respect of approaches to the tribunal must be the same for both sides. If the Crown had sent plain-clothes police men and women posing as members of a market research organisation to make such enquiries of prospective jurors, I do not doubt it would have been generally, and I think rightly, condemned.[5]

Finlay agreed. He wrote in the *Dominion* on 7 March that jury lists had been legally available some weeks before the hearing and the approach to the possible jurors was above the law but, in his view, people representing themselves as conducting a market survey to make enquiries of prospective jurors was 'most objectionable'.

Shirley later wrote an article in which she dismissed the official indignation and public outcry: 'From the outraged reaction of many people, from the then Attorney-General, Dr. A. M. Finlay, down, one would have thought that one of the most precious of our constitutional freedoms had been breached.'[6] She said that there was nothing improper about the defence making enquiries about potential jurors. But she didn't mention the deception involved, not only to ask their questions but to enter homes, look around and note what they saw in way of books, furnishings and anything that indicated liberal or conservative views.

She apparently never mentioned the jury survey to her father before he read about it in the *Dominion* following the *Truth* exposure. He promptly cut short his holiday in Taupō and returned to Wellington. He wrote to Shirley that he was relieved to learn the Attorney-General ruled out allegations of illegal dealings. 'The latest attack in *Truth* raises further problems but I make no comment here.'[7]

David Smith was referring to an article on 11 March 1975 headed 'Sutch: A Man of Property', claiming he was worth about half a million

5 Solicitor-General to Attorney-General, 5 March 1975, 'Truth Comments Concerning Jury Panel: R v. Sutch', Martyn Finlay papers.

6 SHSS, 'Fair Challenge? An Aspect of Trial by Jury', 1979, SHSS papers, ATL MS-Papers-11404-179, published in *New Zealand and the World: Essays in Honour of Wolfgang Rosenberg*, ed. W. E. Willmott, University of Canterbury, Christchurch, 1980.

7 DSS to SHSS, 9 March 1975, SHSS papers.

dollars. (Adjusted for inflation that is over $5 million in 2019.) It noted that over the years Sutch had bought and sold an unusual number of properties and documented with photographs the houses and land he currently owned in Wellington, Paraparaumu and Auckland, with details of what he had paid and speculations about their current values. Some of the land was bought purely for capital gain, including three acres in Paraparaumu purchased in 1967–68, zoned for industrial use. The article noted that in some cases there were mortgages on the properties, but they were very small.

This information could be found in public records. But *Truth* also reported that Sutch held substantial bank accounts in several overseas countries. 'These include in Switzerland which is noted for the banking service it provides for persons wishing to remain anonymous.' Observing that few of Sutch's supporters were aware of the accounts or his property speculation because he had always 'posed' as an opponent of capitalism, *Truth* commented, 'Sutch's associates may well be dismayed to learn that their idol has feet of gold.'[8] And people did wonder, if the revelations were true, how had Sutch acquired such wealth?

Whatever Shirley thought, she continued to portray Bill as a victim of conspiracy. She wrote to Martyn Finlay that when *Truth* was not using Crown sources it was 'abysmally wrong'; for example, she had been described as the daughter of the 'late' Sir David Smith. She added that she had informed the Prime Minister that most of *Truth*'s information must have come from Crown sources and suggested he investigate the matter. She herself had not previously known some of the information published. She concluded:

It has always seemed to me that an attack on the Government has been implicit in the moves against Bill: and the Government, like Bill, has played into the hands of those who are inimical to both. I feel like Cassandra when I say, as I do, that the threat to the Government implicit in the activities of the NZSIS and its Big Brother, the CIA, is real, imminent and almost totally unrecognised by the Government.[9]

8 *NZ Truth*, 11 March 1975, pp.8–9.
9 SHSS to Martyn Finlay, 13 March 1975, Martyn Finlay papers.

Shirley, in her letter to Prime Minister Rowling in March, requested answers to specific questions. This prompted the investigation into the SIS by Chief Ombudsman Sir Guy Powles.[10]

At the beginning of April, Sutch resigned as director of the Queen Elizabeth II Arts Council. When Shirley had to give evidence in Auckland for a client, he went with her and they stayed again with Pat Booth and Valerie Davies at Drury. Bill asked Pat to be his biographer. (Pat Booth was a first-rate investigative journalist whose work on the Arthur Allan Thomas Case – of intense interest to Shirley – ultimately resulted in Thomas's release and pardon.) After considering the proposal, what it would involve and the personal cost, he declined, explaining tactfully that their friendship clouded the objectivity required of a biographer.

During that visit, Valerie was convalescing after a car accident and conversations mostly took place around her bedside. At one point Bill said wearily that he just wished he could crawl into bed with her. Pat pretended to be outraged and they all laughed, but Bill looked exhausted. Shirley put it down to strain and nervous exhaustion.

He refused to see a doctor, but agreed to go with Shirley to a natural health consultant. 'Bill and I are taking all the things you recommended that we can get . . . we both feel sure that we are much the better for it. There seems to be a permanent non-supply of desiccated liver . . . I have never seen Ruvitin tablets but I did get a kind of Ruvitin tea . . . doesn't seem to be any shortage of wheatgerm . . .'[11]

Keith Ovenden recalled that Shirley was 'like a lioness with her cub', preparing special meals and doing everything in her power for Bill. In Keith's view, Bill put on a brave face, but he was a defeated man, cowed, and he was sick. Either he was pretending he wasn't sick, or he knew he was and wasn't going to do anything about it.[12] Others, too, thought that he had lost his will to live. Shirley wrote to Peggy Garland in November 1975 that this made her angry – he was never defeated – his

10 http://www.nzsis.govt.nz/assets/media/SutchOmbudsmanReport.pdf (accessed 15 October 2015).

11 SHSS to Wendy (surname not given), 24 June 1975, SHSS papers, ATL, MS-Papers-11369-193.

12 KWO to author, interview, 26 March 2013.

courage and will were indomitable up to the end.[13]

Helen and Keith were now living in Bill's cottage in Glenbervie Terrace and Helen was expecting a baby in September. They had reverted to attending Sunday evening dinners at Todman Street. Shirley was often flustered and forgetful, but she resisted help in the kitchen. With no help in the house, it was getting out of hand.

With all that was going on, Keith found he was no longer a preoccupation as far as Shirley was concerned. She appreciated his wish to help and what she saw as his loyalty to Bill.

Before the trial, Shirley had asked Keith to come up with possible scenarios. Then Bill had apparently agreed to his writing a book on the trial and told him that Hugh Price at Victoria University Press would be interested in publishing it. After Keith had written and submitted his manuscript, Bill changed his mind.[14] Shirley wrote to Keith to say how sorry she and Bill were for all the labour he had done in vain and that they both greatly regretted their initial agreement.

At the time you asked, of course, Bill had not yet been acquitted, he had not given the TV interview, there had not been the Truth *campaign. You may well ask, why was it left so long before you were told Bill had changed his mind. It was really a matter of accretion – little by little – and crystallization. Another grand conspirator libel, another strong opinion from a friend who deplored the TV interview, the attack by Sir Roy Jack* [National MP, former Attorney-General and Minister of Justice]*; and the growing conviction that Bill's enemies would not let up and would seize any opportunity to reopen the debate: together with the realization that it would be assumed (whatever disclaimer you made) that you were Bill's mouthpiece and also the realization that others could read the Notes of Evidence and write other scenarios, which given the required slant, could be made as damaging as yours was exculpatory.*[15]

Shirley's main concern was how publication would hurt Bill. 'We cannot have any more clobbering of Bill; he has taken all he can. The

13 SHSS to Peggy Garland, 23 November 1975, SHSS papers.
14 The author has not seen the manuscript.
15 SHSS to KWO, 21 May 1975, KWO papers.

election campaign may give rise to further attacks: these we cannot prevent, but we must avoid in any way provoking them.'[16]

Fresh attacks had already started. A week earlier, on 15 July, *Truth* published 'The Sutch File', the first of a series alleging that he had been a grand conspirator in a 'sinister scheme to socialise New Zealand'. An SIS officer had leaked to *Truth* a secret dossier that showed Kirk had set up a secret think tank whose members, Bill Sutch, Jack Lewin and Gerald O'Brien, were to hatch this scheme.[17] National Party campaigners attacked the Labour Government's superannuation scheme as a communist takeover of New Zealand . . . and so it went on.

In this heated environment, there was a lot of talk of 'Bill's enemies'. Twenty years later Shirley was haunted by the memory of someone phoning their home night after night, saying not a word. She recalled that she always took the calls to protect Bill and never told him.

As she remembered, a more sinister call came on the night of the 8 August:

We were both asleep, late at night or in the small hours . . . and the extension went in my ear. I slept next to the telephone on purpose. A voice said, 'Plan three, Shirley, plan three.' I said, 'Who is it?' Or 'Who's speaking?' several times, keeping my voice low, so as not to disturb Bill. He did not wake and I never told him about it. It did not happen again. The voice was male, educated, in itself very pleasant, almost musical. I hung up, getting no answer, and lay in bed agitatedly thinking – plan three? What were plans one and two? The first plan I thought (assuming they were plans to destroy Bill) was the affair with Razgovorov and the trial: the second was the Truth campaign after the acquittal – what would the third be? I was terribly worried and anxious but there was nothing that I could do. And then, shortly after, Bill became ill – obviously ill.[18]

16 Ibid.

17 Redmer Yska, *Truth: The Rise and Fall of the People's Paper*, Craig Potton Publishing, Nelson, New Zealand, 2010, p.161. See also pp.161–170, 173. Concerned by the direction the Labour Government was taking, Sutch, Lewin and O'Brien had written a document setting out an alternative programme and put it to Kirk. This was regarded by some as subversive activity. (Shirley had the document in the house. She thought it eventually went to the Turnbull.)

18 SHSS memoir, 'WBS – departure from I and C', 25 July 1995, p.7, SHSS papers.

Towards the end of August, Shirley finally persuaded Bill to see his doctor who sent him to a specialist. A small tumour was found in his rectum. A biopsy showed it was benign, but the specialist decided to remove it as a precaution. In hospital, further tests revealed that he had advanced cancer of the liver.

On 17 September Helen gave birth to a son, Piers. Shirley drove Helen and the baby from St Helen's Maternity Hospital to Wellington Public Hospital. Shirley always remembered Bill holding their grandson and saying, 'Thou art in me and I am in thee.' She saw it as a simple expression of love, something that she said didn't come easily to him.[19]

As he was dying, Bill remarked to Shirley, 'Now you will never have to decide whether you will be Lady Sutch.' Shirley knew he longed for a knighthood and was glad that he thought a knighthood possible after all that had happened. She was glad, too, that she would never have to hurt his feelings on this account, not because she was a republican – she wasn't – but because of her feminist principles.[20] He also asked her why she had wanted to have her own profession. Shirley just said, 'Oh darling, what does it matter now?'[21]

But he left her with words to cherish. She wrote to Otto Nathan in New York that when she told Bill she would keep his banner flying, he replied, 'Your banner is bigger than mine; and it streams in a different wind.'[22]

He died on 28 September 1975, one year and a day after his arrest. He was aged 68 and Shirley 58.

19 Shirley recorded this several times, first to Peggy Garland on 23 November 1975. The use of 'thou' and 'thee' was the language of Bill's parents. His words reflect the words of Christ to his disciples before he died: 'At that day ye shall know that I am in my father, and ye in me, and I in you' (John, 14:20).

20 SHSS, 'WBS – departure from I and C', 25 July 1995, SHSS papers. 'Today I had a very interesting conversation with Carrick Lewis.' In 1974 Carrick Lewis was National President for the Society for Closer Relations with Russia and trying to get the government to agree to a writers' group, led by Sutch, to go to the USSR. He was also part of the group lobbying for a knighthood for Bill. Bill didn't tell Shirley this, but she knew he wanted a knighthood. SHSS to Brian Easton, 28 August 1998, Brian Easton papers.

21 SHSS memoir, 'Life with Bill – No. 2', undated, p.4, SHSS papers.

22 SHSS to Otto Nathan, 10 February 1977, SHSS papers, ATL, MS-Papers-11369-195.

23

Widow

PUBLIC AND PRIVATE tributes, letters and telegrams poured in lauding Bill Sutch as 'a champion of New Zealand' and a 'man of vision'. This too was the tone of his funeral. Shirley described it to Otto Nathan as 'a brilliant day and a wonderful service'. She herself had that morning picked the flowers from his garden for the coffin. The service, held in the Wesley Methodist Church in Taranaki Street, was conducted by an old friend of Bill's, the Reverend Wilf Ford, who spoke of the triumph of good over evil. Tributes were led by former Labour leader Arnold Nordmeyer, and the Cook Islanders sang, as they had done at the house the night after Bill died. 'It may seem strange to you that I dwell on the funeral. But it was a tremendous occasion, and I felt it did justice to Bill and did end his life on the right note, of joy and glory and triumph.'[1]

For Shirley, Bill was a classic tragic hero, but never so heroic as in his downfall. As she often repeated, he had blamed no one but himself and had apologised for all the trouble he caused. 'I admired him then more than I ever had in my life,' she told journalist Rosemary Vincent in an interview in 1983. 'He was calm, controlled and courageous throughout the whole thing, it showed up his best qualities. No one could have carried themselves better through that crisis than he did.'[2]

Over time, her memory of the whole year took on a kind of euphoria. 'We were never in the lower depths,' she wrote in 1991. 'It was a strange time, a time of heightened experience, a sense of living on the edge. I was luckier than some members of the family; Bill's surviving brother and sister were crushed by what had happened to their brilliant brother, but my adrenalin rose to the occasion, and I was in a fighting mood throughout.'[3]

1 SHSS to Otto Nathan, 10 February 1977, SHSS papers, ATL, MS-Papers-11369-195.
2 SHSS, 'Mongrels Lawyer takes it quietly', *New Zealand Times*, 27 November 1983, p.9.
3 SHSS to Margaret Hall, 6 March 1991, SHSS papers, ATL, MS-Papers-11364-20.

But Shirley had suffered more than she admitted. She was haunted by the anonymous phone caller and his reference to 'plan three'. She understood from Bill's first specialist that no primary cancer had been found and that the liver cancer would have developed over a year. Shirley attributed Bill's death to his arrest a year and a day earlier, but another possibility crept into her thinking when she read that there was a kind of chemical, used in making vinyl, that could fatally affect the liver. She wondered if someone had been poisoning Bill for a year.[4]

Autopsies were not routinely carried out in 1975, so it was probably at Shirley's request that one was performed on Bill. The post-mortem, dated 29 September 1975, shows a massive tumour in the liver with very little surviving liver tissue. The carcinoma in the rectum (that the specialist missed) had completely penetrated the bowel wall, and some adjacent lymph nodes were also involved.

When oncologist Alan Gray examined Sutch's medical history, he concluded that the advanced rectal cancer must have been there for years: 'While sometimes rectal cancer can be quite silent, which is why they are often diagnosed at a late stage, Bill would have suffered symptoms (probably lethargy and weight loss) from the very extensive liver secondary six to twelve months before he died. The benign result of the biopsy showed that either it was taken from the wrong area, or pathologists failed to correctly suspect the appearance of the lesion. . . . At that stage, however, a correct diagnosis would not have altered the outcome.'[5]

The autopsy refers to 'marked atheroma of basilar and middle cerebral arteries', which is to say that he had marked vascular disease of the blood vessels at the base of the brain at post-mortem, which may have affected his mental state. Shirley related to Brian Easton years later that Mr Adams, Bill's specialist before he went into hospital, told her, after he saw the pathology report, that Bill's conversation had been fascinating, and he could hardly believe that it was the product of only *half* Bill's brain, the emotional side at that. 'Adams said, what must he

4 SHSS, addition to 'Note of telephone conversation from EJS to WBS, 22.1.65', 25 July 1995, SHSS papers.

5 Alan Gray, emails to author, 31 January and 5 February 2012.

have been like with a whole brain!'[6]

Shirley took hold of this idea, but in fact the autopsy found no evidence of obvious brain damage. Some atheroma would be expected in someone of Bill's age. Oncologist Alan Gray notes that while other causes of mild dementia could not be excluded by the limited examination of the brain tissue, the post-mortem showed no evidence of these, referring only to a 'healed myocardial infarct'.[7]

Shirley was utterly unprepared for Bill's will. After reading it, she met Deirdre Macken, her former law student, now friend and client, at Parsons. She was in tears.

Bill had changed his will on 15 September and made Mike Bungay his trustee and sole executor. (Shirley circled 'sole', her only marking on her copy of the will.) Later Shirley would say that Bill had wished to spare her the extra worry and responsibility of administering his estate, but, at the time, she thought it implied that she wasn't competent.

After specific bequests were settled, Shirley was to receive a net annual income until her death, when the whole of the residual estate was to go to Helen. Bill also left Helen his cottage at 39 Glenbervie Terrace and bequeathed 103b Mitchell Street to his sister Margaret Shirley, both the mortgages to be paid out of the funds of his estate. The will contained no mention of the family home or its contents. They were therefore part of the 'residual estate'.[8]

Shirley's father wrote a note and filed it for future reference: 'Shirley is not given the contents of the joint family home at Brooklyn. This is not satisfactory and should be corrected by Deed, approved by Court, or under the Family Protection Act.' He later added that he had discussed the matter with Shirley, 'but she thought matter not sufficient to worry

6 SHSS to Brian Easton, 22 August 2000, Brian Easton papers.

7 The heart was of a normal size. Apart from the scar of the healed myocardial infarct, the myocardium was normal. So were the valves. 'The coronary arteries were moderately artheromatous, but quite patent. The aorta was only mildly atheromatous.' Pathologist R. H. Steele, Post Mortem, Sutch, William Ball, Pathology Department, Wellington Hospital, Hosp No. 206207, Path No. 75/208, Ward no. 10; oncologist Alan Gray, emails to author, 28 January and 5 February 2012.

8 WBS Last Will and Testament, 15 September 1975, Archives New Zealand, AAOM W3265 6031 Box 574.

about.'[9] In fact the house remained her home and most of its contents stayed in her possession as long as she lived there.[10]

FEELING LOW on the night of her fifty-ninth birthday, Shirley attended the Wellington District Law Society annual dinner. She didn't feel like going but felt she should to acknowledge that it was for all members, without regard to gender. Earlier in the year (1975) the New Zealand Law Society Conference, for the first time ever, had recognised that practitioners were both male and female and that spouses may be husbands as well as wives.

She arrived late, after everyone was seated. 'As I entered the room, they all rose as one and stood until I was seated. A seat was found for me beside old friends. I was moved almost to tears . . .'[11]

Some months later, in 1976, the New Zealand Council for Civil Liberties demonstrated their esteem for Shirley when they made her their first Life Member. (She had resigned to spare the Council any embarrassment from ongoing media attention after Bill's trial.) Moving the motion, the president, Walter Scott, acknowledged that she had 'done more than anybody else with the actual steps taken to bring the council into being', adding that she had served the cause with devotion and distinction.[12]

9 DSS, 5 & 16 January 1976, file labeled 'Shirley', 1973-82, SHSS papers, ATL, MS-Papers-11369-254. The note refers to the 'joint family home in Brooklyn', but comments only on the contents. Keith Ovenden told the author that Bill left the house and contents to Helen because he knew Shirley wouldn't look after them as she didn't care for such things: 7 December 2017.

10 In 1983, Shirley, Helen and Keith signed a deed requesting variation of the will. Helen and Shirley agreed that the residue of the estate could be distributed during Shirley's lifetime. After setting aside a sum for Piers and Crispin (Keith acted as their trustee) the balance was to be divided equally between Shirley and Helen. Deed of 17 August 1983, marked 'E' between Shirley, Helen and Keith, referred to in the annexed affidavit of Shirley Hilda Stanley Smith, SHSS papers.

11 SHSS, 'My life in the law', *Claiming the Law: Essays by New Zealand Women in Celebration of the 1993 Suffrage Centennial*, eds. Elisabeth McDonald and Graeme Austin, VUW Law Review & VUP, May 1993, p.8.

12 NZCCL President Walter Scott to SHSS, 30 July 1976, SHSS papers, ATL, MS-Papers-11404-21.

New year 1976 saw Shirley at Lake Rotoiti, Nelson, delivering a series of lectures at the WEA summer school. It was hectic but she wrote to her father that she felt quite rejuvenated. At the end she received a standing ovation. She then went on holiday in Golden Bay with Helen, Keith and Piers. She wrote cheerfully about the brilliant weather, her swims and, best of all, her three-month-old grandson. Piers was a happy diversion, but she needed a longer rest after such a year.

Helen worried about her mother. Before Bill's death, Helen and Keith had declined the offer to take over the now derelict house, 105 Mitchell Street, that Bill had bought some years back along with other properties to secure driveway access to Mitchell Street. (He had put 105 in Shirley's name.) Now Helen and Keith decided to move there to be close to Shirley. She transferred ownership to them (they repaid her later) and they had it restored. During the nine months it took to complete the renovations, Helen, Keith and Piers lived with Shirley along with a series of nannies. Helen returned to work at Treasury. Keith continued to commute to the University of Canterbury in Christchurch.

Having a grandson opened up a new avenue of intimacy between Shirley and Keith, but he found her exasperating. Apart from the turmoil she lived in, their situation was bound to create tensions. Keith says that Shirley almost stifled their life in her efforts to take control. She in turn was extremely anxious to have their good opinion. Amanda Russell thought Shirley felt very vulnerable.

It was like she was a naughty girl who'd been told she'd been very wicked and had to stand in the corner, and somebody would come and she would hope that she'd be forgiven. She had a huge guilt complex. . . . On one hand she looked enormously confident, and in a situation where she was in control, she could take on ten policemen and intimidate them, but somehow with her family she seemed to be this little small one who had to justify herself and apologise . . .[13]

The birth on 10 January 1978 of her second grandson, Crispin, brought a shift in Shirley's relationship with Keith. When he came

13 Amanda Rosenberg (formerly Russell) to author, interview, 29 February 2012.

home from the hospital, Shirley opened a bottle of champagne, and as they celebrated together into the night she acknowledged how badly she and Bill had treated him, how wrong they had been and how very sorry she was. Keith said it didn't settle the relationship, but it cleared the air.[14]

Shirley loved being a grandmother. She encouraged Keith and Helen to take off on their own for weekends while she devoted herself to the boys. Piers recalls playing cricket with her in her living room. Surrounded by glass and ceramics, he had to keep the ball low.

While it was a comfort to Shirley to have her family living next door, she didn't feel safe. She was still paranoid that SIS spies were entering her house and she was sure her phone was tapped. She had a security expert sweep the house and advise her what she could do. Stretching invisible thread across doorways was one suggestion. She compiled a list of strange events that occurred at 79a Todman Street between the night of Bill's arrest and February 1977. It included items that were inexplicably moved, like the aluminium foil from her tea caddy, milk bottles in the fridge, brandy and sherry in the cellar, jewellery in her bedroom. That she wasn't entirely rational is in part an understandable reaction to the turmoil she had experienced.

On 10 February 1977, when she wrote to Otto Nathan about Bill's death, Shirley admitted to 'a long period of strain, and I'm tired (tho' perfectly well) and get muddled. I really need a long break but can't see any chance of one at present.'[15]

In the office, Shirley had more than her usual problems. In the months after Bill's arrest, she had carried on with her essential court work. George Rosenberg came back briefly to help. After he left, her law clerk Gordon Webb took on a lot of her work as well as the work he inherited from George, while also studying for his final exams.[16]

Then in January 1975, when Shirley was distracted by her husband's pending trial, her secretary Helen Edwards was diagnosed with breast cancer. Amanda Russell, who had worked for Shirley as a typist

14 KWO to author, interview, 11 April 2013.
15 SHSS to Otto Nathan, 10 February 1977, SHSS papers, ATL, MS-Papers-11369-195.
16 Gordon Webb to SHSS, 17 April 1977, SHSS papers, ATL, MS-Papers-11404-69.

for three years, took over the work of legal secretary. Over the next months, Amanda and Shirley's highly competent legal clerk, Maureen McDonald, referred clients to Gordon when Shirley was unavailable, as was often the case at this time. Gordon explained to Shirley later that he was sometimes fighting blind, but not wishing to add to her worries he didn't mention it to her at the time. Everyone in the office did their best to keep things going.[17]

In May 1976, Gordon Webb left to travel. Shirley was sorry to lose him. She had offered him a partnership but she understood his desire to see the world. His replacement left after only two weeks, just as a case was to open, because he refused to follow courtroom procedure (specifically, to open with 'May it please your Worship . . .'). Shirley had to deal with that case, Gordon's files and the conveyancing work, some of which was complicated and developed snags and problems. She wrote to Gordon that she had 'lost money left right and centre'.[18]

I have done nothing about taking anybody else on. I couldn't face another personality to cope with. . . . but by this time the overdraft was about $8,000 and the bank manager was getting unhappy: so the girls put their heads together and said Can't we all work very hard and manage without taking on anyone else? This was on the basis that Helen Edwards had offered to come back in the afternoons . . . So this is what we are trying to do. I'm the one who hasn't really been pulling her weight, and this is partly because I get enmeshed in my daughter's affairs.[19]

George Rosenberg returned to work for Shirley until he set up his own community law practice in Newtown. Shirley wished he would change his mind about going solo and go into partnership with her. She loved working with George.

But George's work didn't bring in money. He didn't invoice clients who couldn't afford to pay. When she discovered this after he left, she objected to him treating her firm as a charitable organisation. But that

17 Ibid.

18 SHSS to Gordon Webb, 23 August 1976, SHSS papers, ATL, MS-Papers-11404-21; Gordon Webb to author, 8 March 2018.

19 Ibid.

was how she herself ran her practice. She hated asking for money, even to pay a bill. Unable to understand how she could run her practice without making money, the tax department investigated her to see if she was salting income away somewhere. They found her squeaky clean.[20]

By mid-1977 Shirley complained to Valerie Davies that her usual troubles had trebled with a pending rent review and free wage bargaining. She feared another wage increase would make life impossible. At the same time, the law profession was subject to a fees freeze, 'but that makes little difference to me, as my clients are the sort, mostly, that I can't even charge standard rates.'[21]

Cathy Shaw, who still did her books, told Shirley that her overdraft was too high and she couldn't carry on as she was going. Her new rate for annual rent increased by well over $2,000 and, with wages increasing also, she had to radically reassess her practice. She told her staff she had to kiss them all goodbye.

Amanda went with George to his new practice. (They would marry in 1984.) Helen Edwards retired, or so she thought.

Shirley moved into the smaller of her two offices, intending to sub-let the larger office. She wrote to her bank manager, explaining the measures she had taken and that she intended to wind down her existing solicitor's work and concentrate on court work in future. 'This requires little overhead, and if I am strong-minded enough to get my fees in before trial, I should become financial.' She would send her typing out to be done on contract and get an answerphone service in place of a receptionist. The accountant who did Mike Bungay's books agreed to help with the bookkeeping.[22]

She wrote to the Wellington Law Practitioners' Industrial Union of Employers, explaining why she had ceased employing labour:

As far as I am concerned, legal employees had effectively priced themselves out of my office. I do not, in general, have the kind of clients to whom I can

20 This is from the oral history of Shirley Smith with Hugo Manson on 4 November 1988 commissioned by the New Zealand Law Society, Wellington Branch, side 7, ATL, OHInt-0082-02.

21 SHSS to Valerie Davies, 31 July 1977, SHSS papers, ATL, MS-Papers-11404-22.

22 SHSS to her bank manager, 25 January 1978, SHSS papers, ATL, 2013-045-05-38/2.

pass on the increased overheads: and the Legal Aid Committees far from accepting any increases, are cutting down on the rates that existed several years ago. As for Criminal Legal Aid . . . words fail those of us who are on the receiving end.

It is no doubt true, as Maule J. said in 1845, that the law knows no distinction between rich and poor: but the lawyer does, and it is distressing that it is becoming more and more difficult for the poor to get adequate legal assistance. Lawyers facing heavy overheads cannot afford poor clients.[23]

Working on her own, Shirley was soon exhausted. After giving a paper at a law conference in Auckland she arrived at Valerie Davies and Pat Booth's place in Drury and slept, dead to the world, for 36 hours. When she returned to Wellington, Shirley asked Helen Edwards to come back to work again.

SHIRLEY MIGHT have paid off her firm's mortgage easily had she been the wealthy widow people assumed her to be. In fact, she had yet to receive any income from Bill's estate and was scratching along on the state pension she'd received since turning sixty in October 1976. The Inland Revenue was investigating the estate.

It seems their investigations prompted Shirley to write on 20 March 1978 to Bill's surgeon Alan Anderson about Bill's pathology report. She thought she recalled seeing a letter from Anderson to her brother Allan Smith – 'which Allan no longer has and which he is sure is a figment of my imagination' – in which he wrote that Bill was 'operating with only half a brain' and another reference to his liver as 'an event unique in the annals of medical science', meaning, she said, that he kept going for so long in such a state. She explained her reason for her request for this letter:

As it happens, it would be very helpful to Mr Bungay, who is Bill's sole executor, to have your interpretation of that part of the pathologist's report which refers to the state of Bill's brain; including how long it would have taken the atheroma to have developed to that state. I can assure you that

23 SHSS to Secretary, Wellington Law Practitioners' Industrial Union of Employers, 4 February 1978, SHSS papers, ATL, 2013-045-05-38/2.

there would be no question whatever of your having to give evidence or be cross-examined by anyone: I can safely say that the family would put up with anything rather than have Bill's name involved in Court proceedings again.

I know that it is remarkable how normal Bill seemed, up until the last few days; but I had noticed things about his thinking for some time which had disturbed me. In particular, his judgment seemed to be deteriorating (quite apart from his meeting the Russian).

I greatly appreciate the trouble you have already taken in looking up your records, and would be very much obliged if you would let Mr Bungay have your report in answer to the letter from him with which this will be enclosed. It is necessary that it be addressed to him.[24]

The author has found no reply to her letter.

'MY MEMORY is poor about recent events,' she wrote three months later, '. . . but extremely good about the past.'[25]

This was to Peter Crawley, her predecessor at Auckland University College in 1942, in reply to his invitation to write her memories of the Classics Department. As has been quoted earlier, she continued:

I also see that you have a responsibility 'to exercise the utmost discretion', and that causes me another problem, a moral one. If my contribution to your history is to present an incomplete picture of how things were from 1943–1944 (which I realize is probably unavoidable if I am to contribute at all), should I contribute at all? The question is, is there an alternative between silence and telling the whole truth?[26]

This was Shirley's dilemma. When writing history, she saw a moral obligation to tell the whole truth. When it came to Bill, however, the truth was difficult. Shirley would leap into print to correct inaccuracies as she saw them. But when Bill was named as a tax evader she was silent.

24 SHSS to Mr A. F. Gordon Anderson, 20 March 1978, SHSS papers, ATL, MS-Papers-11404-22.

25 SHSS to L. Crawley (Peter), 11 July 1978, SHSS papers, ATL, MS-Papers-11404-70.

26 Ibid. Shirley did eventually write at length, too late for Crawley to do more than minor modifications and additions, but a valuable source for this biography.

Bill's estate had at last been wound up when, on 7 August 1979, the *Dominion* ran a headline, 'Sutch tax disclosure shocks widow'. Shirley said she learnt from a journalist that her husband had been named in the *New Zealand Gazette* as an evader of taxes estimated at $47,241 between 1966 and 1974, the second highest for any individual among about 650 persons listed in the supplementary gazette. In addition, there was a penal tax of $25,000. On top rates of income tax at the time, Sutch's undisclosed income during that period was estimated to be in the vicinity of $100,000.[27]

Shirley told the reporter that several months earlier the executor of Sutch's estate had told her that the Inland Revenue Department relinquishments on the estate had been satisfied. 'But this does not dispose of the fact that my husband may have been in default,' she added. She said that she knew little of her husband's financial affairs.[28]

Shirley's public explanation for Bill's wealth was that it came from thrift. (She was quoted as saying that her financial contribution enabled them to save most of Bill's salary, presumably referring to when she was employed full-time as a university lecturer.) But she was deeply upset by Bill's tax evasion. When her brother Allan asked her about this, she confirmed that had Bill lived he would have been prosecuted and that she had had to deal with it and pay what was owed. Fraud was anathema to her. Allan thought it was the last straw for Shirley. 'Bill almost seemed to cease to exist in Shirley's mind.'[29]

In public, Shirley continued to portray Bill as New Zealand's great patriot. She had been deeply hurt by Prime Minister Muldoon's comments that Sutch was 'guilty as sin' in his autobiography, *Muldoon*, launched in November 1977. In an *Auckland Star* article headed 'Setting the record straight', she pointed out Muldoon's lack of evidence. Ironically, while asserting 'these are facts', she described Bill's travels in 1932, 'walking "round the Arctic Circle", as he put it, through Lapland

27 *Dominion*, 7 August 1979. Sir John Marshall's memoirs, volume 2, published 1989, reported in *Evening Post*, 29 July 1989.

28 Article by Bernard Lagan, *Dominion*, 7 August 1979, clipping in Martyn Finlay's papers.

29 AGS to author, interview, 21 March 2011, track 6. Presumably what was owed came out of the WBS estate.

and Finland and into the USSR . . . He walked down through Soviet Asia and over the passes of Afghanistan into India . . . an epic journey which deserves to take its place with the great odysseys.'[30]

In this and other respects she presented the facts as she knew them. Elsie Locke advised her to get on with her life and leave Bill to history.

In February 1980, Muldoon requested the release of 'Top Secret' text – from the report by Chief Ombudsman Sir Guy Powles – to back up his 'guilty as sin' statement about Sutch (showing that he was not referring to the 1975 trial but to Sutch's activity over a longer period). The *Evening Post* ran a front-page story headed 'Sutch widow "bloody angry"'.[31] The report was a public document, but the part related to Sutch was classified, largely to spare the family further pain. Presumably Sir Guy had conveyed his answers to her questions that had prompted the investigation in the first place, but Shirley said she had not then seen the report and did not know what it said about her late husband.

The *Evening Post* published the report on Tuesday 5 February 1980.[32] The 'Top Secret' annex detailed Powles's enquiries into allegations against the NZSIS relating to the Sutch case. Powles summarised the allegations in paragraph 2:

- *that the investigation and arrest of Dr Sutch was undertaken without the knowledge of either Mr Kirk or Mr Rowling, as the case may be.*
- *that officers of the Service perjured themselves at Dr Sutch's trial.*
- *that the arrest and prosecution were undertaken at the behest of a foreign power or of one of its intelligence service.*
- *That Dr Sutch was 'framed' as a result of collusion between the Service and the KGB.*

My inquiries have satisfied me that there is not a shred of truth in any of these allegations.

30 *Auckland Star*, 11 November 1977.

31 *Evening Post*, 2 February 1980.

32 When Powles presented his report to Parliament in July 1976, Shirley spoke to him about it. The author hasn't seen any written account of their meeting/s or correspondence, but on top of a clipping from *Truth* (17 August 1976) that referred to parts of his findings that had been made public, Shirley has written 'Sir Guy (Dick) Powles told me that his findings wd have been different with a different government.'

After summarising the sequence of events his investigations revealed, Powles continued:

18 I am satisfied that none of the allegations of the kind I have mentioned has any foundation whatever. There was no plot and no sinister invention on part of the Service. There was no collusion between the service and anyone else. The Prime Ministers of the day, both Mr Kirk and Mr Rowling, were kept informed. The evidence presented in court by SIS officers was truthful.

19 In the middle of 1975 'Truth' newspaper published a series of articles under the heading 'The Sutch File'. Members of Dr Sutch's family alleged to me that these articles contained, inter alia, personal information about him and his affairs which could have been obtained only from the files of the police and the service containing the results of the searches of Dr Sutch's house, office and papers. These members said that some of these matters were unknown even to them.

They therefore alleged that the service had given this information to 'Truth'. In answer to my question, the service had denied this charge as it did to the Prime Minister on at least two occasions. So has the editor of 'Truth'. I have been unable to find any evidence to support it, and I have seen some material on the service's files which tends to contradict it.

20 If these allegations against the service are all without foundation, there are one or two aspects of the Dr Sutch case which are disturbing and on which I shall now comment.

21 First, it seems more than likely, from an analysis undertaken by the service of all the evidence after Dr Sutch's trial, that his association with the Russians had lasted for a period of years before the meeting between him and Razgovorov on April 18, 1974.

If this is correct, it may reasonably be asked whether a larger concentration of the service's work on surveillance of the staff of the Soviet Embassy would not have discovered this association at a much earlier stage. This aspect of the case is one of the factors which has led me to make the recommendation contained in Section b, subsection 2 of this report, that there should be a substantial reordering of the priorities of the service as between counter-espionage and counter-subversion.[33]

The Powles Report led to more media discussion about the Sutch case. The public learnt from the report that the SIS had not wanted to prosecute Sutch, that Brigadier Gilbert had been overruled by Kirk and that much of the intelligence the SIS had gathered did not amount to evidence in the law.

It also led to the New Zealand Security Intelligence Amendment Bill 1977, which brought bugging within the law subject to strict criteria.

SHIRLEY OPPOSED the proposed Security Intelligence Amendment Bill. Her viewpoint encompassed fundamental issues within the broad scope of history and human values.

She wrote in her reflections on the Amendment Bill that her main purpose was to look at the philosophy of security. Eliminating terrorism from the scope of her enquiry, she questioned the protection of New Zealand from espionage and subversion. Seeing that espionage and counter-espionage had accompanied the exercise of power throughout history, she accepted that those exercises would continue. The essential thing, she said, was to clearly define espionage. However, she slipped away from this, eliding it with her idea of subversion:

It is the pervasive, hidden political judgments implicit in deciding what should be regarded as espionage and subversion that pose a real threat to a free society. The 'security' which has always concerned governments has been the stability of the established order. If a society is capitalist, then anti-capitalist activities are subversive; in a communist society the reverse is true. But the condition of existence on this earth is change, as Heracleitus pointed out in the earliest days of Greek philosophy . . . Is there not the

33 'Sutch Report' published in *Evening Post*, 5 February 1980, pp.16, 24. The full report was declassified on 6 February 2008 when the NZSIS also released their PF on Sutch. For the full report, see: http://www.nzsis.govt.nz/assets/media/SutchOmbudsmanReport.pdf (accessed 15 October 2018).

whole panorama of human history behind us showing that human affairs are in constant flow?[34]

After identifying Jesus Christ, Joan of Arc, Copernicus, Galileo, Mrs Pankhurst and Gandhi as subversives according to their times, Shirley noted that the proposed legislation allowed the SIS to lawfully survey 'potential subversion' in which no unlawful acts were involved. None of the groups to which she had belonged that had been regarded as subversive were illegal and she claimed none had ever operated unlawfully. What had been considered suspect yesterday was often government policy today.

For example, it is now respectable to oppose the use of nuclear weapons; and to be friends with China. According to Brigadier Gilbert's announcement not so long ago, that to advocate recognition of Communist China was the very kind of thing he regarded as highly suspicious, Mr. Rowling and Mr. Muldoon should now be top equal on the list of subversives.[35]

After she questioned the Prime Minister's assertion that opposition to the Amendment Bill must be giving comfort to our enemies – 'Who are our enemies?' – she noted that our security lay within our own people. She recalled living in the United States at the beginning of the McCarthy era, 'how the miasma of distrust and suspicion grew'. The proposed bill was already having that effect in New Zealand, she believed.

To keep up with the changing world, with 'future shock', our society needs the stimulus of challenging ideas, the clash of debate, the security of received ideas, the acknowledgment that all past history shows that the shocking proposition of today is the orthodoxy of tomorrow.

It does not need an apparatus apt to be used for thought control. Whether or not it was intended for that purpose is unimportant. What matters is that it provides for the willing hand a tool to fashion the very kind of society

34 SHSS, 'Reflections on the New Zealand Security Service Amendment Bill 1977, 14 October 1977, SHSS papers, ATL, MS-Papers-11404-146.

35 Ibid.

that we are told it is designed to protect us from.[36]

Shirley didn't complete her submission in time to send it to the Labour Caucus Committee, but she sent it to the Prime Minister and Martyn Finlay. Finlay found her observations 'very much to the point' and hoped to 'dip into them during the further progress of this legislation through the House'.

Her submission addressed the question of espionage only in passing. She, and the population at large, knew little about espionage. Muldoon's bluster about 'our enemies' only confused the issue. It was now simplistic to see an enemy as a particular country. When Christchurch magistrate Paul Molineaux replaced Brigadier Gilbert (now Sir Herbert Gilbert) as NZSIS director in 1976, he said the security staff would 'shift the emphasis of their work away from gathering information about communists . . . Instead they would intensify efforts to guard against terrorism.'[37]

As Shirley stated, she eliminated terrorism from her enquiry. She may have thought external terrorism a proper matter for police, in which case she may have revised her views in 1985 when the French foreign intelligence service bombed the Greenpeace flagship, *Rainbow Warrior*, in the port of Auckland.

ANOTHER ISSUE that preoccupied Shirley over these years was the Arthur Allan Thomas case. She and her father had together followed the case since 1971, when Thomas was first convicted of the double murder of Harvey and Jeanette Crewe. She became more interested after she talked about it with Pat Booth and learnt of the evidence he and forensic scientist Jim Sprott had uncovered about the cartridge case that police had planted. (They proved that the cartridge case alleged to have fallen from the bullet that killed Harvey Crewe was not in production at the time.) Pat, in turn, was interested in Shirley's explanation of the legal aspects.

On her way through Waikato after one of her stays with Pat and

36 Ibid.
37 'Security guard shifts from communists', *Dominion*, 20 July 1976, p.1.

Valerie, Shirley drove to Pukekawa, an area she knew well from her childhood. She drove down every road that had access to the river from the Tūākau Bridge to below Orton, and decided that the only place where a person could put a body in the river unseen was at Orton. 'Strangely, the house nearest but safely distant was the old farmhouse where Nannie and I stayed with Auntie Annie and Uncle Don when I was a small child.'[38]

She visited Thomas's father in Pukekawa, and also Thomas himself at the Rangipō Prison Farm near Tūrangi. That was the beginning of her small part in the campaign to get Thomas cleared. Among many letters she wrote was one to Prime Minister Robert Muldoon suggesting ways the case could be brought before the court. He replied, but she said it was a 'complete brushoff'. Finally, the government gave in to public pressure and set up a Commission that found Arthur Allan Thomas innocent beyond all doubt. He received a full Royal Pardon and was awarded nearly a million dollars compensation.

Muldoon was no friend of Shirley's but she credited him for the decision. She wrote on 23 December 1979:

Dear Mr Muldoon,

I write to offer you my sincere thanks and congratulations on your Government's decision to pardon Arthur Allan Thomas, of whose innocence I have long been convinced.

It is a great relief to me that the action has been taken, for in my view, right or wrong, *you were the only Prime Minister we were likely to have who would have the guts to buck the legal establishment.*

As a corollary, may I add that it was not the system which is wrong, it was in this case the wrong use of it by police, prosecution and judges who broke rules designed to protect the innocent and serve justice. I can document this generalization and intend to do so, because of course it is the duty of all of us to do whatever we can to see that such a miscarriage of justice does not occur again.

With the compliments of the Season[39]

38 SHSS memoir, 'Arthur Allan Thomas', 27 August 1998, SHSS papers.

39 SHSS to Rt. Hon. R. D. Muldoon, 23 December 1979, SHSS papers, ATL, MS-Papers-11369-181.

She documented her argument in 'Fair Challenge: An Aspect of Trial by Jury', published in Wolfgang Rosenberg's festschrift.[40]

On 1 April 1980, after the revelations about Bill Sutch's income tax and the publication of the Powles Report, Shirley had a visit at her office from her old friend Christine Cole Catley. Now a publisher, Christine was working with Norman Kirk's former private secretary Margaret Hayward on a book about the Third Labour Government, based on her diaries. Christine wanted to prepare Shirley for what it revealed about Bill and had thought of a way to soften this. She had heard a rumour that Bill had suffered a degree of brain damage earlier in his life. If it was true and if Shirley would give permission to use it as a footnote, people would then understand some otherwise puzzling facets of his character.

She showed Shirley the suggested footnote: 'An autopsy in 1975 revealed that Dr Sutch had suffered a degree of brain damage earlier in his life.' As Christine recounted to Margaret Hayward that same day, she explained to Shirley that she and the author would like to put it in a passage referring to Bill's judgment seeming to be impaired.

Shirley said the footnote seemed to imply that the damage had been sudden, as if he had fallen off a motorbike. In fact the condition was similar to arteries gradually becoming blocked except that there are no arteries in the brain. She said the condition was called Athera? [atheroma] *and after some discussion, she suggested the following as a footnote: 'An autopsy in 1975 revealed that Dr Sutch had been suffering from a gradual impairment of brain function.' She told me that the family had wondered whether they could make the autopsy findings public but had decided that as a family they could not. She was therefore pleased, even grateful, that the suggested footnote could appear in a reputable book.*[41]

40 Ed. W. E. Willmott, Professor of Sociology, Canterbury University, 1980, SHSS papers, ATL, MS-Papers-11404-179. Shirley also sent her essay to Frank O'Flynn and Geoffrey Palmer when the Jury Bill 1981 was at committee stage.

41 Christine Cole Catley dictating to Margaret Hayward immediately after her meeting with Shirley, 1 April 1980, Margaret Hayward papers, ATL, 81-48 Box. The footnote appears as Shirley suggested in *Diary of the Kirk Years* by Margaret Hayward, Cape Catley/Reed, 1981, p.249.

Shirley subsequently spoke to the *Christchurch Press* more specifically: 'A post-mortem examination had shown that he had effectively used only one lobe of the brain which she describes as a disease shutting off the flow of blood to the brain which in his case had affected the side of the brain governing reason rather than emotion. The disease had advanced for years without her or Dr Sutch's knowledge.'[42]

It was the truth as she knew it. The thought that Bill had suffered long-term impairment of the brain cast him, even more than before, as a classic tragic hero.

42 *Christchurch Press*, clipping undated.

24

'Her boys'

AT THE END of 1978, financial circumstances forced Shirley to stop her domestic practice and most other legal work (with the exception of long-term clients). She looked forward to focusing on the work she liked best: criminal law. She had known some of her clients since they were children. Invariably they shared backgrounds of hardship.

In the Hutt Valley suburb of Taita, Shirley inherited a troubled group, most of whom were Pākehā. She developed a special rapport with one in particular, Grant Ewen.

Born in 1961, Grant grew up in Pomare where he said he and his older brother were like other 'brats around the neighbourhood'. Things changed for Grant at the age of ten, when their father was killed in a pub fight. Grant had an attitude.

In 1973 Grant was put into a class at Taita College known as '3-I'. It was comprised of twenty 'bad boys'. As a result of this educational experiment, a group emerged that became known as the 'Taita gang'. After Grant was expelled early in the fourth form, he continued to hang out with these mates from 3-I. Periodically they appeared before the magistrate for fighting, under-age drinking and petty crimes. When more serious trouble took them to the High Court, the mother of two of the boys called on Shirley.

Grant recalls the first time he went to see Shirley at her office. Seeing Mike Bungay's now famous name on his door next to Shirley's office, Grant was impressed.

And then this little lady comes out, you know, and we're like, 'Hell, what are we in for here?' We knew we had to go into this High Court, and that was a big step up from getting a slap on the hand in the Magistrates' Court for having a scrap outside the takeaway bar. This was getting a bit serious, you know, and, hell, I didn't want to go to jail![1]

But they found Miss Smith very approachable and she gained their confidence. Grant remembered how, on the first day in court, after their names were called out and they were taken down to 'the dungeons', she went down to see them. She was wearing her barrister's gown 'and we were all laughing at how hers went right down to the ground because she was only little'. But they felt reassured by her attention to them. Whenever they were in the cells she checked up on them.

Grant and two other clients Shirley had from the incident were found not guilty. Shirley acted for Grant in two more cases. Then came the Taita Riot.

On Christmas Eve 1981, with fresh pay in his pocket, Grant had spent the afternoon at the Taita Hotel, ending up at a party at a friend's flat above the Taita shops. Half the Hutt Valley was there, says Grant. They spilled out over the verandas and rooftops above the shops. The police arrived after midnight, then reinforcements from Upper Hutt and Wellington turned up wearing riot gear to face a hail of full and empty bottles. The dairy below the flat had two plate glass windows broken. Its owner told the *Evening Post* that the incident had come out of the blue. 'It's normally very quiet round here. We've had nothing like this since the bodgie days.'[2]

Grant was among 27 people who appeared in court on 19 January 1982. Charged with unlawful assembly and taking part in a riot, they elected trial by jury.[3] Grant was the only one Shirley represented in this case. Again, he was found not guilty, but she warned him that he wouldn't always be lucky.

While the case was proceeding, he was in remand at Mt Crawford Prison. His friends who had lived in institutions seemed at home there, but he hated it. Shirley visited him, saw his misery and said something

1 Grant Ewen to author, interview, 16 August 2011.

2 'Riot gear saves police in hail of bottles', *Evening Post*, 26 December 1981. Bodgies were a subcultural group in New Zealand and Australia in the 1950s, like greasers in the US or rockers in the UK.

3 *Evening Post*, 20 January 1982.

like, 'Oh Grant, you don't really want this kind of life, do you?' She got him to see that he shouldn't be there, to realise that he was a good person, too good to waste his life, and that this was how it was going to be if he didn't stay out of trouble from now on.

Grant did stay out of trouble. When he met Shirley in court she was always relieved to know he was 'just visiting', supporting one or other of his friends. He started sending her Christmas cards every year and keeping her up to date with the activities of her other former clients from Taita: 'Me mate Frank rang me from England . . . he has got a business there . . .' 'The Welsh boys ask after you. . . . Mum sends her regards and all the boys say hello. We all still see each other and have a few beers. Times don't change much.' 'Most of us have settled down now so (touch wood) we haven't seen a courtroom for a while.' 'The boys always ask after you and send their regards.' 'We always remember you when we get together and talk of the old days of Courts and getting in 2 trouble. They all respect you in the highest regards.' 'I know I say this every year, Shirley, but we always remember how you helped us and you are held in high respect in our circle, especially by myself and Mum.'[4]

Shirley replied every year as long as she was able to write. Finally, in 2002 she wrote:

16 April
Dear Grant,

. . . Please give my regards and best wishes to the boys. I was never a normal lawyer, I really cared about my clients and was very fond of most of them, especially the young ones. Do you remember how the police prosecution would refer to the 'Taita gang' and I would leap up and say, 'They're not a gang!' So do please tell the boys I'll never forget them while I live – I'm 85 now . . . Dear Grant, I do like to hear from you.

With love,
Shirley[5]

4 Grant Ewen to SHSS, SHSS papers.
5 SHSS to Grant Ewen, Grant Ewen papers.

From 1978, when Shirley cut back her practice to focus on her criminal law, most of her clients were young Māori and Polynesian men. In her retirement, she reflected that she enjoyed her work with them more than anything else she did in the law.

Shirley Smith was by now a seasoned criminal lawyer with a realistic understanding of the problems her young clients presented. She had acted for Black Power members in the 1970s and had set up the Aroha Trust for gang girls. She had worked at the Porirua Legal Advice Centre in Waitangirua, Porirua; her work for the Society for Research on Women (SROW), Stepping Stones, the Cook Island Society, Maori Women's Welfare League, the New Zealand Council for Civil Liberties, domestic law – all gave her insights into the lives of under-privileged families in the state housing estates populated by Māori and Pacific Islanders. She saw hard-working parents, and family ties of affection and loyalty, but also unemployment, poverty, addiction, mental illness and domestic violence. She understood why their children rebelled and joined gangs.

Shirley became the official solicitor for the Porirua Mongrel Mob in October 1980 following a pitched battle between the Mob and Black Power outside the Wellington District Court House. According to Mob member Dennis Makalio, after appearing in the District Court, a lone Mongrel called the Mob in Porirua to say he was being threatened by Black Power and couldn't leave the courthouse – could they come and get him? The first carload set off to rescue him. They arrived to find Black Power waiting outside, lining both sides of Ballance Street in overwhelming numbers, so they called for backup from Porirua. More carloads of the Mob came in, plus a truck of gang members who had been scrubcutting and were armed with slashers, pitchforks and machetes. They all met up and drove together straight down the middle of Ballance Street, jammed the brakes on, jumped out of their vehicles, grabbed their tools and fought their way right into the courthouse to get their man, then took off in different directions . . . and most of them got pulled up.[6]

6 Dennis Makalio to author, interview, 12 June 2015.

Shirley received a call from their president, Charlie Te Houkamau, 'Big Charlie', asking her to go down to the police station where fifteen of their members were in cells. She went and was greeted with the cry, 'Shirley, your children need you!' From then, she referred to them as 'my boys'.

'I couldn't fit them all in my office,' she recalled, 'so we met in their hall on the Porirua Highway. Loads of others came up asking me to defend them on charges of their own.'[7]

The next day, expecting the Mongrels to turn up for their court appearance, more than sixty Black Power gathered in Ballance Street to get revenge for the damage done to their van in the fight. A special section of police was on duty to keep the factions apart; a police van with two dogs was parked outside, traffic officers were on hand and reporters were there to catch the action. Some Mongrels cruised past in their cars, others sat on a car in Ballance Street, drinking beer from bottles, but nothing happened: Shirley and her clients didn't come.

They appeared the next day. Journalists were on hand but there were no reported incidents. Shirley's clients all entered pleas of not guilty to charges of unlawful assembly. The *Evening Post* photographer caught them outside afterwards, and a photo of Shirley talking to Big Charlie in a group of Mongrels appeared on the front page that night. Outside the photo frame were the rest of her clients, plus those who had come along for support. Dennis Makalio wondered what went through people's minds as they passed by: 'There's this little old lady with glasses, right smack in the middle of us. It felt like she was our little nanny.'[8]

He recalls the hearing in the District Court three months later: 'We were walking proud with her, into the courtroom thinking, 'You look after us, we'll look after you.' All fifteen took the witness stand. Shirley did her best for them, but they knew they weren't going to jail so didn't take it seriously. Dennis explained: 'You get fifteen Mongies all cracking up at once, you know, something's gotta give – everyone bloody cracks up. Even the judge couldn't keep a straight face.' They were all found guilty, fined $300 and their driving licences were disqualified for fifteen

7 Rosemary Vincent, 'Mongrel's lawyer takes it quietly', *New Zealand Times*, 27 November 1983, p.9.

8 Dennis Makalio to author, interview, 12 June 2015.

months. 'We didn't care. It's like a game of cards – once it's over, it's over.'[9]

A FEW WEEKS later the photo of Shirley with her Mongrel Mob clients reappeared in the *Evening Post* with an item about their proposal to take her out in a car one night to see for herself how the police in Porirua hassled them. She agreed to the idea. She saw a 'cowboys and Indians mentality between some of the police and the mob in which neither side was blameless. Each was baiting the other.'[10]

Her father wasn't happy about any of this. He thought her association with the Mongrel Mob reflected badly on the family name and wrote asking her to stop it.[11]

She abandoned her night out with the boys, but she did meet the Commander of the Western Coastal Region in his office in the Porirua Police Station to discuss how they might reduce tensions between the police and the Mob. She recalled, 'We were getting on very well until I said "I do feel it would be helpful if on some occasion your men would use a different approach". Whereupon he froze, and said "*My* men are not going to adapt their approach to suit *your* clients."'[12]

Shirley thought that if people gave them the benefit of the doubt to start with, they'd be rewarded as she was. She explained how she related to them: 'I don't look at the gang patches, the Rastafarian locks, or the tattoos. I look at their eyes. I get on with them because I treat them as individuals. I don't believe in starting with an assumption of superiority – I treat them the same as I do everyone – as human beings with great possibilities.'[13] They found she listened to them and she cared. Her first Mongrel Mob client told her she was the first person who had ever put up a real defence for him, the first to subpoena a witness.

9 Ibid.

10 SHSS as reported in *Evening Post*, 20 December 1980.

11 From author's memory of seeing this letter before SHSS papers went to ATL.

12 SHSS to editor, *Evening* Post, 16 October 1983, SHSS papers, ATL, MS-Papers-11404-138. Most of the letter was published on 20 October in an article headed 'Chase report criticized by Mongrel Mob's lawyer'. *New Zealand Times* published the letter in full under the heading, 'Counsel: Police need to change', 23 October 1983, p.3.

13 SHSS to Rosemary Vincent, feature, 'I look at their eyes . . . not their patches', *New Zealand Women's Weekly*, 23 May 1988, p.10.

Seeing the good in them, she brought out the best in them. She said, 'When you get to know these young men – and I mean really know them, when they know that you accept them and they accept you – you find warmth, trust, loyalty; you find intelligence, abilities of all kinds and their joy in using them when the rare chance comes.'[14]

This describes her relationship with Paul Parker, called Pauli.

Aged seventeen when he came out of borstal in 1976, Pauli developed an affinity with Shirley. She was in regular contact with both him and his partner Jay Marson over the next fifteen years or more. She defended Pauli in court and he was a key to her relationship with the Porirua chapter.

Pauli was both exceptional and representative of Shirley's Porirua clients. She was much more than a solicitor to him. 'She was like a mum to me – because I never had a mother.'[15]

Jay recalls how Shirley took the time to listen to Pauli in a way no one else had ever done: 'Shirley saw the hurt in him. She saw the hurt in them all but with Pauli she had a special rapport. It was very emotional.' And Shirley also saw that Pauli had a heart, Jay says. 'He hid it, but underneath he was kind.'

Pauli was seven when he and three siblings were 'committed Indigent and Neglected' to Welfare, another brother having been put up for adoption earlier. Pauli never accepted the way his family was torn apart. He was placed in a Pākehā foster home out of Wanganui and for a while he seemed to thrive. According to Welfare records, his emotional reaction to being separated from his siblings was his only problem. He had previously missed a great deal of schooling, but he was bright, keen to learn and he made good progress in all areas. One school report typically described him as an 'intelligent child, pleasant, well-mannered, well behaved, very stable, very reliable, co-operative, a keen sportsman, a well-adjusted child'.[16]

He would probably have confided in Shirley how everything changed. Soon after his twelfth birthday he ran away from his foster

14 *Evening Post*, 22 April 1987.

15 Paul Parker to author, telephone interview, 8 October 2015.

16 School report, 30 November 1967, Paul Parker's Welfare Records.

home and refused to return. He was put in another foster home and ran away from there too. By the time he started college he hated school and refused to attend. He was sent from the Wanganui Family Home to Epuni Boys' Home in Lower Hutt, absconding three times from there. (Aged thirteen, he converted cars, including on one occasion a police car in which he got as far as Rotorua in an attempt to find his father.) He was transferred to Hōkio Beach School, where he was beaten in front of the whole school and probably suffered other abuses not recorded. It was anticipated that he could look forward to a lifetime of incarceration. On Pauli's transfer to Kohitere Training Centre in June 1973, the principal wrote:

On the surface he can present as a likable individual but beneath this exterior there lurks a bitter and twisted personality and he harbours strong feelings of hate and revenge. He has constantly challenged the system and has welcomed opportunities to encourage others to adopt the same attitude. It is the opinion of most staff that he has caused more dissentions in the place than any other boy.[17]

He left Kohitere when he turned fifteen and in 1974 he lived among the Mongrel Mob in Porirua.[18] The mob became his whānau. But he was soon in trouble and he ended up in borstal.

Shirley knew of the abuse and brutality that inmates experienced in the boys' homes and borstals and believed imprisonment was not the answer for people like Pauli. She argued that much of the money spent on prisons would be better spent on seeing children had a fair start in life.

She made herself available for her boys at any time, day or night. She did whatever she could for them, regardless of the cost to her. 'I cared so much that none of the boys should go down for something they were innocent of,' she said.[19] In court, she showed an exceptional empathy for her clients. After one trial a juror wrote to congratulate her on her

17 Hōkio Beach Principal T. K. North, 29 June 1973, (903), Paul Parker's Welfare Records.
18 Social worker J. C. Harwood, Case Report (843–844), Paul Parker's Welfare Records.
19 SHSS to Rosemary Vincent, 'Shirley – battler for the Mob', *Evening Post*, 30 December 1993.

'dedication and devotion and acute sensitive and astute representation for Paul Parker'. Seeing she was deeply involved in helping 'our Maori brethren', he thought there might be some way of assisting her.[20] Shirley was very willing to take up his offer.

Employment was one issue they surely discussed. From time to time they had labouring jobs (when the government's Project Employment Programme work schemes were still operating), but more often the boys were unemployed and spent their time drinking. Shirley found that most of their offending was either caused by or associated with alcohol – much more than drugs.[21]

Mongrel Mob member Dennis Makalio agrees that, back then, alcohol was the problem. 'I think our pad was one party for twenty years, 24/7. We just had groups of shifts running it. . . . And when you party you get drunk . . . then there'd be some trouble and they'd say, "Well I'm gonna ring up Shirley".'[22]

Sometimes she went out to them. Pauli's friend Harvey Uiti recalled how Shirley conducted herself when she came out to the gang pad: 'She was short but she walked tall among the Mob. She was held in high esteem. Pauli was very protective of her and he always championed her.'[23] Pauli recalls, 'We didn't comb our hair, we were dirty . . . we were ugly and greasy but we behaved like gentlemen around Shirley. There was no swearing around her. We treated her with respect.'[24]

More often they saw her in her chambers. Helen Edwards recalls feeling intimidated the first time they jostled their way into the small office, but they were courteous. Shirley always looked them straight in the eye, ignoring their gang regalia. She never talked down to them.

Pauli's partner Jay, who often accompanied Pauli to appointments with Shirley, remembers how Shirley insisted on telling the truth. 'If she knew you were telling lies she'd cut you off quick as lightning. . . . She was straight and shrewd, and they knew where they stood with her.'[25]

20 James W. Cornish to SHSS, 23 August 1981, SHSS papers, ATL, MS-Papers-11369-200.
21 SHSS, 'Commentary', *Evening Post*, 22 April 1987.
22 Dennis Makalio to author, interview, 12 June 2015.
23 Harvey Uiti to author, telephone interview, 13 June 2015.
24 Paul Parker to author, 8 October 2015.
25 Jay Marson to author, 3 July 2015.

But sometimes Shirley had doubts. In a letter to Eoin Jury, who had provided photographic evidence for an identification case she'd lost for Pauli Parker, she wrote that it was awfully distressing, and she was only then (about a week later) coming out from under the cloud.

There were some very odd things about the whole case, I must confess, and I had a great urge to implore the boys to tell me, now that it was all over, just what the truth was. I have had these urges before, and always resisted them, as I did this one. You can't win. If the boys have *been telling the truth, you will destroy the trust between you; and if they haven't, they will in all probability continue to lie.*[26]

She chose to believe them. 'Paul said that he was only thankful that it was over at last. I am often amazed at how they accept what seems to me injustice; they have no great expectations. An amazing contrast to white middle class liberals – a friend went down in a very minor Small Claims Tribunal claim, and you should have heard her carrying on about it.'[27]

As paranoia about gangs increased, Shirley countered what she saw as prejudice by speaking up for the Porirua Mob. In an interview for *New Zealand Women's Weekly*, she told Rosemary Vincent that she'd read about robberies, rapes and other serious crimes carried out by members in other parts of New Zealand, but the Porirua group she knew best was 'different from the usual conception of gangs'.

They don't live in a fortified gang house. They live in their own homes with their parents, their wives or their de factos.

They're devoted to their children and one of the most striking things about them is their concern that their kids don't grow up like them and become jailbirds.[28]

Interviewed for the same article, Pauli Parker said, 'She likes us – that's what makes her different. Just about every member of our gang

26 SHSS to Eoin Jury, 28 April 1987, SHSS papers, ATL, MS-Papers-11404-190.
27 Ibid.
28 SHSS to Rosemary Vincent, *New Zealand Women's Weekly*, 23 May 1988, p.10–11.

has a lot of respect for her. If it wasn't for her getting us off, which she does do a lot, some of us wouldn't have our families and our kids. We'd be in prison.'

Shirley saw that it was Jay's good influence and his children that kept Pauli out of jail most of the time since they had been together. Jay says Shirley was their rock. They visited her at her home, she came to tea at theirs and held their babies. When Jay's mother died, Jay gave Shirley first pick of her mother's clothes. 'She was my friend,' says Jay.

Shirley visited other Mongrel Mob members at their homes, but Pauli was probably the only one who went to her home, apart from his friend Harvey Uiti, who went with Pauli. Harvey recalled that their conversations were wide-ranging.

Her relationship was more with Pauli . . . but we were a trio, me, Pauli and her. She talked to us about social justice and our responsibility to each other but also to the wider community. We talked about the injustice of the police and the way they conducted themselves, the undercurrent of institutionalized racism. . . . And yes, she talked to us about the injustices within our own system, creating our own victims. She was passionate about the role of women and the way we treated them. I'd think, OK Shirley. I didn't really listen. Her voice came back later when I started CART [Consultancy, Advocacy and Research Trust]. *Hers was the first voice to talk about social justice that I remember.*[29]

Before his death in 2017, Harvey Uiti coordinated anti-violence programmes in Dunedin. Dennis Makalio works with his wife Lizzie McMillan-Makalio in Porirua on similar programmes. They speak with authority, having served their sentences for violent crimes.

The Porirua Mob may have been less violent than other chapters, but Shirley defended some serious cases. In an interview with Neville Glasgow, broadcast in January 1989, she admitted, 'Every now and then some of the boys I know have been involved in something nasty . . . I can't win every time and very often they don't deserve to win. Often I

29 Harvey Uiti to author, telephone interview, 13 June 2015. Harvey Uiti and Gary Victor Martin set up CART in 1989 to meet the needs of 'Nga Mokai', people on the social periphery. http://www.cart.org.nz/page/history.html (accessed 15 October 2018).

am making just a plea for mitigation, I am not really defending them. But they know they can rely on me to do my best for them.'[30]

Helen Croft recalls the deep impression Shirley made on her when she acted as Shirley's junior in a vicious mass gang rape trial. Shirley showed her how to approach it, putting all emotion aside, looking at the theory of law. 'She was totally principled, absolutely non-judgmental. It was hard not to judge when the girl's injuries were so apparent, but Shirley articulated why they would do their best. She was genuine, real, passionate about justice being done, and her final address to the jury was inspirational. She said, "We all sympathise with the victim, we all have prejudices, but you have to put them aside, put aside what happened, and think about whether the Crown has proved its case. *It has to be proved.*"'[31]

The accused were all found guilty, but they had a fair trial. This was what underpinned Shirley's criminal work. She proclaimed the basic principle of British justice that everyone is entitled to a fair trial as 'our bulwark against the lynch law'.[32]

IN 1981 SHIRLEY was called in to represent the Petone Mongrel Mob after the police mounted an assault on their fortified gang house. Her new clients included a young Māori man called Paul Chase.

After serving a prison sentence, Paul Chase left the Mongrel Mob. He lived with his partner and child in Petone and had a steady job at Ford Motors, where he was well liked by colleagues and his employer. On 16 April 1983, he went on a drinking binge with his friends Erwin Babbington and Ramon Tangitutu, who were still in the Mob. They ended up at the Hutt Park Hotel, considered to be Black Power turf. After getting into a fight they left, then returned with a double-barrelled shotgun. During a further altercation a shot was fired in the air inside the bar. Police concluded that Babbington had fired it and that Chase and Tangitutu were party to the shooting. Witnesses gave

30 SHSS to Neville Glasgow, interview, broadcast on National Radio, 18 January 1989, published in *Directions: New Zealanders Explore the Meaning of Life, Shoal Bay Press*, Christchurch, 1995, p.199.

31 Helen Croft to author, 22 April 2015.

32 SHSS to editor, *Dominion*, 4 June 1982, written 25 May under heading, 'Mob Justice'.

contradictory descriptions of the weapon, the course of events and Paul Chase's involvement.[33]

The next day, Sunday, he stayed at home, waiting for the police to call, having heard that they would. Expecting reprisals from Black Power he barricaded his door that night before going to bed. On the Monday morning before dawn, members of the Wellington Armed Offenders Squad, who were trained as an anti-terrorist squad, broke down his door in a four-minute operation. Apparently thinking his attackers were Black Power, Paul Chase picked up an exercise bar to defend himself, whereupon the police shot him. He died two hours later.

Babbington and Tangitutu went into hiding. Police mounted a manhunt, which ended a week later when, as Shirley later recalled, she received a phone call from one of them saying they wanted to give themselves up and hand in the weapon used in the Hutt Park Hotel shooting.

Would I come and collect them, and the gun, and arrange for them to appear, with me, at the police station? If they went on their own they were terrified they would be shot.

So this was done and another sad mistake was discovered. The police believed that the gun was a bright shiny weapon. But no, it was dark and not shiny. They could hardly believe it. It was because they mistook the shiny exercise bar for a shiny gun that they shot Paul.[34]

Dick Werry of Lower Hutt had earlier phoned Shirley to tell her about the shooting and ask her to represent Paul Chase's partner, Dee. He recalls Shirley's horror, not only at what had happened but that it

33 SHSS to editor, *New Zealand Times* (original), 9 November 1983; SHSS to editor, *Evening Post*, 16 October (published 20 October) 1983, SHSS papers, ATL, MS-Papers-11404-138.

34 SHSS to editor, *Evening Post*, published 1 July 1997. SHSS to editor, written 16 Oct 1983: 'The police originally did not content themselves with "shiny" and "chrome". They were convinced that the barrels of the gun were silver, and the depositions apparently made no dent on their belief, because when at the end of the hearing I delivered the gun up to them, on behalf of my clients, they at first could not believe that it was the gun used because it was not silver-barrelled.'

had happened to Paul. She said that even when he had been a gang member he had done nothing – just a couple of assaults. She thought it better that Mike Bungay represent the family. She would represent Babbington and Tangitutu.[35]

Meanwhile the community was angry and anxious. Only four months earlier, another Lower Hutt man, John Morgan, had been shot dead by police in circumstances that left many worrying questions unanswered. Looking for action, more than 200 people attended a public meeting in the Lower Hutt Town Hall on 25 April. George Rosenberg took a leading role, arguing that any homicide inquiry would clear the policemen of blame. What was needed was not an inquiry into the guilt or innocence of the policeman who pulled the trigger; they needed to know why he was put in that situation, why he was armed with such a weapon, why the situation was set up where he thought he had to use that weapon. What had happened in the past few months, George said, was the development of a system by the police that amounted to 'a licence to kill'.[36]

The meeting unanimously called for a full public inquiry into the death of Paul Chase and an investigation into the police procedures that led to the shooting, including the issuing of firearms. They formed a committee to bring this about.

When the Paul Chase Public Inquiry Committee met with Minister of Police Ben Couch he refused to agree to a full public inquiry. Instead, the government appointed Auckland QC Colin Nicholson as independent assessor of an internal police inquiry, allowing no opportunity to cross-examine witnesses. The report found that the police had acted scrupulously.

In a letter, published by both the *Evening Post* and *New Zealand Times*, Shirley asserted that 'preconceived ideas, strongly held' contributed to the unnecessary death of Paul Chase. 'I believe that an open-minded enquiry among those who knew the three would have shaken their belief that the three were desperadoes ready to shoot on sight.'

In her view, the most serious question unanswered by Nicholson was

35 Dick Werry to author, interview, 9 October 2015.
36 *Evening Post*, 28 April 1983.

why Māori wardens were not used. Nicholson considered it would have been inappropriate to involve them in the armed offenders operation. Shirley saw this as 'Alice in Wonderland stuff':

No one would have expected Maori wardens to be involved in the armed offenders operation. The whole point of their offer of help, surely, was to obviate the need for any armed offenders operation. They would have made contact with Paul using words, not guns. It was not only Maori wardens who could have helped; there were elder members of the Chase family, Albert Babbington as leader of the gang, or myself as solicitor of the Petone Mob. If any of us had been asked, or allowed, to make contact with Paul independently, he would not have died.

. . .

I knew Paul Chase. He was not an angel but he was a young man of great vitality and attractive personality. The life force that flowed so strongly through him, sometimes ill-directed, would in time, I feel sure, have been turned to the service of the community and made him an outstanding leader. As it was, he had a family, a wife and child, friends and a job. By many people and in many places he is missed and mourned, with anger as well as sorrow. For the offences in the Hutt Park Hotel, Babbington got three years imprisonment, Tangitutu got two, but Chase got death, and without even being found guilty.

For the future, whatever is necessary to prevent such a death must be done: and in my mind there is no doubt that this requires changes in police attitudes and procedure.[37]

The Nicholson Report had one positive outcome in that it proposed a total review of armed offenders squad training, and this in turn led to armed offenders' squads having basic training in negotiation techniques. As for gang–police relations, they were set back for years.

A CONTRAST to the tragic shooting of Paul Chase is a story told at Shirley's funeral, about a hostage situation in Porirua in which a young

37 SHSS to editor, *Evening Post* (original), 16 October 1983 (published 20 October), SHSS papers, ATL, MS-Papers-11404-138.

man with a gun was holding a baby. The police tried to negotiate with him but the only person he would speak to was Shirley Smith. She was hastily brought to the scene, entered the house alone (unarmed of course) and emerged carrying the baby.[38]

38 MHS to author, 27 April 2017.

25

The flood

IN THE 1980s Shirley's circumstances allowed her to travel. It had always been a passion and now her family was living in Europe. In 1981 she followed Helen and Keith and the boys soon after they moved to Paris, where Helen, on unpaid leave from the New Zealand Treasury, joined the Social Affairs Directorate of the OECD. The following year, 1982, Shirley took a longer trip of over two months that included a fortnight with the family in Italy, based in a Tuscan village north-west of Florence. She was as thrilled as ever by Europe.

In London she attended the Privy Council for George Rosenberg's landmark victory (with George Barton QC) against the Crown for his client, Falema'i Lesa, a Western Sāmoan facing deportation. Both Georges were heroes, at least for around 150,000 Sāmoans who became New Zealand citizens overnight.[1] Shirley was ecstatic and proud, especially of her former law clerk.

Meanwhile her father's health was declining. Aged 94, he was still writing legal opinions, but his eyesight was failing, he suffered from arthritis, an operation on his knee had complications with regard to medication, and he had a recurrence of prostate cancer.

When Shirley returned home at the beginning of September, she was very attentive to his needs. He noted in his diary her every phone call and visit, their routine lunches together, the dinners she cooked on his housekeeper May Ives's night off and other indications of her devoted care. She thought of things of interest and people he'd like

1 The key to the success was the 1928 British Nationality and Status of Aliens (in New Zealand) Act, which held that the Cook Islands and Western Sāmoa were 'in the same manner in all respects . . . [and] for all purposes part of New Zealand'. The Privy Council's ruling was overturned by the 1982 Citizenship (Western Sāmoa) Act. Privy Council Appeal no. 42 of 1981, http://www.bailii.org/uk/cases/UKPC/1982/1982_30.pdf (accessed 15 October 2018).

to see – all this while catching up with her own work. But he wanted more. His last entry on 19 October reads, 'Shirley will not stay here.' As he had both May Ives and a nurse, it wasn't necessary that Shirley move in, but she later reproached herself.[2]

He stayed at home until after Christmas, when he was scheduled for surgery. Allan recalled visiting him in hospital with Shirley on the morning of 29 December:

We were talking away. The physician in charge, who was a lady, came in and asked us to leave the room . . . We were out there not terribly long, just a few minutes, and she came and said, Come quickly, come in – and we came in and Pop was unconscious and died before our eyes.[3]

Māui Pōmare and Steve (now called Tipene) O'Regan offered to give Sir David a Māori farewell at his funeral. Shirley later wrote to Māui Pōmare's widow, Louise, that this was 'unsought, unexpected, and totally heart-warming. Maui spoke wonderfully. I remember one phrase – he spoke of Dad's "beloved playground of Taranaki", and farewelled him in Maori. They put feather cloaks on the coffin. It moves me now, unspeakably, to remember.'[4] Shirley gave the main eulogy. It made a deep impression on those present.[5]

A few weeks later she expressed how she felt over her father's death in a letter to Keith Ovenden:

I think of him a lot, and find that absorbing into oneself the 'finality of death' is quite different from the rational knowledge one has always had (more or less) and thought one accepted. He was the one person who had always been there, from the beginning of my life. And I am haunted by the thought that I didn't really give him all the care and comfort that I should have. I think more of the mystery of mortality . . . it is as if one sees familiar country in a new and sharper focus.

I am more and more grateful for what I have had – so fortunate I have

2 SHSS to KWO, 3 March 1983; DSS diary, 1982, DSS papers.
3 AGS to author, interview, 12 August 2011.
4 SHSS to Louise Pōmare, 8 April 1995, Cecilia Johnson papers.
5 Helen Edwards to author, interview, 8 April 2011.

been. I wrote to Helen that I felt 'translated' when I gazed at my book of pictures from the Louvre; I feel the same when I think of many experiences in my life, not least those of last summer. With the flick of a thought I am in Colle, looking across at Montecatine Alto, in Volterra, Pisa, in Florence . . . these names stand for all. I feel part of them, they part of me, and that gives me a share – not in immortality, for nothing human can be immortal – but in an immeasurably greater existence than one mortal life.

And then of course there are the children. I, too, greatly value their link with Dad and that he loved them so – and their unique selves.[6]

When her family moved to Paris, Shirley thought that one consolation would be that she would get on top of her work and the maintenance of her house and garden. Now, with her father gone too, she may have thought the same, but old clients kept getting into trouble, new ones flowed in and she seemed as pressured as ever. Before joining Helen and Keith on a holiday in Crete in July 1984, she moved out of her downtown office.

Shirley decided to work from home when the lease on her chambers expired. Bringing home all the files she had accumulated since 1961 was a major operation, and then she had to find room to store them among all her other papers – her own, Bill's and now also her father's. The storage space in the basement had long since filled.

She had deposited the legal papers her father had selected for the Alexander Turnbull Library. Turnbull Librarian Jim Traue had tried to get Shirley to deposit Bill's papers in accordance with an informal arrangement he had with Bill. Shirley denied there were papers Bill had promised and said that she didn't have them – the SIS had raided the house and taken them.[7] But before her 1984 trip she deposited 17 cartons. According to her, the papers didn't include Bill's research material on Gordon Coates, which the Coates family wanted returned. She couldn't find the Coates papers.

In March 1984, the final distribution of her father's estate left her comfortably off. She painted the house and replaced the roof on the

6 SHSS to KWO, 3 March 1983. May Ives died suddenly nine months later, aged 95. She had been with the family since 1940.

7 Jim Traue to author, 29 October 2013.

upper level. For years she had dealt with leaks by placing buckets strategically around the house, leaving her sister-in-law Margaret Shirley the job of emptying those buckets when Shirley was travelling. She was glad she no longer had to worry about that.

Before she left, George and Amanda Rosenberg moved to Hong Kong, where George joined the Government Legal Department – the beginning of his international career. He wrote Shirley a note on 21 March 1984 thanking her for all she had done for him and Amanda:

Your influence has been pivotal in both our lives and I really cannot imagine life without you somewhere in a 3-mile radius!

The consolation is that I know we will be seeing you when you pop into H.K. to or from Europe and I am looking forward to that eagerly.

Love,

George[8]

GREECE WAS BLISS. Shirley feared that returning to the country she had fallen in love with in 1937 would spoil her memory, but she fell in love all over again. Travelling ahead of Helen and Keith, she rediscovered the classical sites of Athens and the Peloponnese before meeting the family in Patras, then going with them to Crete. They stayed in a hillside villa at Limenas Chersonisou, a 90-minute drive east of Heraklion on the north coast, a good base from which to visit Minoan archeological sites. Shirley was most captivated by the ruins of the ancient city of Lato near the village of Kritsa. Keith would remember that he never saw her so happy as on those sites 'where the atmosphere can steal your breath away, and much has to be imagined.'[9]

Adding to her happiness at this time came the news from home that the National Government had been overthrown in a snap election. Rejoicing in Muldoon's downfall, she was oblivious to the disaster that occurred two days later when a torrential rainstorm caused her new roof to fail.

Shirley and the family left Crete together on 24 July, making their

8 George Rosenberg to SHSS, 21 March 1984, SHSS papers, ATL, MS-Papers-11404-74.
9 KWO, Eulogy for SHSS, January 2008.

way to Florence, where Shirley stayed on after the others returned to Paris. On 31 July, while still in Florence, she learnt about the flood, but only when her brother Allan phoned her when she was back in Paris did she realise how serious it was. The roofers had blocked an internal drainpipe that went through the middle of the house.

Determined to deal with the whole thing herself, Margaret Shirley had contacted Shirley's insurance company and lawyer but otherwise involved only her friends Jack and Kate Shallcrass, until she had to inform Helen Edwards, who was looking after the law practice. Helen decided that Shirley had to be told, and also Allan Smith. When Allan saw the damage, he was appalled. Carpets were sodden, mould had already formed on books, paintings and prints, water had collected in cups hanging on the hooks in the kitchen and some of Bill's precious ceramics were broken.

Shirley decided that the damage was done and there was no point in rushing home. Helen Edwards assured her that things were in hand, and that there was nothing sinister in the removal of legal files and receipt books to the Crown Law office. Shirley's lawyer Gerald Fitzgerald (acting on behalf of Ian McKay) had simply arranged for them to be taken there to be stored and dried.

Allan contacted Turnbull Librarian Jim Traue, who took some of his staff to the house to see what could be done. They arranged for a private conservator, Rosemary Collier, to take books away to dry. And they found the missing boxes of Bill's papers, including some of the Coates material. When he told Shirley that they had found and rescued them, she seemed quite miffed. (There were in fact more of Bill's papers in other parts of the house.)[10]

10 Jim Traue to author, 23 October 2013. Rosemary Collier to author, email, 26 July 2012. SHSS to John Barr, c/- ATL, 5 March 1988:

It was only last Thursday that I learned that more of the Coates family material had been recovered from my house after the disastrous flood of 1984. . . .

. . . I located some further items that clearly belonged to the Coates family among the contents of a carton that was set aside as purely Sutch material.

. . . it was not in the cartons that I delivered to Mr Traue just before I went overseas in 1984. I itemised the entire contents of those 17 cartons . . . Mr Traue explained that this extra material had been found when his people went up to remove my own books which had been badly damaged in the flood.

Of course I do not doubt this, but I am amazed and baffled that there was Coates material still

Allan was anxious to dry the house by turning on the under-floor heating. He also wanted to ensure that the roof didn't flood again. He wrote to his sister Shirley in exasperation, 'It is not possible to get past [Margaret] Shirley Sutch, she has the key, will discuss nothing, and accepts neither help nor suggestions. I have the impression she regards herself as the guardian of Bill's relics and wants nobody else, particularly me, near the place.'[11]

Writing in defence of her friend, Kate Shallcrass warned Shirley that 'a very large part of the house was affected. . . . Shirley, be prepared to return to a very different house from the one you left in June but know that it has been lovingly cared for by Shirley Sutch each day since the flood.'[12]

WHILE COMING to terms with this disaster, Shirley was mugged by gypsies in Paris. She was on the Metro with Crispin when the teenagers, one carrying a baby, descended on them chanting, dancing and holding in front of them a huge piece of paper. She kept hold of Crispin while fending them off with the other hand but under cover of the paper they took her wallet.[13] Though shaken and greatly inconvenienced, especially by the loss of her driving licence, she made light of it.

Every letter from home brought more bad news. She asked Allan about the ceramics in the house, in particular two ancient Indonesian pots and the Chinese horses, both unglazed burial pieces, and learnt that some works of art had been swept off their shelf by the flood. Margaret Shirley reported that the Chinese horses weren't damaged and that she had put them 'in a safe place', but later sent photos of the Han horse lying on its side with one leg broken, its rider and plaque separate, damaged by the workmen who removed the carpet. She had it assessed by museum staff, who doubted its authenticity. On top of all this, Margaret Shirley referred to the T'ang horse as a 'replica'. Among Bill's papers she had come across a Brentano catalogue with an

in the house. I cannot think where it can have been . . .
Anyway, I'm glad you will be able to restore these items to the family.

11 AGS to SHSS, 24 August 1984, SHSS papers.
12 Kate Shallcrass to SHSS, 9 October 1984, SHSS papers, ATL, MS-Papers-11404-76.
13 SHSS to Helen Edwards, 16 August 1984, SHSS papers, ATL, MS-Papers-11404-24.

illustration and description of the T'ang horse, whose original was in the Museum of Fine Arts, Boston.[14]

Shirley was vexed. She recalled being with Bill when they bought the horses in New York and thought they came with certificates of authenticity. What further shocks awaited her, she wondered? She was in no hurry to find out.

She eventually booked her flight home, planning a four-week return journey from London that included six days in Israel (travelling on her own in a hired a car) and a week in Hong Kong with Amanda and George, now married. In Auckland she spent another week catching up with her old friends Rona Edwards (formerly Lewis, now remarried) and Cecil Algie (formerly Upton), all her Auckland relatives and Pat Booth and Valerie Davies. She travelled to Rotorua to visit more people, and to Taupō, where she stayed a further week, arranging that on her arrival in Wellington she would go straight out to Allan and Helen Smith's at Tītahi Bay.

Eventually she had to go home to her ruined house with its empty bookcases. And she had to face her sister-in-law.

ASIDE FROM the problems of the house itself, Shirley found piles of legal work, some of it urgent, needing her attention. Where previously she escaped to the office, she now worked at home and the environment was more chaotic than ever. 'My papers and files were just stuffed into cartons and carted away to Crown Law, no lists, no marks on the cartons,' she complained. '. . . what I need may be anywhere, in the living room, the corridor or bedrooms or at Crown Law. . . . there is

14 'Art of the Far East', Catalogue of the Brentano Collection of Sculpture Masterpieces in Replica, 1955, Brentano's Inc., p.30 (MSS to SHSS, 17 October 1984, SHSS papers, ATL, MS-Papers-11404-76):
Figure of a standing horse Chinese T'ang dynasty (618–907 A.D.) . . .
'The original of this is pottery and is from the collection of Mr and Mrs Paul Bernot on loan to the Museum of Fine Arts, Boston,
No M.F.A. –56 Price $75
Height 17 ½"
Length 16"
(shipped express collect)
'All pieces unless otherwise noted have been reproduced in Alvastone*'.*

always the fear that something I need is gone for good.'[15]

In view of Margaret Shirley's secrecy about the flood, she was surprised when her local dairy owner mentioned it. 'I asked him how he knew, and what he said struck a chill into my soul.' He said that 'Shirley' had been taking so much stuff to the tip that he asked her about it, and she told him. All Margaret Shirley had told her was that she'd thrown out some photos from Bill's file drawers. That alone had appalled Shirley. 'How could she throw away photos?' She feared she would never know how much had really been thrown away.[16]

FOUR WEEKS later, Shirley confessed to her daughter Helen that she had done nothing about architects, insurance, lawyers, books and so forth. Halfway through the following year she wrote to Keith's father that the house was still not in order, nothing had been done and she was 'just camping out'. She had to find the house plans for the architect. 'Nothing is where it should be. . . . Also I am appallingly busy; my old clients keep getting into more trouble and new ones flock in. I feel beset. As usual.'[17]

THERE HAD BEEN floods at 79a Todman Street before and would be more after, but the 1984 flood was a defining event, not only because the Sutch–Smith House was regarded as an architectural classic. Shirley always referred to it to explain the state she lived in. She always intended to organise the historical papers, but instead she was creating new material with her voluminous writings, clippings and other printed matter. As for the house itself, there was too much to do on her own, she resisted help and anyway the world at large was more important. She preferred to attend to her clients and her causes.

The campaign for homosexual law reform was coming to a head. Shirley had spoken on behalf of the movement at a time when it was dangerous for homosexuals to speak for themselves, and she was still a spokesperson and vice-president of the Homosexual Law Reform Society, but gays and lesbians now made themselves seen and heard.

15 SHSS to MHS, pp.6–7, 15 November 1984, MHS papers.
16 SHSS to MHS, 15 November 1984, MHS papers.
17 SHSS to Alf Ovenden, 19 June 1985, SHSS papers, ATL, MS-Papers-11369-198.

People discovered family members, friends and colleagues were gay.

Shirley's sister-in-law Margaret Shirley was a lesbian. Shirley of course had always been comfortable with that, and though the law reform referred to male homosexuality, Margaret Shirley was someone with whom she could discuss her ideas for her submission to the Statutes Revision Committee. In her submission, Shirley proposed that the Homosexual Law Reform Bill 'should be seen as placing homosexual love on the same basis as heterosexual love, equally acceptable in itself and subject to the same restraints against force, deception and the exploitation of minors.'[18]

To the Salvation Army Public Relations Officer, she wrote that though it hurt her not to enclose a donation to help them in their good work, she could not in good conscience do so while the Army opposed homosexual law reform.

To my mind it is not relevant whether one likes or dislikes any particular sexual practices, whether homosexual or heterosexual (and in my legal practice I have encountered sodomy only among heterosexuals, as a charged offence); or even whether or not there are Biblical dictates against them: the point is that the public law of the country should not concern itself with sexual practices, as such. Of course force, fraud, injury and harm to children are properly proscribed by law whether combined with sex or not. I also believe, on the basis of my reading of many civilizations, and my experience, that homosexual preference is not a matter of choice, but is a natural variant of sexual behaviour, and that homosexuals should be accepted as normal people. I do hope the Army will change its collective mind.[19]

To Minister of Defence Frank O'Flynn, who was opposed to the Bill, she wrote that a phenomenon that had been so persistent in all ages and cultures could not be called 'unnatural'. As for sodomy, she explained, it was neither necessary nor exclusive to homosexuals. It certainly took

18 SHSS, submission to the Statutes Revision Committee on the Homosexual Law Reform Bill 26 April 1985, SHSS papers, ATL, MS-Papers-11369-026.

19 SHSS to Major Major, Salvation Army Public Relations Officer, 19 December 1985, SHSS papers, ATL, MS-Papers-11369-026.

place in the marriage bed. Furthermore, it was impossible to police a law that forbade sodomy, except when it was allied with rape when it could equally be dealt with as sexual assault. 'As a lawyer, you will undoubtedly agree that an unenforceable law is a bad law.' And she added a word to him as Minister of Defence:

It is a pity that the study of Classics has practically died in NZ: if these military wallahs who see all homosexuals as limp-wristed effetes had read their Greek history they would know that the most celebrated and successful army of Ancient Greece was the Spartan army, in which homosexuality was institutionalized, and that the elite corps of the Theban army, the Sacred Companions, was composed exclusively of pairs of lovers, whose devotion to each other ensured military prowess, rather than the reverse, as feared by our military.

Finally, she asked him 'to vote in accordance with the Labour Party constitution, which outlaws discrimination based, *inter alia*, on sexual discrimination.'[20]

By the time the Bill got to its third reading, public opinion had changed to the point where it was recognised the legislation had to be passed. The final vote for homosexual law reform was on 9 July 1986, 49 in favour, 44 against. The debate had changed not only the law but also attitudes. The next step, removing discrimination against homosexuals, would be written into the Human Rights Act in 1993.

THE THORNDON TRUST was still one of Shirley's highest priorities. She had been the prime mover in the Trust's purchase of artist Rita Angus's former cottage at 194a Sydney Street West, thus saving it from developers. They bought it for $50,000 and raised a further $20,000 to restore the cottage for use as an artist residency. The Rita Angus Memorial Cottage had opened while Shirley was overseas in 1984.

Beyond her clients and causes, her correspondence extended to people she knew and didn't know, congratulating, commiserating,

20 SHSS to Minister of Defence Frank O'Flynn, 21 October 1985, SHSS papers, ATL, MS-Papers-11404-119.

advising, sharing. When she enjoyed a book, she invariably wrote to its author, considering it a moral obligation to do so. When she sent off donations, she wrote accompanying letters giving her reasons for her support and sometimes why it wasn't more. She was never short of suggestions.

All this, together with her correspondence with family and friends, clients and colleagues, amounted to a prodigious engagement with the world, the cumulative effect of which is immeasurable; yet she felt guilty about letters she hadn't written and the mess around her as she generated ever-increasing volumes of paper. Amanda Rosenberg had one word for how Shirley saw herself: 'Guilty!' She was always saying, '*mea culpa*!'[21]

'New Zealand has been full of excitements,' she wrote to her nephew David Smith and his American wife Cookie in California. 'It can no longer be said that nothing happens here. The bombing of the *Rainbow Warrior*, the All Black tour row, Bob Jones trying to sink his own NZ Party and punching up journalists (for which he has been charged), Muldoon attacking McLay and so on and so on. Stirring times, apart from the ANZUS row.'[22]

Adding her voice to the 'ANZUS row', on 12 September 1985 she wrote to Deputy Prime Minister Geoffrey Palmer:

Dear Geoff,

In the hope that you will get this before you leave for the United States, I write to add my voice to the body of opinion which I have no doubt you know exists, to the effect that little would please me more than to have the United States continue to exclude New Zealand from ANZUS.

New Zealand's only hope of safety – or comparative safety – in this mad world, in my view, is to stay entirely clear of both power blocs. I not only do not want nuclear warships of any nation in our harbours or our waters, I do not want any warships of any nation other than our own anywhere near New Zealand. Frankly, I regard Bob Jones's defence policy as the only

21 Amanda Rosenberg to author, interview, 15 February 2012.
22 SHSS to David and Cookie Smith, 2 August 1985, AGS papers.

sane one.

I hope that you will have a nice trip, with results pleasing to me.

Yours sincerely[23]

Public opinion helped keep Prime Minister David Lange on course with regard to nuclear weapons, especially after the sinking of Greenpeace flagship *Rainbow Warrior* by French agents in July 1985. The anti-nuclear movement had now become mainstream. As a leader of the movement's earlier incarnation in the 1960s, Shirley might have taken some credit, but apparently did not. When asked by an Auckland journalist to give her account of the Committee for Nuclear Disarmament (CND) from a woman's point of view, she replied sharply:

Dear Judy Smith,

Do I know you? Are you one of the Smith clan to which I belong? I must say that at my age I find it extremely difficult to adapt to this recent practice of using first names at first blush, or, I suppose, without blush.

I must confess that the thought of having to try to give you a coherent account of my CND activities in the '60s does not give me any joy. I am extremely busy, my house is in a terrible mess as result of a flood: back in the early '70s my husband got sick of all my CND cartons cluttering the basement and threw them out. I have absolutely no records. What I did anyway, I did as a person, not specifically as a woman: I am allergic to sex specification when (in my view) it is irrelevant. I am a very old-fashioned type of feminist, although a fierce one.[24]

In November 1985, when Helen was appointed an economic advisor to Prime Minister David Lange, the family returned to live in Wellington, not to their house next door to Shirley but to Tinakori Road, Thorndon. Shirley had planned to visit them in Europe in 1986 and went anyway, first to England for St Hugh's centenary Gaudy, then to meet George and Amanda Rosenberg and Amanda's teenage son Ben in Athens to travel with them through Greece, Turkey, Syria and Jordan.

23 SHSS to Geoffrey Palmer, 12 September 1985, SHSS papers, ATL, MS-Papers-11404-78.
24 SHSS to Judy Smith, 20 June 1985, ATL, SHSS papers, ATL, MS-Papers-11369-200.

For Shirley, the only disadvantage of travelling with these friends was that she didn't have time to write. Sometimes she went off on solo adventures, as when she walked the spectacular 16 km Samaria Gorge walk, emerging at the foot of the White Mountains at Agia Roumeli on the Libyan Sea.

George and Amanda flew back to Hong Kong from Amman, leaving Shirley with a day on her own before returning to Greece for rest and recovery. Having seen Petra – driving down the ancient King's Highway, riding on horseback down the narrow gorge that led to the ancient city – 'and it *was* fabulous' – Shirley decided on her last day to visit Jordan's other great ancient city, Jerash.

Some thoughts I had in Jerash I should like to record. When walking through the remains of this beautifully proportioned, elegant city, I thought what an effect it must have on people to live in such surroundings, where there was nothing mean or tacky or chaotic . . . and then I remembered what the Romans were capable of, cruelty, trickery, vulgarity. They were just as human as we are. Still, I cling to the thought that the capacity to build in such a way must proceed from noble and generous qualities of mind and spirit, and such buildings must in turn encourage the development of such qualities in those who live in them. Wishful thinking, no doubt, but to live, one must hope, and Jerash engendered such thoughts in me.[25]

Recording this two years later, she also recalled her less edifying experience with the guide who took her on her own down into the crypt and passages under the temple.

When we were down in the gloom, stumbling (at least I did) through underground passages, he took my arm, and proceeded to tell me about his sexual prowess, and how he was especially partial to older ladies. He told me of an extraordinary relationship he had had with an elderly English woman, who had recently died, to his great distress. It seemed time to make my position clear, so I told him he was out of luck this time, I had no interest

25 SHSS, account of 1986 trip written from Sougia in August 1988, pp.64–65, SHSS papers, ATL, MS-Papers-11404-26.

in sex since my husband died. . . . I was thinking what a time I would have telling George and Amanda (I was going to spend a night with them on the way home) all the amazing things he told me, when he suddenly said, 'You will not repeat what I've told you, will you?' And I had to say I wouldn't. All I have given here is the merest outline; as to the substance, I have kept my word.[26]

'Turkey, Syria and Jordan were interesting and we saw some fabulous sights, and the people were friendly . . . But it's almost like coming home to come back to Greece,' she wrote to Helen Edwards from Athens.[27] She left her suitcase there and travelled light, back to the south coast of Crete, this time to Sougia, west of Agia Roumeli, where she had stayed a month earlier. 'Here I am now in my refuge,' she wrote, sitting under a great tamarisk tree on the seafront.[28] This small, undeveloped seaside village became for her a home away from home. In later years, when other reasons drew her to Sougia, she would lament the changes that came with its popularity, but now it was all she wished for. Her time there seemed timeless.[29]

Before returning to Athens, she took a ferry to Sfakia, further east along the coast.[30] There in the little bay where she swam, she saw small children diving fearlessly from high rocks. Hearing them speaking both English and Greek, she called out to their mother in English something about the water babies.

And so she met Jennifer Sivitos, an Australian, and an interior designer like her Greek husband Andreas. Jennifer invited Shirley for drinks to the little house they had reconstructed from a ruin high up on the hillside. Shirley climbed the winding narrow lane with its steep steps, arriving at a little eyrie: small, bare, with only essential furniture in the Greek style that she so admired, and a shaded terrace where they sat watching the setting sun.

26 Ibid, p.62.
27 SHSS to Helen Edwards, 15 August 1986, SHSS papers, ATL, MS-Papers-11404-25.
28 SHSS to Helen Edwards, 23 August 1986, SHSS papers, ATL, MS-Papers-11404-25.
29 SHSS to Helen Edwards, 27 August 1986, SHSS papers, ATL, MS-Papers-11404-25.
30 Also known as Chora Sfakion, it was from here that New Zealand and Australian soldiers were evacuated from Crete on 31 May 1931, after the Battle of Crete.

By chance, the next night the family was returning to Athens on the same boat as Shirley. Finding Shirley preparing to sleep on the deck, not having eaten, Jennifer brought her down to share their bunk room and their picnic evening meal. They took a shine to Shirley and invited her to their Athens home in the seaside suburb of Kifissia. Shirley came to regard them and their four children as her Greek family.

She came home to the chaos she had left behind, plus some new disasters perpetrated by misguided tradesmen in her absence. 'It would break your heart to see the house as it is now,' she wrote to Peggy Garland, explaining why she couldn't invite her to stay.[31] At home, Shirley was becoming a recluse.

HAVING TURNED down the invitation of a client, Hungarian Paul Lanczy, to join him in Yugoslavia in 1986, Shirley surprised those who knew them both by now agreeing to go to Eastern Europe with him the following year. Paul was domineering and that, said Helen Edwards, was something Shirley wouldn't tolerate. 'I am not sure I would commit myself to Paul Lanczy for two months!' wrote George Rosenberg.[32]

Shirley planned not two but three months with Paul Lanczy. They lasted two-and-a-half weeks. 'I told him in Prague that I wouldn't go any further with him. We were not compatible travelling companions and he had reduced me to a nervous wreck twice in three days by his rages at me,' she explained to George and Amanda.[33] She flew to Amsterdam, then spent August in England and most of September in Italy. In Rome, while staying with Helen's old school friend, Denise Almao, she collapsed in exhaustion. Denise, grateful to Shirley for all that she had done for her in the past, was happy to look after her but worried as she slept for days on end. There seemed to be nothing wrong. She just needed to sleep.

31 SHSS to Peggy Garland, 26 September 1986, SHSS papers.
32 George Rosenberg to SHSS, 8 March 1987, SHSS papers, ATL, MS-Papers-11369-198.
33 SHSS to George and Amanda Rosenberg, 1988, SHSS papers, ATL, MS-Papers-11369-198.

26

Privy Council

SHIRLEY'S NEXT trip to Europe in 1988 was to take a case to the Privy Council. Her client was a misfit for whom even Shirley saw little redemption. That did not deter her from doing what she recognised as her duty as a lawyer.

Noel Kerr, a Pākehā man in his mid-thirties, started life with all the cards stacked against him. After his violent alcoholic father was convicted of incest with Noel's ten-year-old sister, Noel and his siblings were put into foster care. From there, Noel was sent to Otekaieke Special School, a residential school for boys with mental disabilities and behavioural problems. He was virtually illiterate when he left the school, aged sixteen.

A year later, after appearing in court for indecent assault, he was committed to Sunnyside Hospital in Christchurch. Following further violent outbursts, he was transferred to Lake Alice Hospital, where he received electroconvulsive therapy. Shirley later wrote to Lake Alice's Medical Superintendent Dr S. L. Pugmire, who explained that Noel was a 'typical sex offender who is struck every now and again by a sudden urge to commit an offence. The urges hit him like epileptic seizures hit epileptic patients, unexpectedly and often completely beyond their control'. In answer to Shirley's question about whether Noel could be held responsible for his actions, Dr Pugmire explained that he was 'never fully responsible. Some urges were resistible and some completely irresistible. With medication, the majority of cases would be resistible.'[1] Noel Kerr's offences usually occurred when he had stopped taking his medication and had been drinking heavily.

After some eleven years in psychiatric hospitals, Noel Kerr formed a de facto relationship in Porirua with a former fellow patient from

1 S. L. Pugmire to SHSS, 6 April 1982, SHSS papers, ATL, Record ID 2013-045-22.

Stokes Valley, a young Māori woman Shirley had known for some years. She brought Noel to Shirley in 1981 when he was up on a charge of Burglary and Assault with Intent to Rape. Noel pleaded not guilty, but in the High Court he was found guilty. Justice Jeffries noted that Miss Smith had correctly pointed out that aspects of his background were appalling and they no doubt contributed to his sexual offending. He also agreed with her submission that her client, despite his limitations, would be able to understand leniency if it was positively his last chance. He passed a sentence of six months' non-residential periodic detention and Kerr was released on probation for a period of one year.[2]

On 14 May 1982 he was in court again. He denied a charge of indecent assault on a girl under twelve, but was found guilty and sentenced to two years' imprisonment.

The day after Noel was released he assaulted a woman in a public toilet in the town hall. The *Evening Post* reported on 16 November 1983 that a passer-by, hearing the woman's scream, had come to her aid, chased her attacker out of the building and eventually caught and held him, with help from another, until police arrived. As usual, Kerr vehemently denied he was the attacker. Shirley tracked down the first witness and got permission to interview him at the police station. Later, the police showed her their briefs of evidence. They didn't believe Kerr would change his plea, as he never had before. They were astonished that Shirley persuaded him to plead guilty.[3]

Then came the case that tested how far she would go to fight for a legal principle. Noel Kerr, in trouble again, pleaded not guilty in a High Court jury trial on 10 July 1987, once again before Justice Jeffries. Shirley described the case to George and Amanda Rosenberg (now in London where George had just joined a law firm as Head of Litigation):

Now the latest case involves Noel seeing, from the house where he was staying, one fine Sunday just over a year ago (1st Feb 1987) the neighbour lady lying out on her concrete backyard sunbathing, very scantily clad. Noel, who had been drinking all morning, hops over the fence and is seen

2 Sentence of Jeffries J., 27 November 1981, SHSS papers, ATL, Record ID 2013-045-22.
3 SHSS to Registrar, District Court, 18 January 1984, SHSS papers, ATL, Record ID 2013-045-22.

out of the kitchen window by the lady's daughter standing over her mother holding an axe. It emerged that the lady had got the axe from her garage to hold down her hat which was blowing away in the wind. Noel had picked it up. The girl said he was swaying on his feet looking confused. She ran off to (a) get dressed – she was dressmaking, nearly nude, I gather . . . and (b) see if she could find some help. Succeeding in (a) but not (b), she opened the kitchen door and seeing Noel now standing some distance away, having put down the axe, in the act of lowering his trousers, yelled out, 'What do you think you're doing?' This woke up Mum – I see I have omitted the only important fact, for my purposes, that is; and that is, that up to this moment Mum had slept peacefully through all. Mum also yells out the same question, Noel says 'I'm only having a piss' and takes off over the fence.

Noel is quickly found, and charged with two separate charges of assault, first, 'while in possession of a weapon, with intent to use it' and second, 'with intent to commit sexual violation, namely rape.'[4]

It occurred to Shirley during the trial that both charges depended on the same alleged 'assault', and that had to be by way of a threat since there was no physical contact. She found a statement from the English High Court to support her definition of 'threat'. She told the jury that legally you could not threaten a person who was unconscious. Justice Jeffries in his summing up said that was nonsense. He ruled that, 'As a matter of law it is possible to threaten a person even though the object of the threat may not have been aware and that would be the case in a sleeping person.' Shirley held that the judge was not only wrong in this, but that he also misdirected the jury on the facts in his summing up, putting the case for the Crown, that Kerr was holding the axe in a chopping position. She pointed out there was nothing in the notes of evidence to show that he did more than pick up the axe and was standing with it when he was observed by the daughter.[5] Nothing he had done amounted to a threat.

The jury was undecided on the second charge and returned a verdict

4 SHSS to George and Amanda Rosenberg, 20 February 1988, SHSS papers, ATL, MS-Papers-11369-198.

5 Court of Appeal Judgment; Application for leave to appeal to Privy Council, SHSS papers, ATL, Record ID 2013-045-22.

of guilty on the first, for which he was sentenced to two-and-a-half years' prison.

Shirley saw that Noel was actually better off in prison and, with his history, she thought it reasonable he was declined bail. 'Kerr always looks 100 per cent better in health and spirits when I visit him on the Hill than the pasty bedraggled individual I meet when he is at large,' she wrote to Crown Prosecutor Jim Larsen. 'It is sad, but I'm afraid he needs an institutional environment, and does well in one.'[6]

She decided he was nevertheless entitled to justice. And also, as a legal principle was at stake, Shirley decided to appeal. She wrote to Noel Kerr, who was on remand, on 21 June:

I have spent some time looking into the law relating to 'threatening', and as far as I can see I was right in saying that you cannot threaten someone who is asleep.

Therefore, I think it worthwhile appealing. I shall bring up a form for you to sign as soon as possible.[7]

She ended her letter encouraging him to join the Alcoholics Anonymous group. 'Deirdre and Peter will be pleased to see you again.'[8]

Regarding the retrial of the second charge, Justice Eichelbaum decided that as the same point of law, the statutory definition of 'assault', was involved in both the retrial and the appeal, the appeal should be heard first. Shirley explained to Kerr that if the appeal succeeded, there wouldn't be a second trial – unless the Crown came up with some new charge. 'So I shall be doing my very best to put across my view of the law to the Court of Appeal [then the highest court in New Zealand]. I think that I have a very good argument, but you can never be sure what view the Court will take.'[9]

The appeal took place on 24 November. She was taken aback when

6 SHSS to Crown Solicitor Mr Larsen, 5 July 1987, SHSS papers, ATL, Record ID 2013-045-22. The letter is about setting the date of retrial for the second charge.
7 SHSS to Noel Kerr, 21 June 1987, SHSS papers, ATL Record ID 2013-045-22.
8 Ibid.
9 SHSS to Noel Kerr, 10 November 1987, SHSS papers, ATL, Record ID 2013-045-22.

Justice Casey asked her if she approved of her client's conduct, but she was confident that her legal case was sound.

Delivering the Court of Appeal's decision on 16 December, Justice McMullin referred to the meaning of the key words, 'threatening by any act or gesture' to apply force: 'In their ordinary meaning those words do not make the state of mind of the recipient of the threatening act or gesture relevant.' He dismissed the appeal with an acknowledgment to counsel for their help with researches.[10]

Shirley was incensed. She wrote to Noel Kerr:

. . . they agreed with everything I had said, but decided they saw no reason why the law under the New Zealand Crimes Act should be the same as the English law on which it is based: although there has been no Act of Parliament that has changed it. Normally this would mean that it stays the same as the English law.

All the lawyers I know, who know about the case, believe that the Court of Appeal judgment is wrong, and approve of my intention to take it to the Privy Council. This, however, will take a considerable time. I have been speaking to a senior barrister about it . . . He knows that there is no money in it, but he is very willing to help me prepare the papers – a complicated matter which he is familiar with, while I am not.

As far as money is concerned, there is no legal aid for an appeal to the Privy Council, and I know that you can't pay: but I am prepared to do it for nothing, and pay my own expenses. The biggest item will be the English solicitors' fees – you have to have English solicitors to act for you in London – but I think I can manage that.

I have to be honest and tell you that I am not doing this just *for you, although of course I do want to help you, but because I think an important point of law is at stake, and also because it is an opportunity for me to do something that I very much want to do – take an appeal to the Privy Council.*[11]

10 CA Judgment delivered 16 December 1987.

11 SHSS to Noel Kerr, 26 November 1987, SHSS papers, ATL, Record ID 2013-045-22. The senior barrister referred to was her old friend George Barton QC, who had helped her with the Konia case and many others.

To George and Amanda, she wrote that in the Appeal she *proved* that New Zealand's first Criminal Code Act took over English Common Law and the law could not now be changed except by the legislature.

They agreed that everything I had said was correct but then they said that they did not have to follow English law, and they preferred the view that you could threaten someone who was not conscious. It was outrageous.

So Noel Kerr is going to appeal (or apply for leave to appeal) to the Privy Council. Of course the CA know he is penniless, and if they thought about it at all, would have thought they were quite safe. But little Shirley, who never thought she would ever have a chance of appearing in that august chamber, is going ahead. If anyone asks who is paying, I shall say, 'I shall of course bill Noel, and I do not mind if he takes a while to pay'. I have a feeling I could be vulnerable under those old English sins of Champerty and Maintenance if I confess that I am prepared to pay myself! . . .

You will understand, of course, that it is not only for my glory that I want to go (they can't turn me down, can they?) but for the sake of the law and to deliver a blow while there is still time at the arrogant and 'creative' CA. Other lawyers around the Courts and the Library tell me that the CA has been much too 'creative' lately. They are all unanimously on my side. It has excited quite a lot of interest. (Geoff Palmer has announced that the right of appeal to the PC will be abolished.[12] *He thinks the CA can be relied on!!)*[13]

Shirley took advice initially from her old friend and colleague George Barton QC until he departed for his own Privy Council case, and he referred her to a London law firm, Macfarlanes, who agreed to accept instructions from her. On 26 April she wrote to them that while she realised it would be cheaper to instruct a barrister in London to present her petition for special leave to appeal, she wanted to do it

12 Appeals to the Privy Council were not abolished until 2003 and a local Supreme Court was established. This had a different status to the court of the same name on which Sir David Smith had sat.

13 SHSS to George and Amanda Rosenberg, 20 February 1988, SHSS papers, ATL, MS-Papers-11369-198. Champerty and maintenance are doctrines in common law jurisdictions that aim to preclude frivolous litigation.

herself. She nevertheless sought advice from their barrister on the form of the Petition. She also sent a draft to the Solicitor-General.

Her petition stressed that her appeal was exclusively concerned with questions of law, that the issues were of statutory interpretation and that the Court of Appeal's departure from settled principles of law resulted in a serious miscarriage of justice:

If the decision of the Court of Appeal of New Zealand stands, it will be the first and only time in any common law jurisdiction or in any statutory jurisdiction derived from common law, so far as your Petitioner has been able to ascertain, that it has been held that criminal liability attaches to an alleged assault by way of threat which is not apprehended any way by the alleged victim.[14]

Macfarlanes advised her that her petition appeared to be in order but, as they did not normally handle criminal cases, they recommended briefing a London barrister, a Mr Goldberg, to settle its final form. Shirley now considered briefing him to present the petition instead of doing it herself. Time was short – the dates set were 27 June or 4 July. Bill Gazley, whose case *Nakhla v McCarthy* [1978] had been the only New Zealand criminal case ever to succeed at the Privy Council, strongly advised her to do it herself. Still she dithered, considering the cost. Then she read an article about Lowell Goddard, recently appointed QC (with Sian Elias, the first women QCs in New Zealand), who had taken an Application for Special Leave to the Privy Council. Shirley wrote to her explaining that she was under pressure to decide who was to present her petition. 'The lovely woman actually rang me from Auckland as soon as she got my letter, and she said, "You do it". So that settled it.' Shirley continued to George and Amanda:

She is going to send me a transcript of the proceedings on her application, so that 'you can see what they're likely to throw at you'. She thinks they could well take the view of our CA, that there would be no substantial

14 SHSS, draft of petition, Kerr v. The Queen, Appeal to the Privy Council, p.2, sent to the Solicitor-General, Crown Law Office, 30 May 1988, Archives NZ.

miscarriage of justice (though of course the CA went further, it changed the law to suit), because they too would disapprove of my client's conduct. I suppose I wouldn't mind so much as long as they stated firmly that our CA was totally wrong on the law. What's happened to the maxim 'Fiat Justitia, Ruat Caelum'? I actually quoted it to the CA but they weren't impressed.[15]

Bill Gazley suggested she write to Auckland QC Paul Temm, who had taken his successful Nahkla case to the Privy Council, about how to get into rapport with their Lordships. Temm responded immediately. His first point was that their Lordships' main underlying question with any petition for special leave to appeal in a criminal case was simply 'Why should we trouble ourselves with this matter?' An applicant usually had ten minutes in which to speak. One had to persuade them to grant leave without getting to the merits of the appeal. 'It is quite the most difficult technical argument that I have ever had to mount, and it is because of the technical difficulty that so many petitions for special leave fail.' But if their interest was aroused, they would extend the time, and in fact he had addressed them for nearly an hour and a half, which was quite exceptional.

He advised her to spend at least a week in London before the hearing, to go to the Privy Council and listen to the course of events and familiarise herself with the atmosphere.

It is very different from anything we know here although there is some truth to the saying that it is rather like the Court of Appeal only their Lordships are much more polite! They are however extraordinarily quick mentally, quite ruthless and frequently do not call upon the respondent to reply. Do not take this as a personal slight in any way if it should unhappily occur in your case. It is the usual routine because they will not waste a minute. After all it is good to remember that we can't go in to criminal cases in particular always expecting to win. The most that we can do is do the best that we can and when you do win I like to remind myself that it does no more than prove you can't lose them all!

15 SHSS to George and Amanda Rosenberg, 27 May 1988, SHSS papers, ATL, Record ID 2013-045-22. 'Let justice be done, though the heavens fall.'

I hope you do not find this letter depressing. I do not intend it to be so.[16]

He offered to talk about it in person if she would come to Auckland. 'I regard a trip to the Privy Council as the highlight of counsel's experience and I would like to do whatever I can to enable you to enjoy it – as I say, win, lose or draw!'[17]

Shirley replied that she was overjoyed to get his letter. Crown Law had now asked her to delay until the end of July, so she had more time to prepare. She explained that she had done more work on her petition after Solicitor-General Paul Neazor had arranged for her to see precedents in their possession.

I have always liked Paul Neazor and that is now an understatement: for this meant that I saw and took notes from your Nakhla *application for special leave. This made me realize that what I had already drafted was on quite the wrong lines . . . it might help if I sent you my latest draft, just finished. It seems to me that my case has quite a lot in common with* Nakhla, *but unfortunately it is not quite so uncomplicated, although a decision on the word 'threat' would settle it. I notice that you did not cite a single authority, but kept them for the hearing, so I have followed suit. I do have some quite formidable authority, at least I think so. It has occurred to me that it might be counter-productive to tell their Lordships that one is going to quote at them, from themselves.*

My poor chap Kerr, of course, is in himself quite unmeritorious . . . but even so sad a case – I know him all too well – is entitled to be dealt with according to the law as it stands, and not have it twisted out of all recognition simply to catch him, regardless of the future effect on NZ law.[18]

She added that she wished to take up his offer to see him in Auckland. 'I do truly regard this as the highlight of my legal life and am desperately keen to do well. I did sit through the Samoan overstayers case in the PC, so have some idea of the atmosphere.'[19]

16 Paul Temm to SHSS, 31 May 1988, SHSS papers, ATL, MS-Papers-11404-81.
17 Ibid.
18 SHSS to Paul Temm, 8 June 1988, SHSS papers, ATL, MS-Papers-11404-81.
19 Ibid.

Shirley also arranged to see Lowell Goddard. As well as the law, there was the question of dress. She had seen photographs of English women barristers with drifts of lace from neck and wrists. Lowell Goddard lent Shirley her Bar jacket.[20]

From London, George Rosenberg applauded Shirley's decision:

I can hardly wait to reciprocate your acting as an audience for me in 1982, by acting as an audience for you in 1988, hopefully with an equally successful impact on the result. . . . I think your legal point is a good one . . . Obviously your tactic is going to have to be to emphasise the importance of the legal points over the question of whether or not there has been a substantial miscarriage of justice in the particular circumstances, and it seems to me that even if the narrow point is not one of earth-shattering importance (perhaps that is the distinction from Nakhla), the general one about the way in which the Crimes Act should be construed is, and it is important in the interests of the certainty of the criminal law that it be unequivocally decided that where the Crimes Act is silent on a point which is dealt with in the common law, that the common law should bind the NZ courts. Otherwise the law will never be certain until the courts legislate upon it, and then what benefit would NZ derive from its common law heritage?[21]

It was not until early July that Shirley received Goldberg's advice:

There is no great mystique about the Petition in a criminal cause in the Privy Council. It will not be construed like a civil proceeding. Their Lordships are a robust and pragmatic bunch, Miss Smith will find, who simply wish to know from the Petition what the nub issues are. If I may say so, they emerge with clarity here, and if I had any criticism at all, it would simply be that she has given too much detail, not too little, of her argument, if anything.

To speak plainly, she will have an uphill task in getting leave I guess

20 SHSS to Lowell Goddard, 9 June 1988, SHSS papers, ATL, MS-Papers-11404-81; Dame Lowell Goddard DNZM QC became a High Court judge in 1994; from February 2015 to August 2016 she chaired the Independent Inquiry into Child Sexual Abuse in England and Wales.

21 George Rosenberg to SHSS, 2 June 1988, SHSS papers, ATL, MS-Papers-11404-81.

however. The Statute does seem at first glance to amend the old Common Law. The Court of Appeal Judgment reads well. All turns round the meaning of the word 'threaten' and in common usage, A can threaten the absent B in the presence of C. Where then the argument that B must be present and apprehending violence?

I see no point therefore in reissuing the draft Petition under my own name. It would add nothing to do so.[22]

Shirley noted dryly that his enthusiasm seemed to have waned. At the same time Macfarlanes warned her that less than one-third of the petitions presented to the Privy Council were successful, but assured her that if Goldberg had considered that her petition had no merit, he would not have advised her to proceed. Shirley faxed them her redrafted petition requesting it be lodged forthwith. She was anxious to be heard before the vacation, fearing that she would be in danger of being disallowed through delay. At the same time she couldn't book her flight without a confirmed date. When that was settled for 27 July, the only available seats on flights to London were Business Class – $3,000 more than she had intended to spend on her fare.

She arrived in London three days before her hearing. She stayed with George and Amanda and they attended the Privy Council hearing with her. Despite Paul Temm's warning, Shirley was shocked that their Lordships rejected her case so quickly. She wrote to Margaret Shirley Sutch a week later from Heathrow Airport before flying to Athens:

It wasn't that they considered I had no case – they did not even look at the merits. Lord Keith, presiding, when I had hardly got started, said, 'We do not care to interfere with the decisions of the New Zealand Court of Appeal.' Fancy letting one come so far – when they still do have jurisdiction – if they've decided in advance that they're not going to interfere with NZCA decisions. I'm told they're so hurt at our projected abandonment of them that they're abandoning us in advance. (On v.g. *authority.) I did*

22 Jonathan Goldberg to Macfarlanes, 30 June 1988, forwarded by fax from Macfarlanes on 4 July, SHSS papers, ATL, Record ID 2013-045-22.

battle on and they called on the Crown to reply, which they did in no other application that morning, including two NZ ones, which people told me was a feather in my cap, but the result was the same.[23]

The abandonment she referred to was the government's intention to abolish New Zealand's relationship with the Privy Council, President of the Court of Appeal Sir Robin Cooke having approved this policy.[24] In a Law Conference speech in 1985 he had said we 'must accept responsibility for our national legal identity and recognise that the Privy Council has outlived its time'.[25]

FOR SOME ten days her disappointment put a pall over everything, even in Athens. 'I felt tired and lacking in energy as rarely in the past,' she wrote to Helen and Keith. 'But Crete – I feel there's life after the PC. I feel a new vitality and joie de vivre.'[26]

She had arrived in Chania in Crete in the early evening and, with just a small backpack, had walked to the old quarter, found a hotel next to the mosque, taken a room overlooking the harbour and was writing from her balcony, enjoying a drop of single malt Scotch, 'the most perfect single malt I have ever tasted'.[27]

Next morning she headed for the south coast. 'Here I am, where I long to be,' she wrote from Sougia on 9 August. She spent her time in solitude, swimming in the crystalline Libyan Sea, lunching on figs and nuts, sipping beer under her favourite tamarisk tree, reading and writing. She had brought pads and pens for the purpose of recording

23 SHSS to MSS, 3 August 1988, SHSS papers, ATL, MS-Papers-11369-203. The authority to which Shirley refers was probably the Registrar of the Privy Council.

24 SHSS to Warwick Gendall, 10 October 1988, SHSS papers. Shirley explained to Gendall (who had not represented the Crown in London) that the Privy Council's decision not to grant her leave was 'all to do with pique at Robin Cooke's turning his back on them at the last NZLS Conference'. The government soon lost its enthusiasm for Privy Council law reform. This was because of the CA decision in 1987 concerning State-Owned Enterprises and the effect of transferring to them assets, in particular land, which was subject to Treaty of Waitangi claims: Sir John McGrath to author, email, 7 August 2015.

25 'The New Zealand National Legal Identity' (1987) volume 3, *Canterbury Law Review* 171 at p.172.

26 SHSS to MHS and KWO, 7 August 1988, MHS papers.

27 Ibid.

her 1986 Syrian and Jordanian journeys with George and Amanda, and this she did, but she found it easier to write about the here and now.

One morning she rose before the sun and walked over the ridge to Lissos, where she had been two years before. She wrote through the heat of the day. 'The haunted peace of this valley (it has seen at least three civilizations come, build, stay and vanish) was disturbed earlier by family picnickers who had come by small boat . . .' But she was pleased later when she met a former resistance fighter, Nikos Papagrigorakis. During their brief conversation in broken English, he expressed his great wish to find two New Zealanders he'd known in Rodovani (near Sougia) in 1941. Shirley took this on as a mission.

Back in New Zealand Shirley had still to deal with the retrial of the second charge against Kerr. She wrote to Crown Prosecutor Warwick Gendall that she hadn't given up the fight – far from it! 'In fact, my main desire is to get the "assault" issue back before the CA, a full bench this time, so I count on your battling me all along the line! In the meantime it goes without saying, I have to do my best for my client . . . the first time, I think, when I've had to cope with a strong pull in the other direction.'[28] But when the retrial was held in May the following year the jury still couldn't agree. It seemed Kerr could neither be acquitted nor committed.

Noel Kerr had been out on bail since March 1989 and he was doing quite well, attending the Wellington Alcohol and Drug Centre, Alcoholics Anonymous and the Full Gospel Church in Stokes Valley. Shirley had excellent reports of his behaviour, including one, supported by blood tests, that he was 'entirely abstinent' and was continuing the anti-alcohol medication under supervision. All this she presented to the new Solicitor-General, John McGrath, who was to decide whether there was good reason to have a third trial. He duly halted further proceedings.[29]

28 SHSS to Warwick Gendall, 10 October 1988, SHSS papers, ATL, Record ID 2013-045-22.

29 Warrant for stay of proceedings signed by Solicitor-General John Joseph McGrath to the Registrar, High Court, Wellington, 17 August 1989, Crown Law Office.

Then, in the retrial, she found herself torn between wanting an acquittal and wanting a conviction so that she could take her point back to the Court of Appeal and this time *win* – but she had to do her best for her client.

SHIRLEY'S EGO was clearly a driving force in taking the Kerr case to the Privy Council. Also, there was no real hope for her client, who reoffended according to pattern. Possibly, Shirley regretted in retrospect taking the case so far. She never mentioned her appeal to the Privy Council in the extensive oral history interviews she gave to mark her retirement, nor in her written memoirs of her life in the law.

To have ended her career with the triumph she envisaged would have been a personal victory but that is not how she rated herself as a lawyer, nor how others have rated her. She had many successes in court, but they weren't high-profile cases. Few of them were reported. But they brought respect from her colleagues and the satisfaction of having given people who fell between the cracks access to the law. Besides her advocacy as a barrister, her work as a solicitor, not only for her individual clients but also in addressing underlying social inequities, was significant and important.

During her last years in practice when she narrowed her focus she was associated most closely with the Mongrel Mob, but in former years, when she took on a wide range of cases and causes, it was in family law that she made her greatest impact. Here again, one can never know the true value of her work. While client confidentiality limits any assessment, her advocacy undoubtedly had immeasurable benefits for her clients' children, and their children down to the next generation.

Shirley acknowledged the good work other small firms did looking after people. By 1989, when the Wellington District Law Society commissioned Hugo Manson to record an oral history of Shirley Smith, quite a few young women had started their own practices. She sent them work and was pleased to hear how busy they were. Some regarded her as a personal mentor; others were encouraged by her example and, for some, she was the inspiration to become a lawyer, the equivalent of the woman in the black dress at the United Nations who led Shirley to think, 'If you can do it, so can I.'[30]

In due course, they and the next generation of women in law were to acknowledge her importance to them.

30 Rachael Dewar to author, 11 June 2018. Rachael's flash of inspiration came on seeing the published photograph of Shirley Smith with her Mongrel Mob clients.

27

Gods and heroes

SHIRLEY GREW increasingly despondent about the world and especially the state of the nation. She was disgusted that the Labour Government had been hijacked by Roger Douglas and his monetarist policies. In September 1989, when she wrote to congratulate Geoffrey Palmer on becoming Prime Minister, she referred to the appalling situation he had inherited:

The results are clear to see: social and economic division, each man (and woman?) for himself, I'm all right Jack, crime, an increasing gulf between rich and poor. Even your attempt to do justice to the Maori people by recognizing the Treaty of Waitangi, which I applauded, has brought more problems than it has solved.

Only your nuclear-free policy remains, and it is not enough. Only if you changed direction could I support you, and I have not much hope.[1]

She was gloomy, too, about stopping her law work. Her retirement might have brought some relief had it not been for a threatened lawsuit hanging over her – in this case, a suit against her, by a client. When she moved her practice from her downtown office to Todman Street, the client's files relating to a paternity case went missing. Shirley assured her she would find them but never did. The threatened lawsuit was serious enough for Allan Smith to think that Shirley should put her half-share of the Taupō property into a trust to avoid the risk of losing it. Shirley was furious at the suggestion. As late as November 1993 the case was unresolved, though Shirley wrote to Amanda Rosenberg that she hardly ever thought of it and assumed it wouldn't go ahead.

1 SHSS to Rt. Hon. Geoffrey Palmer, 21 September 1989, SHSS papers, ATL, MS-Papers-11404-119.

Apparently it didn't. But according to Keith Ovenden, it cost Shirley $60,000 in legal fees.[2]

She continued to look after a few old clients until she gave up her solicitor's certificate in 1992. Though she kept her barrister's certificate until 1994, she had to give up the court work she loved, she said, in order to deal with her house and garden. She complained that it was not a life of her own choosing.

Helen, Keith and the boys had recently moved to Washington, where Helen had a job with the World Bank. 'Helen had to get out,' Shirley wrote to Peggy Garland, 'the atmosphere here was so antipathetic to everything she believed in, as it is to me.' As for what she called her 'domestic disasters', only she could deal with the accumulation of junk ('not all junk, of course'). She could not leave it to Helen.[3]

She intended to go through all the boxes of papers that now filled every corner of the house and garage, but other things got in the way. As she managed to free her mind from these other matters when she was away from home, a friend suggested she take a notional holiday for six months. Where she would like to be? 'Greece'. But being there simply in her imagination didn't work.

In reality, Shirley longed to be in Greece and Europe, but she had lost heavily in the 1987 share market crash and now shares had plummeted again.

In 1990 she visited her family in Washington, but her trip was cut short when her house was burgled. She came home to find things were pulled out of cupboards and drawers and locked cupboard doors had been forced open. Among things that were missing were some items of jewellery that had sentimental value, and the Chinese horses were gone.

The horses had recently been restored by ceramicist Janet Clougherty, who had been an expert restorer of ceramics at the British Museum.

2 The author found no files relating to the case among Shirley's papers in the Turnbull. Correspondence between her and Helen Sutch briefly referred to it and in her letter to Amanda Rosenberg, 19 November 1993, Shirley referred to 'my persecutor'. At that point she hadn't spent any money on the case. All that had been before the Court was Shirley's 'motion to strike out on the law'.

3 SHSS to Peggy Garland, 26 January 1990, SHSS papers.

They looked spectacular when Shirley got them back in the house, just three days before leaving for Washington. After the burglary, the T'ang horse was never found but, through a tip from the Mongrel Mob, Shirley eventually recovered the Han horse – in pieces once again. And again Janet restored it.

Helen, Keith and the boys came home on a visit in August 1991. They didn't stay with Shirley and she felt her relationship with them was fragile. She offered to throw them a party, then became 'almost paralysed with terror' at the prospect. In the event it went well. Shirley noted in her diary, 'Both H and K sd spontaneously that it had been a v happy party. I was so relieved and pleased.'[4]

In the days after they left, Shirley felt low. She noted in her diary that she had no energy and her memory was failing. But two weeks later, in mid-September, she was off and away to France, then Greece.

SHIRLEY HAD been as good as her word regarding her promise to Nikos Papagrigorakis. After she met him in 1988 she placed a notice in the *Dominion*, appealing for news of Cretan veterans Joe Stratford and Bill Hoani. Another veteran Jim McDevitt replied that Bill had died but he put her in touch with Joe Stratford. This led to Joe and Nikos having a wonderful reunion in Crete in 1989.

Now intensely interested in the Cretan resistance, Shirley closely followed the commemorative events of the fiftieth anniversary of the Battle of Crete. She read about the New Zealander, Special Agent Dudley Perkins, whom the Greeks code-named 'Kapitan Vasilis', whose wartime exploits made him a legend in Crete. (Murray Elliott, author of *Vasili: The Lion of Crete*, later visited Shirley in Wellington to compare their research.) She met other veterans and their families, and John Irwin, whose documentary *In Rich Regard* explored the relationship between Crete and New Zealand arising out of the war. The film showed Cretan families who had risked torture and execution to shelter New Zealand soldiers left behind after the Allies withdrew from Crete. Footage of leading resistance fighters from the small mountain village

4 SHSS diary entries, 6, 7 August 1991, SHSS papers.

of Koustogerako included the Paterakis brothers. These *andartes* were great heroes to Shirley.[5]

Celebrating her seventy-fifth birthday in Athens, Shirley treated herself to a splendid lunch in the main square. 'I just love being in Athens. The smog has gone, the sky is blue, it's warm but not hot, and I'm happy,' she wrote to Helen Edwards.

She met up with her new friends, the Sivitos family, and travelled with them from Athens to Crete and on to Sfakia, where Jenny and Andreas were transforming another bigger ruin into a holiday home. Instead of then taking the ferry to Sougia, Shirley returned over the mountains to Chania to meet Antonis Kosmadakis, Secretary of the Crete Resistance Association and President of the Greek–New Zealand Association, to get information about Nikos Papagrigorakis. She knew he had been Chief of Police in Chania and had written to him of Joe Stratford's death earlier in the year, but he hadn't replied. Antonis Kosmadakis told her she would find him in Sougia at the beachfront café-bar and 'rooms to rent' that he ran with his wife and mother-in-law.

Before Shirley left, Antonis Kosmadakis ceremoniously presented her with a certificate of membership of the Greek–New Zealand Association. With this furled up under her arm, she caught the bus south.

In Sougia she found the 'rooms to rent' and introduced herself to Nikos, who neither recognised her from their brief meeting years earlier, nor understood her introduction. 'After some fairly heavy-weather conversation, he said, churning the words out with effort, "There is a woman in New Zealand who wrote to me every month: her name is Shirley Smith." "*I* am Shirley Smith," I said, and then what a welcome!'[6]

He introduced his wife Ririka and her mother. As neither woman spoke English, communication was mainly by smiles and gestures. Nikos insisted Shirley was their guest and wouldn't allow her to pay for her room.

5 Manolis Paterakis had helped Patrick Leigh Fermor capture General Kreipe in April 1944.

6 SHSS, 'Visit to Crete, 1991', p.7, SHSS papers, ATL, MS-Papers-11404-46.

Jim McDevitt had asked Shirley to go up to Koustogerako to photograph the new war memorial to which New Zealand Cretan veterans had contributed. It commemorated the families of three villages destroyed in 1943 in German reprisals. He suggested that she also go to the 'water cave' where New Zealand soldiers had hidden. Finding neither rental cars nor taxis available, she decided to walk to Koustogerako. 'Impossible!' she was told, but she was determined. Nikos then arranged to drive her up there and he asked his friend Adonis Paterakis to take her to the water cave. 'I was overcome,' Shirley wrote. 'To be taken by one of the famous Paterakis brothers, was more than I had ever dreamed of.'

The hour-long hike to the water cave took them around the side of the mountain along a path that became little more than a narrow uneven ledge with large chunks of slippery marble. Shirley followed Adonis, their silence broken only when he looked back to check she was all right. 'I was so grateful for his attitude to me: he did not fuss or offer patronising help: he took it for granted that I was capable, and looked back only when we came to a more difficult place: when I did need a hand it was there. It was the perfection of courtesy.'[7]

At the cave, while Shirley took photos, Adonis spoke of Patrick Leigh Fermor, who had organised the Cretan Resistance (with Xan Fielding) and who had translated George Psychoundakis's book *The Cretan Runner*, where Shirley had read about the water cave. He would also have talked of how his family regarded New Zealander Dudley Perkins, 'Kapitan Vasilis', as a brother, and how their mother wept at his death as if he were her son.

Back in the village, at the kafenion, Shirley met Adonis Paterakis's wife, Sofia. They went to lunch with a cousin of Nikos's, Vardis Gentekake. Vardis and his wife Katerina made an impression on Shirley that shows as much about her as about them:

They were, I would think, in late middle age. One little incident touched me deeply. While we were sitting at table, talking, Vardis, with complete lack of self-consciousness, put his arm around his wife's shoulders (they were sitting

7 Ibid. p.10.

side by side) and hugged her, then he put his hand up and stroked her hair. She turned her head and smiled at him, and gently patted his hair. In the way they looked at each other there was the essence of love and companionship. It was quite simply accepted by everyone present, without remark.[8]

At the end of the day Shirley found she'd run out of film and had no photographs of the War Memorial. She felt she couldn't ask Nikos to take her again, so before dawn next morning she left a note saying that she had gone for a walk and set off.

She missed the turn-off to Koustogerako and walked some considerable distance uphill in the wrong direction before realising her mistake. Retracing her steps, she found the turn-off. Apart from a lift for a short distance, she walked most of the way up the mountain. After taking her photographs, she lingered at the memorial, enjoying the mountain air in the early morning sun, the peace and the poignancy.

Then she walked on up to the village square to photograph the cliffs above, imagining the famous scene she had read about in *The Cretan Runner*:

There had been a lot of trouble at Koustogerako on the twenty-fifth of September. The Germans, after repeated reports about Koustogerako, went there and surrounded the village, but they found only women and children as all the men had remained outside the village. So the women and children were assembled and the interrogation started. Where are the English? Where is the wireless? Where are the arms? Nobody talked but the Germans had positive information. They lined them all up, and, as they refused to speak, prepared to execute the lot. But before they could press the trigger of their heavy machine-gun, ten Germans fell dead. For some of the village men – about ten – had taken up position along the top of a sheer cliff above the village, from where they could watch every detail, and, at just the right moment, had opened fire. Not a bullet went wide.[9]

8 Ibid. p.12.

9 George Psychoundakis, *The Cretan Runner*, translated by Patrick Leigh Fermor, published by John Murray, 1955, Penguin Books, 1998, reissued 2009, p.232.

The telling point for Shirley was Patrick Leigh Fermor's footnote: 'Costi Pateraki actually fired the first shot which killed the machine-gunner, at a distance of over four hundred yards. It still seems to me one of the most spectacular moments of the war.'

Murray Elliott later explained to Shirley that it was not in the square but in an olive grove about 50 yards behind the kafenion, that the women and children were assembled for execution. The backside of the grove was tiered for crop-growing and it was on one of those tiers that the Germans mounted their machine-gun. In the grove is a memorial with the names of the seven who were, in fact, shot dead before Costis Paterakis fired.[10]

Then, as Shirley knew from George Psychoundakis, 'The Germans fled, leaving their machine guns and most of their rifles. Koustogerakiots pursued them and shot many more. The men from the three villages (the other two were Leivada and Moni), expecting reprisals, took their women and children higher into the mountains to hide out.'[11]

While imagining all this and the reprisals that followed, Shirley was seized upon by a man who introduced himself as Epimenides Paterakis (not one of the brothers). Assured that she was a New Zealander, he invited her to his house and, with his arm around her shoulders, steered her to one of the white houses on the square, where he fed her souvlaki and a glass of the local liqueur.

He told me, with fierce emphasis, that the New Zealanders and Australians were wonderful people and fighters but the English were no good; he practically spat with contempt. I thought I would have to speak up for Patrick Leigh Fermor and Xan Fielding, and he agreed they were fine . . . Then all of a sudden he got up, and said 'I have business!' and again with his arm around my shoulder, propelled me out of the door into the sunlight, and with barely a goodbye, strode off into the distance.[12]

10 Murray Elliott to SHSS, 4 January 1993, SHSS papers. To Shirley's argument for her own account, he replied, 'I note what you say about certain aspects of yours and my research. People's memories after so many years tend to be clouded while some accounts are hearsay. And even when the Cretans have the wrong end of a story and are confronted with evidence to the contrary they tend to stick to their own version of events.'

11 George Psychoundakis, *The Cretan Runner*, p.232.

12 SHSS, 'Visit to Crete, 1991', p.17, SHSS papers, ATL, MS-Papers-11404-46.

She headed for the kafenion for a beer before heading down the mountain. Sofia Paterakis sat down beside her and with the help of Shirley's little dictionary they conversed. While they were talking, a man came striding by. Sofia called him over and introduced Shirley to Costis Paterakis. They shook hands and he moved on. For Shirley, it was a crowning moment: 'I felt, up there in the dazzlingly clear air of the Cretan mountains, that I had briefly entered the ancient world of gods and heroes.'[13]

In the hot afternoon sun, she found the homeward journey more difficult than her way up the mountain. Not a car came by. When she reached the main road, she sat down in the shade of some bushes and there discovered the signpost she had missed earlier, knocked over by a vehicle and flattened. It may have crossed her mind that she too could fall by the wayside.

On she went. Eventually she heard a small truck coming towards her. It stopped, she waited hopefully, watching the driver and his wife have an urgent conversation. He shook his head and drove on, but minutes later he returned, much to Shirley's relief, and delivered her to the Café-Bar Maria.

Ririka knelt at my feet and pulled off my trainers, found a chair for my feet, someone brought me a small black coffee, Ririka disappeared and emerged with a bowl of yoghurt and honey, which alas I simply couldn't face. I managed to make it known that I was pining for a beer, and it came, at once.

. . . Everyone was amazed at what I had done, and thought I must be stiff and aching; so, vaingloriously, I stood up and shook my legs and said, No, I was fine. At length I managed to leave all these kind people and plunge into the heavenly Libyan sea, which I had been longing to do.[14]

Back in New Zealand she discovered her camera's shutter had jammed and none of her photographs had come out.

13 Ibid. p.19.
14 Ibid. pp.18–19.

28

Once more into the breach

BACK HOME, Shirley was beset with worries about Bill's papers falling into the wrong hands.[1] She had turned down everyone who had approached her wanting to write a biography of Bill and she refused to collaborate with anyone. Now she considered writing it herself.

Hearing of this, Alister Taylor, now living and running his publishing company in Auckland, wrote to her in May 1991 to ask her if it was true. He didn't wish to preempt her but he thought it important that an independent biography be started.

If a researcher could be assigned to this, would you be prepared to co-operate, and make available the documentation and records you have, and also be available yourself to record some taped interviews? If you say no, of course that will be an end to it; in the past you have avoided my inquiries in this area, but the passage of time now makes such avoidance a real handicap to a project which should *proceed, and relatively quickly.*[2]

He also proposed establishing a scholarship in Bill's name. Shirley replied:

The idea of a scholarship sounds good. It's subject, however, to what I feel about doing anything public about Bill. This affects the project of a biography too. I have been more concerned to protect the living than to celebrate the dead. Bill's brother and sister suffered so much over the whole affair that I don't want them to have the past raked up again. Because

1 Shirley wanted to see Bill's work on a biography of Gordon Coates completed but not by Michael Bassett. She was upset that he managed to get hold of some of Bill's research notes that she hadn't known existed. (Bassett's biography, *Coates of Kaipara*, AUP, 1995, hardly acknowledges the Sutch papers.)

2 Alister Taylor to SHSS, 24 May 1991, SHSS papers, ATL, MS-Papers-11369-151.

you may be sure that if anything faintly approving is said or written about Bill, the other side will raise its ugly head and throw dirt again. I am also concerned about Helen who still has quite a lot of life to live (I hope) under the Sutch name; she may not always be overseas. . . . I'm sure you will know that it's not that I'm concerned for myself, I'm always ready for 'Once more into the breach . . .'

There are other reasons why I haven't collaborated with anybody over a biography. I do feel that Bill is mine; I know him better than anybody, and I know a lot about his life before I met him: his old mother used to talk to me, she actually liked me. My problem is trying to get free to write anything: I'm also under pressure to write my own life, not only from Helen and others, but at least one publisher. . . .

No, I'm not prepared to collaborate with anybody at present, if ever. . . .[3]

Despite this explanation, Alister's partner, journalist Deborah Coddington, wrote some months later asking Shirley for permission to write the Sutch biography. Shirley replied that she had turned everyone down, from her son-in-law (Keith Ovenden says he never wanted to write a biography of Sutch) to Alister himself. She added that Helen had asked her friend Rosslyn Noonan to tape some interviews and she had consented to this. 'I have *not* agreed to Ros's writing the biography.' She still wanted to do it herself, if only she could get herself 'disentangled from the problem of sorting out and disposing of the stuff in this house . . . There is a lot I want to write about, not only about Bill.'[4]

More than two years later Shirley learnt that Rosslyn Noonan had assumed that she would write the biography. According to Aileen Finucane, people from far and wide, including Alister, knew of it. In a quandary, Shirley wrote to Helen:

Should I say anything to Ros? It's difficult; we let her state her hope of getting something written within the three years and said nary a word. And I can hardly go behind her back and tell Alister and others that she got it

3 SHSS to Alister Taylor, 29 May 1991, SHSS papers, ATL, MS-Papers-11369-151.

4 SHSS to Deborah Coddington, 7 November 1991, SHSS papers, ATL, MS-Papers-11369-013. The author has not seen Rosslyn Noonan's research material.

wrong. It puts me in a false position with people to whom I said, truthfully, that while I wouldn't give them permission, I was not going to give it to anyone. Oh dear, the problems . . .[5]

One problem had been people requesting access to the Sutch papers in the Alexander Turnbull Library. Shirley and Helen solved that by giving Rosslyn Noonan sole access, but when PhD student Simon Emsley requested to see papers relating to John A. Lee, Shirley was sympathetic. She explained to Helen that Simon said he would 'never write anything to harm Bill, he admires him so much; and he can't wait as long as our restrictions would bind him to.'[6] They came to an arrangement and in December 1993 Shirley and Rosslyn were working through the boxes in the Turnbull, sorting them, clearing them for Emsley and for another PhD student, Tim Bollinger. Shirley had earlier helped Bollinger write a paper on Bill. He went on to complete his PhD on 'The administrative career of Dr W. B. Sutch 1958–65' (2001).

There would be other requests down the years, all of which demanded her time and attention. In 1999, when she was helping Brian Easton with both his entry on Sutch in the *Dictionary of New Zealand Biography* and the two chapters devoted to Sutch in his book *The Nationbuilders* (Auckland University Press, 2001), she conceded that a biography should be written about Bill's public career, 'but heaven help anyone who tries to write about the whole man. This is why I have not wanted one written, although Helen is keen. Luckily Rosslyn has had no time!'[7]

ALTHOUGH SHIRLEY thought she knew her husband best, she continued to be perplexed and surprised as she made fresh discoveries about him. When, in the late 1980s, she eventually had herself substituted as executor of the W. B. Sutch Estate (which was still not wound up), she

5 SHSS to MHS, 18 November 1993, MHS papers.

6 SHSS to MHS, 24 September 1993, MHS papers. Simon Emsley wasn't desperate to publish, but he was concerned that the conditions under which he was to view the material and the restrictions proposed on what he could write might bring into question his independence and the value of his work.

7 SHSS to Brian Easton, 23 March 1999, Brian Easton papers.

found one of the outstanding items was land Bill bought in 1970 on an estate called Stella Maris on Long Island in the Bahamas. When she made enquiries, she started receiving bills for road maintenance.

Shirley wrote to the manager that she had no idea Bill had bought this land and why he did was a mystery. He had taken out a membership for one, in perpetuity, of the exclusive Stella Maris Tennis and Cabana Club and planned to visit, intending to use the complimentary vacation certificate for one person. Was this certificate still valid, she asked?

She found herself in an impossible situation. Mike Bungay, as Bill's executor, had failed to apply for re-sealing of probate and Shirley could not sell the property until it was completed. She let the matter lie. In 1998 she and Helen had still not taken possession of the property. Neither of them expected to take holidays in the Bahamas.

Unhappy about how Mike Bungay had managed Bill's estate, Shirley was also worried that his file on the Sutch trial could get into the wrong hands. She had asked Mike for it, formally through her lawyer, back in 1984. He had replied that it was *his* file. 'It contains a number of matters of a confidential nature including the result of certain enquiries. My file does not form part of the estate property. For that reason I am not prepared to hand it over to the beneficiaries.'[8]

Shirley heard that he intended to write a book about the trial and thought that she had blocked this. She tried unsuccessfully to stop Bungay's episode on the Sutch case in his 1992 television series *Bungay on Crime*. When Mike died in August the following year, she wrote to his widow Ronda, whom she had never met, about both the book and television programme. 'He had been my friend for so long, and Bill regarded him as a friend: I felt that he had betrayed that friendship. I trust you will accept this in the spirit of sorrow in which it is written: you won't expect me to write platitudes.'[9]

8 Bungay to McKay, 21 June 1984 (copied by Helen Edwards), SHSS papers. Bungay offered to consider Shirley's request to see a specific item, but she wanted the complete file.

9 SHSS to Ronda Bungay, 1 September 1993, SHSS papers. She had earlier, on 20 November 1992, complained to the New Zealand Law Society, her main objection being the impropriety 'for counsel to use their knowledge, gained in defence of a client, in a manner which is prejudicial to their client, especially, of course, when death has robbed the client of any remedy.'

Once again she tried through her lawyer to get the trial papers but was told that the file had been destroyed long ago. Shirley did not believe this. She thought that if she couldn't get it back, she wanted an assurance that it was in fact destroyed. She visited Ronda in Rotorua and found her sympathetic. Ronda told her that after Mike died she had asked the police to shred his files, but she had kept a slim file, and she gave it to Shirley.

And she told Shirley that Mike had never intended to write a book about the Sutch case. Shirley was puzzled. If he did not intend to write a book, why didn't he say so when she confronted him about it? Instead he had said that a book should be written.[10]

What had distressed her most about the *Bungay on Crime* programme was an interview with Martyn Finlay, who said that the profiles Sutch had prepared on prominent New Zealanders had had a direct bearing on his decision to proceed with prosecution. That they weren't then given in evidence in the trial suggested that justice did not appear to have been served, he said.

Then on 10 October 1993 came a bombshell in an article by Geoff Chapple in the *Sunday Star*. Retired diplomat Alexei Makarov, who had been Chargé d'Affaires at the Soviet Embassy in Wellington in 1974, decided that with the breakup of the USSR and its secret police he had nothing to fear from writing his version of the Sutch affair. Geoff Chapple tracked him down in Moscow.

Russian diplomat Alexei Makarov breaks 19 years of silence on the Dr William Ball Sutch spy affair, claiming that before the New Zealander was arrested in 1974 he passed a package to a Soviet KGB agent.

Makarov, speaking exclusively to the Sunday Star, *has revealed the first evidence that written information was passed by Sutch and reached the Soviet Embassy.*[11]

Makarov told how the driver of the Soviet Embassy diplomatic car had shaken off a hot pursuit and taken Sutch's package back to the embassy

10 SHSS to MHS, undated [June] 1995, MHS papers.
11 'Russian revelations on Sutch spy affair', *Sunday Star*, 10 October 1993.

and handed it directly to him, telling him the package was KGB material. When Razgovorov later returned to the embassy, Makarov gave it to him, unopened.

In the same article, Chapple reported that Martyn Finlay confirmed what he had said on Mike Bungay's programme about the profiles. Shirley wrote to him giving her explanation of why the profiles weren't used. She stressed that he didn't need to talk about the profiles to justify his decision to prosecute and that by doing so he damaged her, her daughter and other members of the family. With this letter she enclosed a personal note in a card:

Dear Martyn,

I am sorry it has come to this. No doubt I should have written to you after the Bungay show (which I tried to stop but couldn't). People who spoke to me about it all thought that what you said was more damaging to Bill than anything else in it.

I know Bill was stupid in this and from before we married, I knew his judgment was poor. And he got to know that I would advise against things he proposed and I disapproved of. So when he knew I wouldn't approve, he wouldn't tell me. So I knew nothing about his meeting Razgovorov until that awful night. But it is also true that though I hoped you wouldn't allow the prosecution, I realized, thinking rationally, that you really had no choice – quite apart from these profiles. And so I have always told people.

Hector MacNeill has passed on to me your kind thoughts about me, and I am glad you so think of me. I too have never forgotten that train journey, nor have I forgotten how you sent me New Yorkers while I was ill in Switzerland. And I have never thought ill of you.

Yours sincerely,
Shirley[12]

Martyn replied that he was saddened by her letter but somewhat relieved by her card. He explained that the profiles had not convinced him that the case should proceed, as the Chapple article reported, but that he thought he had told Bungay that they had 'tipped the scales' and

12 SHSS to Martyn Finlay, 14 October 1993, Martyn Finlay papers.

had caused him the greatest anxiety. He had never felt the need to justify his decision, but he explained the considerations on which he based his decision as best as he could recall. He ended with a handwritten note:

Meanwhile I trust the Suffrage Medal Administration didn't pass you by. It's only one distinction and recognition that you deserve – but not really the right one. Some other gesture by the Law Society of Criminal Bar Assn would be more like it. Plus an honorary 'bro'-ship from the many you've served so well.

And it was nice, and thoughtful of you to recall earlier and happier times.

My very best to you, and, with feeling,
Martyn F.[13]

Shirley laughed off the idea of a suffrage medal, but the Wellington District Law Society had invited five practitioners in their seventies to the dinner as the president's guests, and she was one of them. 'Not a special Suffrage effort, as I was the only woman. I was rather pleased, actually, to be treated as just a lawyer. And as for the "Bro's", they don't forget me, and I don't forget them . . .'[14]

She was also pleased to be part of a proposed legal drama series called 'Old Bailey' about a small-scale homely law practice in Thorndon run by Pat Bailey, an eccentric but brilliant 'older' lawyer. Shirley was both the model for this character (to be played by Pat Evison) and advisor to director/writer Peter Coates and producer Bill Sheat, who was also a lawyer and an advocate for the performing arts. The proposal included a synopsis of scenes, a detailed budget for the first episode and an outline of further episodes on topics such as sexual harassment at university, street kids and their rights, elderly people ripped off by lawyers and difficulties with a car repair man. Peter and Bill thought Shirley was a 'fantastic' person to draw on for such a character, but TVNZ's commissioning editor, Jane Wrightson, thought she was 'too old' to be of interest.[15]

13 Martyn Finlay to SHSS, 20 October 1993, Martyn Finlay papers.
14 SHSS to Martyn Finlay, 23 October 1993, Martyn Finlay papers.
15 Bill Sheat to author, 16 August 2014; Peter Coates to author, 2 July 2018; 'Old Bailey'

Public interest in the Sutch case flared again in the new year of 1994. Alexei Makarov had tracked down Razgovorov, living in retirement in Moscow. He reported their conversation to the *Auckland Star*.

Razgovorov reportedly told Makarov that he had 'inherited' Sutch from the KGB officer he had replaced in Wellington. This was Yuri Drozhzhin. (The Mitrokhin files that identified Drozhzhin as Sutch's contact would not be released until 2014.)

Razgovorov said that he and Sutch had several meetings over eight months and that usually he drove to a place they had pre-arranged. When Makarov asked what was in the package he received from Sutch in Holloway Road on the night of 26 September, Razgovorov replied, 'Oh a lot of interesting things.' He said the text was written in capital letters. Makarov referred to the embassy speculation that the package contained only economic reports clipped from newspapers. 'It depends how you view the matter,' Razgovorov replied. Makarov moved on to ask about how the driver, Vitaly Pertsev, managed to get away while Razgovorov had been detained. After explaining that he personally had planned every step of the operation, Razgovorov continued:

I received the package, then quickly came up to Pertsev, who was waiting for me in his car at an agreed close by place, and I gave it to him. The package should be brought immediately to the Embassy. I did not go with Pertsev because I wanted to continue with our meeting with Dr Sutch and I returned to him. But when I came to him closer, the circumstances had changed. I saw him surrounded by Police.[16]

He told Makarov he had been repatriated to the Soviet Union, worked there for seven years, then served as a counsellor in the Soviet Embassy in Syria until his retirement in 1986.

Three days later Shirley was still shaking. She decided that the only

format concept written by Peter Coates, prepared by Bill Sheat, producer, Avalon Television, 2 May 1993, Peter Coates papers.

16 Geoff Chapple, 'Russian inquiry tells more about famous spy scandal', *Sunday Star*, 30 January 1994. Chapple didn't interview Razgovorov directly. Makarov refused to give them Razgovorov's telephone number, fearing it could get him into trouble on some level.

thing she could do, if asked, was to say that she didn't believe a word he said, that he was a psychiatric case.[17]

Privately she couldn't dismiss the implications of Razgovorov's reference to Drozhzhin, nor that he had met Sutch and received a package from him on the night of 26 September 1974 (which she knew was Sir Guy Powles's conclusion), nor the fact that Razgovorov had not defected to the west, which dispelled that conspiracy theory.

Hector MacNeill, now retired and living in the far north, had done a lot of research on the Sutch case and had his own theory. He wanted to 'go public' with his rebuttal of the establishment story that Bill Sutch was a spy against New Zealand. Shirley had urged him not to, but after Razgovorov's 'Lazarus act' he decided it was a 'whole new ball game'. He wrote to Martyn Finlay on 24 February 1994:

I have a feeling that dear Shirley, at a deep intuitive level must know that these meetings with the Russians over a number of years had a sinister connotation. I wrote her a long letter expounding my theory that Bill's conduct is best explained on the basis that he was spying for the KGB, against the NZ Israel Assn. and while she did not agree, her response was couched in a form of words that left me with the impression that she does not wholly reject it, deep down.

You and I know that Bill could be immensely persuasive, and exceedingly charming to his male acquaintances. I imagine that he had an even greater charisma for the women he knew. Shirley, I think, is to this day a victim of that charm.[18]

Hector never published his manuscript. He sent Shirley drafts and she drove up to see him at Maunganui in 1995. She feared his manuscript would be damaging but conceded, looking at his copy of the trial transcript, that there was about a minute when Bill might have met Razgovorov on the night of his arrest. She no longer took Bill's word that they hadn't.

17 SHSS to MHS, 2 February 1994, MHS papers.
18 Hector MacNeill to Martyn Finlay, 24 February 1994, Martyn Finlay papers.

At this time, her belief in Bill had taken another blow. In March 1994, their friend from their New York days, Jim Weir, wrote to Shirley that the Russian Studies department at Victoria University proposed to publish a volume of essays commemorating fifty years of diplomatic relations between New Zealand and the Soviet Union. As he had been New Zealand's Ambassador to Moscow in 1977–80, he had been asked to contribute. He proposed to write about New Zealanders who visited the Soviet Union in the 1920s and '30s and asked for approval to see the Sutch papers in the Alexander Turnbull Library, identifying those he thought relevant. He asked Shirley if Bill had kept an account of 'perhaps the most fascinating journey ever undertaken by a New Zealander.'[19]

Shirley found about four letters from Bill to his mother from the USSR in 1932. 'I was shattered when I read these letters,' she later told James McNeish.[20]

Bill had told her he had walked around the Arctic Circle. Now she learnt he took a boat. He hadn't '*walked* across the Soviet Union' – he took the Trans-Siberian railway. He flew in a commercial plane from the border at Termez over the mountains to Kabul. He was in the Soviet Union for just a fortnight.

She didn't show Jim Weir the letters at this stage. She told him that Rosslyn Noonan had been commissioned to write Sutch's biography and earlier publication of the letters would pre-empt that. Then Maurice Shadbolt, in his memoir *One of Ben's*, proposed that Bill had been recruited by the Soviets when he spent two months in the USSR in 1932. To quash that idea, Shirley finally showed Jim Weir the letters.

They talked about them over lunch and continued by correspondence, discussing also their time in New York when Jim was Bill's Third Secretary. Just one thing from these conversations stuck in Jim's mind, something on which he was able to reassure her. Shirley asked him something about Bill's membership of the Social Commission and the Economic and Social Council, 'and she ended up by asking, "Did he lie to me about that too?"'[21]

19 Jim Weir to SHSS, 7 March 1994, SHSS papers.
20 SHSS to James McNeish, 2 November 1998, James McNeish papers; others.
21 Jim Weir to SHSS, 7 March 1994, SHSS papers.

When Jim Weir's story was published in the *Journal of Slavonic Studies* in 1997, it created headlines: 'Sutch's Soviet trek debunked.'[22] Shirley told Brian Easton that Bill had written a book about his Soviet journey. She had always told him he should write it, but he never told her that he had. Now she wished he hadn't. It was total fantasy. 'I don't trust *anything* he said about that trip except what he wrote to his mother as recorded by Jim Weir.'[23]

In public she continued to proclaim Bill's loyalty to New Zealand. In private, with George and Amanda, she asked, 'What if he had been a spy?' Amanda would say hotly, 'I'd be proud!'

Shirley would thank God she went to Oxford, not Cambridge, or she might have been recruited.[24]

EUROPE STILL beckoned, and her family on the other side of the world continued to lure her to wherever they were. Every trip took her to Oxford. Few of her contemporaries were still alive, but she had the pleasure of seeing both Piers and Crispin at Oxford. And always she went to Greece. When George and Amanda bought a house in Mani in the Peloponnese, they suggested Shirley sell up and join them. 'I cannot tell you what your affection and warm welcome to your new home in Greece means to me,' she wrote. 'I am overwhelmed.'[25] She wished she could – it was so tempting. But she had always felt that she should keep the house for Helen. 'And I *can't* just junk all the stuff it's stuffed with; a lot of it is not rubbish, tho' no doubt a lot of it is.'[26]

She visited Mani with her friend Julie Grenfell in 1996, and she took Julie to her favourite places in Crete – Sougia, Koustogerako and Sfakia. In 1998 Shirley made a farewell visit to Sougia, alone.

22 *Dominion*, 1 April 1997, p.12.
23 SHSS to Brian Easton, 22 August 2000, Brian Easton papers.
24 SHSS to James McNeish, 9 May 1998, James McNeish papers; others, including SHSS to Keith Ovenden, 10 February 1993 (see introduction), KWO papers. In fact, there was an Oxford spy ring, recruited during Shirley's years there. In 1992 the KGB released files relating to 'Agent Scott', identified in 2009 as Arthur Wynn, who sent reports on members of the Communist Party in Oxford, possible recruits and at least 25 potential Soviet spies of whom five were considered highly suitable.
25 SHSS to George and Amanda Rosenberg, 21 June 1995, SHSS papers.
26 SHSS to George and Amanda Rosenberg, 8 July 1995, SHSS papers.

What Shirley wanted to do, besides travel, was write. Since she had learnt to use a computer, Helen and Keith had given her a laptop to write her story. She had written her family history and made a tentative start on her own life, but the major task lay ahead. At home, her distractions now included the final decline of Bill's surviving sibling, Margaret Shirley. Bill's brother Ted Sutch, of whom Shirley was fond, died of cancer in 1995.

Margaret Shirley was then suffering from memory loss, depression and alcoholism. Shirley Smith and their friend and neighbour Gay Saker did their best, but Margaret Shirley wanted to die. 'Nothing in my life has so debilitated me as dealing with Shirley Sutch's problems,' Shirley Smith wrote to Brian Easton, adding to Helen that as well as the house and mess, she had to deal with 'the problem of all her stuff, the stuff that can't be thrown out! As if I didn't have enough of that myself.'[27]

Margaret Shirley died on 3 January 1998. Shirley Smith rushed back from Taupō to organise the funeral. There was no one else to do it.

Meanwhile the World Bank had posted Helen to Warsaw as 'lead economist' responsible for Poland and the Baltic States, pioneering work on governance and anti-corruption. Helen invited her mother to join them there. They lived in a quiet area, half an hour's drive out of the city. She should bring her laptop. They had a little hunting lodge on the property where she could stay and work without distraction.

It was Shirley's last overseas trip. She went to Oxford for the St Hugh's Gaudy and later returned to attend Piers's graduation in Law. She made her final trip to Greece and across northern Europe, visiting favourite sites and museums. For a new experience, Helen took her on a World Bank trip to Latvia, Riga and the seaside resort of Jūrmala on the Baltic coast.

When she wasn't travelling she was writing up topics Helen set her. 'I enjoyed writing about my childhood,' she wrote to Brian Easton, 'but as I get older I find different emotions get stirred up.'[28]

She wondered how different her life would have been if her mother

27 SHSS to Brian Easton, 15 April 1997, Brian Easton papers; SHSS to MHS, 12 April 1997, SHSS and MHS papers.

28 SHSS to Brian Easton, 27 August 1998, Brian Easton papers.

had not died – but then she wouldn't have had the life she had or been the person she was. She wouldn't have gone to Oxford, or married Bill, and there would have been no Helen. No Helen was unthinkable.

She was proud of Helen and the important work she was doing and saw any criticism of the World Bank as an attack on her daughter. Her long friendship with Aileen Finucane and Max Wilkinson had ended in 1995 when Max said Helen had 'sold out' by going to work for the World Bank and words to the effect that she had let Bill down.[29] There were other rifts – as Shirley grew older she was more inclined not only to take offence but also to cause it (compelled to speak 'the truth' as she saw it, even if it was hurtful) – but none was so distressing as her break-up with Max and Aileen.

On the other hand, her relationship with her son-in-law Keith Ovenden continued to improve. She adored her grandsons, who were a credit to his, as well as Helen's, parenting. In 1994, after reading *Stalin's Nose* by Rory MacLean, an exposé of the crimes of the Stalinist regime in Eastern Europe, ending in Moscow, she sent the book to Keith with a 'mea culpa'. Helen was pleased. Her mother's residual defence of Soviet Russia in some things had apparently stood between them.[30]

In 1996 when Oxford University Press published *A Fighting Withdrawal*, Keith's biography of Shirley's old friend Dan Davin, she wrote to Keith that she was awed by his deep research, the appropriate and elegant way he used it, his content and style and much more besides. Dan Davin's later years were marked by depression and alcoholism. She read the end with tears in her eyes and wrote that they brought to mind her favourite lines by Meredith:

'In tragic life, God wot, No villain need be! Passions spin the plot. We are betrayed by what is false within.'

By 'false' to my mind, nothing blameworthy is necessarily meant: it can be some genetic inheritance, or some conditioning by family or society –

29 Correspondence between Shirley and Aileen Finucane and Max Wilkinson, December 1995–January 1996, SHSS papers; SHSS to MHS, 18 January 1996, MHS papers. Max and Aileen accepted what Shirley subsequently wrote about Helen's motivation, but held to their views about the ideology of the World Bank.

30 MHS to SHSS, 8 February 1994, MHS papers.

something out of kilter. We are what all the factors of our birth and early life have made us. Even our ability (when it exists) to rise above these – that is, above harmful ones, derives from those same beginnings.

. . . Bill's tragedy comes under the same head.[31]

The saddest thing for Shirley as she grew older was that she suffered increasingly from what she called logorrhea, excessive talkativeness. She had always been chatty, but this compulsion to communicate was quite different. The problem was compounded by deafness. It made intimacy more difficult and she became increasingly isolated.

She still regularly lunched at Parsons' coffee shop in Lambton Quay with various younger friends. She and her sister-in-law Helen Smith, Allan's wife, met there every week. Their close friendship was deepened by shared Christmas and new year holidays with their families in Taupō. Helen and Allan had built a new house with an expansive view across the river to the boat harbour, but Shirley preferred to stay in the old house with its memories.

She was quietly gratified by recognition she received from the law profession. Back in 1995 the Wellington District Law Society made her an Honorary Life Member. In 2000, newly appointed Chief Justice Sian Elias thanked Shirley for her letter of congratulations. Elias added, 'Of course you are right up the top of the list of pioneering women in the law and we are all both proud of you and grateful for what you accomplished.'[32] Shirley wasn't present when Elias made a similar remark about her at an Auckland District Law Society dinner. Despite Shirley's absence, the audience rose as of one accord and gave a standing ovation.

Remembering this, when the Wellington District Law Society hosted a farewell dinner for Ted Thomas on his retirement from the Court of Appeal, he invited Shirley to sit at the top table and he too made a special tribute to her in his speech. As in Auckland, everyone rose spontaneously and gave her standing ovation. Shirley wrote to Helen that she was so stunned that she didn't really know what had

31 SHSS to KWO, 20 November 1996, KWO papers.

32 Sian Elias, Chief Justice, to SHSS, 3 March 2000, SHSS papers, ATL, MS-Papers-2013-045-32.

happened until someone told her that he had praised her for what she'd done for women lawyers.

I'd have preferred Maoris and Polynesians and the Black Power and the Mongrel Mob. I strove to have women lawyers simply accepted as lawyers, regardless of gender, and felt absolutely betrayed by the women who formed the Women Lawyers' Society. Two of them, Sian Elias, now Chief Justice, and Lowell Goddard, on the Court of Appeal, were at the table. Although I told them, when they called a meeting in Wellington to form their society, what I thought of it, and having made a speech, walked out, they were friendly and joined in the applause.[33]

She had been only dimly aware that the applause was for her until a letter from George Barton QC, who hadn't been present, made it clear. He wrote that everyone who had spoken to him about that dinner, without any prompting on his part, had spoken of the universal delight in seeing her honoured. Shirley thought of her father. How pleased he would have been.[34]

By 2000, Shirley had changed her thinking about a biography of Bill. She now wanted it written. Shirley realised before Noonan's appointment as Chief Human Rights Commissioner in 2001 that she should find someone else.

In February 2000, she phoned Wellington author Chris Maclean, asking him to bring her a copy of his latest book, *Kapiti*. In his 1994 book, *Tararua*, Maclean had written of the survival of the 'Sutch party' – the missing trampers that prompted the 'Sutch search' in Easter 1933. He was the first to tell the story as an extraordinary feat of survival. Having won the confidence of Morva Sutch when he interviewed her about it in 1990, he was now to learn from Shirley much more about the life of Bill Sutch. In *A Way with Words* (2018) Maclean recalls how his Sunday afternoon visit to her Brooklyn home turned out rather differently from what he expected:

33 SHSS to MHS, 22 October 2001, MHS papers.
34 Ibid.

Shirley was sharp and engaging. Soon the conversation turned to Bill. Unprompted, Shirley spent much of the afternoon describing her late husband. She had much to say and almost all of it suggested ambivalence. He was, she told me, an unusual, complex and secretive man of many contradictions whose early life in Brooklyn revealed curious formative experiences. . . . Eventually, Shirley made an explicit request: she was looking for someone to write about Bill – would I be interested?[35]

Chris Maclean felt inadequate in the fields of economics and international politics and declined. It must have been clear to Shirley that Bill's biography would not be written in her lifetime.

Shirley's last foray into defending Bill followed a TV One *Assignment* documentary in March 2000 that claimed Sutch was a spy. Her complaint to the Broadcasting Complaints Authority was reported in the *Evening Post*:

She said the programme contained inaccuracies, was unfair to Dr Sutch, was unbalanced, failed to respect the principles of law, and used deceptions which took advantage of the confidences viewers had in the integrity of broadcasting.

In addition, she complained that she, as a participant, had been misled by the producer as to the purpose of the programme.[36]

The authority acknowledged that some facts had been interpreted in a light that could be seen as unfavourable to Sutch and that there was another possible version of events, but it didn't find the programme to be materially unfair, unbalanced or partial to an extent that it breached standards.

In response to Shirley's assertion that the matter had been put to rest with her husband's acquittal, the authority responded:

35 Chris Maclean, *A Way with Words: A Memoir of Writing and Publishing in New Zealand*, Potton & Burton, 2018, pp.106–107. The author has seen the notes Chris wrote, 'Notes on a Conversation with Shirley Smith, 6 Feb 2000'.

36 *Evening Post*, 5 October 2000, p.14.

In the complainant's view that matter had been put to rest with his acquittal . . . however, journalists and lawyers come from a different perspective when analysing a set of facts.

The authority emphasises that there is a distinction between legal processes on the one hand and journalism on the other. For example, in counterpoint to the legal principle that a case will not be relitigated, for journalists there is no point at which matters of public interest become finalised: there will always be ongoing review of historical events, including court trials.[37]

She had understood that the programme was to be based on information from the Mitrokhin Archive in Cambridge. Nothing of note had come out of the latest release of the documents. The ruling carried a caveat: when the second volume of the Mitrokhin file was published, there would be further opportunity for the facts to be revisited.

Shirley accepted that the Mitrokhin files would have the final word on Bill's relationship to the Russians. She objected to Brian Easton describing Bill as a 'source' in his *Dictionary of New Zealand Biography* entry. 'I don't think you should publish anything on all of this until the "Pacific" edition of the Mitrokhin files comes out. If Bill doesn't figure in them, he's clear, if he does, it will be quite soon enough to say "he was only a source".'[38] (Shirley would not live to see the Mitrokhin Archive with its entry on 'Maori' declassified in 2014.)

SHE WAS NOW ready give up the fight. To James and Helen McNeish she wrote, 'I know that you – at least Jim, who made his views very clear – think that I should drop all this now and get on with more important things, and with June now well on the way to July, I agree.'[39]

The 'more important things' were, of course, sorting out her own life.

37 Broadcasting Complaints Authority, NZPA, *Evening Post*, 5 October 2000, p.14.

38 SHSS to Brian Easton, 22 August 2000, Brian Easton papers, Appendix to notes, p.12–13.

39 SHSS to James and Helen McNeish, 19 June 2000, James McNeish papers.

29

He hau toa

For some time now, Shirley had been having trouble with her short-term memory. It was later found that, as the result of multiple small strokes, which may have happened over a long time, she had multi-infarcts dementia (now described under the umbrella of ADARDS, Alzheimer's Disease and Related Disorders). Something had to be done to help her manage her day-to-day living, but she resisted help. When she broke her arm and was entitled to help through ACC she chose not to apply. She said she would have to clean and tidy up first and anyway, she liked the spiders.

When things went missing she suspected the SIS. Her paranoia led her to hand over to the Alexander Turnbull Library four bundles of 'precious letters' from Bill that she had retrieved from his parents' house. The only bundle she had read were those she opened for Jim Weir, dated 24 September to 19 October 1932. The others remained bound. She explained in February 2000 to David Colquhoun, Curator of Manuscripts at the Alexander Turnbull Library, that the disappearance of papers relating to Bill's trial and now some other letters 'had put the fear of God into me, and I decided that these letters should go to you as soon as possible. To think that the SIS is still trying to prove that Bill was a Russian spy! Who else could it be?'[1]

She was genuinely afraid. She wrote to Helen later in the year that she was looking forward to getting out of the house.

Strange things keep happening, the sort of things that happened after Daddy died. Silly little things, the telling of which would lead people to think that I'm going round the bend. . . . It's spooky. Of course I had set the alarm. I'm told that the SIS can easily neutralize an alarm. . . . I have always

1 SHSS to David Colquhoun, 22 February 2000, SHSS papers.

believed that they do these things to frighten me out of the house, because they are convinced that somewhere in this house is proof that Daddy was a spy.[2]

Helen and Keith had bought her a town house at 33 Hobson Street in Thorndon. Shirley had chosen it but, despite feeling spooked, she wouldn't move until she had finished her impossible task of dealing with all the stuff at Todman Street. In January 2002 they finally moved her.

The Todman Street house was to be restored and the garden re-landscaped. On Helen's insistence, Shirley had put the house in a trust. The sale of the art works, including Alexander Calder mobiles, which had dramatically increased in value since Bill bought them, helped pay for the restoration by architect Alistair Luke of the major art work – the house – and made it possible for Helen and Keith to live there.[3] In 2003 the house won the New Zealand Institute of Architects Resene Award for Enduring Architecture.

Helen hoped her mother would have an easier life without the burden of the house, but Shirley thought her work there was unfinished. For the first months, she returned every day to sort boxes in the garage. She had achieved a lot, setting up a new filing system, annotating letters for the benefit of unknown readers. She explained to Amanda Rosenberg that one had to see all the stuff to understand how much she had to do, but she couldn't explain why it was important or even what it was for.

Meanwhile the cartons of her belongings in her new flat remained packed. She had greatly underestimated what would be involved in moving house after more than forty years. She attributed her state of fatigue and disorientation to the move. She now needed a map to find her way around Wellington.

In January 2003, less than a year after the move, she was in Taupō with Allan and Helen Smith when she had a bad fall. It was decided that she would go direct from Taupō to a studio in the Malvina Major Retirement Village in Johnsonville. Though this was explained to

2 SHSS to MHS, 4 November 2000, MHS papers.

3 MHS to SHSS, 24 August and 1 November 2002, SHSS papers.

Shirley, she didn't absorb it and was outraged when Allan 'dumped' her there. She hated losing her independence – especially her driving licence – but she realised her mind was not what it used to be.

In due course she was moved to a more dependent unit, but Helen wanted her mother to stay in her studio as long as possible. She engaged Elder Family Matters, who provided Shirley with a carer, who, along with a few devoted friends, helped her with various tasks, took her on outings and provided companionship.

Shirley's last letters to Helen show her awareness of her world contracting on all fronts. '. . . you lose part of your life when you don't remember the past,' she wrote on one occasion. She didn't know the date. For one who meticulously dated practically everything she ever wrote, this must have bothered her. Typically, her letters described her view of the harbour across to Days Bay and Eastbourne and the Orongorongos. In February 2003, after setting this scene for Helen, she continued:

Wish you were here. Keith, of course, is, and I understand that he is doing a big job with my stuff. What I don't understand, everyone who has dealt with my stuff hasn't thought it necessary to tell me what they're doing with it! Perhaps they think I shouldn't be bothered. I asked Keith this morning and he told me, and he's doing a good job, but why do people think I don't need to know? I'll not know if things are in storage and if so, where?[4]

In her studio, besides pens and writing paper and recent correspondence, she had her personal diaries and accounts of trips, belongings of her mother, Eva, her family photo albums and larger photographs, including a photo of herself as a baby with her mother, portraits of Helen Coates and Cecil Upton as debutants, and also her daughter Helen as a debutant. On her wall hung the certificate from the Greek–New Zealand Association. But visitors were surprised that she had no photo on display of Bill. The day came when, seeing him in one of her albums, she remarked, 'Who is that handsome man?'

What she retained was her pleasure in poetry, especially the poems

4 SHSS to MHS (from Malvina Major), February 2003, MHS papers.

she knew from childhood in her Palgrave's *Golden Treasury*. Later towards the end, when visitors read them to her, she would mouth the words or say them with the reader, stumbling as she lost control of her speaking muscles. The last time Brian Easton read to her, she read her favourite, the ballade, *Fair Helen*. 'She did so with alacrity, with pleasure and with perfection . . . in a strong Scottish accent.'[5]

While her daughter Helen was working overseas, Shirley was still capable of writing, always in a clear hand and with impeccable grammar. 'People seem to think that if one is alone one is lonely,' she wrote to Helen in September 2003. 'I am perfectly happy on my own – I always have been, though of course there are people one likes to see, such as you – well, you especially.'[6]

Then Helen came home for good, and so did Piers and Crispin.

On Boxing Day 2007, after a battle with cancer, Shirley's sister-in-law Helen Smith died. After her funeral, when the family were gathered together at the Karori crematorium, Crispin received a call that Shirley had suffered a fatal stroke. She was ninety-one.

It was 29 December, the day on which Shirley's father had died twenty-five years earlier.

A celebration of Shirley's life was held in St Andrew's on the Terrace, where her grandfather, the Rev. John Gibson Smith, had ministered a century earlier. The occasion brought together friends and family, past and present judges, Shirley's former students, colleagues and clients, members of the Mongrel Mob and their Black Power rivals. No one present will ever forget Black Power's haka led by Denis O'Reilly. 'This is the mother of our tribe who showed us how to do things in this land. . . . who did her best to balance things and we love her for it,' he said, explaining the significance of the special haka, reserved for one of their own:

5 https://www.eastonbh.ac.nz/2008/01/shirley-smith-1916-2007/ (accessed 7 February 2018).

6 SHSS to MHS, 4 September 2003, MHS papers.

Te rongo toa	*I am a warrior*
O oku tipuna	*Who listens to the teachings of my ancestors*
Ka hinga au, aue	*If I should fall in battle*
Ka mate au,	*If I should die*
Ka takoto toa	*Even if I am surrounded*
Tena i karawhuia,	*By fallen comrades*
Kia piki,	*Another will stand in my place*
He hau toa	*A warrior wind blows*
Aue hi! Aue hi![7]	

The wind of her inspiration still blows. In 2008 the New Zealand Law Society's Women in Law Committee established the annual Shirley Smith Address in her memory. In the inaugural address, the Hon. Margaret Wilson, DCNZM, explained that Shirley Smith appeared in court when it was almost unheard of for women to do so and that she epitomised the hope and possibility of women practising in all facets of the law. 'She not only practised the law but also she challenged the profession and the legal system to recognise the rights of women and those who lacked access to law. It is hard to describe the importance of women such as Shirley Smith not only to women entering the profession but to the development of our legal system.'[8]

While Shirley was much more than a woman of the law, the Shirley Smith Address is a fitting tribute to her memory. As their internationally acclaimed speakers challenge and provoke thinking on issues related to justice and human rights, they too acknowledge how Shirley Smith showed the way.

7 Black Power composed the haka at a national hui at Jerusalem in 1989 when the gang was trying to pull itself together. John Newton, *The Double Rainbow*, VUP, 2009, pp.166–167.

8 Hon. Margaret Wilson, inaugural Shirley Smith Address, 2008.

Bibliography

PRIMARY SOURCES

People interviewed or consulted

Denise Almao, Robin Anderson, Hazel Armstrong, Ailsa Barton, Elizabeth Bayliss, Tom Bayliss, Kathleen Bell, Véronique Bernard, John Billington QC, Maureen Birchfield, Pat Booth, Kobi Bosshard, Kristen Bunn, David Burke, Russell Campbell, Isobel Cassey, Maureen Cassey, Peter Coates, Rosemary Collier, Megan Cook, Helen Croft, Rowena Cullen, Valerie Davies, Anna Davin, Dana de Milo, Mark Derby, Pip Desmond, Michel Devin, Alex Dickie, David Dunningham, Brian Easton, Helen Edwards, Jennifer Edwards, Grant Ewen, Aaron Fox, Judith Fyfe, Tony Garstang, Alan Gray, Janet Green, Phillip Green, Ian Greig, Julie Grenfell, Ray Grover, Nicky Hager, Margaret Hayward, Richard Hill, Sue Hirst, Chris Hodson, Shirley Hope Evans, Cecilia Johnson, Jim Kebbell, Sir Kenneth Keith, Rebecca Kitteridge, Geoff Lewington, Bill Logan, David Long, Margaret Long, Steven Loveridge, Chris Maclean, Hector MacNeill, Betty MacNeill, Sir John McGrath, Sir James McNeish, Emma Maddison-Ross, Dennis Makalio, Phillip Mann, Hugo Manson, Jay Marson, Keith Matthews, Jackie Matthews, John Morrison, John Newton, Paul Oestreicher, Noelene O'Keefe, Pauline O'Regan, Denis O'Reilly, Elizabeth Orr, Vincent O'Sullivan, Keith Ovenden, Ririka Papagrigorakis, Paul Parker, Dorothy Pascoe, Vardis Paterakis, Susan Price, Beverley Randall, Nonnita Reese, Tina Reid, Hugh Rennie QC, Dennis Rose, Amanda Rosenberg, George Rosenberg, Margot Roth, Eugene Ryder, Gay Saker, Elspeth Sandys, Ben Schrader, Dick Scott, Bill Sheat, Dame Margaret Shields, Andreas Sivitos, Jenny Sivitos, Richard (Dick) Skinner, Tepaeru Skinnon, Alastair Smith, Allan Smith, Dame Margaret Sparrow, Roger Steele, Helen Sutch, Harry Tam, John Tannahill, Alister Taylor, Philip Temple, Sir Edmund Thomas, Jim Thomson, Judy Tindall, Jim Traue, Julia Traue, Warren Tucker, Fuiamaono Tuiasau, Harvey Uiti, John Upton, Dina Viatos, Gordon Webb, Jim Weir, Denis Welch, Dick Werry, Chris Wheeler, Max Wilkinson, Fran Williams, Sir Owen Woodhouse, Peter Woodhouse, Jack Woodward, Mary Woodward, Joan Wooler, Sir Kim Workman, Redmer Yska.

Interviews with Shirley Smith

Interviewer Hugo Manson, Wellington District Law Society Oral History Project: 1989, 4 November 1988, ATL, ID OHA LAW / 2528.
Interviewer Neville Glasgow, first broadcast on the National Radio programme *Directions* on 18 January 1989, published in *Directions: New Zealanders Explore the Meaning of Life,* Shoal Bay Press, Christchurch, 1995, pp.186–201.
Interviewers Martin and Selina Powell, 1999.
Interviewer Megan Cook about Committee on Vietnam.
Celebrating One Hundred and Twenty Five Years of St Hugh's College: Recorded Memories of Senior Members from 1930s–1990s, St Hugh's College, Oxford.

Private papers

Russell Campbell
Peter Coates
Rosemary Collier
Brian Easton
Grant Ewen
Martyn Finlay
Aaron Fox
Helen Garrett
Margaret Hayward
Cecilia Johnson
Hector MacNeill
Chris Maclean
James McNeish
Keith Matthews
Keith Ovenden
Hugh Price (Susan Price)
Amanda Rosenberg
George Rosenberg
Dick Scott
Allan Smith
David Smith
Helen Sutch
Judy Tindall

Further correspondence provided by people interviewed for this project.

Alexander Turnbull Library collections

Christine Cole Catley
Margaret (Peggy) Garland
Elsie Violet Locke
David Stanley Smith
Shirley Hilda Stanley Smith
Margaret Shirley Sutch
William Ball Sutch
Ormond Wilson

Other repositories

Archives New Zealand
Auckland University
Auckland University Special Collections
Auckland War Memorial Museum

J. C. Beaglehole Room, Victoria University of Wellington Library
Canterbury Museum
Christchurch City Libraries Archives
Crown Law Office, Wellington
L'Office du Tourisme, Leysin, Switzerland (Véronique Bernard, local historian)
McMillan Brown Library, Christchurch
National Archives, UK (MI5 Security Service files)
National Archives, USA (FBI Files)
National Criminal Investigations Group, Police National Headquarters, NZ
New Zealand Courts
New Zealand Law Society Library
New Zealand Security Intelligence Service
Nga Tawa College, Marton
Petone Library
Queen Margaret College, Wellington
Radio New Zealand Archives
St Cuthbert's College, Auckland
St Hugh's College, Oxford
United Nations Archives
Wellington City Archives

Unpublished memoirs by Shirley Smith

Typescripts of reminiscences under subject headings, 1992–2002.

'Classics Department, AUC – 2nd term 1944' by Shirley Smith, Temporary Wartime Appointment, March 1979, ATL MS-Papers-11404-70.

'Reminiscences for St Hugh's Centenary Book', 1986, SHSS papers, ATL, MS-Papers-11404-35 (extracts published in *St Hugh's: One Hundred Years of Women's Education in Oxford*) .

Published memoirs by Shirley Smith

St Hugh's: One Hundred Years of Women's Education in Oxford, ed. Penny Griffin, Macmillan Press, UK, 1986.

'Shirley Smith', *Directions: New Zealanders Explore the Meaning of Life,* Shoal Bay Press, Christchurch, 1995, pp.186–201 (interview with Neville Glasgow for National Radio first broadcast 1989).

'My Life in the Law', *Claiming the Law, Essays by New Zealand Women in Celebration of the 1993 Suffrage Centennial,* Victoria University of Wellington Law Review Special Issue, Monograph 6, Elisabeth McDonald and Graeme Austin (eds.), VUW Law Review & VUP, May 1993.

Unpublished memoirs of Shirley Smith

Sir David Smith, handwritten manuscript labelled 'Reminiscences' and 'Biographical notes and jottings', started October 1966. Two copies, one in DSS papers, ATL, MS-Papers-11112-034; better copy with a recent transcription in KWO and MHS papers.

Ormond Wilson, 'Memories of my contacts with Bill Sutch, for the eyes of a serious biographer', typescript, ATL MS-Papers-10506.

Shirley Smith, *Fair Challenge: An Aspect of Trial by Jury*, published in Wolfgang Rosenberg's festschrift.

Submissions on behalf of the Organisation of Human Rights to the Statutes Revision Committee with Regard to Certain Aspects of the Police Offences Bill, 1951.

Shirley Smith, Submission, 1970, Archives NZ, Ref. No. COM7 7, Royal Commission on Social Security.

Shirley Smith, 'Reflections on the New Zealand Security Intelligence Service Amendment Bill, 1977'.

Shirley Smith, Submission to the Statutes Revision Committee on the Homosexual Law Reform Bill 26 April 1985.

Tributes to Shirley Smith

Judge Ema Aitken
Rosslyn Noonan
Crispin Ovenden
Piers Ovenden
Keith Ovenden
Helen Sutch
Keith Matthews (published)

Court records

New Zealand Law Reports
Legal opinions
Judicial decisions
Court reports in media
Coroner's reports
Depositions and transcript of Supreme Court trial *The Queen v. William B. Sutch.*

Diaries and journals

Shirley Smith, travel journals, 1935–98
—personal journals, 1935–36, 1951, 1991
—work diaries, 1980s

Margaret Smith, travel journal, 1938
David Smith, diaries
Dan Davin, diary, 1947
Theodore Philip Toynbee diaries, Bodleian Library Special Collections, Oxford

SECONDARY SOURCES: SELECT BIBLIOGRAPHY

Alington, Margaret H., *Unquiet Earth: A History of the Bolton Street Cemetery*, Wellington City Council, 1978.

Andrew, Christopher, and Gordievsky, Oleg, *KGB: The Inside Story of Foreign Operations from Lenin to Gorbachev*, Hodder & Stoughton, London Sydney Auckland Toronto, 1990.

Auckland University College (University of New Zealand) Calendars, 1942–44.

Barton, Susan, *Healthy Living in the Alps: The Origins of Winter Tourism in Switzerland 1860–1914* (Chapter 'Leysin' pp.78–88), Manchester University Press, Manchester, 2008.

Beatson, Peter and Dianne, eds., *Dear Peggy: Letters to Margaret Garland from her New Zealand friends*, Sociology Department, Massey University, Palmerston North, 1997.

Barrowman, Rachel, *A Popular Vision: The Arts and the Left in New Zealand, 1930–1950*, VUP, Wellington, 1991.

Barrowman, Rachel, *Victoria University of Wellington, 1899–1999*, VUP, Wellington, 1999.

Bennetts, C. H. Kit, *Spy: A Former SIS Officer Unmasks New Zealand's Sensational Cold War Spy Affair*, Random House NZ, Auckland, 2006.

Birchfield, Maureen, *Looking for Answers: A Life of Elsie Locke*, Canterbury University Press, Christchurch, 2010.

Booth, Pat, *Deadline: My Story*, Viking/Penguin Books (NZ) Ltd, Auckland, 1997.

Campbell, Russell, *Codename Intelligentsia: The Life and Times of the Honourable Ivor Montagu, Filmmaker, Communist, Spy*, The History Press UK, Stroud, 2018.

Carey, John, *The Unexpected Professor: An Oxford Life in Books*, Faber & Faber, London, 2014.

Carey, John, *What Good are the Arts?* Faber & Faber, London, 2005.

Clements, Kevin, *Back from the Brink: The Creation of a Nuclear-free New Zealand*, Allen & Unwin New Zealand Ltd in association with the Port Nicholson Press, Wellington, 1988.

Cooke, Robin Q.C., ed., *Portrait of a Profession: The Centennial Book of the New Zealand Law Society*, A. H. & A. W. Reed, Wellington, 1969 (Chapter 7 'Bench and Bar 1928–1950' by Sir David Smith, p.90).

Davies, Valerie, *Heaven is a Place on Earth: Eight Years of my Life*, William Collins Publishers Ltd, Auckland, 1989.

Davies, Sonja, *Bread and Roses: Sonja Davies, Her Story*, Australia and New Zealand Book Co with Fraser Books, Auckland, 1984.

Davies, Sonja, *Marching on*, Random House NZ, Auckland, 1997.

Derby, Mark, *White-collar Radical: Dan Long and the Rise of the White-collar Unions*, Craig Potton, Nelson, 2013.

Desmond, Pip, *Trust: A True Story of Women and Gangs*, Random House NZ, Auckland, 2009.

Dictionary of New Zealand Biography volumes 1–5, general editors W. H. Oliver and Claudia Orange, Department of Internal Affairs/AUP, Wellington, 1990–2000.

Easton, Brian, *The Nationbuilders*, AUP, Auckland, 2001.

Easton, B. H., and Beaven, W. H., eds, *The Future of New Zealand Medicine: A Progressive View*, Introduction by W. B. Sutch, N. M. Peryer Ltd, Christchurch, 1974.

Fraser, George, Fraser, Pauline, *Both Eyes Open, A Memoir*, J. McIndoe, Dunedin, 1990.

Fraser, George, *Seeing Red: Undercover in 1950s New Zealand*, Dunmore Publishing Ltd, Palmerston North, 1995.

Freer, Warren, *A Lifetime in Politics: The Memoirs of Warren Freer*, VUP, Wellington, 2004.

Gambrill, Mollie D., *A History of Queen Margaret College*, Board of Governors, Queen Margaret College, Wellington, 1969.

Gilbert, Jarrod, *Patched: The History of Gangs in New Zealand*, AUP, Auckland, 2013.

Grant, David, *The Mighty Totara: The Life and Times of Norman Kirk*, Random House NZ, Auckland, 2014.

Griffin, Penny, ed., *St Hugh's: One Hundred Years of Women's Education in Oxford*, Palgrave Macmillan, London, 1986.

Healey, Denis, *The Time of My Life*, Penguin Books, London, 1990.

Hayward, Margaret, *Diary of the Kirk Years*, Cape Catley Ltd, Queen Charlotte Sound, and A. H. and A. W. Reed Ltd., Wellington, 1981.

Elsie Locke, *Peace People: A History of Peace Activities in New Zealand*, Hazard Press, Christchurch and Melbourne, 1992.

Maclean, Chris, *A Way with Words: A Memoir of Writing and Publishing in New Zealand*, Potton & Burton, Nelson, 2018.

MacLean, Rory, *Stalin's Nose: Across the Face of Europe*, Harper Collins Publishers, London, 1992.

MacMillan, Margaret, *The Uses and Abuses of History*, Profile Books, London, 2010.

Marx and Engels, *The Communist Manifesto*, first published anonymously by the

Workers' Education Association, London, 1948.

McGibbon, Ian, ed., *Undiplomatic Dialogue: Letters between Carl Berendsen and Alister McIntosh 1943–1952*, AUP, Auckland, 1993.

McGibbon, Ian, ed., *Unofficial Channels: Letters between Alister McIntosh and Foss Shanahan, George Laking and Frank Corner 1946–1966*, VUP, Wellington, 1999.

McNeish, James, *Dance of the Peacocks: New Zealanders in Exile in the Time of Hitler and Mao Tse-Tung*, Vintage, Auckland, 2003.

Mead, Margaret, *Male and Female: A Study of the Sexes in a Changing World*, William Morrow, New York, 1949.

Moore, George Edward, *Principia Ethica*, Cambridge University Press, Cambridge, 1929 (first published 1903).

Mowat, Charles Loch, *Britain between the Wars, 1918–1940*, Methuen & Co. Ltd, London, 1955.

Mowat, John, *Random Reminiscence: An Autobiography*, New Cherwell Press, Oxford, 2001.

Mowat, John, *One Man's War: A Memoir*, New Cherwell Press, Oxford, 1997.

Mulgan, John, *Report on Experience*, Oxford University Press, Oxford, 1947, reprinted by Blackwood and Janet Paul Ltd, Auckland, 1967, this edition 1984.

O'Sullivan, Vincent, ed., *Intersecting Lines: The Memoirs of Ian Milner*, VUP, Wellington, 1993.

O'Sullivan, Vincent, *Long Journey to the Border: A Life of John Mulgan*, Penguin Books, Auckland, 2003.

Plischke, E. A., *On the Human Aspect in Modern Architecture*, Kurt Wedl, Vienna, 1969.

Powles, Michèle, 'A Legal History of the New Zealand Jury Service – Introduction, Evolution and Equality?' *Victoria University of Wellington Law Review*, 1999 29(2) 283.

Richardson, W. F., and Crawley, L.W.A., *Classics in Auckland: A Centennial History of the Department of Classics and Ancient History in the University of Auckland*, The Department, Auckland, 1983.

Ross, W. D., *The Right and the Good*, Oxford at the Clarendon Press, Oxford, 1930.

Sanger, Margaret, *Woman of the Future*, booklet in SHSS papers published in 1937 refers to speech in 1934, typed draft of speech dated 3 September 1933, Margaret Sager papers, Smith College.

Schwartz, Laura, *A Serious Endeavour: Gender, Education and Community at St Hugh's, 1886–2011*, Profile Books, London, 2011.

Scott, Dick, *Would a Good Man Die? Niue Island, New Zealand and the Late Mr Larsen*, Hodder and Stoughton, Auckland, 1993.

Scott, W. J., *Indecency in Literature*, New Zealand Council for Civil Liberties, Wellington, 1959.

Sinclair, Keith, *A History of the University of Auckland, 1883–1983*, AUP/OUP, Auckland, 1983.

Sinclair, Keith, *Walter Nash*, AUP/OUP, Auckland, 1976.

Slate, Nico, ed., *Black Power Beyond Borders: The Global Dimensions of the Black Power Movement*, Palgrave Macmillan, New York, 2012.

Smith, Helen, *Keep Telling Stories*, published by the Smith family, Wellington, 2008.

Soutter, Anne M., with Mary Clapinson, *St Hugh's College Register 1888–1959*, St Hugh's College, Oxford, 2011.

Steiner, George, *Errata: A Life in Ideas*, Weidenfeld & Nicolson, London, 1997, first published in ebook by Weidenfeld & Nicolson, 2011.

Sutch, W. B., *Poverty and Progress*, Modern Books, Wellington, 1941.

Sutch, W. B., in collaboration with Robertson, W. L., Smith, Shirley, and Webster, L. D., *Goodbye to Gold: A Guide to the International Monetary Fund*, Progressive Publishing Society, Wellington, 1944.

Sutch, W. B., *Guilty of Manslaughter?* Progressive Publishing Society, Wellington, 1944.

Sutch, W. B., *The Quest for Security in New Zealand: 1840 to 1966*, Oxford University Press, Wellington, 1966.

Sutch, W. B., *Poverty and Progress: A Re Assessment*, A. H. & A. W. Reed, Wellington, 1969.

Sutch, W. B., *Takeover New Zealand*, A. H. & A. W. Reed, Wellington, 1972.

Sutch, W. B., *Women with a Cause*, New Zealand University Press, Wellington, 1973.

Turnovsky, Fred, *Turnovsky: Fifty Years in New Zealand*, Allen & Unwin, Wellington, 1990.

McDonald, Elisabeth, and Austin, Graeme, eds., *Claiming the Law: Essays by New Zealand Women in Celebration of the 1993 Suffrage Centennial*, Victoria University of Wellington Law Review Special Issue, Monograph 6, VUW Law Review & VUP, Wellington, May 1993.

Victoria University Law Review issues from 1954.

Weir, Jim, *Eat, Drink and be Wary: A New Zealand Diplomat Looks Back*, Dunmore Publishing Ltd, Wellington, 2011.

Wharton, Miriam L., *The Development of Security Intelligence in New Zealand 1945–1957*: a thesis towards the degree of Master of Defence Studies at Massey University, 2012. *http://muir.massey.ac.nz/bitstream/handle/10179/4251/02_whole.pdf?sequence=1*

Willmott, W. E., ed., *New Zealand and the World: Essays in Honour of Wolfgang Rosenberg*, University of Canterbury, Christchurch, 1980 (includes 'Fair Challenge? An aspect of Trial by Jury' by Shirley Smith).

Yska, Redmer, *Truth: The Rise and Fall of the People's Paper*, Craig Potton Publishing, Nelson, 2010.

Booklets

Clinique Miremont: Air and Sun in High Altitudes
The Sun Cure in Professor Rollier's Clinics at Leysin (Switzerland)

Papers

Orr, Elizabeth, *Equal Pay for Work of Equal Value in New Zealand: A History of the 1960 and 1972 Equal Pay Acts*, paper to the Women's Studies Conference 21–23 November 2003, Palmerston North.
Ben Schrader, *Residential E and the 'Saving' of Thorndon*, Research Roundup Seminar Series, Stout Research Centre, Wellington, 18 October 2017 (forthcoming book *Won + Lost: A History of Historic Preservation in New Zealand*).

Shirley Smith Addresses:
George Barton (Introduction), 2008
Hon. Margaret Wilson, 2008
Dame Sian Elias, 2009
Nicola Lacey, 2010
Sir Kenneth Keith, 2011
Professor Hilary Charlesworth, 2012
Justice Teresa Doherty, 2013
Dame Susan Glazebrook, 2014
Dame Sylvia Cartwright, 2015
Professor Ngaire Naffine, 2016

The addresses are published on https://shirleysmithaddress.org/past-addresses/

Newspapers and magazines

Auckland Star
Christchurch Press
CRACCUM, 1940–46
Dominion
Eve Magazine
Evening Post
Here & Now, 1951–57
Landfall
New Zealand Herald
New Zealand Listener
New Zealand Times

New Zealand Truth
New Zealand Women's Weekly
New York Times
Nga Tawa School Magazine
Northern Advocate
NZ Magazine November–December 1944: New Zealand National Journal for All Readers
Poverty Bay Herald
Sunday Star
Te Karere, Queen Margaret College magazine, 1924–29
The Cygnet, St Hugh's College magazine, March 1936, June 1936, March 1937
The Kiwi, annual magazine of the Auckland University College Students Association

Media

Middle Class Recruits to Communism in the 1930s, conference, Gresham College, Oxford, March 2013, published by Gresham College (http://www.gresham.ac.uk):
http://www.gresham.ac.uk/lectures-and-events/middle-class-recruits-to-communism-in-the-1930s
http://www.gresham.ac.uk/lectures-and-events/the-radiant-illusion-middle-class-recruits-to-communism-in-the-1930s-seminar-0
http://www.gresham.ac.uk/lectures-and-events/the-radiant-illusion-middle-class-recruits-to-communism-in-the-1930s-seminar
http://www.gresham.ac.uk/lectures-and-events/middle-class-recruits-to-communism-in-the-1930s-seminar-panel-discussion

Leysin, 100 Years of History 1860–1960, DVD produced by Véronique Bernard and Pierre-Alain Frey.

Dr W. B. Sutch, U.N.R.R.A. Supply Officer: Dr W. B. Sutch returns to New Zealand to ask the public for financial support in the post war effort in Europe, New Zealand National Film Unit presents Weekly Review no. 201 (1945), Archives New Zealand, YouTube, published on 6 January 2015, https://www.youtube.com/watch?v=9q4WcDaqRQI

Additional websites

Dr Aaron Fox, kiwispies.com, *The Price of Collective Security: State-sponsored Anti-communism in New Zealand during the Cold War*, 2009
https://shirleysmithaddress.org/past-addresses/
Te Ara: The Encyclopedia of New Zealand, teara.govt.nz

Index

n denotes references in the footnotes
italics denotes references to the page in the photograph section